COUNTY

Woodville

RANDOLPH
CHURCH

BETHESDA
CHURCH

ASBURY
CHURCH

COUNTY

Union Point

BROWNS
CHAPEL

SIBLEY
SCHOOL

BETHANY
CHURCH

Siloam

ANDREWS
SCHOOL

Ogeechee

River

ROCK HILL
CHURCH

TALIAFERRO

White
Plains

MOONS
ACADEMY

FAIRVIEW
SCHOOL

COUNTY

CHURCH
SCHOOL

COUNTY LINE
CHURCH

HANCOCK

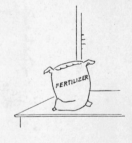

FERTILIZER

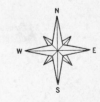

N
W   E
S

TENANTS OF THE ALMIGHTY

THE MACMILLAN COMPANY
NEW YORK · BOSTON · CHICAGO
DALLAS · ATLANTA · SAN FRANCISCO

MACMILLAN AND CO., LIMITED
LONDON · BOMBAY · CALCUTTA
MADRAS · MELBOURNE

THE MACMILLAN COMPANY
OF CANADA, LIMITED
TORONTO

Here is a book for the people of Greene County, Georgia. It is dedicated to the County Historian, Dr. T. B. Rice, who is most at home among his heirlooms.

Tenants of the Almighty

BY
ARTHUR F. RAPER

FSA PHOTOGRAPHS BY
JACK DELANO

1943
THE MACMILLAN COMPANY
NEW YORK

PRINTED IN THE UNITED STATES OF AMERICA
AMERICAN BOOK–STRATFORD PRESS, INC., NEW YORK

"We are tenants of the Almighty
Entrusted with a portion of His earth
To dress and keep
And pass on to the next generation."

LOUISIANA DUNN THOMAS
NEGRO FARM TENANT MOTHER
GREENE COUNTY, GEORGIA

FOREWORD

HERE IS our third study of Greene county, Georgia. The first was made in 1927 and 1928, and can be found among the 1931 Ph. D. dissertations at the University of North Carolina. It was called *A Study of Two Black-Belt Counties*. The report dealt with living conditions in Greene and Macon counties, Georgia; it showed why so many farmers had left Greene, why almost none had left Macon.

The second study was made in 1934 and 1935. It was published the following year by the University of North Carolina Press, under the title *Preface to Peasantry*. It presented a summary of the earlier study, and showed how the New Deal was affecting the people on the farms and in the towns of these two counties.

The third study was begun in September of 1940. The plan was to take a ten-month's look at Greene's Unified Farm Program. Trying to understand why different people felt as they did about the Program, we decided to make a full study of what had happened to the people in the county over the years. Soon we were engrossed with the story of the Indians, white settlers, self-sufficient frontier farmers, slavery, war and reconstruction, wage hands and sharecroppers, time-merchants and Populists, "weevil-free" land and boom times, boll weevil and deflation, hard years, and then the launching of the Unified Farm Program.

So for two years, rather than for ten months, we have lived and worked in Greene county. We saw, heard, and felt much as we read the grand jury presentments from 1786 down to the present, as we looked through the other old records of the county in the courthouse and in the Duke University Library, as we read the newspaper files in the Ordinary's Office and in the Rene Collection at the University

vii

of Georgia Library, in Athens. We talked to the old people, visited
the ante-bellum houses, read the inscriptions on the tomb stones,
hunted out the sites of abandoned towns and roads, homesteads and
churches, tramped over the mounds along the Oconee, looked
through the Indian relics a dozen farmers and their families had
collected, made notes from a score of scrapbooks, listened to the
farmers and townsfolk talk of their ups and downs, their fears and
hopes.

Our work with the background study of the county was made
simple and pleasant by the gracious cooperation of Dr. T. B. Rice,
the County Historian. He laid open his full files, was always ready
with counsel and encouragement, and he and Maymie Bowen Rice,
his wife, read the manuscript from the first page through to the last.

Other elderly people who gave generously of their time and infor-
mation are Judge James B. Park, John Gentry, Sam Turner, Estelle
Colclough, A. J. Boswell, Waide Durham, M. L. Jernigan, A. S.
Parker, Hart Sibley, Jennie Sibley Lamb, Charles Jenkins Thomton,
W. R. Corry, and Charles O'Neil. Ex-slaves from whom we got
stories of the old times are Alfred "Preacher" Parrott, Tilda
"Grandma" Lawrence, Tony Thompson, and Frances Griffin.

We would like to acknowledge the contributions made by many
other persons, but to write down all their names would make too
long a list. Everybody helped us compile this story of Greene—
county officials, representatives of the various agencies in the Unified
Farm Program, and most of all the farmers and townspeople themselves, white and colored, men, women, and children.

How does one go about thanking a county? And how can we
express our appreciation to those scores of families who sat down
with our interviewers and filled out that 13-page schedule which
asked for information about everything? Or the 500 fathers and
mothers who told us what they thought of the county-wide farm program, and of the world situation. Then there are the school teachers
and pupils who assisted us in filling our blanks for the oldest child in
school from nearly a thousand homes.

In compiling the story of the activities of the Unified Farm Program, launched in 1939, we had the cooperation of representatives of every phase of the Program, and so we acknowledge our indebtedness to Hamp McGibony, Chairman of the County Commissioners; H. C. Stewart, Chairman of the County War Board; T. B. Rice of the County Welfare Board; Sheriff L. L. Wyatt; Dr. Goodwin Gheesling and Dr. W. R. Richards of the Health Department; Chairman M. H. Tappan of the County Board of Education, Superintendent Floyd T. Corry of the county schools, Superintendent C. C. Wills of the Greensboro schools, Supervisors J. D. Salter and Mary Jernigan Holmes of the white schools, and Jeanes Supervisor Lucille Stone Welch of colored schools; Francis Bowen, Nelle Thrash, and C. L. Tapley of the Extension Service; E. H. Downs, S. L. Van Landingham, Pearl Wheeler Tappan, and Joel E. Thomas of the FSA; W. M. Jernigan of the AAA; E. D. Brender and George F. Powers of the SCS.

We appreciate especially the cooperation of Carey Williams, editor of the *Herald-Journal*. He has carried the study in his paper in weekly instalments, and helpful suggestions have come in from all over the county.

Will W. Alexander, former FSA Administrator and for many years interested in Greene county, has always encouraged us to look deep, think straight, and write plain.

People in the Department of Agriculture and outside of it have been interested and helpful: M. L. Wilson, Director of Extension Service; George S. Mitchell, Constance E. H. Daniel, and Tarleton Collier of the FSA; Carl C. Taylor, Raymond C. Smith, and Conrad Taeuber of the BAE; Margaret Mead of the Museum of Natural History; Fred Wale of Chicago and Washington; Howard W. Odum of Chapel Hill, North Carolina; Willis A. Sutton and Ira de A. Reid of Atlanta, M. R. Little of Louisville, and many more.

A number of people assisted directly in the study of Greene county: Roy E. Stryker of the Historical Division of FSA made available Jack Delano, one of the expert photographers of his staff. Delano made pictures throughout the county. Stryker also sent Edwin Rosskam to help us select and arrange the illustrations for

the report. Lee Coleman, of the Atlanta Area BAE office, worked
in the county several weeks making detailed community delineation
maps. The NYA furnished us three clerical workers for several
months.

We are, of course, especially indebted to those who worked with
us in the office: Caroline Blue, Margaret McGibony, Madison C.
Wright, Jr., C. A. Edwards, Carolyn Chapman, Sybil Meadows,
Elizabeth Smith, and Katherine Cheyney.

With the materials all in hand and a rough manuscript through the
typewriter, one inevitably comes to that last month when the whole
study has to be revised. It was late July. Morning, afternoon, and
evening, U. T. Miller and Martha Jarrell Raper worked with us,
watched out for misspelled words, poorly expressed ideas, and
"dumb" sentences.

At last the job was done, and it was time to leave Greene county
again. With some sadness we set about disposing of our cow and calf,
chickens, dog and cats, and the little white horse that the three boys
and Margaret loved so well.

For two years we have lived in the old J. B. "Punch" Dolvin plantation house with its large hall, big rooms, high ceilings and spacious
porches. All about us have been farm and sawmill folk, owners and
workers, who have been affected in one way or another by the
county-wide farm program and by the world situation. We listened,
tried to help.

We leave with the hope that our efforts while here will make it
a little easier for our neighbors—and their neighbors' neighbors—to
live over into a better day. We leave, too, with the hope that one
spring we will come again to this hard-pressed and hopeful county
of Greene—to make a garden, gather eggs, milk a cow or two, ride
a white horse, listen and learn what has happened since we went
away.

ARTHUR RAPER

Greensboro, Georgia
January, 1943

TABLE OF CONTENTS

TENANTS OF THE ALMIGHTY

BOOK ONE

If you like your story short . . .

PLATE I

The rivers and creeks and trees were here. Here, too, were the wild animals, and fish and fowl. The years were recorded in the rings of the trees, the centuries in the deepening soil—an inch every thousand years.

The first men to live along the Oconee were red men, moundbuilders. They hunted and fished, planted patches of corn, made stone axes, hickory bows and

PLATE 2

pots of clay, chipped flint arrowheads for hunting and for battle. They respected the forests they lived in and the wild animals that gave them meat.

They revered the counsel of their old men, depended on the skills of their old women, expected after death to reach the happy hunting ground.

White men from Spain came to the Oconee with compasses and guns, steel knives and "fire water." They asked the red men about gold, and went away.

Englishmen came with their wives and children, cleared the lands and grew their food, built forts and churches and one-room cabins of hand-hewn logs.

PLATE 3

The white settlers brought black men to work for them, black men sold into slavery by African Chiefs and carried to America in New England ships.

The white men drove the red men out, made them stay beyond the Oconee. Other white men soon drove them beyond the Chattahoochee, and then beyond the Mississippi.

Within fifty years after the red men were pushed out, there were twice as many slaves as Whites in Greene county. Slave prosperity built a railroad, three cotton mills, two colleges, and a half hundred plantation homes.

PLATE 4

As the slaves were brought in, white people moved out, until as many had left as stayed. Of the white families who still lived here, half of them never did own a single slave.

Then came fear, and the War of the 1860's. The slave-owning and nonslave-owning Whites gave freely of their lives and fortunes, but they were overwhelmed in battle. The slaves were freed and given the ballot. And for a time Federal troops supervised the affairs of the county with the help of Northern "carpet-

baggers" and local "scallawags." Bluecoats camped on the courthouse square.

The small landowners went back to their neglected live-at-home farms.

The masters' slaves were free, their money worthless, but they owned the land. The Negroes were still here, and nothing had come of the talk of giving them

40 acres and a mule.

Cotton was selling at 40¢ a pound, and bankers in the North and East would lend landowners money to grow a cotton crop.

So farming was begun again on the old plantation with freed Negroes as wagehands, and then as tenants. The former masters and overseers were in their accustomed places, but they were living on borrowed money.

Year after year, bankers and money lenders held mortgages on the cotton

PLATE 5

land. Year after year the planters held first claim on the growing crops of the farm tenants for the food and clothes advanced to them in spring.

The fields leached and washed as the money lenders pressed the planters for payment, as the planters pressed the tenants for full settlement.

To force the failing land, costly guano was bought and put on it.

The small landowners, too, were growing cotton, needed fertilizer and supplies on a credit, gave their land as security.

PLATE 6

A few planter-merchants made fortunes selling food, feed, and fertilizer to the debt-ridden cotton farmers, taking over their lands when they could not pay.

By the 1890's the hard-pressed tenants and small landowners were supporting a new party, the Populists. This third party wanted lower rates of interest on small loans and landownership for more farmers.

When the national Third Party broke up, the white Populists in Greene joined with the local Democrats to set up a White Primary, which made an end of the Negro voting that began under the Reconstruction government.

In the meantime about five hundred white people found work in the county's three new cotton mills. More than a thousand Negroes were shipped by labor agents to the new plantations in the Mississippi Delta and Texas.

The fresh lands of the Delta and the Southwest could grow cotton cheaper than the tired hills of Greene, so farmers here began to turn to dairying.

Then the weevil in the West and World War I made cotton go from 15¢ to 40¢ a pound. Greene's fields again were all planted to cotton and corn, even the new pastures. But soon the weevil came and ruined one cotton crop after the other. And the price dropped 'way down, too.

The tenants could not pay their bills. The landowners could not pay back their loans. There was not enough credit left to keep on farming. Most of the land lay idle, and thousands of people left the county.

Then were hard years.

After a while a plan was worked out to help the farmers of Greene live better and take better care of their land.

Look out of the past toward the future—look through the columns of Old Mercer to the low white vocational building across the way.

PLATE 7

Out of the tall white columned plantation homesteads and the close-to-earth houses and lives of the live-at-home farmers, the government program has brought its low white homes and school-houses, with their air of work and promise.

Because of the county-wide program in Greene, World War II finds our people better prepared to work together in serving their country.

Now let's look at some representative scenes in Greene county.

BOOK TWO

and so we live . . .

PLATE 8

PLATE 9

PLATE 10

We live and work in the country. We know the smell of fresh plowed earth. To break and plant and cultivate one acre of cotton, we walk 40 miles. At chopping time and picking time, everybody helps.

PLATE II

Corn feeds the pigs that feed the cotton farmers. Corn feeds the mules that pull the cotton plows. The yield is low, but it is cheaper to grow it than to buy it.

Over half of Greene county's 260,000 acres are in second-growth pines. Seedlings spring up wherever the land is not plowed. In a generation they are big enough for sawlogs—rough plank for tenant cabins, finished lumber for the market.

There are now 97 sawmills in the county. Many of them are small, and can be moved from place to place. When the wage and hour legislation came, the operators speeded up the mills, put more tractors in the woods. The workers like the shorter day and the better pay, begin work on Monday mornings just as they did before. Pines have helped the sawmill owners, landowners, and landless workers of Greene through many a hard place, are now the county's greatest single source of income. The good price for pine lumber in recent months has caused most of the sawable timber to be sold.

PLATE 12

PLATE 13

This house has been empty since the boll weevil came. Farmers left nearly half of the farms between 1920 and 1930. The farmers who left the land took their families to the cities, South and North. There they found jobs as common laborers, were first to be laid off when hard times reached the cities. They stood in breadlines, asked for relief, longed for home. But only a few came back, for there was little to come to.

PLATE 14

Years and years before the boll weevil came, the land in Greene was washing away. Some of the old red-land plantations along the Oconee had galled and gullied before the slaves were freed. Growing cotton with borrowed money after the War of the 1860's made the land wash still more. Houses and barns, churches and schoolhouses go down as the soil goes out. Gullies are the earthy receipts for our misuses of the land.

PLATE 15

The old is still with us. At public expense a ferry is operated at Park's Mill over the Oconee. In dry weather the boat cannot be used, for the river bed is now choked with mud from the hills. No farmer has a better yoke of oxen than Frank Barnett, who lives where the town of Scull Shoals once stood.

PLATE 16

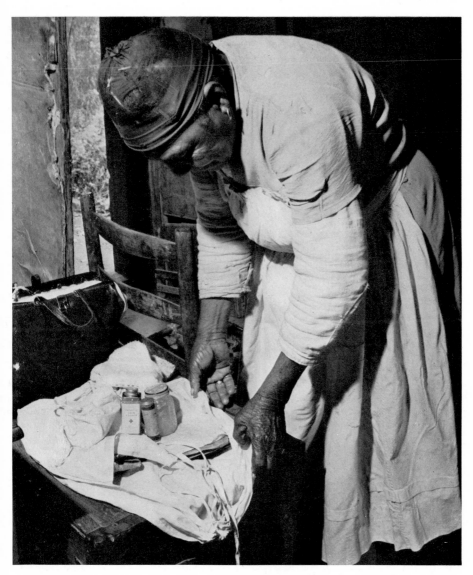

Three-fourths of the colored babies born in the county, and a fifth of the white babies, are delivered by the fifteen Negro midwives. They go to monthly meetings at the county health office, have a handbag full of supplies, charge from five to ten dollars. Only three of the fifteen can fill in a birth certificate.

PLATE 17

PLATE 18

The Negro woman knows work and worry. "Sorrow has played upon my heart, and trouble is weaved there like a vine."

Colored convicts work on the public roads. They sleep and eat behind bars, and will dance like the dickens for your dime.

PLATE 19

We borrow some money to grow a cotton crop, and we live by hard work. Mostly we use the same kind of tools our fathers used before us. But we have to buy more fertilizer, and the weevil is here now. Sometimes it looks like things are stacked against us. Looks like we get too little for what we grow, and pay too much for what we buy. But we love the land and want to rear our children on it. We know no other way of life. When these plowlines give out we will get some more.

PLATE 20

PLATE 21

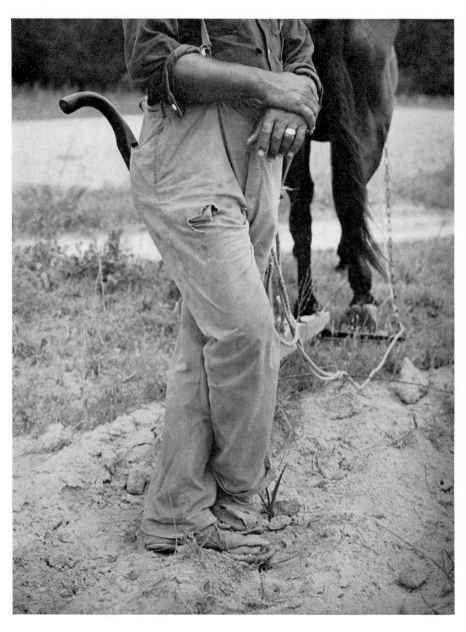

PLATE 22

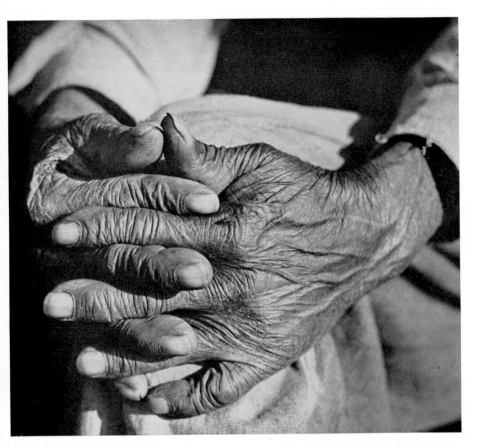

Our hands and feet know the feel of this land, and of trace-chains, plow handles and hoe handles, of washboards and cotton to pick. Black feet on the red land of Greene, black feet on the white lands—in the field by day and along the roads and paths at night. And we go on, feelin' maybe something is coming, coming for to help us along to a better living and better schools, better churches and the chance to be somebody.

PLATE 23

Year in and year out we've grown cotton in Greene county. We have stuck to cotton simply because it was the best way we have found to get money for our creditors and for ourselves.

Nowadays we can't grow cotton cheap with fertilizer and soda, and we can't grow it at all without them.

We've always worked as tenants on somebody else's land, and we guess we always will.

PLATE 24

PLATE 25

PLATE 26

When we farmers were having a hard time in the late 1930's, the government agencies got together and began to work out a county-wide program to help us live better and care for our land. Trained supervisors sat down with us, helped us work out farm plans, secure terraces from the SCS, new fences from the CCC, legumes and fertilizer from the AAA and the County Agent, and rehabilitation loans from the FSA.

PLATE 27

The old plantation tenant house was poor at best—sagging floorboards, leaky roofs, no inside ceiling, no screens, perhaps no window sash. Chickens came through the windows, pigs through the doors, wind through the cracks.

PLATE 28

A steady new house and barn, a chicken house and smokehouse, pasture and hog lot, and 140 acres of land cost about $3,500—with from 20 to 40 years to pay. Family-size farms are being laid out on 20,000 acres bought by the FSA.

PLATE 29

Most FSA borrowers were living on farms the government had not bought. How could their houses be made better without money from the landlord, or the tenant, or the government? Ed Downs and Joel Thomas, FSA officials here, figured it out. The landlord could sign away a part of his rent for 5 or 7 years. Against this future rent the FSA would loan the money to fix up the farm buildings and terrace the land.

PLATE 30

This is the same house after it was repaired and creosoted with advanced rent money. Over a hundred other tenant houses were fixed up, five new ones built; fifteen barns were repaired, ninety built. Barrels of white creosote were sprayed on 200 unpainted houses. Altogether $50,000 worth of future rents have been signed over to FSA by landlords to make tenant houses and barns better and to terrace the land.

PLATE 31

The Brooks children near Siloam. Billy and little Sara Nell, Dorothy, Thomas and Virginia. Their father had an accident five years ago, and it left him lame. He has done WPA work for four years. Thomas and his older brother Robert get up the wood and help with the garden and cow. The whole family listens to the battery-radio. Son Franklin is in the Army, "somewhere in the Pacific."

PLATE 32

The L. H. Cooks of Woodville obligingly pose for a picture in the house they bought and repaired with a Tenant-Purchase loan. They have 40 years in which to pay for it. They work on their own farm, and in the hosiery mill at Union Point. There are eleven other T-P families in the county, seven white and four colored.

PLATE 33

An FSA borrower has had no assurance of a comfortable place to live. Not every landlord is willing, or thinks he can afford, to sign over advance rent.

PLATE 34

Curtains and shades, a table cloth and paper flowers, and mail-order wallpaper can be bought if you have a little money to spare.

To keep the flies out of the kitchen and the frogs out of the well—235 FSA houses screened, 220 new pumps put in. Nearly 600 fly-proof privies have been installed within the last five years.

PLATE 35

PLATE 36

We know there are no virgin forests left to clear for new grounds. We know some of our land is washed so badly it will not grow crops, and that some of the slopes are too steep to cultivate. The SCS has bought nearly 30,000 acres to set aside as forests—a sort of "social security" for tired lands to sit down and rest a century or two. Anybody can see the work the SCS, with the CCC, has done— new wide terraces on 7,500 acres, kudzu on 1,700 acres, 30,000 rods of new fence, and more lespedeza, sericea, hegari, oats and barley than ever before. But as we ride along, we still see a lot that needs to be done.

PLATE 37

We've always seen some good gardens here. Then a few years ago the farm agencies began to help more of us have good gardens. There are over 500 families on the FSA, and each of us has a fenced garden and some extra vegetables in the field, enough to eat during the summer and to can for the winter. First we were taught to have good spring gardens, and now we are learning to make gardens the year 'round.

PLATE 38

The garden is the most valuable piece of land on the farm. There is deep satisfaction in a good garden close to the house. On this patch of earth a farmer and his wife perform nobly. Here they deal justly with the Almighty and here they reap abundantly. Year after year the garden yields up its dishes to those who tend it. A good garden can whet the appetite, balance the diet, and make a family proud of their farm home.

PLATE 39

Our canned stuff is like a garden in the house all winter. The whole county is canning more than ever before. In three years those of us on the FSA have canned over a half million quarts—almost 500 quarts to the family last year—and most of us used to have hardly a dozen jars. Last year, eleven families canned over 900 quarts each. We eat better than before and leave the store-bought tin cans for our soldiers.

PLATE 40

PLATE 41

Growing meat and bread at home makes your cotton money go further. FSA families all have pigs. Many have grown all the meat they needed for the first time in their lives.

The FSA borrower usually buys a cow with his first loan. Thirty-five thousand chicks were sent around in 1941, 40,000 in 1942. Children are getting milk and eggs. Their faces are brighter, their bodies stronger.

PLATE 42

PLATE 43

The county health program has been paid for by the County, State and FSA together. It has a full time doctor, two nurses, and a sanitary engineer. When the public health workers find a new case of TB, they teach the family how to care for the sick one, and keep well themselves.

At the monthly VD clinic anybody can be tested for "bad blood" and get his "shots."

The baby clinic is most popular. The mothers readily learn to fix bottles and prepare food. The nurses weigh the children, and give them the scratches and shots that keep them from having diphtheria and smallpox.

PLATE 44

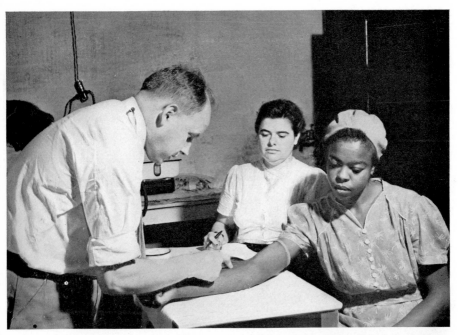

PLATE 45

This is Arthur Burtling and his wife near Watson Springs. Old-Age Assistance checks are making life more pleasant and hopeful for 218 white people and 202 Negroes. The Whites average $9.00 a month, the Negroes $7.00.

PLATE 46

Says 93-year-old Alfred "Preacher" Parrott: "Lived right 'round Siloam all my life. Belonged to the white folks in slavery times, worked, plowed in slavery time for my master. And I'm thankful to be here and be with the guv'ment. They give me bread to eat, they give me clothes to wear, they give me coffee to drink, and I'm thankful fur it. Don't know how we'd git along if it wasn't fur the guv'ment helping us old people in this country. You see the guv'ment has to help a lot of old people just to be certain it helps the deserving old people like me. Come to think about it, you know the guv'ment is better able to take care of me now than I am to take care of myself."

PLATE 47

The school lunch program pleases just about everybody, and the children thrive on it. A hot school lunch may change a "bad boy" into a good student. Last year hot lunches were served in the seven white county schools and in eight of the largest colored schools. Cold lunches were served at all the rest. The coming of the war makes the lunch-room program all the more important.

PLATE 48

When the WPA and NYA and Surplus Commodities couldn't keep on helping, the school patrons in the local communities began to try to figure what to
do. The new canneries, for Whites at Greensboro and for Negroes at the Alexander Community School, are canning vegetables, some for the school children
next winter.

PLATE 49

Five years ago most of the Negro schools convened in lodge halls and churches, and most of the teachers had only county licenses. Last year 37 out of 52 Negro teachers had college training, and 20 new buildings were used.

PLATE 50

A farmer sharpens his plowpoint at the forge in the school shop. Under a trained teacher, the girls learn to sew a good seam.

PLATE 51

The vocational teachers of each race help their students make brooders and ironing boards, show them and their fathers how to build truck frames, bedsteads, porch furniture; how to mend tools; how to inoculate farm animals. The girls are taught to make aprons, then dresses, and some can already make their own clothes without help. They learn what foods are healthful and how to cook them, how to can, how to set the table and serve.

PLATE 52

"I want the schools to teach our people how to live better here," says Floyd T. Corry, Superintendent of Schools.

PLATE 53

"We've worked hard. And we're coming up. We farm with the 'government.' The way things look now, we'll pay out this fall."

When work is done we can dress up a bit, visit the neighbors, or go into town.

It's a big job—wife, mother, housekeeper, gardener, and dairy maid.

PLATE 54

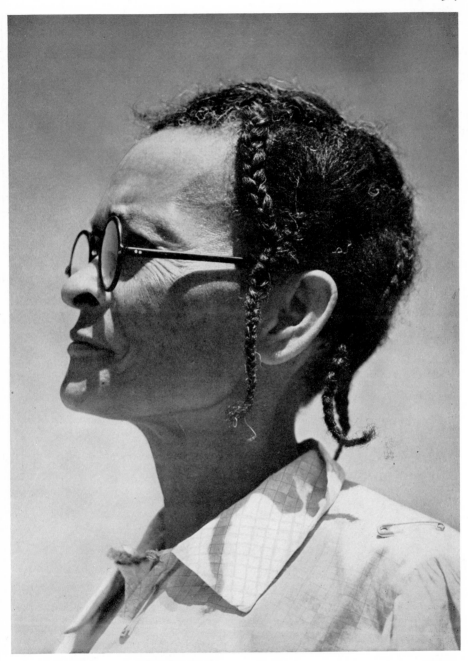

I know what it is to work in the field and cook, wash, iron, and can. Of course, the children help out a lot.

PLATE 55

But comes Saturday afternoon, and off to town we go in a buggy, wagon, automobile, or on foot. We men and women look forward to it, and the children work better all week if you promise to let them go to town on Saturday.

When we get to town we listen for the news and gossip, look around to see who else is here. If we get tired, we step in a hot dog stand and get a wiener or hamburger—no fun in town unless you got at least a little money to spend. On the bench by the Bank of Greensboro great and small sit and talk about everything—the war and the weather, farm prices and politics, the countrywide farm program and the newcomer who just went up the street. Perhaps no one ever told the Negroes not to sit here, but they never do.

The farmers make most of their money out of the land and spend it in town. The stores are full of pretty things, and it's hard to keep any cash in pocket. By the time we buy the clothes for the family and all the things we've got to have for the farm, there isn't much money left. The merchants know they can prosper only when the farmers have money to spend.

PLATE 56

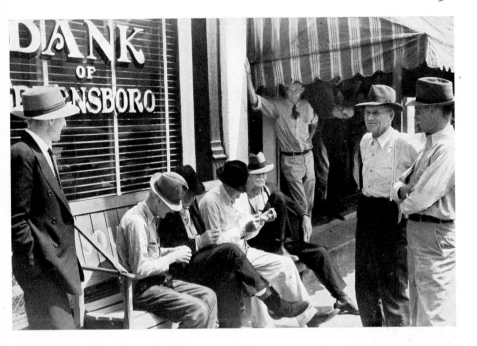

PLATE 57

Judge James B. Park of Greensboro was 89 years old recently. He has been a lawyer here for 67 years, still carries on an active practice. He was judge of the Ocmulgee Circuit Court for 28 years, has served as State Legislator and State Senator. He thinks the farmers get too little for what they sell, and pay too much for what they buy.

PLATE 58

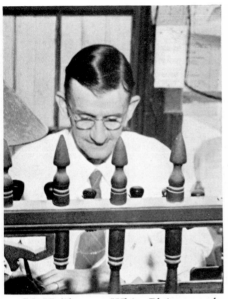

M. H. Tappan, White Plains merchant, chairman County Board of Education.
E. J. Stanley has been Clerk of Superior Court for 22 years.
Lloyd Lewis is County Ordinary, active leader in County Home Guard.
Sheriff L. L. Wyatt says the "moonshine" business dropped off after the Unified Farm Program got under way.

PLATE 59

Merchant Hamp McGibony is chairman of the County Commissioners, member of the County Board of Health and the City Council, friend of thousands.

PLATE 60

The editor of the *Herald-Journal*, Carey Williams, sometimes composes his syndicated column "Sense and Nonsense" at the linotype.

PLATE 61

PLATE 62

The Greensboro Lions Club backs the Unified Farm Program.

One of the oldest bridge clubs in the county is at Siloam. White Plains has the only Federated Woman's Club in the county.

Everybody had a good time at the countywide May-day celebration.

When we tire of hot weather, we stop and have a barbecue.

The county fair in the fall is the time for visiting and fun.

PLATE 63

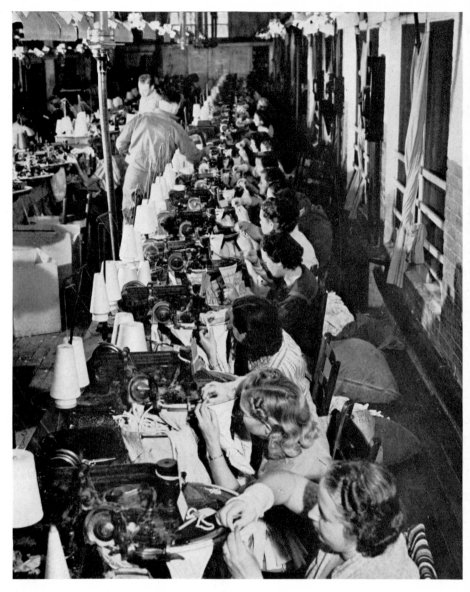

Knitting socks in the Union Manufacturing Company at Union Point. Greene's first three cotton mills were built in the 1830's, were closed by the War of the 1860's. By the 1890's the sharecropper plantations were in decline. Knitting mills were started at Penfield and Union Point and a cotton mill at Greensboro.

PLATE 64

For four months early in 1941, the spindles and looms in the Mary-Leila Mill at Greensboro stood still. The management called it a "strike"; the workers called it a "lockout." The local TWUA, a CIO Union, now has a contract, and the mill is busy again. Scores of farmers have turned from field to factory. The cotton mill means shorter hours and better wages for men, and women.

PLATE 65

The Carl Lingolds live in the mill village at Greensboro, work in the mill. Just now he is going into the Army.

PLATE 66

The Harold Lambs of Union Point live on top of the hill at Hawthorne Heights, have a controlling interest in the Union Manufacturing Company.

PLATE 67

There are 30 white Churches in Greene—Baptist, Methodist, Presbyterian, Episcopal, Church of God. Altogether there are nearly 3,500 members. Many rural and village churches are small and weak. Bethesda Baptist, Bethany Presbyterian, and Liberty Methodist were started before 1800. It is claimed that the first mourner's bench in the country was at old Liberty Church.

PLATE 68

Revival meetings are held in mid-summer when fried chicken and water-melons are at their best. Most churches have women's missionary societies; only the largest ones have young people's organizations.

PLATE 69

The Negroes have had their own separate churches since soon after Emancipation. Today there are fifty of them scattered across the county, mostly Baptist, with goodly groups of Methodists here and there. Many of the churches have small memberships, and most of them have once-a-month preachers. Some of the ministers are seminary graduates. Others are local farmers who answered "the call." The Negroes have improved their church buildings since the Unified Farm Program began. A few have been rebuilt, many painted. The church is the Negro's most important institution. It is his own, and he supports it.

PLATE 70

PLATE 71

Down through the fifteen-year-old pines of an abandoned cotton field go the REA lines. Electrical current went into many sections of the county. Perhaps REA can complete its job when the war is over.

PLATE 72

The radio sits proudly in many a farmer's home where the printed page is hardly known. With their sons and kinsmen now in the armed forces, these people listen—learn of the Atlantic Charter, hear of the four freedoms, find out about new places and new peoples around the world.

PLATE 73

Though we never knew it so well as now, the big world has long affected our lives here—for we grew cotton for the world market. This plantation homestead, Jefferson Hall, has stood through over a century of plantation expansion and decline. Here they are—yesterday and tomorrow. An old house and a young boy. History and hope.

We are getting into a strange new world, and we know it. A couple of hundred tractors are taking the place of a half thousand mules. We are beginning to put a part of our fertilizer on the pastures. The grass grows thicker, and our cows get along better. Maybe we can get some cash from cows and not have to depend so much on cotton. And now we can get work in war industries.

PLATE 74

PLATE 75

We know the land and the pines stand back of our homes, back of our churches and schools, cotton mills and sawmills. We know, too, now we are in war, that this land of ours is called upon to feed us at home, feed our fighting men wherever they are, and a portion of the hungry world.

PLATE 76

We farmers are taking this war more and more seriously. We are close to the land, and we love it. We want to help our boys who have been in the thick of this thing from the very start. We'll grow more livestock, help our womenfolk put up more jars of fruits and vegetables, do all that we can.

PLATE 77

The county's leaders spoke to the Negroes at their schools and churches. They listened, understood their country's needs, went home to do what they could. And today our people, white and black, work and hope for a better Greene County in a better world.

PLATE 78

PLATE 79

BOOK III

TENANTS OF THE ALMIGHTY

But a short story and representative pictures leave much untold. If you have the time, let's begin at the beginning and tell the whole story of this one county-full of tenants of the Almighty.

PART ONE

BACKGROUNDS

I

IN THE BEGINNING

The Almighty had spoken.

Time was.

Life was.

A hill and a hollow, and beyond them more hills and hollows. To the northwest higher hills and mountains, to the southeast lower hills, coastal plain, the ocean.

On the ridges and slopes stood together the oak, hickory, beech, maple, and chestnut, with pines here and there; and under them the flowering dogwood, azalea, redbud, chinquapin, huckleberry. In the hollows grew the ash, gum, willow, alder, and wild magnolia. On the forest floor in deep beds of decaying leaves and rotting logs came trillium, heart leaf, and violet. Winding and climbing up through the trunks and branches were grape vines, muscadine, cowslip, poison ivy, and yellow jasmine.

Down in the forest at the foot of the hills, water bubbled out of the ground at one or two or a dozen places. The overflow was cool and clear. Rivulets, fed by many springs, joined with creeks from other hollows to swell the waters of the Oconee and the Appalachee, and to form the headwaters of the Ogeechee. A picture of one of these rivers, from its mouth to its sources in the hills, would look something like a forest oak with more cool clear springs feeding into it than there are leaves feeding sunshine to the tree. The rivers, and creeks, and spring branches were alive with fish and frog, terrapin and snake.

3

Along their banks and on the ridges ran the paths of rabbits and raccoons. Partings in the grass were worn slick by weasels and minks. The deer and bear made larger paths. But largest of all was the trail which buffalo herds beat out when they visited the salt lick by the headwaters of the Ogeechee.

In and out among the trees, bushes and vines, flashed the sheen of many wings. Transient small birds of bright colors and lively tunes lived on bugs and flies. The owls made lonesome moans for songs at night and slept by day. Great silent birds ate flesh, caught it alive with talon feet, or found it long dead and stayed until the stench was consumed. Others, just as large, gobbled and stayed on the ground most of the time, fed on grasshoppers, berries, and wild grain. With the first cold weather, geese and ducks flew in high formation from over the northern horizon and were soon lost to sight in the south; the flight back north of these methodical high flyers was a sure sign of spring.

Sometimes a ball of fire fell from the clouds and split a chestnut wide open, or peeled the bark off an oak; or kindled a flame in a dead pine that burned for days, and with a wind roared up through the tree tops until another thunder storm drowned it out. The water from a single creek put the river over its bank for an afternoon. The wolf killed the wild boar and ate him. The hawk hovered against the sun and dropped upon a rabbit. The eagle carried off a fawn.

For unnumbered seasons acorns sprouted and pine seeds scattered on the winds. Birds built their nests. The animals nursed their young. The fish spawned, and the turtles came up out of the water and buried their soft-shelled eggs in the warm sand.

II

THE FIRST MEN

ONE DAY smoke was seen where no ball of white fire had fallen. A deer was tangled in a strange strong vine. A turkey fluttered with a sharp stick in his breast. At night fish swam up toward a new light, were run through with a spear and hung over a fire.

The fire was tended by creatures that walked upright, and communed with each other by much jabbering. They lived long years by the rivers and larger creeks. They built a mound in the swamp west of the Oconee, a short walk above its junction with the Appalachee. It was a stone's throw across the base, half as high as the nearby trees, with sloping sides, and a flat circular top as wide as the river.

The mound was built up over a long period of time, with one layer of mud added and burned and then another and another. Between the mound and the river was a pond from which the mound dirt came. On the east side of the river was a smaller mound. Up the Oconee near the shoals was the largest mound of all. Smaller mounds were built here and there along the rivers and creeks. A day's walk to the southwest was a hilltop on which the early men arranged rock to form a giant eagle in flight.

Years passed. And the bones of their dead, charred posts, pottery, bone needles, the streaks of baked clay in the mounds, and the rocks —these outlasted the moundbuilders, the first people along the Oconee.

For a time smoke rose in the forests only when fire fell from the clouds. The deer and turkey neither saw nor heard those that walked upright. The holes by the mounds became havens for fish. First weeds grew on the mounds, then grass, and finally trees. The trees grew old, and younger trees replaced them again and again.

OTHER RED MEN

Then once more men walked the paths of bear and buffalo. They came out of the west, and were red of face, as were the mound-builders before them. They brought fire with them, put it in a clearing, fed it sticks and poles, and sat hunched around it at night. There were men, women, and children, and pet animals that growled after every strange noise in the dark, and in the daytime yelped off through the woods after rabbit or deer.

The women stayed near the fire all day, scratched the leaves into piles and burned them. With stones they bruised the living bark off big trees, so the trees would die and the sunshine could come through to their patches. They poked about in the dirt with sharp sticks, pressed in white or yellow grains that grew in mid-summer into tall stalks of sweet green corn. The corn could be scraped from the cob and made into succotash, or left to ripen on the stalk. Then they shucked and shelled it, parched the grains, crushed them between stones. Of the meal they made a batter, which they wrapped about with wet shucks, and baked in the hot ashes of the camp fire.

With big knuckled fingers the women also made baskets of willows, clay pots into which they pressed designs with pieces of reed. They cleaned skins to make blankets, or tanned them for clothes and thong.

The older men stayed about the camp, chipped arrows, rubbed down stone axes and made bows. It was they who repeated the sacred words on feast days. The younger men followed the paths through the forests, blazed new trails, and drew their bows on deer and bear, turkey and bobwhite.

Along the Oconee and in the headwaters of the Ogeechee the woods and streams and Indians lived together. Sometimes deer would be killed out, or the fish would leave the river; a brave would tell of a place where these were plentiful. The tribe would agree to leave their dead and tramp through the woods to set up another home. In the new place huts were set up, the bark was rubbed off some trees, the women's patches planted. Canoes split the waters above fresh fishing grounds.

A young brave sits by the fire. He watches the work-slick hands of the old men and women form the articles upon which his life depends. He marvels at the arrow maker's deft use of stone on stone, the canoe maker's skill with wood and fire. His sister, now working with the older women, in a few more years will be making baskets and bowls.

He knows that old men are young braves of many summers, that wrinkled women are his squaw and his sister grown old. There will always be those who will make good arrowheads and axes, bow strings and pots. Thinking so, he looks forward with a singing heart to steamed corn, a couple of days in camp, and then to other days in the woods with his dog watching for antlers.

There were stories of quarrels within his clan, and of extended wars with other tribes. Behind these were legends of how the Creeks and Cherokees came out of the west to live along the Chattahoochee and the Oconee and Ogeechee. An older brother goes from his village to the meeting of the Nation on the banks of the Savannah. He is happy that his people are now permanently settled, that forced treks are of the long ago.

A NEW KIND OF PEOPLE

Then one day the brother returned from the meeting of the Nation, and told a strange story to the people living on the banks of the Oconee. A new kind of people had been seen to the south along the shores of the Great Water. Their skin was reddish, but not so red as their own; their nostrils were thin, their hair fine, and dress curious. They talked in unknown words. They came from another world across the Great Water, in boats wider than the council ring and many times longer. They had rocks you could see through, that drew fire down from the sun. Out of their hard, hollow sticks came a loud noise, smoke, and sure death for buck and bear, or turkey in full flight—death for the red man, too, if he did not help them find the heavy yellow rocks they were looking for.

The people gathered to listen. They had the report told over and over. The oldest men and women pondered, remembered how they had been told of some daring pale men with light hair who in the long, long ago had come from across the Great Water to the north country. It took more men to row one of their boats than there were moons from one summer to the next and the next. Those men traveled far and wide among the red men. They burned clay to make a rock that would last forever. They made a heavy black thing harder than bone that they put on the end of a stick to beat with. They left behind them squared posts with each of the four corners shaved off until all eight sides were alike. Whether those first white men ever reached the Oconee and Ogeechee is not known. But the red men who lived on the east side of the Oconee, below where the Appalachee joins it, had one of their bricks, one of their eight-sided posts, and a claw hammer.

The old men and the braves may have thought that these new white men would go as the old ones had gone, leaving only a legend with the red men. But these newcomers never turned back. They kept coming. The very winds of the sea were bringing them in boats with great white blankets above them.

The next council meeting of the Nation, and the next and the next brought more reports of the Spaniards to the south, and how they were going here and there throughout the red man's farthest domains. They were looking always for the yellow rock, even little ones inside the other rocks. They called it gold, and would do anything to get it. Far over the plains and mountains, the red men sickened and died of a new malady. More than one camp fire went out amid the dead. Or a half dozen survivors, skin heavily pocked, might go through the woods until they came to paths that led to some other camp.

Other councils met, and one year stories came of paler white men who lived in the lower Chesapeake country. Soon after the men, came their women. The settlers cut back the trees, planted the red man's maize and tobacco. They sold the corn and tobacco across the ocean to get more ships which brought more pale men and their wives who in turn cut down the trees farther inland. These English settlers didn't live like the Spaniards, they stayed in one place and raised a family. They pushed the red man off his land, forever.

A few seasons later, news came of white families still farther up the shore of the Great Water. The white people kept coming. Always coming, coming. Each year more of the coastline was taken up. Red men forced back and back in the north by the English and the French.

There were reports too of more newcomers in the south, more women and children among the Spaniards now, more villages and towns. The Indians there yielded ground, too. The Creeks moved the meeting place of their council from the Savannah westward to the banks of the Ocmulgee.

The Creeks and the Cherokees had heard how their kinsmen disliked to lose land in the north and in the south, but how they liked the new things the white men brought. They wanted "fire water" to drink, "fire sticks" to shoot with, glass beads and mirrors, the compass, iron hoes and axes, and scalping knives very much better than their stone tomahawks. And there were always white men who would give them these things to gain favors for themselves or to arm the Indians to fight against their foes. Red men who had worked with stone implements for a thousand years learned to use a rifle in a single afternoon.

Though the red men in the Oconee country saw white men now and then, had some of their trinkets, and died of the white man's smallpox and measles, they were still at home in the stone age.

Their lands lay in the wide strip between the French and English
to the north and the Spaniards to the south, bitter enemies the one
of the other. In the region where the Altamaha runs into the sea, first
the English and then the Spaniards camped. At first they did not
bring their women and children nor build houses and clear land.
But the Creeks moved their council meetings still farther inland,
from the Ocmulgee to the Chattahoochee.

Stories began to come of fighting to the north, where the French
over the mountains and around the Great Lakes had allied themselves with the red men to make war on the English along the sea-
shore. With the help of the mother country, the English came to
rule in the north over the Indians and the French.

The English were determined to control the land that lay between
them and the Spaniards, as well as the north country. So the red
men along the Oconee knew why a few shiploads of men from
England had been sent to occupy all that coast where the Savannah
and Altamaha empty into the sea. There men built forts; soon other
men with their women and children came to live near the mouth
of the Savannah River, and called their town Savannah. The colony
was named Georgia in honor of the English king.

The Englishmen at Savannah made a treaty with the Lower
Creeks. The chiefs agreed to let them have some land along the
coast, to give no encouragement to any white settlers except the
English, and to keep their promise "as long as the sun shall shine,
or the waters run into the sea." This was in what the white men
called "the year of our Lord 1733."

Two summers later the fort at Frederica was built below the
mouth of the Altamaha. And in 1739 the chiefs of the Creeks,
Cherokees, and Chickasaws met with the Englishmen at the
new town of Augusta, far up the Savannah, and there agreed and
signed for Englishmen only to settle along the south side of the
Savannah River.

For three more decades the Creeks and Cherokees along the
Oconee had little reason to fear being pushed off their lands. The

English were busy with the French and Indians in the north, busy with the Spaniards in the south. The English settlements in Georgia grew slowly, remained fast by the sea and the Savannah. Shortly before the 1770's, white men with their families began to follow the fur traders into the forests west of Augusta, and then there was talk of driving the Indians from these hunting grounds.

In 1773 the chiefs of the Creeks and Cherokees were called to Augusta. There they reluctantly signed a treaty ceding two million acres of land to the State of Georgia as settlement for debts owed by the Indians to the merchants of Georgia.

WHITE MEN ON THE OCONEE

The lands given up by the Indians in the treaty of 1773 cornered in the headwaters of the Ogeechee at Great Buffalo Lick, an easy day's walk east of the mounds on the Oconee. A party of surveyors, astronomers, hunters, Indian guides, and gentlemen interested in land speculation went to Great Buffalo Lick to lay out the boundaries of the ceded territory. With this party was the English botanist, William Bartram. In his diary he told of the four-day journey from Augusta. He wrote that Buffalo Lick "contains about three or four acres, is nearly level . . . the earth . . . to an unknown depth is almost white . . . tenacious, fatty clay, which all kinds of cattle lick into great caves, pursuing the delicious vein . . . horned cattle, horses, and deer are immoderately fond of it."

Soon after this the English along the seaboard were at war freeing themselves from the English across the sea. For nearly a decade more the Georgians were friendly with the Creeks and Cherokees, to keep them from becoming the allies of the Spaniards or of the English across the sea, and to carry on a profitable fur trade with them.

When the War of Independence was over, the soldiers were offered free land in Georgia. Settlements grew rapidly. Territory ceded in 1773, named Wilkes county four years later, was soon taken up. In 1783 the State of Georgia called upon the Indians to give up the lands lying between Wilkes county and the east bank of the Oconee. Such a treaty was signed. Now the leaders of the Creeks were aroused. They complained that the treaty had been made with but two of their hundred chiefs and was not valid. Another treaty followed shortly. The Indians claimed that it was even worse than the first, for six of their number had been carried away as hostages to Augusta by the white men who came to hear their complaints about the first treaty.

While the Indians and the State of Georgia haggled over these treaties, the legislature in 1784 created Washington and Franklin counties out of the disputed territory.

A stream of settlers poured into these counties from Virgina and the Carolinas. Scotch-Irish Presbyterians from North Carolina came with their families to the upper forks of the Ogeechee. They called their settlement Bethany. The rich red lands on the east side of the Oconee, above and below the upper shoals, Scull Shoals, were also soon taken up.

GREENE COUNTY ON THE MAP

Early in 1786 by an act of the Georgia Legislature, the westmost section of Washington county was set aside and named Greene county, in honor of the Revolutionary hero Nathaniel Greene. The same Legislature created the town of Greenesborough.

The Indians easily crossed the Oconee River, the western boundary of the land the white men got by the treaty of 1783. Every able-bodied white man was a soldier. Jonas Fauche of Greenesborough, a Swiss already famous as an Indian fighter, was placed in charge of military protection of the Whites. Shortly after the county was formed, Fauche made a survey and recommended twelve forts along the Oconee between Scull Shoals and the shoals at the lower end of the county, Long Shoals. The forts were built.

Some of the settlers with most means had already built private forts. Isaac Stocks' was on his farm about six miles south of Scull Shoals. His son, Thomas, was born there two days before Greene county was laid out. Davis Gresham's fort was two miles to the north, Andrew Armour's and Kimbrough's several miles to the south. When Indian raids came, the settlers took their families to the forts. A sentry kept watch during the night. At daybreak trained dogs were sent out to see if there were any Indians around.

Despite the row of forts, bands of Indians crossed the Oconee from time to time. The Shoulderbone Treaty of 1786 made the Indians even more hostile. The settlers retaliated. Requests were sent to the Congress of the United States for an armed force against them. Congress sent James White, Indian Superintendent, to inquire of the difficulty between the Indians and the settlers of Greene county, whom White called "the Virginians of Georgia." At a meeting with the Indians in the spring of 1787, White pleaded for an "amicable settlement," agreed that the trouble had "perhaps ... been a little the difficulty of both parties," and hoped that "now each will yield a little to the other." He went on to tell the Indians that the Georgians "had lately made provisions for severely punishing their bad folks, who shall disturb their friends, the Indians." Speaking to the red men and Whites together, he said: "We are countrymen, we live in the same land, we breathe the same air; we should be brothers. The Kings and the people who live over the Great Water, will wish to subdue us all ... Ought we not, therefore, to grasp one another with a strong arm of friendship, the more easily to repel these foreigners."

But the Creeks did not agree to go down and run the boundary line, as Superintendent White advised. They repeated that the Virginians of Georgia had "falsely persuaded the rest of the white people they had purchased the land from the Indians." Superintendent White explained that it was impossible to move the white families off the land they occupied and restore it to the Indians. He said he could promise them, however, that the white men would push them off no more of their lands. The Hallowing King of the

Cowetas, in reviewing the continued advances of the white people, said: "These last strides tell us that they never mean to let their foot rest; our lands are our life and breath; if we part with them, we part with our blood. We must fight for them."

This meeting occurred in mid-April 1787. During the summer and early fall the Indians made repeated raids upon the white settlers along the Oconee, killed and wounded several, carried off a few slaves and a good deal of livestock. The settlers pursued them far into their own territory, killing any Indians they found.

In the fall of that year the Indians crossed the Oconee at the lower shoals, came up the ridge to Greenesborough, burned the courthouse and all the houses, killed thirty-one settlers, wounded about twenty more, and took four prisoners.

George Matthews, then Governor of Georgia, penned a letter to President George Washington. He asked that the federal government help arm the 3,000 men he had just called out to carry the war on the Indians into their own country.

In December 1787 the Creeks, in a letter written to Superintendent White by their spokesman Alexander McGillivray, explained their undeclared war on the Greene county settlers: how the chiefs from only two towns had agreed to give up the land, how the chiefs of all the towns soon met at Tookabatcha with ninety-eight of them denying "the right of any two of their countrymen" to give away land that belonged to the whole Creek Nation. The Creeks, he said, had "warned the Georgians of the dangerous consequences that would certainly attend the settling of the lands in question," and "if, after every peaceable mode of obtaining a redress of grievances proved fruitless, a recourse to arms to obtain it be a mark of a savage, and not of the soldier, what savages must the Americans be."

Indian raids and reprisals continued through the 1790's. White settlers were killed and their property stolen. The Indians were pursued, many killed, some captured, and some of their towns burned. In the fall of 1793, a group of armed settlers returned to Greenesborough from over the Oconee with eight Indian prisoners.

Peter Williamson, who was in command, wrote to the Governor: "I now await the pleasure of your Excellency respecting the prisoners and request that they may be kept at some interior place, or the prejudice of the people on the frontier may operate materially against them." The records do not show what became of the captives.

The threat of the Indians to the settlers diminished in the late 1790's and faded out only after the treaties of 1802 and 1804, by which the lands between the Oconee and Ocmulgee were ceded to the Whites. In one of the treaties of this period there was an invoice of goods the Whites were to deliver to the Indians. Among the items were blankets and cloth, axes and hoes, tobacco and whiskey, guns, rifles and ammunition, and "two dozen scalping knives at $2 per dozen."

III

HARDY PIONEERS

By 1767, the year the Indians burned Greenesborough, a Superior Court had been set up and the Grand Inquest (later called the grand jury) made its presentments. It asked for a state constitution with "a full bill of Wright," that would "give the people the blesings of a lasting, hapy, easey, and good government."

Judge George Walton, a signer of the Declaration of Independence, then presided over the Superior Court in Greene county. In one of his early charges to the grand jury he observed that since the county was newly settled and near the borders where there were savages, "a various description of characters may be expected constantly to be found among our citizens whose point of view and practices are not the most honorable and honest." Another part of his charge was directed to the lawyers: "It had crept into practice for gentlemen of the Bar to return thanks to juries for verdicts favorable to their clients. This is indelicate and highly improper."

WESTERN GEORGIA—"THE RICHEST JEWELL"

During the time that the Indians were warring with the Whites east of the Oconee, other white men went over the river and formed the Trans-Oconee Republic, a state to be separate from the United States. A Revolutionary hero, Elijah Clark, was the leader of this group, which sometimes furnished the Indians with guns and ammunition to carry on their raids against the settlers. Clark was arrested, carried to Augusta, and tried for treason.

At the trial when Judge Walton charged the grand jury, he spoke of Clark as a personal friend and pointed to his fine record in the War of Independence. The judge was sure that Clark himself would forgive him for "detailing the laws against a scheme, which tends to undermine the fair fabric which he helped to raise." In reviewing the many treaties with the Indians, the judge said he did not believe that treaties with savages "be of the same rank as those with civilized nations." He made it clear, however, that the President of the United States had given orders against settlement of the lands over the Oconee, and that if necessary arms would be used to prevent it. He concluded by saying western Georgia was the "richest jewell the State possesses, and the real basis of her future wealth and rank in the Union," and that settlers should not be allowed to move in except with the consent of the state and federal governments.

Commenting on the trial the *Augusta Chronicle* said, "The intention is to bring General Clark from the south side of the Oconee that all may have a fair start for that rich jewel, the last territory belonging to Georgia." General Clark was acquitted. He faithfully agreed to stay east of the river.

Elijah Clark was not the only man interested in land grabbing. There was the Yazoo Fraud: The Georgia Legislature of 1794-95 was bribed to sell some thirty-five million acres of land for $500,000 to a group of speculators. When the news leaked out, the people rose up and demanded that the sale be declared illegal. The next Legislature burned the records of the deal on the public square, that no evidence of it might be left.

Jonas Fauche, the Indian fighter, and another legislator from Greene voted for the Yazoo land deal. A Greenesborough citizen condemned the legislators. Fauche challenged him to a duel at Love Spring just outside of Greenesborough. He felled his opponent, dropped to his knees by the dying man and burst into tears. Afterward he often made visits to the grave. When it was hinted his conscience was bothering him, Fauche proudly said: "I killed him, it is true. I do not weep that I did wrong, for I did not. I weep that so brave a man and so noble an opponent was forced to die. That is all."

Along with the grand schemes of the Trans-Oconee Republic and the Yazoo Land Fraud went the commoner forms of land-grabbing. One of Greene's first grand juries presented as a "great grievance" the disclosure that there were more land warrants than there was land. Deeds, notes, and other legal papers were of first importance. The Legislature made forgery a capital crime. In 1800 four men from Greene were convicted of forgery and sentenced to be hanged. Two of them were sons of a leading family. The Governor had requests from all over the state to pardon them. He did. But the accused were told nothing about the pardon until they had mounted the gallows, felt the noose around their necks, and heard their funerals read. In a letter to the minister who was to preach the funerals, the Governor explained: "My intention is by making them taste of death to render them back to the community members worthy of it . . . and to their families as renovated characters."

AN HONEST LIVELIHOOD

The majority of Greene's early settlers came here with their families to earn a livelihood honestly. Their ideal was expressed in the epitaph which Jeremiah Sanford dictated for his tombstone:

> HE WAS A SOLDIER OF THE REVOLUTION,
> A FRIEND OF WASHINGTON,
> AND AN HONEST MAN

The backgrounds and experiences of the pioneers were varied. Some were sons and daughters of plantation families who had left depleted lands in Virginia, where for generations tobacco had been grown with slave labor. Most were from the older sections of Georgia and the hill country of the Carolinas. Ex-Revolutionary soldiers were attracted by headright offers of 287½-acre tracts, with 50 acres added for each child and each slave.

Nearly all the families made their own living at home. They built log houses, cleared the land to cultivate, put rail fences around their fields and patches, and let their cows, sheep, and hogs range the countryside. Every large landholder had a registered mark for his livestock. For example, James Park's mark was "a crop in the right ear & a nick in the under part of the same ear." Most of the families planted enough cotton for their own needs. They also made clothes of wool which the women carded into thread and wove into cloth. They made shoes from tanned cowhide. Beaver, mink, coon, and rabbit provided meat for the table and fur for hats or the market. Clear streams furnished plenty of fish for the family, and now and then fertilizer for a garden patch.

Tobacco and indigo, their cash crops, were marketed in Augusta. Indigo was usually carried in wagons. Tobacco was rolled in wooden hogsheads six feet high and eight or ten feet long. A part of the route near Augusta came to be known as Tobacco Road. Tobacco was so important that it was often used for currency in local transactions. In 1791 it was a capital crime to give two receipts for the same hogshead of tobacco, or to change the markings on a hogshead. With tobacco and indigo, the farmers bought what they could not produce at home: coffee, iron tools, medicine, needles and buttons, guns and ammunition, and sometimes a book or magazine. A few families needed schoolbooks for their children who attended the academy in Greenesborough.

ACRES AND SLAVES

While they lived simply at first, a few of the families owned large tracts of land. The tax returns of 1788 showed twelve landowners with more than 1,000 acres each. The largest was John Swepson, with 7,294 acres—5,519 "oak and hickory land" and 1,775 "pine." The next largest owners were William Danniell 3,796 acres, Robert Middleton 2,750, Peter Coffee 2,737, Jesse Battle 1,900, James Adams 1,887.

By 1795 two dozen men owned over 1,000 acres each; several of them had over 10,000. These big tracts were in the rich, red lands of the northern and western parts of the county, except for a few in the strip of red land around Bethany in the southeast.

Some of these early settlers brought slaves with them. In 1788 there were 192 slaveowners in the county. One hundred and thirty-six of them owned five or less, and only five owned fifteen or more. The largest owners were James Showet with 32, John Mitchell with 23, Charles Abercrombie and William Lawson with 19 each, and John Thomas with 15. The largest landowners were not always the largest slave owners.

The number of slaves increased rapidly. Joel Early of Scull Shoals was the largest slaveowner in the county in 1800. He had 70. The next largest were Thomas Grimes with 26, William Green 25, Redmond Thornton and James Park 24 each, John Crutchfield 22, George W. Foster 21, Absalom Lawrence and George Dawson 20 each, and Oliver Porter with 19. Over a third of the population were Negroes—all slaves but "seven free persons of color."

By 1810, half of the 12,000 people in the county were slaves. But half of Greene's white families owned no slaves at all.

JOSEPH SMITH AND JOEL EARLY

Men representing the two types of farmer in Greene county in the pioneer period were Joseph Smith and Joel Early. The first will on record in the county is that of Smith, a surveyor. He left 300 acres of land, 17 cows, 4 horses, 3 Bibles, 3 testaments, 3 sermon books, surveying instruments, and 4½ yards of grey cloth. He had no slaves.

Joel Early's large home, which he named Early's Manor, over-looked the shoals. It was built of brick brought over from England, and was said to be the most elegant country place north of Savannah. He lived like an English lord, had his children wear formal dress to dinner at six. He owned 1,400 acres where his manor was located, 1,300 acres across the Oconee, the place in Wilkes county which he left when he came to Greene, and unsurveyed lands on the frontier. In his will he left specific instructions for the care of his fields and orchards.

Other substantial houses in the county in 1800 included those of Jonas Fauche and Nicholas Lewis in Greenesborough; Benjamin Weaver, two miles south of Greenesborough; and Redmond Thornton, eight miles to the northeast. Thornton's house is said to be the first frame house built in the county. He was a great grandson of Matthew Thornton, Virginia signer of the Declaration of Independence, and was named for his paternal grandmother, an Indian woman of a family named Redmond (sometimes spelled Redman, or Redmen).

Joel Early's taxes were nearly $50, the next largest in the county was scarcely one third that amount. Eight other men in the county paid as much as ten dollars each.

Most of the white families of this early period, like Joseph Smith, had few or no slaves and worked their own land. Their double log cabins soon began to replace the usual one-room type. Roofs were made of boards rived from oaks or chestnut. Floors were commonly of hard sand, though brick and planks from hand-operated sawmills were being used more and more. Neighbors often got together to build a house or a barn, clear out a road or harvest a crop. Much of this working together was arranged from day to day; some of it was well planned.

Two pioneer cooperatives were the Yazoo and Methodist Fisheries. They operated on the island in the Oconee River at the mouth of Richland Creek. Each fishery was composed of twenty-six families, each of whom devoted two weeks a year to taking fish from the traps and distributing them equally among the members. The company as a whole kept the dam and traps in good condition. Any member who failed to tend the traps during his two weeks, or failed to report for emergency repairs, was given no fish for the remainder of the season. Both fisheries flourished for years.

"A HAPY, EASEY, AND GOOD GOVERNMENT"

The erection of the first courthouse and "gaol" was authorized in the same legislative act that created the county. The buildings were made of wood. A stronger "gaol" was soon needed, so in 1806 a two-story, rock one was built—twenty-eight feet square and twenty-five feet high.

The Governor's action in pardoning the young forgers, after he had scared them good, expressed the current idea in regard to punishment in those days: "To renovate" the evil doer, if possible; if not, to make him a gruesome and ridiculous example. Hangings were public events. Branding was not unknown. Ducking was considered a sure way to cure a woman of tongue wagging, and more than one felt the chill waters of Richland Creek. Men were imprisoned for their debts, though in one instance the jailer released a debtor because he had not been paid upkeep for him.

The early presentments of the grand jury contained several grievances of interest: in 1789 it was regretted that "profane swearing" was tolerated by the magistrates of Greenesborough "in their hearings;" and that there was "no stocks erected for the confinement of disorderly persons." In 1795 it was lamented that duelling is so common and that the law "has not made more effectual provision against it;" that "the law now in force in this state respecting the protection of negroes and their lives is not adequate."

The grand jury asked the legislature for a law "to prevent hawking and peddling in this state" for it drains off "much circulating specie." A later presentment told how the itinerant merchants and peddlers (many from New England) "sell superficially good looking goods but shoddy." And most important, they discouraged honest local merchants, for "in the sunshine of peace they are subject to no taxation because they have no permanent place of residence whilst our local merchants enhance the treasury of this state."

In 1796, the grand jury brought to the attention of the citizens that "the streets of Greenesborough are so enclosed that carriages can scarcely pass." The Inferior Court was asked to "compel the citizens not to exceed the front and sides of their lots." Enforcement of patrol laws for slaves was recommended by 1798, and early in 1800 this: "We present as a grievance the little attention paid to the presentments of the grand juries in general." Later in that year two Justices were presented "for suffering and admitting the disorderly and unwarranted conduct of profane swearing, drinking, fidling, and dancing at the time and place of holding their courts." Gambling and card playing at public meetings were condemned, as was also "the custom of leading and parading stud horses in the main street of Greenesborough on public occassions . . . and the profane and indelicate practice of showing stud horses on the Sabbath day at places of public worship."

HORSE RACING, MOURNERS' BENCH, SCHOOLS

With more settlers coming and the threat of the Indians waning, there was some leisure and money for sports. In the *Augusta Chronicle* in 1801, the Greenesborough Jockey Club advertised a three-day horse race. The first day's purse was $250 for a three-mile heat; second day, $150 for two-mile heat; third day, one-mile heat for entrance money.

Along with pioneer cabins, Indian raids, forts, land-grabbing, duels, courts, jails, and horse racing came the churches. Not all the people approved of horse racing any more than they all did of land-grabbing and duelling. Some minutes of the Bethesda Baptist Church read: "Charges of immoral and un-Christian conduct will be brought against Brother ———. He is charged with aiding and abetting in the un-Godly practice of horse racing, in that, he allowed visiting horse owners to quarter their horses on his land, and that he sold them corn and hay for said horses." The accused claimed he had a right to sell his provender and rent his barns to any person visiting in his neighborhood. After lecturing him on the sins of the day, particularly horse racing, the church leaders withdrew the charge.

Bethesda Baptist Church was organized in 1785, in territory that was Wilkes county until its transfer to Greene in 1802. Bethany Presbyterian was established in 1786 with Reverend Francis Cummins pastor. He had been a delegate to the Independence Conventions at Mecklenburg, North Carolina in 1775 and at Philadelphia in 1776. Shiloh and Scull Shoals Baptist churches came soon after.

Liberty Chappell, in the lower part of Greene county, was meeting in a brush arbor, called "Bush's" in honor of the Bush family near by who helped maintain the arbor. In 1799 Bishop Francis Asbury held a Methodist conference at Liberty. And there he ordained Lovick Pierce into the Methodist ministry. The institution of the "mourners' bench" is supposed to have been begun "at Old Liberty" by the revivalist Reverend Stilth Mead. His preaching brought so many "under conviction" that he gave up trying to instruct each one separately and invited them to take the front seats where he could talk with all of them at once. From this developed the custom of going up to the altar to be prayed for.

Reverend Cummins of Bethany early established an "arm" of the Presbyterian Church in Greenesborough. The few Methodists and Baptists in town worshiped with the Presbyterians in the Siloam Meeting House on Cemetery Hill. From these parent churches in Greene county sprang many another through schism, division, and growth of population.

The schooling of the young was limited largely to what little book instruction the parents gave at home. In creating Greene county and Greenesborough, the legislature had ordered that six tracts of land, of 5,000 acres each, be used to build and support a state university, to be located in Greene. The county-seat town was laid out on one of these tracts, and in 1796 the county authorities had $3,188.57 in hand from the sale of lots. But the early Greenesborough families wanted no university boys making way with their apples. So a little later the university was founded thirty miles to the north, on a tract of land given by Governor Milledge, valued at the price of a horse and saddle.

The only record of a school in Greene in the early years was the one-teacher Greene County Academy, set up by the legislature of 1786 which created the county and Greenesborough.

THE COUNTY GROWS UP

By 1800 the young county of Greene was beginning to grow up. It had a population of more than 10,500. A Greene county cotton gin was in the courts in 1802: William Ellison was suing William Veazy for the $160 promised him for a saw gin he had made and delivered the year before. Court records show that this was not the type of gin for which Whitney got a patent in 1791.*

Early in 1803 plans were under way to provide Greenesborough with a regular weekly mail service. A scheduled weekly mail was a great improvement over sending a message by one's own servant, or waiting for an undetermined mail departure.

In 1803, also, a road was laid out across the Cherokee Nation from Greenesborough to Walnut Hill on the Mississippi River. It was called the Three-Chop Road. Samuel Dale, well known in Greene, helped lay out the route that was marked by three chops in one tree after another through the hundreds of miles of virgin forests.

Unoccupied land in Greene was distributed by lottery in 1806. The next year a newspaper was set up, the *Greenesborough Observator*. Yelverton P. King, a citizen of Greene, had been made custodian of Georgia's gold mines, and Templeton Reid was coining ten-dollar gold pieces.

The first paper mill in Georgia was established in 1810 at Scull Shoals, with a loan of $3,000 from the legislature to Zachariah Sims.

The rising plantation owners needed a way to get their cotton to the sea. One grand jury after another had advocated opening the

---

* Also non-Whitney were the "two cotton wheels" appraised at 24 shillings in the estate of Benjamin Gilbert, recorded January 1791.

Oconee to navigation. In 1811 the Oconee Navigation Company was granted a charter by the Georgia Legislature, and given an appropriation for the removal of rocks and other obstructions from the river. A half dozen stockholders of the Company were from Greene. Small grist mills and sawmills operating along the river were no longer allowed to dam it; they were ordered to take water from the head of falls. And so the small businessmen began to feel the power of the plantation owners.

River boats soon churned the Oconee from Scull Shoals to Long Shoals, and back again. At Long Shoals the cotton had to be unloaded and carried around the shoals to boats below. This happened at several other points farther down the river where the channel remained rockbound.

Further evidence that the county was growing up was that Joel Early's son, Peter, already powerful in state and national politics, was headed for the Governor's chair during the War of 1812. Elected, he helped win the war by making state funds available to the United States Army. Governor Early was asked if he did not think each state might have to protect itself, and, if it did, would not Georgia need all her own resources. He said he hoped "such a thing would never happen, but if it should" he had no wish "that Georgia should survive the general wreck." He wanted to sink or swim with the other states.

Men prominent in politics, slave-owning, and plantation management were emerging in the county. They could meet in the county seat of Greenesborough, and dine together at Ye Eagle Tavern, which proudly advertised: "Regularly supplied with the best provender the county affords . . . cellars are abundantly provided with liquor of the first quality, stables are extensive and airy."

By the time of the War of 1812, white families had taken up nearly all the land, though one more lottery * was to distribute free land, and the final boundaries of the county had not yet been fixed.

---

*In 1826, a land lottery distributed tracts to 92 soldiers and widows.

The forts along the Oconee were falling in. Treaty after treaty with the Indians had put the white man's frontier well into Alabama.

Tallow candles were used for lighting houses. The girl who had a parasol was the envy of the other girls, and the boy with new home-made boots stirred his rival to desperate efforts to distinguish himself. Wagon trains still hauled cotton 600 miles to Baltimore, and brought back supplies. Some of the worshipers at Bethesda Church remained jittery about the Indians, carried their guns. And when Garnett Andrews, then a small boy, drove his mother to church in the four-wheel vehicle his father had built for her, the church folks frowned upon such display of worldliness. Even more flashy was planter Harrison Watts' $80 gold watch, and the $3 silver slippers he had bought for his womenfolk.

In 1813 a white woman was tried and convicted as a "common scold and tattler." For punishment she was "ducked" in Richland Creek. And throughout that year a professional pensman, with an "M" burned into his left thumb, sat in the jail transcribing the court proceedings and tax digests for permanent binding. He had been employed for this task in the office of the clerk of court, but before completing it he killed a man and was convicted of murder. The jury recommended mercy. The judge had him branded and sentenced to jail, and allowed him to shorten his stay by completing his work on the records.

Frontier rowdiness was common for many years. The grand jury of 1817 presented as a grievance "the firing of cannon in the town of Greenesborough particularly in the public square to the material injury of property situated therein; and also to the interruption of families in the town." And many were the men presented for "an affray which took place . . . to the terror of the citizens and great disturbance of the public tranquility."

Something of Greene's raw frontier life was written down by

Augustus B. Longstreet in his book, *Georgia Scenes*. He came to the county as a young lawyer in 1817. In a few years he married Frances Eliza Park, daughter of James Park. He left the county in 1829 a Methodist minister and a respected judge. Repentant of what he had revealed in *Georgia Scenes,* he bought up all the copies he could find in an effort to remove it from circulation.

Most of the white families had few or no slaves and worked their own lands. But in the decade after the Battle of New Orleans, more and more of the best lands were being bought up by the larger slave-holders. They were building plantation houses on the knolls along the Oconee and Appalachee rivers and larger creeks. In the red-land sections of the county, a landed aristocracy was emerging through the use of slave labor, the commercial production of cotton, and the home production of practically all the food, feed, clothing, and fuel needed on the plantation. In a single generation the Indians had been driven out and slaves from Africa outnumbered the white people. To the landed Whites, accumulation and security was becoming a profession.

The creeks were all named by the early settlers: Richland, Beaver Dam, Towns, Fishing, Greenbrier, and the smaller ones. And the waters of these English-named creeks ran into Indian-named rivers. New water kept bubbling up through a hundred springs to make the creek that swelled the river. Boats on the rivers carried cotton to the sea.

Time, too, moved on: the present ever turning back to join the past, the future always coming with sunups and seasons. And already the seeds of Greene county's golden age of slaves, cotton, politics, and manners were rooted in the fertile soil along the Oconee and the Appalachee, and in the headwaters of the Ogeechee.

IV

THE GOLDEN AGE

When the planter families around Bethesda Baptist Church erected a beautiful brick building in 1818 they put balconies on three sides for their slaves.

The masters gave written permission for the slaves to join the church. Penned notes to the official church bodies would read: "Jane has permission to be baptized," "Phoeby has leaf to join the church," and "John has my permission (as far as I have a right to give my permission) to join the Baptist denomination." Negro deacons served the Negroes just as white deacons served the white group.

"OUTLANDISH" SLAVES AND POLITICS

Some slaves had been brought in from the older communities of Virginia and the Carolinas. They were familiar with the white man's way of life, and had learned many skills. Even after the slave trade was supposed to have stopped in 1808, a larger number was brought here by smugglers direct from Africa or from the sea-islands off the coast of Georgia. These were wholly unaccustomed to living conditions here, and were called "outlandish" or "new" Negroes. A few claimed to have been princes and princesses in their native land. Some found the slave's lot intolerable and killed themselves so their spirits at least might return to their native country. It is reported that one slaveholder overcame this practice "by cutting off the head of the suicide," and telling the other slaves that even if the dead man did return to his country he would be without a head.

29

Under supervision the "outlandish" slaves did well enough clearing new-grounds, planting, cultivating, and harvesting the crops. After a few years a number of them, too, had learned to do the skilled work around the large plantations: build the house and barn, tan the leather, make the shoes, sharpen plow points, mend trace chains, repair wagon wheels, build carts. On nearly every plantation, one or more slaves looked after the livestock—fed them and "doctored" them when sick.

Inside the house, under the general oversight of the wife and mother, slave women and a favored man servant tended fires, cooked and served meals, swept the floors and made beds, kept milk and butter cool in the spring-house and carried water to the kitchen, mixed white clay or calcimine to brighten hearths and walls, made tallow candles and lighted them at dusk.

The children of the house slaves were usually the playmates, errand-runners, and confidants of the owner's children. The sons and daughters of the slaveowners were little masters and mistresses themselves. A little white girl and her slave playmate played dolls. When the noon bell rang, the Negro mammy tidied the white child for dinner and told the slave child to make up the doll's bed, clean off the little dresser, and put all the dolls back on the shelf.

White boys and slave boys played together all over the yard. Slave boys hitched to a home-made wagon. Two white boys riding in it calling "gee," "haw," "gid-up," "whoa!" Sometimes one of the colored boys rode, sometimes two of them, but they all knew that if any argument arose, the little Negroes would be reminded that they were slave children.

The children of the house slaves felt they could treat the field hands' children much as they were treated by their little masters and mistresses. One child tired of his color, put flour all over his hands and face only to find a little later that he was black as ever. Twice daily he watched from the back porch of the big house, saw his mother put milk, bread, and Spanish potatoes in the scrubbed poplar trough where the children of the field hands were given their extra food. Every day he heard her call: "Little niggahs, little niggahs, little niggahs!" Saw the children come running. With cups and fingers they went for it. Often he saw his mistress come across the porch, say with satisfaction: "Just look at my little niggahs eat, keeps them fat and nice." One day, needing to prove that he was different, he went out and walked in the trough, felt the warm food squeeze up between his toes. The field children yanked him out and pommeled him. After a time, his mistress stopped them: "You've beat him enough now. He wants to be white, but he can't. From now on, though, he'll know not to walk in the victuals of my hungry little niggahs!"

The county's leaders were aware that Greene was part of the slave South. Local attitudes were revealed in this toast to the Missouri Compromise: "It has excited much argument. It has exposed individual views. May the King of the North be confined to his own dominion." The occasion was a dinner in 1820 in Greenesborough in honor of Andrew Jackson, who was here visiting his uncle, Gwynn Allison's father.

Six years later, at an Independence Day program, other revealing toasts were drunk: "May his political days be few and another take his office," ran a toast to John Quincy Adams. A toast "to the general Government" said, "So long as it was administered by wise and impartial hands, so long and no longer were individual states bound to respect it and submit to its decrees." At the same dinner a toast was drunk to the citizens of Georgia: "Free, honest, and enlightened, may the prejudice of education or the force of party never make them guilty of treason against themselves."

The largest slaveholder in Greene in 1834 was Dr. Thomas N. Poullain of Scull Shoals. He owned 145. The second largest was his neighbor, James K. Daniel, with 117. Eight families owned between 50 and 100 slaves. Eighty-three more families owned between 20 and 50 slaves. In 1810 only 31 families had owned 20 or more slaves, in 1788 but two.*

_____
* For names of largest slaveowners, see Appendices 2, 3, and 4.

How completely slaves were thought of as property is shown by a grand jury presentment of March 1822. The carrying off of a certain woman slave named Rachel was called "larceny" and condemned as a "great damage" to the man who owned her. The presentments of nearly every grand jury contained complaints against the ineffectiveness of the patrol laws.

SMALL WHITE FARMERS PUSHED OUT

As the slave population of Greene increased, the white population decreased. Between 1810 and 1840 the slave population rose from 5,281 to 7,049. The county's white population dropped from 6,398 to 4,641.

As the slave plantation expanded many live-at-home white families sold their land and moved out. A few found haven on the coarse grey lands in the southeastern part of Greene. The old Fort Wall settlement on the lower edge of the white lands moved two miles west to some good springs, and in 1828 took the name of White Plains. Many families left the county. Some went to the Alabama and Mississippi frontiers. Some moved into the foothills of the Blue Ridge or deep into the wiregrass and pine barren region.

Plantations took up more and more of the land. The two-room pioneer log cabins of the family-size farmers were largely replaced by the few homes of the planters and their slave quarters close by.

Many of the larger plantation owners developed proud country places, made beautiful with magnolia and boxwood, mimosa and azalea, crepe myrtle and jasmine, roses and verbena. Wide cotton fields had already cleared most of the original forest except for the wooded tracts around the "big house." Thomas Stocks called his place "Oak Hill," his neighbor Colonel Willis lived at "Dover," the Greshams at "Oakland," the Harts at "Oak Grove," Lemuel Greene at "Jefferson Hall." Other plantation homesteads, too, bore the names of the trees which the slaves were chopping back, as well as Anglo-Saxon family names.

GREENE'S BOUNTIFUL DECADE

During the 1830's Greene forged into the period of her greatest prosperity. She had advanced beyond the hard pioneer days, yet she still had much virgin soil. In 1837, Georgia was the leading cotton state—earning the title of "Empire State of the South." Greene, just fifty years old, was producing most of the foods and feeds she needed and more cotton than any other county in the state.

As wealth accumulated on banner crops from virgin soil and slave labor, a railroad was constructed, a university founded, and three cotton factories built.

In 1834 one of the first cotton mills in Georgia was opened at Scull Shoals on the Oconee, fourteen miles northwest of Greenesborough. The factory was operated partly with slave labor, as was Ligon's public gin which had been doing business here since 1807. Many people in the county believed the cotton mill would be as important in cotton history as the gin. Before the end of the 1830's two other cotton factories were built: one at Greenesborough, the other at Long Shoals on the Oconee fifteen miles to the south.

A census of a few years later listed 47 manufactures in the county. This included the three cotton mills, several wagon shops, blacksmith shops, cotton gins, clockmakers, and others. Northern people played an important part in the business life of the county. The owners of the mills hired experienced men from northern mills to supervise their laborers, many of whom were slaves. Greenesborough's clockmakers, Barber and Davis, were from Connecticut.

GEORGIA'S FIRST RAILROADS

A Greene county mud hole is said to have been responsible for the building of the Georgia Railroad. English-made cotton mill machinery was being taken from Augusta to Athens on six-mule wagons. The wagons got stuck in the mud on the eastern side of Greene, and could not be moved until the land dried out the following spring. As a result, the factory promoters applied for a charter to build a railroad from Augusta to Athens. The Georgia Legislature granted the charter late in 1833, and work began at once out of Augusta. After some months the railroad was finished as far as Jefferson Hall, Lemuel Greene's place nine miles east of Greenesborough. Jefferson Hall became a thriving community overnight, as wagon trains from Greenesborough, Athens, Madison, Eatonton, Sparta, and Covington brought cotton to load on freight cars and carried back supplies.

After the road was built two miles beyond this terminus, it was decided to construct a branch line through Greenesborough to Marthasville. Later the road on to Athens was completed. Their junction was called Union Point. Nearby Thornton's Crossroads, earlier Scruggsville, soon became a part of the new railroad town. Here the trains stopped to take on water and wood for fuel, and give passengers an opportunity to get a meal and change trains. Repair shops were built. As Union Point grew, Jefferson Hall shrank back into a plantation homesite.

There was some opposition to the building of the railroad. The town of Lexington, in nearby Oglethorpe county, would not let it come nearer than four miles, nor were all the landowners in Greene pleased. Andrew Jackson's cousin, Gwynn Allison, who lived midway between Greenesborough and Union Point, was an unyielding opponent. He disregarded court orders, took his gun and drove the railroad surveyors off "his" property. He was tried for contempt of court and lodged in jail for a short time. Pride injured, he refused the money the arbitrators awarded him for his land.

Allison's neighbor, Thomas Hart, on the other hand befriended the railroad in every way he could, and a courtesy stop was maintained at Oak Grove, his home. The very first passenger train stopped to celebrate a wedding breakfast here, with passengers and crew taking part in the festivities.

Only two other railroads in the United States had trains running when the Georgia Railroad began its schedule. Greenesborough was the terminus from 1835-1837, while the road was being built into Marthasville (later Atlanta). The train crews had to spend one night in Augusta, the next in Greenesborough. It was against the law to run the train at night: neither man nor beast could sleep along its route.

The cross-ties were six feet apart, and the rails were strong wooden beams with a strip of iron three inches wide nailed to the top. Horses drew the first cars between Athens and Union Point. The first engine running between Union Point and Athens was called the "Fire-Fly;" the fire did fly as one cord of wood after another was fed to it. Woodville took its name from the great piles of wood stacked near the station for the engines.

THE PROGRESS OF MIND

Some of the larger planters began to pay more attention to education and manners. Brockman United Academy was incorporated in 1826, the first after the Greenesborough Academy of 1786. Lafayette Hall Academy was opened in 1827, Thornton Academy 1831, and White Plains Academy 1834.

Greene's most outstanding educational development was Mercer University. In 1829 it was announced at the Georgia Baptist Convention in Milledgeville that Josiah Penfield, a deacon of Savannah, had bequeathed $2,500 to the Convention for education on condition that an equal amount be raised. Fifteen minutes later the amount had been subscribed by Jesse Mercer, Adiel Sherwood, William Flournoy, Thomas Stocks, all of Greene county, and other Baptists at the Convention.

The Convention decided to locate the school in Greene county as a result of the wealth and influence of the Greene county Baptists. Oliver Porter, Billington Sanders, James Armstrong, and Absalom and Thomas James all assisted in getting the school located here. In due time a 450-acre tract of land seven miles north of Greenesborough was purchased. The town of Penfield came into existence.

The school was named Mercer Institute for Jesse Mercer, then the most influential Baptist divine in the state, and the school's largest financial supporter. Mercer gave more than $40,000 to the school. Much of his financial resources had come to him through his second wife, a Gentile woman who had inherited considerable wealth from her Jewish husband, Captain Abram Simons, a Revolutionary soldier.

In 1837 the Georgia Baptist Convention raised $100,000 as a permanent endowment fund, and changed the name to Mercer University.

The report of the Mercer Endowment Committee tells the story of Greene county's new prosperity, and the passing of the Pioneer Age: "This age of our republic is characterized by the march of mind. The time is passed when the attention of our nation is chained down to arduous toil for the necessities of life. Plenty and peace are ours . . . The sinews of our mighty nation cannot be employed solely in felling the forests, tilling the soil, or in mechanics. We have been compelled to employ our minds, to advance in the arts and sciences for our political and social good. The pleasures of intellectual study are now generally indulged. The character of common schools is elevated, and the literary character of the mass of people as a consequence is also raised . . . All denominations are wisely engaged in making preparation to keep pace with the progress of mind, and to meet the intellectual wants of the age."

With their wealth and position grounded in slavery, Mercer's founders wanted a university where due recognition would be given to Southern values and practices. The University was established to train young Southern men for the various professions, especially the Baptist ministry.

Mercer pioneered in helping students earn their way through school, and in providing free textbooks. The church leaders apparently realized that most of their ministers were coming from the poorer families. Students at Mercer University could get board at the "Commons" for $7 per month or at the private homes for $10, washing $1 per month, and room rent and fuel in the college for $10.

The University attracted intellectual and cultural activity. Well-to-do families from different parts of Georgia and neighboring states moved in to educate their children. The Penfield Female Academy was chartered in 1840.

The Temperance Crusader attacked the practice of drinking in taverns and hotels, and listed "Temperance Hotels" in many Georgia towns. Penfield became the headquarters of the state's temperance movement, as it was already the capital of Georgia Baptists. Mercer University, the townspeople, and outlying plantations made it a thriving business center, and for a time, Greenesborough played second fiddle to Penfield.

POLISHED DAUGHTERS AND POOR SCHOOLS

But Greenesborough, too, had educational institutions of which it was proud—its old academy and the Greenesborough Female College established in 1852 by the Georgia Synod of the Presbyterian Church. United States Senator W. C. Dawson and Congressman Francis Cone of Greenesborough were trustees. Dr. I. S. K. Axson was president. The Academy's motto was: "That our Daughters may be as corner-stones, polished after the similitude of a Palace." One of the early commencement sermons was on the text, "Let your women keep silence in the church." The preacher was Dr. Joseph R. Wilson. Unfortunately the record does not show whether he was accompanied by his little son, Thomas Woodrow, who years later married the daughter of President Axson.

The Greenesborough Female College used some teachers from the North and East. One was Anne Maria Lyman, sister of the famous New England clergyman. She married Junius Poullain, son of Thomas N. Poullain, chief owner of the Scull Shoals factory and the largest slaveholder in the county. William H. Seward, when a young man, is locally reported to have spent some time in Greenesborough and White Plains.

The growing need of the poorer white children for schools had been revealed in the grand jury presentments. In March of 1844 it was recommended that the Inferior Court "levy a tax of 16-2/3 per cent on the state tax for the education of the poor children of the county." Two years later the county had raised and spent $270 through the "Poor School Fund." Five years later a little over a thousand dollars was spent. One fourth of it came from the state, the other three fourths from county taxes. The jury reported that many children were staying away from the "free" schools. It pointed out that the parents should send their children to the schools without any sense of shame since they were maintained by money from all the taxpayers.

The Poor School Fund made it possible for about 450 white children who could not attend an academy to get some schooling. In Greene's Golden Age of slaves, cotton, politics, and manners, her leaders were busy with the new railroad, new cotton mills, a new university, and a new Female College. Through the Poor School Fund they recognized the presence in their midst of non-slaveowning Whites.

V

THE GOLDEN AGE

(*Continued*)

IN THE heyday of slavery, Greene county had many thriving communities; there were over a dozen post offices. Some of these communities declined after a few years, and the post offices were discontinued.

STAGE COACHES AND TALLOW CANDLES REMAIN

Public Square was at its height in the 1820's and early 1830's. It boasted the leading country store, first in the county to sell factory-made clothes. With the coming of the railroad, its importance declined. Temperance Bell got its name from two popular school teachers, Temperance Daniel and a man named Bell.

The best mill on the Oconee was six miles southwest of Greenesborough at Park's Mill, sometimes called Riverside, where there was also a ferry and later a toll bridge. Here lived James B. Park and his uncle, "Dickie" Park, who built a strong hickory chest with a coin slot in the top of it. The ferry and bridge tolls went into it; nothing came out. When "Dickie" Park died, his administrators opened the chest, counted out over $100,000 in gold and silver.

Travel was still slow and expensive. Railroad fare was five cents a mile; the speed was fifteen miles an hour, when running. It took eight hours to go from Greenesborough to Augusta, a distance of 85 miles. The county's other scheduled transportation was the old stand-by, the stage coach—five miles an hour at ten cents a mile.

Stage coaches came to Greenesborough from Athens, Washington, Sparta, and Eatonton. Convenient stops were made along the way to change horses, and allow passengers to get meals and lodging.

Grantville was four miles northeast of Union Point on the Greenesborough-Washington stage coach route. There was a tavern here, and a station for changing stage coach horses. It was general headquarters for gaming—horse races, cock fights, gander pullings, greased-pole contests, and the like.

Things were astir in Greenesborough throughout the day: coaches coming in, lathered animals unhitched and led away. Fresh teams harnessed, the coaches went out again. Four horses to the coach. Great was the excitement when runaway horses pounded down Broad Street, the coach lurching after.

But the arrival of the train at the railroad station was a thrill the town could always depend on. After five and ten years many townsfolk were still attracted to the station. And country people hardly thought they had been to town at all if they hadn't seen a train screech to a stop, and the passengers get off and get on. Friends to greet, strangers to wonder about.

Postage rates ranged from 12½ cents to $1.50, depending on the distance. The letter was folded and sealed with wax, and the address written on the outside of the same sheet. Almanacs were beginning to appear, and cost from 25 to 50 cents. Calendars were few. The *Christian Index* carried one in its first issue each year. In most homes it was given a special hiding place, often inside the clock on the parlor mantel.

Tallow candles remained the means of lighting homes in country and towns. Kerosene oil was just coming into use in the wealthier homes. It cost $1.75 a gallon. Many of the fine early oil lamps would hold only a half pint of the precious fuel.

Soap was made at home. Into the ash-hopper in the yard were poured the powdery ashes of hardwoods burned in fireplaces, where most of the cooking was done. A couple of buckets of water in the hopper every day rewarded the housewife with a few gallons of lye by the end of the week. The lye, with fat meat or lard added, was put into an iron pot and boiled until "done." When it was cooled, the soap was cut into pieces of the desired size and shape. Toilet water could be added to a portion of it for milady's hands and face.

HOG KILLINGS, CORN SHUCKINGS, LOG ROLLINGS

Most of the slave plantations produced their own shoes and clothes, meat and bread. In field and forest the slaves worked. Now and then a slave woman plowed, or chopped and split two-foot logs with the best of the men. A few house slaves became highly skilled in the making of thread and the weaving of cloth, as well as tanning hides and making shoes.

Hog killings were a great occasion for everybody, especially the slaves. The meat for a whole year was butchered, as many as 75 hogs in a single day. Among the slaves, the position of hog-sticker was an honored one. The younger slaves would get the hogs to the sticker, sometimes by jumping on their backs and riding them, often being thrown off. Another slave was expert at cutting up the carcass, and yet another at frying out the lard. All helped clean and dress and pack away the meat in the barred smokehouse. All ate freely from the pot of "haslets"—the traditional hog-killing dish made of bits of liver, lights, sweetbread, marrow from jaw bones, and liberal chunks of fat.

Corn shuckings, too, were popular, and afforded an opportunity for the slaves of two or more plantations to come together for an evening. On an appointed night, when the dry corn had been piled in a long rick in the barnyard, neighboring planters met here with their slaves. The slaves would select two leaders, who in turn would cast lots to see who would have the first choice for his team. Then the other leader chose the next best shucker, and so on down to the last child. The corn pile was divided into halves. Each leader mounted his pile; shucking and singing, he spurred his team on. Husks rustled hoarsely as they were peeled and snapped from clean ears. Tossed across the rick, the ears fell on the growing pile like heavy rain, falling rhythmically until all the corn was shucked. Two or three cribs full, and maybe more. The planters then gave the slaves supper, or sometimes whiskey to drink.

Some slaves were strong, so strong that only the best white men would "come up" with the other end of the biggest logs they lifted at log rollings. Vigorous young white men would sometimes match strength with the Negroes to prove that they were just as strong.

WHEN A MAN'S WORD

Bigger and better houses were built throughout the red land sections of the county. They were centers of gracious hospitality to friends and accepted strangers.

Plantation families who were inhospitable were looked down on by the planter community. A stingy man was ridiculed. There was a popular story about such a man. When company came he would stand on his front porch and order his slave to put up the visitor's horse in a voice loud enough for everyone to hear: "Take this horse and feed him. Feed him good, I say." All the while he would be holding up two fingers, and the slave knew that meant two ears of corn, not ten—the good feed for a horse.

Looked down on, too, were the slaveowners who did not feed their slaves well enough for them to compete in the log-rolling contests.

The families developed a strict ethical code. The fact that in their world a man's word was as good as his bond cost Vincent Sanford and John Bethune of Greene their lands. Each had endorsed large notes for an unscrupulous fellow who cashed them, put the money in his pocket and left the county. When his creditors could not locate him they turned to Sanford and Bethune, who sold their lands and paid the notes. Bethune, broke, moved to Alabama; Sanford stayed in Greene and became the clerk of court. Vincent's father was "Honest" Jeremiah Sanford. His son, Shelton P. Sanford, taught at Mercer University, and was the author of arithmetic and algebra textbooks as classic for the upper grades as the old "Blueback Speller" was for the lower.

One year when crops were bad, Thomas Stocks loaned his neighbor, Richard J. Willis, $20,000 to keep him from losing his plantation to creditors. Willis repaid the money in a few years. Stocks would accept no interest. On another occasion a small farmowner across the Oconee from Stocks and Willis was burned out. They took their slaves and rebuilt his house and barn within a week.

Neighborly acts were common. Greene pioneered in the delivery of mail. On Sundays Judge Godkin, the postmaster, would get the mail from the train, mount his white horse, and deliver the mail as he went through town. Rural mail delivery was anticipated by Peter Curtwright's wagon trains as they made regular trips from his cotton mill at Long Shoals to Greenesborough. His drivers were instructed to accept and deliver letters and packages free of charge. Small bells on the horses' harness announced their coming and going.

Greene's neighborliness also sent $300 to the starving Irish from Penfield in the late 1840's. Greenesborough Baptists sent two missionaries to Africa. The Reverend Thomas J. Bowen went to Nigeria in 1849 and had reduced the Youraba language to writing by 1853, when he came home on a furlough and married Lourane Davis of Greenesborough. In her letters to her sister, the second wife of Thomas Stocks of Oak Hill, she wrote in great detail of Africa and the people there. The real concern of the Bowens for the Africans is revealed in their request for seeds, plants, and roots from Greene which might grow in Nigeria and improve the diet of the people. They asked that the package "be small, not weighing over 50 pounds, because it will be brought to us in the interior on the head of some native man or woman, and the above weight is considered a good load."

The churches and Masonic orders in Greene remained powerful. For over twenty years the Presbyterians and Baptists of Greenesborough made joint use of the Union Meeting House which was built in 1830. The Methodists of the town had had a church since shortly after Bishop Asbury's visit here at the turn of the century. As a reading of the minutes reveal, a man might be dismissed from either church or lodge for too much drinking or for too little payment of debts.

In spite of the strength of the churches, the court records abound with indictments against card players and men who "gambled at dice." More than once was noted the "unwarranted practice of blacking a man's face and riding him around town on a rail."

THE SOUTHERN CENTRAL AGRICULTURAL SOCIETY

Slave-grown cotton had built the plantations, factories, railroads, schools and churches. And cotton came out of the ground. Increasing signs of erosion followed the big cotton years of the 1830's. Yields began to decline. Old fields were abandoned. Slaves kept on chopping hardwood trees, kept on clearing new-grounds. Small owners continued to leave the plantation sections.

Some planters moved to the new lands of Alabama and Mississippi. Other planters began to discuss the need of conserving and restoring the county's failing soil. One of the county's most successful planters, Richard J. Willis of the Oakland community, recommended a compost of leaves, manure, and cotton seeds.

County fairs here and there were set up to call attention to better farming practices. The Planters Club of adjoining Hancock county organized a fair in 1842. John W. Bonner, of White Plains, just across the line in Greene, was an officer of the Club and an active promoter of the Hancock Fair.

Among the stock exhibited by Bonner were a Berkshire boar, Rip Van Winkle, and several Berkshire sows: Nonesuch, Flower of Orange, Black Rose, Kitty Clover, Young Victoria, Sarah Jane, Mary, Miss Ontario, Neopolitan and a "beautiful China sow, Anna White." His Durham bull, Sam Houston, won a premium of $5.00. Bonner carried away over half the prizes that year. Before the fair the next year, he had added to his exhibit Lady Huddleston, an imported Berkshire sow. William Daniel, also of Greene, exhibited a jack two years old, which the judge praised as "one of the finest animals of his race, either as to form or size."

The first prize for crops was awarded for an acre of corn that yielded "73½ bushels to the acre, without manure." This must have been bottom corn, for the second prize went for "an acre of corn on old upland, medium quality soil, red clay, manured with stable-manure."

Looking at the popularity of the scattered county fairs and at the need for saving the soil, a group of interested people from over the state met at Stone Mountain in 1846 and organized the Southern Central Agricultural Society. Thomas Stocks of Greene was made president.

The Society featured state and county agricultural committees and fairs. Two years later the Jefferson Agricultural Society of Greene County was organized, with headquarters at Penfield, and sponsored a county fair. Leading planters cooperated, and their womenfolk served on committees to award prizes for canned goods and home-crafts. Several slaves were among those who won prizes for needle-work and carpentry.

WE HONESTLY BELIEVE

Greene's leaders were not only concerned about the thinning land; they were ill at ease because of the anti-slavery sentiment in the North and East. The grand jury of September 1835 presented "The interference of abolitionists" as a "grievance to the whole South." An "abolitionist" was spoken of as an "infatuated deluded misguided man." The jury asked that Southern people refuse "to trade with an avowed abolitionist" or with anybody in a city that would allow any individual or society "to circulate any abolition pamphlet, tract or newspaper to the prejudice of these peaceable,

Southern States." The jury said Northern people had profited by the sale of slaves in the South, that "the streets of your commercial cities testify, to you as well as us, the truth of this." The jury went on to say, "we honestly believe the negro is better off in slavery, than if free."

Something of the attitude of people born in the North and living in Greene can be gathered from the same grand jury report: "We tender our thanks, in behalf of our county to our Northern friends, and especially those who have at their recent meetings come out so decidedly, pledging themselves to use all their influence in putting down any interference in any matter touching our slave population, as entered into, by compromise in the adoption of the Federal Constitution."

In protest against the attacks on slavery, southern churchmen were setting up organizations of their own. It was a Greene county slave, Kitty, who precipitated the organization of the Methodist Episcopal Church, South, in 1844. She came into the possession of Bishop J. O. Andrew when he married her owner, the widow Greenwood. The objections of the northern Methodists to a bishop's owning a slave led to an extended discussion of slavery, and to the withdrawal of most of the southern churchmen.

Among the leaders most active in setting up the Southern Baptist Convention at Augusta in 1845 were the delegates from around Penfield. Within a few years, also at Augusta, and also over the slavery issue, people from Greene county helped form the Presbyterian Church of the United States; that is, the "Southern Presbyterian Church."

Greene county's leaders also found things they did not like at home. Ever since the founding of the county, grand juries had recommended a new state constitution, and a state court of errors. In 1820, while pleading for "a convention to alter and amend and consolidate the constitution of our state," the presentment had pointed out that "the constitution of any country ought to be viewed and respected as the grand palladium of our liberties and the sacred limit of legislation and official action."

With no relief, in 1827 the jury grieved that the weak, ignorant, and peaceful citizens were not protected "from the arbitrary aggression of the strong, the cunning and the froward. How much then is it to be lamented when by a loss of half a century we find our system of jurisprudence to be incompetent to the attainment of this desirable object." Still no relief, in 1843 the jury agreed with Judge Francis H. Cone's charge "that the law on this subject requires amendment. Experience has shown that under the law as it now stands persons charged with crime who have money and friends escape punishment no matter how guilty they may be in the eyes of the community or how conclusive may be the evidence of this guilt upon trial."

In 1846 the jury deplored "the alarming state of things in our country, arising out of the inexcusable negligence in executing the laws against murderers, robbers, and other notorious criminals . . . Of what use are our courts of Judication if our laws are not to be executed?" The grand juries of Greene continued to point out the inadequacy of the state government even after they had begun to proclaim the sacredness of the South's cause on the basis of States' Rights. The Georgia system of jurisprudence did not seem adequate to the leaders of Greene, and they felt it was their responsibility to help make it so.

The mounting slave population was kept under control, plantation by plantation. Outward signs of unrest were limited to complaints against the too lax enforcement of the patrol laws, and those who sold spirituous liquors to the slaves. A measure of the apparent tranquillity of this period is shown by the fact that eleven of the thirty-eight grand juries which convened in the two decades prior to 1847 reported "with much satisfaction" that "so much good order has prevailed" not a single presentment had to be made. Many a plantation was a law unto itself.

A FEW PLANTERS TIRED OF SLAVERY

Vigorously as most planters defended slavery, some did not approve it. Daniel Grant, of Grantsville, freed his slaves and had a guardian appointed for them. Grant contracted to build a portion of the railroad to Marthasville, later moved there and so got in on the "ground floor" of the Atlanta real estate bonanza.

Joel Early, son of the first large slaveowner in Greene, found no satisfaction in the ownership of slaves. He lived in a big country house on a knoll between Greenesborough and the river, owned several thousand acres of land, and scores of slaves. He advised his slaves to go back to Africa, offered them their freedom and passage over. As tradition has it, some forty accepted his offer. He had them put on a ship at Norfolk, with a gift of $100 each. Among those who went to Africa was a mulatto house boy who had learned to read and write. Every few months a letter from him would come to Early, telling of fever and death, how those who were still alive wanted to come back. Then there were no more letters. The house boy, too, must have died. Early was greatly grieved, and is said to have sought relief in excessive drink.

PART TWO

TENSE TIMES

VI

UNEASY PLANTERS

ALL ALONG the Georgia Railroad, men, women, and children learned the schedules of the trains. They knew the whistles—the one for Woodville, for Union Point, Greenesborough, the river bridge, and the numerous road crossings.

TRAIN WHISTLES AND CROWING ROOSTERS

A whistle which meant one hour to Athens to trainmen meant two hours 'til dinner to the slave. And the whistle that announced "off the rail" to the train crew brought hope to black field hands; maybe they would be allowed to help get it back on the track. The engineer merely pulled the cord for Madison, but the slaves in Greene who heard it groaned, for a breeze out of the west meant dry weather and work. When they heard the whistle for Crawfordville, to the east, they knew there was a chance for rain and rest. They watched the smoke and were glad when it flattened out and settled over the creeks.

The whistles of the scheduled trains divided up the slave's day as the crowing of roosters divided his night. After many years a night train was put on, and then another. Cross-ties were laid closer together, and solid iron rails were spiked to them. The trains went faster, made less noise, and stayed on the track better. The passengers rode in softer seats. Chattel slaves up and down the railroad ordered their days and nights by scheduled trains—trains to Augusta, Athens, and Atlanta that made connections with other scheduled trains to all parts of the slave country, and beyond.

The masters rode on the trains the slaves listened to. They owned and controlled the railroads just as they did the slaves, the factories, and the land along Richland Creek and the other lands of the county which would grow the best crops.

So when the trains on the Georgia Railroad blew for the stations and crossings in Greene, two thirds of the people who heard them were Negro slaves, and half the whites who heard them lived in a slave society without slaves of their own. Three fifths of those who did own slaves had ten or less.

In 1850 the planters of Greene bought over 200 additional slaves. And maybe they bought too many. At any rate, the grand jury of March 1851 was of the opinion that "the immense introduction of slaves into this state for the last eighteen months caused by the repeal of the law prohibiting the introduction of slaves for sale is operating injuriously to the best interest of the state" and recommended that "the next Legislature favor such action . . . as will be an effective remedy of the evil complained of."

Greene's plantation economy did not expand any further. During the ten years following 1850 the slave population increased less than the natural gain of births over deaths. The number of families with 20 or more slaves dropped from 144 in 1854 to 139 in 1859. Greene was exporting less cotton, and had begun to export slaves. Six Georgia counties, all of them newer than Greene, now had more slaves than she had: Burke, Houston, Monroe, Troup, Meriwether, and Talbot.

In 1854 there were 8,326 slaves in Greene, in 1860 scarcely 100 more. They were valued on the tax books at $8,895,600, or $1,058 each. Slaves represented 56 percent of the total tax value of the county. Though the slave population was scarcely increasing at all, only one third of the population of Greene in 1860 was white, the other two thirds black and slave. There were now only twenty-five free Negroes, the smallest number at any time since 1800.

Even though two thirds of the population were slaves, half of the white taxpayers owned no slaves at all. Twenty-two taxpayers owned fifty or more slaves each, while 557 did not own a single one.

"RUN, NIGGER, RUN!"

The presentments of the grand juries during the 1850's make it clear that the control of the slave population was becoming burdensome. "We present as a grievance," said the jury of November 1853, "the facility and seeming importunity with which our slave population procures intoxicating liquers in the face of the law." A dealer's license fee of $500 was recommended. Along with the saloons, some of the county's best stores stocked liquors and rum, especially at Christmas. "Moe" snuff, too, for the gentlemen to sniff could be had at the better stores.

The grand jury of March 1854 lamented that "the patrol laws are but partially executed in the county." The jury asked for "regular and efficient patrols." The slaves referred to these officers who were responsible for the regulation of their movements as "patter-rollers."

> "Run, nigger, run! The patterroll'll get you
> Run, nigger, run! It's almost day."

One grand jury after another in the late 1850's recommended strict enforcement of the patrol laws.

Many planters realized that stricter enforcement of patrol laws would work a real hardship on slave mothers and fathers who lived on different plantations. Sunday visits only were officially permitted, but in the early years it was not alarming if Sam slipped off in the night to neighboring slave cabins. The nervousness about the Abolition movement and perhaps a new restlessness among the slaves, who kept hearing snatches of talk, made it seem necessary to keep a stricter vigil.

When the patrol officers found a slave away from quarters without a pass, a whipping usually sufficed, though chronic offenders might be hung up by the thumbs. All were agreed that slaves had to be controlled through punishment, but they were valuable as property and therefore were not subjected to death penalties.

A slave named Mit belonged to Travis Carlton. His wife belonged to Thomas Redmond Thornton. Thornton's son Charles tells this story:

I remember one night my mother was in Augusta, and a cousin of mine was spending the night with me. In the night we were awakened by someone calling my father from outside. When my father raised the window and asked who it was, he said, "It's Mit. Come out here Marse Tommy, I've killed Nat." Nat was a carpenter, doing some finishing work at a house we were living in. Nat belonged to Mr. Moore over near Siloam.

Of course, Mr. Moore and Mr. Carlton, and the other neighbors were sent for, and considered what to do. Mit was too valuable a Negro to be hung, so they had him whipped, I do not remember to what extent, and branded with the letter "M" on each cheek. I do not know if Mr. Moore was ever paid for his negro or not.

Sometimes slaves were punished almost as severely for less serious things. There is the story of a slave cook who had her mouth sewed up with two stitches, so *all* the Sunday dinner would be on the table for her master's family when they returned from church. Provoked at the stitches, the shut-mouth cook once carried to the dinner table a "smothered hen"—undressed, with feathers and head intact. The mistress had asked her to smother two hens for dinner. The stitches out of her mouth, the cook explained that in mid-morning she had put two hens under the washpot banked with mud, and that only one of them had smothered to death. Whipped and further reminded that she was a slave, the cook went to church that night. She moaned loudly, swayed and shouted: "Oh sookie, sadness, sadness, sadness"; under her breath, "White folks is de debil!" and loudly again, "Oh sookie, sadness."

By the middle of the 1850's the slaves were permitted to hold religious meetings apart from the whites, with a white man always there to keep order and to keep up with what was being said. One of the early Negro preachers here was a slave named Cyrus, who preached to the slaves in the grove at Bethesda Church. He could neither read nor write. He would tell his master, Thomas Redmond Thornton, what he wanted to preach about, and his master would look up a scripture bearing on the subject and read it to him.

LOCKED AND BARRED

The greatest honor that could come to a slave woman was to be allowed to carry her mistress's basket of keys. Charles Jenkins Thornton tells that Ophelia, the youngest of their three cooks, was the smartest. When company came in unexpectedly, his mother would give Ophelia the basket of keys to smokehouse, cellar and pantry, and tell her to get dinner and call her when it was ready. Without further instructions to Ophelia, she could take her company to the dinner table with perfect confidence.

Everything on the plantation was locked—corn crib, wheat house, carpentry tools, gears and saddles, closets and trunks, and even the attic. The smokehouses were built of brick or stone, with thick walls, heavy doors, and barred windows to keep the slaves away from the meat. Smokehouses far outnumbered all other brick buildings in the county.

Brick buildings had come with the maturing of the slave economy. The town of Penfield boasted Mercer University Chapel, built in 1845, Ciceronian Hall and Boys Dormitory a little later, then Science Hall and the Penfield Steam Mill. The first brick buildings in Greenesborough were the courthouse and the Greenesborough Female College. The courthouse was built in 1849 by the county and a Masonic lodge, San Marino Lodge # 34.F. and A. M., which owned and used the third floor of the building. A few years later two office buildings, one of them three stories high, were erected. The first brick stores, six of them, were built in 1859 and 1860. About this same time, the Presbyterian and Methodist churches were built. The other brick buildings in the county were Joel Early's manor, Bethesda Church, the Long Shoals cotton factory, the plantation house of Reubin Armour near Long Shoals and the Janes house west of Penfield.

"THEIR GULLIED MOUTHS SPEAK"

In 1850 a few farmers produced two bales of cotton to an acre and realized from $300 to $500 worth of marketable goods from each worker. So reported the County Agricultural Society to the Southern Central Agricultural Society. "Midland Georgia is now," said the report, "not only the safest, but the surest and best planting country in the United States . . . few or none of our citizens are seeking new-grounds in the West, whilst many of our former citizens are wishing they were back in old Greene. Our citizens are giving the best evidence of their intention to live and die on the old homestead."

But Greene's prosperity was not secure. It was built on the land, and the land itself was already leaching and washing. As stated in the report of the County Agricultural Society: "To review the early history of agriculture in Greene, would afford the present generation no benefit, certainly none in the way of good example, but would only act as a beacon to warn them to steer clear of the errors of the past." The report then stated hopefully that many farmers had commenced to straighten creeks, drain swamps, and to understand the need for the application of more barnyard manure. Some were "side hill ditching their rolling land."

In 1851 Judge Garnett Andrews, of Greene, in addressing the state fair at Macon, spoke of the rapid increase of population and the "fearful deterioration of our soil." "Some in this audience," he said, "will be alive when there shall be one hundred millions to feed in the United States—four times the present number." He wondered how they were to be fed when "the destroying millions shall, like flocks of locusts, have passed over the land, and swept off the virgin

soil from the face of the earth, as the famine licks up the stubble."
With heightened oratorical fervor he added, "These bleak hills, with
their gullied mouths, speak more eloquently and convincingly on
this subject than I can."

Andrews went on to say that agriculture was the most profitable
vocation in the world, and that cotton culture with slaves was the
most profitable type of agriculture. He said that within a lifetime
"more than the whole of our present crop will be consumed in the
United States, and we will not be so dependent on foreign markets."
He expected cotton lands to become the most valuable lands in the
nation; he thought soil erosion could and would be stopped; he
seemed to assume that slavery would be permanent.

But the wasting soil from the fields continued to fill up the
spring branches, pour into the creeks and then into the Oconee and
the Ogeechee. The fish were failing in the muddy waters. Floods
and droughts were worse as forests were cleared and springs dried
up.

Slaveholders and non-slaveholders alike faced the problem of depleted fields, with but little more new-ground to replace them. Big
farmers and little ones were coming to realize that if they were to
live as heretofore the fertility of the land then in cultivation would
have to be conserved and restored.

NOBLESSE OBLIGE WILTS

Once slavery had become the dominant issue in national politics
it was clear that the county's leaders feared the outright loss of their
slaves more than the gradual loss of their soil. To restore the soil,
the planters would need to make some shifts in crops and perhaps
some basic changes in the relation of the worker to the land he
worked. It would be a slow and tedious job. At any rate the defense
of slavery became the all-important subject of the day. With much
zeal, the Abolitionists were making speeches and printing pam-
phlets to rid the country of human bondage. Their attitude toward

the slaveowners became generally known, and as generally resented. The planters complained that more than one New England village which had grown rich on a hundred years of slave trade was now a center of anti-slavery agitation.

Slaveowners who among themselves had earlier expressed misgivings about the system were now becoming united in their unqualified defense of it. Planters who had had their own slaves taught to read and write now advocated making this illegal. White men and women who owned no slaves, and who had groaned under their competition, now began to defend their region and its way of life against holier-than-thou critics from the outside. The slaves themselves soon began to speak of the "Yankees" as sassy meddlers.

With the agitation over slavery came distrust of outsiders, strangers, Northerners. Every man had to prove himself: he certainly had a position on slavery, and he must make it known. Any person whose attitude was not known to be for slavery might be an agent of some anti-slavery group. All who came and went were under observation.

People around town with little to do had become watchers for the busy planters and businessmen, a few of whom were thoroughly acclimated Northerners, such as the county's leading cotton buyers, Wakefield and Murray, from Saratoga, New York. The watchers were unorganized and unpaid. They led rather uneventful lives, and were glad to be on the lookout—it promised excitement and plantation-owner appreciation. And their vigilance did not go wholly unrewarded. For in Greenesborough in March of 1855 a young man, an alleged Abolitionist from New England, was chased through the streets; young ladies at the College suggested "tar and feathers." He was soon caught, his face blackened. A slave was made to call him "brother," and lash him "all in fun between us equals." He was then ridden on a rail through the streets and put on the night train with his face unwashed.

The affair originated at a grog-shop. The planters and wealthier townspeople disclaimed any part in it, but no one of those who did take part in it was arrested or indicted by the grand jury. Similar man-handling might await anyone who criticized the practices of the best people; and defenders of Southern traditions could expect the police and courts to grant them a similar immunity.

The grand jury of 1860 again advocated a very high license fee for liquor dealers in view of "the great difficulty of reaching the slaves with the wholesome laws of the land." It complained that because of the ineffectiveness of the patrol officers, the slaves were "becoming more or less insubordinate, often being found under the influence of liquor and even on the Sabbath day at church, thereby disturbing the worship of the sanctuary."

The county was also asked by the jury of 1860 to be on the lookout for strangers: "As we have reason to believe that there are at this time quite a number of suspicious white men straggling about the country and visiting Negro quarters and conversing with negroes and otherwise disturbing the good order, peace and quietude of the country and in view of the political excitement of our country we recommend proper vigilance throughout the county in the enforcement of the law, in bringing all such characters to justice."

The planters, businessmen, small landowners, plantation overseers, and the piddlers about town were feeling more at home with each other. A common outside foe lessened the inside strain from differences in wealth and social position. Nearly all the small owners aspired to become planters. They were flattered when the large slaveholders acknowledged a fellow feeling with them, as were the town piddlers when they were encouraged to keep an eye out for Abolitionists and other "meddlers." The planters, too, liked it—liked to feel they were warmly cherished by the rank and file of Whites, rather than just coolly and distantly respected by them. A new unity between the white groups was well under way.

As the agitation between the North and the South became more intense, something happened to the planters themselves. They were no longer certain of the Negro's desire to remain in slavery, nor of their ability to maintain their bargaining position in the national

Congress. Nothing wilts so quickly the noblesse oblige of the master to the slave, of the stronger to the weaker, as does the master's fear for his own security.

Why was Greene county's agricultural society of 1850 called the Jefferson Society? Perhaps because a Virginian gentleman, a slave-owner, had said the least government was the best. But Jefferson had discussed the freeing of the slaves, and had proclaimed the family-size farmer the backbone of American democracy. In Greene, and especially around Penfield where the Jefferson Society had its head-quarters, the slave system had already pushed out most of these small independent farmers. Even so the planters may have found some satisfaction in acknowledging values contrary to immediate trends but in harmony with their long range ideals.

The family-size farmer—the Jeffersonian ideal—lost his first round in Greene to the slave plantation system, which rose to its height in the 1840's. The plantation remained regnant for the next two decades, though in the late 1850's it began to wane. It was not being displaced. It was weakening from within through the loss of soil fertility and the loss of planter security. It was being censured from without by unyielding critics and threatened by national politics.

UNANSWERED QUESTIONS

At the time that the South's way of life was being proclaimed by the people of Greene, they were faced with real questions. The county's population elements gave rise to some. Was it desirable for the population to remain only one third white? If more white people were wanted, how could they be induced to come? And from where? And if they came, were they to be farmowners with slaves, or without slaves? Or were they to be landless and compete with slaves? Then there was cotton. Could it be grown profitably for the next quarter century as it had for the last? Or in view of the spent soil, had it been grown profitably then? If cotton could not be relied upon, what substitute crop could be grown with local labor?

Such were the questions implicit in the plantation economy. They could have been asked soberly had not the slavery issue become involved in sectional interests and feelings.

And what if slavery itself should go? Without slavery, what would become of the houses and lands of the leading white families? How could any kind of plantation farming be carried on? How could the three cotton mills be operated? How could the colored population be controlled? Who would provide for faithful old "Aunt Fanny" and "Uncle Joe?"

The questions about States' Rights and the continuation of slavery had become so pressing by the end of 1860 that all the other questions were put on the shelf.

"IRREPRESSIBLE CONFLICT"

The ties between the North and the South had about reached the breaking point. Abolitionists thundered the inhumanity of holding Negroes as chattels; the slaveowners clung to the sacredness of the national Constitution and of local self-government.

An outstanding representative of the anti-slavery sentiment in the North was William H. Seward, who had spent some time teaching school in Georgia in the late 1820's or early 1830's. During the 1850's, while Senator from New York, he had said that there was "a higher law" than the Constitution, and that it demanded the extinction of slavery. He had also spoken of the "irrepressible conflict" between those forces in the nation that were for and against slavery. People in Greene read these words of Seward's. Some were white hot with anger; others let them pass as political harangues, for Seward was the ranking Republican leader in the late 1850's, and a likely candidate for President.

Seward's brief sojourn in the South was recalled, and his later anti-slavery sentiments rhythmically resented in William J. Grayson's, *The Hireling and the Slave:*

> A village teacher then, his style betrays
> The pedant practice of those learned days,
> When boys not demagogues obeyed his nod,
> His higher law, the tear compelling rod;
> While Georgia's guest, a pleasant life he led,
> And slavery fed him with her savoury bread.

Then out of the North came Harriet Beecher Stowe's *Uncle Tom's Cabin*. It dramatized slavery's ills. But the planters of Greene recognized in their midst no such slaveowner as Simon Legree, and felt that anyone who believed all the brutal scenes was to be pitied. Soon there was little patience left, for that fiery Abolitionist, John Brown, seized the arsenal at Harper's Ferry in an attempt to lead a slave insurrection. True, the slaves there did not follow him—but who knew what would happen if other such efforts were made! Then there was the national election in the offing, and another book—this time out of the South—was put to use by the Abolitionists. It was *The Impending Crisis,* written by Hinton Rowan Helper of North Carolina, a small white farmer of modest means. He catalogued the bad effects of slavery on the non-slaveowning Whites of the South, and urged them to vote the national Republican ticket to deliver the South from the control of the big slaveowners.

The presidential campaign of 1860 was all-important. If the Republicans won, the underground railroads would carry still more slaves across the state lines to free soil, and the fugitive slave laws would be worth little or nothing; the Dred Scott Decision would be ignored, and the new country of the west would have no chance to become slave territory. Greene county was of the deep South. It stiffened to these threats.

As the months passed grand juries convened and made their presentments, public men delivered their orations, men, women and children, white and black, listened and wondered. News came that Lincoln and the Republicans were elected, and close behind it that South Carolina had seceded from the Union. Shortly afterwards, the legislature met in Milledgeville and Georgia seceded; and so, too, did Alabama, Mississippi, Louisiana, and Florida. The Confederate States of America was soon formed, with Jefferson Davis as president, and Alexander H. Stephens, vice-president. Stephens' home, Liberty Hall, was at Crawfordville, Georgia, twenty miles east of Greenesborough. Robert Toombs, also active in the organization of the Confederacy, lived at Washington, but thirty miles from Greene.

The South's way of life had been challenged, and Greene county was getting ready to fight and die for it.

VII

"WAR IS HELL"

Within a month after the formation of the Confederate States, young men from Greene had volunteered for the army, and officers were being selected. In early April news came that Fort Sumter had been fired upon. The war was on, and Greene county set forth to battle for things she held more dear than life itself.

"better give much than lose all"

The first record of the emerging military activity in Greene is this letter, written three months before the war began, by Thomas N. White to Governor Joseph E. Brown:

> Georgia Greene County
> Curtright factry January 15 1861
>
> to your excelancy Joseph
> E Brown Gov of said state

dear sir   after my respects to you   I write you a fu lines stating to you that we have some 40 or 50 stout yong men at work in this factry and larger potion of them has never yet bin at a muster and as we believe that we will probly be neaded as solders shortly we have organisd a splendid compny at this place as the long shole factry company   we have not a gun in the compny   wish to know of you if we cant draw about 60 muskets from your town so that we ma drill wonst a weak at any rate and if we can get the guns we want them as

62

soon as posible if they could be sent to Eadtonton our factry waggons
goes to that place 2 a weak we could get them from their
yours very respectfuly

Thomas N White

N B the compny expect me to try to command them I would be glad
     you would put me in strait sword if their is any as I am not able to
     by one or otherwise probbly you make a presant of one

There is no record that this company was ever mustered into
service, but the letter is evidence of the readiness of the propertyless
whites to defend the South.

The first three companies to be raised, equipped, and sent from
Greene were the Greene Rifles, from in and around Greenesborough; the Dawson Grays, from around Penfield; and the
Stephens Light Guard, from various points throughout the county.
There were more than 250 men in the three companies. Some of
them could equip themselves, most could not. Though men volunteered readily, the raising of equipment for them seemed not easy.

In late April of 1861, the Greene County Inferior Court issued
bonds to the mount of $5,000 "to relieve the necessities of the families
of indigent volunteers in companies now raised or hereafter to be
raised . . . and also to aid in equipping said indigent soldiers." Committees of leading citizens were named to distribute "bacon or beef,
or other fresh meats, corn meal or flour, and in case of sickness,
sugar and coffee, or tea." These bonds were floated in response to a
resolution presented by Greene's most prominent men at a mass
meeting held in the courthouse two weeks after the war broke out.
The resolution was unanimously adopted.

In an open letter in *The Planters Weekly* of Greenesboro, * June 5,
"A Citizen and A Soldier" inquired: "Shall it be said that Greene
has not supplied absolute necessities to her gallant soldiers?" He
pointed out that some of the people had contributed beyond their
means, while others "hold on to their purse strings with a cold iron
grasp." He went on to say:

---

* Note change in spelling of Greenesborough to "Greenesboro."

This is emphatically the People's war, and the people must sustain it or perish. Our base and merciless enemy boast that they will divide our lands among them, and claim our wives and daughters as their own. The motto of some is "Booty and Beauty" . . . The very men who have not contributed are frequently men of wealth, having lands and negroes, and wives and daughters to defend. The very women who grumble when requested to make soldiers clothing are the wives of rich men! Thank God such men are few, and such women are fewer. Yet such exist; I know it and it makes my heart burn . . . Friends and fellow citizens, down with the dust and equip your defenders. Better give much than lose all. Finally it is not in Greene only, but everywhere, that some give grudgingly or nothing. They really seem to think it is like a *missionary* contribution.

As the months passed more men from Greene went to the Confederate Army. By special executive order, early in 1862, the students of Mercer University were inducted into military service. By March, 128 more men marched off to the battlefields. They were ill-equipped, had only 12 rifles and 86 muzzle-loading shot guns. Other companies were formed as the war wore on: the Rebel Defenders, composed of 57 privates and officers, and a company from the Scull Shoals factory. The latter company of 45 men, ages ranging from 17 to 58, was organized the third year of the war. Thirteen of these men had a horse and saddle; fourteen of them had some kind of a gun.

Many men from Greene entered companies in adjoining counties. Around 600 men from Greene served in the Confederate Army. This number represented nearly one third of the white male population, over two thirds of all the white men between the ages of 18 and 58.

The conscription of soldiers for the Confederate Army, begun in 1862, affected Greene but little. Well over two thirds of Greene's 600 soldiers had volunteered before conscription began. The county records show no evidence of "bushwhacking" to escape military service; only a few owners of 20 or more slaves claimed for themselves the military exemption allowed by the Confederate government.

MEN ON THE BATTLEFIELDS

The suffering and death of war were not secrets. Letters came from the battlefields; men came home on furlough. Some who had been mortally wounded reached home before they died.

From Manassas Junction, Virginia, on July 28, 1861, young G. C. Butter wrote his sister who lived across the Oconee in Putnam County:

i am glad that i am still permited to write to you   i am well though very sore and tired after fighting the hardest battle that has bin fought since the Revolution   the battle commenced on Sunday 21st at 8 o'clock and lasted till 5 in the Evening   we was in it about 5 ours   our Redgement win the Victory   we fight against 40 thousand men & 30 thousand of them was the old U. S. Soldiers   we taken the best batrey they had   we taken 700 prisoners 70 pieces of cannon and i can't tell how many was killed our loss was considirable   i never want to See Such A sight a gaine   the ground was covered with the ded and the grones of the dying.

Still at Manassas on October 19 of that year, the soldier boy wrote:

being as i am at leisur i thou would drop you a few lines   i has nothing new to rite   the armery has fell back some 6 miles in Order to draw the enemy *Out So We* can get a fight out of them   they hav cut of Rimbrells leg and I herd to day that he war ded but i dount no that it is true but i no if he aint ded he Will die for they aint no chance for him to live   i am Very Sorry for his family   in the last three weeks i rote a dozen letters and havent any ancer to none Only that you sent

Thomas F. Colclough from near Penfield wrote from Chatta-nooga on July 15, 1862, telling of his brother "Dock's" severe illness, and the extreme heat in the tent in midday. And a little later word came that "Dock" (Franklin W.) was dead, and shortly after that "Tom," too, had died—one in Chattanooga, the other near Atlanta. Letters from soldiers often reached home after their names had been posted on the fateful board at the courthouse.

As the war wore on the casualty lists lengthened. Listen to the casualties of the Copelands of Greene: J. O., "killed at Gettysburg;"

W. D., "killed at Knoxville;" W. H., "killed at Franktown;" J. J., "wounded at Gettysburg," and W. R., "discharged of bad health." Or look at the notations opposite the alphabetical names in the full muster-roll of Stephens Light Guard: "killed," "killed," "killed," "died from sickness," "killed," "discharged on account of wounds" and on through the 120 men and officers, to find 36 were killed, 17 died of sickness, 41 were wounded, 20 were discharged for wounds and bad health, and 2 on account of old age. A mere remnant of Stephens Light Guard hobbled back to Greene when the war was done. The other companies, too, had suffered heavy losses.

WOMEN AT HOME

When the men went off to the army, the women and old men and boys took over the farms and ran them as best they could. The slaves remained loyal and worked the harder, and the white womenfolk of the non-slaveowning families often took the places of their men in the fields.

Women stepped into men's shoes in other walks of life, too. At White Plains in the fall of 1863, Emma B. Howell became the first woman principal of the academy there.

The leaders in Greene early saw that food and supplies were essential, and that the local people had a responsible part to play. Cotton had to give way to foodstuffs. The war put new demands on land and labor. Said the grand jury of March 1862: "The most important part of our battle is to be decided *at home* this year, by the planters. *The next six weeks* will determine whether a cotton crop will be pitched to the neglect of Provisions, or whether the planters will resolve that our people and our army shall *first be fed.*" As an evidence of their earnestness in the matter, the jury took a vote and resolved unanimously: "that members of this body individually will plant no cotton except enough for domestic use during the year of 1862." It took occasion to urge "a similar course upon the whole planting community," and to plead with the people to produce more "corn, grains, peas, potatoes, vegetables, and pork."

The September presentment of that year noted the rise of prices and urged the people "to discountenance every attempt to exact exorbitant prices for things offered for sale and that they sell their manufactures, goods, wares, and agricultural products, upon such terms, as will place articles of necessity, within the reach of all classes of our People." But prices went higher and higher as England's interest in the South cooled and the blockade was tightened, as production within the Confederacy was crippled and reserves were depleted.

Supplies from farms and towns were drained off with the men. One tenth of the crops was assessed for the army, and many families gave more. The volume of purchasable goods shrank. Adjustments had to be made. Without a supply of three-cent Confederate stamps, Postmaster Godkin, who had an office in the courthouse, would cut six-cent stamps crossways and use the halves. Everything was getting scarce. Prices rose rapidly.

By early 1865 cotton sheeting was $6 a yard, flour $450 a barrel, corn $50 a bushel, bacon $7 a pound, coffee $70 a pound, salt $5 a pound, cooking soda $20 a pound, cotton—no market. Confederate money was almost worthless, and there was little or no other currency in the county. At this time only one small shop in Greenesboro had anything to sell. It belonged to a boy, Charles A. Davis. Every store building in town was devoted to the care of sick and wounded soldiers, as were also all school buildings and churches. The Greenesboro Female College was used as a hospital.

Wayside Home at Union Point was organized in the fall of 1862, and at once began to provide food and entertainment for hundreds of soldiers every week. A score of local women under the leadership of Maria Jennie (Collier) Hart did volunteer duty day and night. Seventeen wounded soldiers died at the Home; scores of others were nursed back to health; thousands were given meals. Each day three ladies boarded the trains with food for soldiers unable to walk over to the Wayside Home. Substantial donations were made by people throughout Greene, by citizens from nearby places, and from more distant points in Georgia and the South. The Georgia Railroad carried bundles to the Wayside Home free of charge.

Nor were all the fatalities on the battlefields or among the soldiers. Old men and old women, young mothers and children felt the pinch at home of high prices, scarce food, and disorganized medical care. Illnesses which would have been overcome proved fatal. Then there were the deaths of two girls. Here is the story of Secessia Heard as told in *Preface to Peasantry:* *

A young Greene county father volunteered for service in the Confederate Army, leaving to the care of the family slaves his wife and a young daughter named Secessia in honor of the Southern cause. Three years later he was home on a furlough to secure additional men and supplies. In preparing to return, he and his slaves were on the front porch repacking some gun powder. A spark from the father's pipe fired the cotton about the powder, which he quickly brushed off the porch. The burning cotton fell on little Secessia, who was playing among the boxwood in the yard. She died. The heartbroken father returned to the army on schedule time with men and supplies.

At White Plains shortly after the war began, fourteen-year-old Laura Alfriend, lineal descendant of Pocahontas, was also accidentally burned to death. She was symbolizing "The Southern Confederacy" in a patriotic allegory. As the curtains rose, her robes caught fire from the candle footlights. The horrified audience saw the flames flare up and envelop her, saw the Confederate flag burn in her outstretched hand. "So perished," says a family letter, "a Georgia descendant of Pocahontas, first representative of the South's cause . . . and like the little burned flag with its fading stars, left but an ashen memory." A tombstone was placed in the White Plains cemetery:

HER BRIGHT AND USEFUL YOUNG
LIFE WAS SUDDENLY LOST IN
AIDING THE CAUSE OF THE CONFEDERACY.

* Page 26, University of North Carolina Press, 1936.

THE WAR AFFECTED EVERYTHING

Most of the Northern residents here went home soon after the war began.

The cotton mill at Greenesboro was turned into an arms factory. Gun powder was made in the basement of the town's drug store and stored for shipment in a rock building by the railroad station. The Bowens were called home from Africa. The *Temperance Crusader* was moved from Penfield to Atlanta and became known as the *Georgia Crusader*.

The Planters Weekly of Greenesboro published its last issue in early June 1861. In it was carried a piece from the *London Press,* which assumed that the British Government would recognize the Confederacy as an independent nation: "The recognition . . . cannot be avoided, nor do we desire to avoid it . . . The calamity to the Union . . . was favorable to our own interests, both political and commercial . . . With the establishment of a Confederacy of purely agricultural States in the South, the restrictive tariff of the old Union, and the still more restrictive one recently adopted, will no longer suffice to prevent the entry of our manufactures in the American Continent. Free trade, pure and simple—free trade of the most absolute kind is opened to us by the new Confederacy." England did not recognize the sovereignty of the Confederacy. The owners of the *Weekly* found no ready buyer for their paper.

During 1862, Dr. Thomas N. Poullain of Scull Shoals made successful experiments with cotton bagging for baling cotton.

Slaves continued to work in the cotton mills at Scull Shoals and Long Shoals, and on the farms throughout the county. The grand jury of March 1863 recommended that a bill be passed by the Legislature to reimburse the owners of the slaves ordered out by Governor Brown to complete the defenses of Savannah.

William H. Seward was Secretary of State in Lincoln's cabinet. From the firing on Fort Sumter to the end of the war, he advised caution and delay. But Lincoln showed Seward and everybody else

that he would not turn aside from his determination to preserve
the Union at any cost.

THE MARCH TO THE SEA

Late in the war when Sherman's army marched through Georgia,
his main force passed to the south of Greene. But bands of foraging
soldiers came through here for nearly a week, carrying off much of
the livestock and provisions still in the county. They burned James
B. Park's mill and the bridge across the Oconee. The mill burned
for three days. Park's house, close by, was saved only because a slave
named Cyrus took a wet quilt to the roof and put out the fires one
after another that were started by falling embers.

James B. Park, Jr., then a small boy, saw Federal soldiers stand
guard at the doors of his home. His mother, in the name of her
absent husband who was a Mason, had sent for an officer and requested protection. The house was not bothered. But everything was
carried off from the yards and smokehouses, cribs and barns—everything except the boy's pet speckled hen. The hen flew into the house
ahead of a pursuing soldier, who ran past the guard and caught her;
but the guard made him drop her as he came out the door. The
boy's speckled hen fluttered back into the house and stayed there
until the last soldier was gone.

The river bridge at Long Shoals was burned, but the cotton mill
was spared. The manager of the mill was a Northerner, and he convinced Sherman's scouts that he owned a considerable part of it.
The bridge at Scull Shoals in the upper part of the county was also
burned, and the mill spared.

Day after day groups of Sherman's men walked the roads of
Greene—the red roads of the plantation area, the white roads of
live-at-home farmers in the southeastern part of the county. At
Siloam a small Negro boy, Alfred, owned by Hardy C. Peek,
watched the bluecoats kill and skin a dozen hogs, leaving the heads
attached to the hides. All of his life he had seen hogs scalded and

scraped free of hair, but never before had he seen them hideless and headless.

Two miles away, "Pete" O'Neal's small son Charles looked out of the window and saw his first Federal soldier, saw him take the saddle from the bony mule he was riding, put it on his father's best pony, and dash off at a gallop. The swap proved a boon to the O'Neals, for the mule was lean enough to be passed over by the other soldiers that came that way, yet young enough to respond to feed when spring came.

One of history's greatest tributes to Southern barbecue occurred in Greene during the famous march to the sea. William P. McWhorter, then a young man, killed and barbecued forty hogs and fed Sherman's soldiers. In return, they allowed him to select what he wanted from the property they had seized. He chose 300 bales of cotton, took it to Augusta, and sold it. He brought the money back and divided it among his neighbors from whom the cotton had been taken.

Over in "The Forks," at her uncle's summer house, Lourane Davis Bowen, recently returned missionary from Africa, stood helplessly beside her trunk, which Federal soldiers were about to run through with bayonets. Without bothering to open it, they would leave her clothes in shreds. Slave women rushed in, begged that the dresses be given to them. "Help yourselves!" said the soldiers. Bluecoats gone, the Negro women restored the trunk to their mistress.

Many slaves, upon hearing of the advancing Federal troops, had been led to believe that they would be freed, and that the "Acre-Right Law" would be put into effect at once. They liked the idea of this law, for they had heard that it promised each family forty acres of land, a wagon, a mule, and a year's supply of rations.

Sherman's soldiers walked through Greene unchallenged. The planters were relieved that only a few slaves followed them out of the county. The presence here of Federal soldiers, the slaves realized, had not meant freedom, had done nothing about the Acre-Right Law.

Some months later the slaves heard that the Confederate forces had surrendered at Appomattox, and soon afterward that President Lincoln's Emancipation Proclamation of January 1, 1863, would become law in the conquered Confederacy.

FREE AT LAST

"Free at last!" was the cry of the black folks when their masters called them together and told them that they were slaves no longer.

"You all is just as free as I is. You ain't obliged to call me old Mahster no more. You can call me Mister Peek, if you want to." As Alfred Parrott remembers it, that is the way his master, the Reverend Hardy C. Peek, broke the news to his slaves when he called them to the house. Then he said to the men: "You just go now and catch your mules. I'll give you a third of all you make."

But they did not catch any mules that day. Shouting, laughing, singing, crying, the men, women, and children made for the big road, joined passing slaves from other plantations. Hundreds of them gathered on the road, walked along together. After a time they stopped, and Joe Peek, an old slave who had wanted to preach all his life, but had never been allowed to do so at the white people's church, delivered his first sermon. The idea of freedom was all mixed up with salvation. The ex-slaves sang the old ring shout:

> I'm glad salvation's free
> I'm glad salvation's free
> I'm glad salvation's free
> For us all

Another chant they had made up, and sung quietly among themselves when they were out of the hearing of the white folks, was:

> No more Monday morning
> No more Monday morning
> No more Monday morning
> Bye and bye

With Freedom, the "Bye and Bye" was changed to "Free at last." They made up new stanzas, sang loud enough for everybody to hear them:

> No more getting up 'fore day
> No more getting up 'fore day
> No more getting up 'fore day
> Free at last. Free at last.
> Thank God A'mighty, I'm free
> at last!

The Negroes stayed out until it got dark that night. Children fell asleep in the road.

The next morning the troughs in the yards where the children of the field hands had been given their extra milk and potatoes were taken up. If the Negro men and women were going to be free, they would have to feed their own children from now on.

A few men who had families elsewhere went to join them, others with families here came in. There was a general shifting around among the plantations everywhere as families got together. Many of the Negro men and women who had been living together went to a preacher or public official and were legally married. In several instances the couple's own children took an active part in the ceremony. The bride-mother might even come in on the arm of her son or daughter, who at the altar would give her to the father in marriage. Other couples let common-law marriage suffice.

Some slaves left the county completely, and were never seen or heard of again. Others when they had got their fill of freedom on the highway, came back to live where they had been living, took the family names of their ex-masters, got their rations from the same smokehouse, worked the same land.

James B. Park's former slave, Cyrus, was among those picked up by the town constable at Madison as a vagrant. Park learned of Cyrus' arrest late at evening when he returned home from Greenesboro. He drove over sixteen miles that night in the rain to arrange bond for his release. At the trial Park told how Cyrus' work with the wet quilt had kept his house from burning. Cyrus was acquitted.

WAR'S END

The most direct route from Washington, Georgia, to Milledgeville, crosses the Oconee at Park's Ferry. On that fact hangs a war's end story. The gold and silver of the Confederacy, packed in kegs and carried in wagons, reached Washington on its way from Richmond to Nashville. The cabinet of the Confederacy met for the last time at the home of Robert Toombs. The treasure-train proceeded from there toward Milledgeville. Enroute the wagons were disbanded, and the gold and silver disposed of to keep it from falling into the hands of a pursuing Federal officer. Greene county legend has it that part of the treasure was buried above Park's Mill Ferry.

Certain it is that the evening after the meeting at Toombs' house, a distinguished stranger crossed the ferry and asked for lodging at the home of James B. Park, Sr. The stranger asked that his horse be left in saddle and hid near the house. He went straight to his room. Next morning he rose early, inquired how to avoid the main road to Eatonton, the next town south toward Milledgeville. He rode off at daybreak.

Soon after he left, several Federal officers appeared on the other side of the river and demanded to be brought across at once. They asked whether a stranger had crossed, but got the non-committal answer that this was a public ferry and little attention was paid to passengers. When they inquired the best way to Eatonton, they were sent on the longest route. After a few hours they returned empty-handed, went back across the ferry toward Greenesboro. Two days later Jefferson Davis was arrested at Irwinville, in south Georgia.

Many hundreds of the "wearers of the Gray" came through Greene on their way home from Appomattox. On foot and in wagons, picking up refugee slaves along the way. One night 1,600 soldiers camped in a wood near Bethesda Church. The men wanted food for their horses and themselves. Though much of the county's food supplies had been carried away, eaten, or stolen, the bottoms of the flour barrels were scraped again, and the corn cribs hidden away in the pine thickets were opened. The plantation mothers rounded up the Negro women and set food on their dining room tables as long as there were hungry soldiers to eat. At the command of the officers, the farm stock was driven away to a safe place so no Southern soldier on foot would be tempted to take a mule or a horse.

It was about this time that young James B. Park, Jr., bought a mule, his first one. He paid for it in Confederate money—$1,000 of valueless money for an almost valueless mule. He bought the mule from a Confederate soldier on his way home to Texas. And the Texan was happy enough, "Bein' as how I am on my way to Texas, and I believe the war will start again, Confederate money will pass where I am goin'."

But the war didn't "start again," nor was its full meaning yet known. Some of Greene's own soldiers had nearly starved to death. D. M. Goodwin of Greenesboro and James B. Boswell, who had been prisoners of war, reported that they had to kill and eat cats.

So, too, had the captured Federal troops imprisoned at Andersonville, a hundred miles southwest of Greene. For "letting prisoners starve" there, the superintendent, Dr. Wortz, was hanged. Dr. W. F. Credelle, of Greene county, had served at Andersonville with Wortz. He fled the prison to British waters for fear he might suffer like treatment.

Two hundred of Greene's six hundred soldiers did not return at all. They were killed in battle or died of sickness. Two hundred others were crippled or wounded. Those who came back found the farmhouses and barns in need of repair, smokehouses empty or nearly so, most of the livestock gone and much of the land idle, their money worthless, their slaves freed.

VIII

THE VICTORIOUS VANQUISHED

THE WAR over, Federal troops were a common sight in Greene county. They were in control for a time, but they were not the whole government. For the grand jury still met twice a year and made its presentments; the county officials remained around their courthouse offices; the *Greenesboro Herald,* started in 1866, recorded the feelings of the white leaders of the community, be they ever so critical of the way the Bluecoats were handling things.

The grand jury of March 1866 found that "there has been nothing done by the 'county treasurer' since the 'Surrender.' " * Roads were in bad condition, and "owing to the impoverished condition of the county, we are of the opinion that there ought not be any tax levied this year for 'poor school' purposes." In deeper despair the September grand jury said, "We cannot congratulate ourselves as in other days upon a bright and hopeful future. We have just emerged from a mighty revolution . . . the consequences of which will never be written, they cannot even be imagined. We began the war in good faith, we were honest, upon its results we stayed our future and our sacred honor. But we have been beaten, by our defeat we have lost millions in Confederate issue, millions in the emancipation of our slaves, millions in the repudiation of our state war debts, we have virtually lost every Bank note . . . All these things have come upon us . . . the debts of our people are gradually lengthened out and today we are overwhelmed in debt and unable to pay."

* Despite the general hard times of this period, there were still at least some islands of prosperity in Greene. See Appendix No. 5.

76

EX-SLAVES WITH CONTRACTS

But the land was still here, the long-suffering, patient land. And after the winter months, spring came as usual. Cotton was selling at a high price in 1865 and 1866. The large plantation owners could readily borrow operating capital from bankers in Baltimore and New York.

Most of the ex-slaves were still here, and though nominally free, were dependent upon their former masters. The white overseers and Negroes were just as landless after Appomattox as before it, and almost as dependent upon the landed families for work and protection.

After the havoc and hurts of war, a new agricultural economy was formed of the same pieces as the old. Wage hand plantations supplanted slave plantations. The same families were in control, the same families in the fields, and in many cases the same overseers.

But there were differences, too. The menfolk in the overseer families had been severely thinned by the war; in some families all of them were killed or wounded. The Negro population, on the other hand, was alive—all of it—anxious for freedom, groping for it.

What now is freedom with the same "Monday mornings" and the same "getting up 'fo day" we had as slaves? Or what would freedom be without work? What is freedom with the same food and the same house we had as slaves? Or what could it be without a house and food?

On a few plantations they received a third of the crop instead of wages, and rations from the smokehouse as they needed them.

These were the days of written contracts with ex-slaves, and real wages. Deductions were to be made for failures of the workers to live up to the contracts, and there were many clauses about the amount and quality of work to be performed.* The slaves signed the contracts by making their marks, and went to work.

---

* See Appendix No. 6 for a copy of a typical contract.

Hopeful and dazed, flustered, fumbling and afraid, most of the Negroes settled down on the cotton plantations as wage hands, with rations in lieu of wages. Some had misgivings about their freedom, but they were not inclined to give it up. They thought about the promise of the "Acre-Right Law," and, until it got here, wanted higher wages. In search of them, they pushed this way and that.

What happened on the James R. Sanders' plantation near Penfield during this period is shown by detailed records. Beginning in January 1866, ex-slaves were hired under written contract at $1.00 per day. Purchases were charged against them, and deductions made for not working, or for misbehavior. A few names in the overseer's book have no deductions after them, but most of them have many: "25c" when a laborer "refused to measure a load of corn;" "25c, stealing 10 guinea eggs;" "50c, hen killed by Henry;" "5c, Charley refused to feed mules;" "25c, Tildy refused to shuck corn at night;" "25c, refused to attend making syrup;" "50c, Sam Cary positive refused to take dog home;" and 25c against a worker who "refused to blow horn in the morning." A few large deductions appeared: $8.00 against George McWhorter who "was taken sick March 5 until March 23 which makes 16 days @ 50 cts;" and $10 against Sam Carey for "breaking Lil's head with a rock." Provisions and deductions sometimes exceeded the month's dollar-a-day wages.

One part of the record was captioned "Disobedience of Freedmen." The first entry was July 4, 1866, when "Alfred absented himself contrary to orders and went to Greenesboro and Richard Dun absented himself and went to Greenesboro withe out saying aney thing to me about it." An entry of Saturday, August 5 that year reads: "Adam Dun stoped works withe out my consent ½ day with all hands. They would have worked on had it not been for Adam he sed he would stop at twelve he did not cear what nobody sed. Mr. J. Davison was present. I called on him he tried to reason they cuse with him and avail nothing." The account of Jane Lyne for June 1867 ended on the 18th: "Jane left she took her child un be knoing to aney one   that was the last of her." Equally final had been the account of Dennis Thackery in February of that year: "Dennis absented himself withe out permission and was killed by a train."

The plantation records also show the crops made. It usually took J. C. Carlton's thresher and men two days at the Sanders plantation. In 1867 the tally stood: 232½ bushels of wheat, 68 bushels of oats, 20½ bushels of barley, and 36 bushels of rye. Into the stubble fields were turned 48 large hogs, 38 shoats, 35 pigs. The cotton crop that year was sold for $880; 15 bushels of cottonseed were sold at 10 cents a bushel, the remainder, except that saved to plant the next crop, was fed to the stock or hauled out on the land. The feed crops that year were 301 bushels of corn "including 36 bushels of nubbing corn;" 10,714 bundles of fodder and 1,200 bundles of hay.

By the spring of 1868, a straight wage of 50¢ for each day's work was being paid. An occasional ex-slave was getting $1.50 to $2.00 a day for some types of shop work and shoemaking. Whether as dollar-a-day laborers with deductions, or 50-cent wage hands, the mass of Negroes lived much the same as when they were slaves.

The Whites found their lot little more tolerable. The plantation owners were hard-pressed to hold their debt-ridden land. The continued decline in the price of cotton made it difficult to maintain even these low wages, much less raise them. The overseers found the Negroes restless, some of them demanding. The poorer Whites were still in competition with them for bread.

Painful to the Whites as were these economic conditions, the political situation was even more distasteful.

BLUECOATS AT THE COURTHOUSE

Confederate soldiers had been deprived of their citizenship. Georgia was without statehood rights. It constituted the Third Militia District. Federal soldiers were encamped on the courthouse square at Greensboro. They listened to the complaints of ex-slaves, and sometimes took their word in preference to that of a white man.

One story of the period goes like this: Asa Rhodes, an ex-slave-holder near Bethany, tired of the thefts and threats of a freedman named Sam. Rhodes appealed to the garrison at Greenesboro for protection. He was told to arrest Sam and bring him in for trial. With the help of some neighbors, he arrested Sam late one evening, took him to his home and set a watch over him, planning to take him to Greenesboro next morning. But Sam's friends rushed off to the Federal troops at Greenesboro with the report that white men had seized Sam and were planning to kill him during the night. Bluecoats proceeded to the Rhodes house, reaching there just before day. They shot into the house and killed Rhodes' brother-in-law and brought Rhodes back to Greenesboro. He was carried to Augusta for trial and was about to be hanged "when a hitch in the evidence saved his life."

For a little while in the late 1860's, Greene county and its neighbors were in many respects just a part of the "Third Militia District of the United States."

In the first year after the surrender, one of the officers in charge of the army of occupation was shot from ambush and killed on the streets of Greenesboro.

THE *Greenesboro Herald* SPEAKS OUT

The disfranchised Whites detested the Bluecoats who supervised the elections in which ex-slaves cast ballots.

An editorial in the *Greenesboro Herald* of January 9, 1868, said: "People of this great country, wherever they have been permitted to speak their sentiment, have declaimed that the Anglo-Saxon race shall rule America according to the Constitution. This is all that the people of the South desire. Our colored citizens must be protected in their rights, persons and property, but we are resolved by the blessings of Divine Providence to keep out of office those who are disqualified for discharge of duties by ignorance—or, what is worse, by renegade principles. Who would not prefer Aaron Alpeoria Bradley, negro, with all his stupidity, as a representative in Congress, to any of those recreant white men?"

The "recreant white men" referred to were those Confederate soldiers who, having agreed to cooperate with the "Carpetbag" leaders of the Reconstruction government, were relieved of their political disability by the Congress of the United States. Ten of these were in Greene county. Each and every one of the ten bid for Negro votes, and were elected to county and state offices. "Scallawags" they were called, and were hated by most "wearers of the Gray." Typical was this notice in an Augusta paper: "No native Scallawags or their money are wanted in my store from this date. Negroes and Eastern men are excusable, even if they are in some ways in opposition to the people of the South; but a native that turns traitor to his country ought not to be tolerated by law abiding people." The scallawags explained their position by saying they did it for the "good of the country."

An editorial of the *Greenesboro Herald* on February 13, 1868, said: "Absolutely essential to the return of Southern prosperity is the establishment of confidence and increasing good will between the two races. Occupying the same country, the interests of the Southern negro and of the Southern white are bound up together. The improvement of their condition must be based upon the improvement of ours —and vice versa. He who would alienate the races . . . is guilty of a high crime against God and man."

"COME WITH US," PLEAD THE WHITES

On March 26 the *Herald* carried a notice of a meeting of white citizens in the county courthouse, to discuss the political situation. The meeting was held, and as reported in the *Herald* the following week, "a motion was made and unanimously adopted requesting the colored voters to attend the next meeting." On the front page, alongside the report of the meeting, appeared a two-column statement to the Negroes about their political participation. The piece was entitled, "Address: of the White people of Greene County, Georgia to the Colored people of the same county."

The statement was direct and friendly. It urged the ex-slaves not to form a black man's party, not to listen to or follow after the "scallawags" or Yankee adventurers:

So if those people want you to vote, it is not because they love you; it is only because they think they can make something out of you . . . the advice they give you is bad advice . . . Now, we don't want you to go with these people. We want you to come with us. If you come with us, then we who live together can all be friendly together . . . we remember how faithful you were when you were slaves. We remember how you stood up for us during the war. We remember you as members of our families—we were boys together, we were raised together. We have not forgotten our old friendships. We do not wish to break them, we hope that no impertinent yankee will come in between us . . . These Yankees have told you that we wish to put you back into slavery . . . They are miserable liars . . . we never made slaves of you in the first place. It was the yankees who did it . . . It was Yankee money that brought you from Africa. You came in Yankee ships manned by Yankee soldiers . . . If the money which they got for you, together with the interest on it, were divided out among you, it would give every one of you a farm and a fortune . . . no, we do not wish to make slaves of you again . . . we would not if we could, we could not if we would . . .

In closing, the Address advised:

We know that we are the stronger party and we can afford to be magnanimous. We offer to you the right hand of friendship. We do not think you are qualified to vote. We know you are not qualified, and so do you know it. Still at present you have the right to do it. We acknowledge that right . . . We wish to live in peace. We wish to be like one family. Your interest is our interest, and our interest is your interest. Let us stand together. We invite you to cooperate with us . . . When voting time comes you had best go to your old master and get him to get you a ticket, that is the little piece of paper, and he will tell you what to do with it. You had best get your old master to go with you to the voting place. For if one of these stealing Yankees gets hold of your ticket, he will take it away from you and give you another in place of it, which will not do so well . . . it will be impossible for the white people and the black people in Georgia to get along together if they are voting in a body against each other . . . we are in all sincerity and truth your friends, and desire to remain so forever, and if we have any trouble it shall start with you and the Yankees, not with us.

This statement was signed by leading white citizens, including the President of Mercer University and a half dozen of the county's largest planters.

An editorial in the county paper of the next week, April 9, said: "Let the white Georgian, the black Georgian, the State, and all that are true to their homes and their families rise triumphant over the vile measures that are being taken to destroy all that is pertaining to a republican form of government." The paper referred to the "carpetbaggers" as members of the Radical Party opposed to a government established by white men, and repeatedly censured the local white men for having "sold out" to it. "This party seeks office," cautioned an editorial of June 4, "because it PAYS; it loves the country because it has a treasury; courts the negro because he votes."

SCALLAWAGS REJOIN DEMOCRATS

On July 9 the *Herald* reported that citizenship had been restored to all those who had participated in the war. Two weeks later it warned the scallawags to "flee from the wrath that is coming." Everyone was invited to come out of the "radical party" and join the Democrats. "We will receive him with the right hand of full fellowship, knowing it is human to err—we hope to see those who say they are not radical in principle, to give their fellow citizens assurance of the fact, and make good their faith by their works."

To make it easier for the scallawags to rejoin the Democrats, the editorial pointed out: "We are fully satisfied that there are many, some of whom we have heard say, that they did not consent for their names to be associated with the party because they were pleased with it, but for the benefit they expected to derive from the adoption of the measures contained in the constitution . . . We appeal to them to retrace their steps and save their honor."

The scallawags did rejoin the Democrats—all ten of them—and their "relatively brief excursion in iniquity" was forgiven. They agreed to remember that they were taken back into the Democratic fold upon repentance of their pro-Negro activities and their promise to "make good their faith by their works." The old-line Democrat, big landowner and little alike, could be open and friendly when dealing with the Negro. Not so the ex-scallawag, for he knew he had promised the Democrats—that is, the white community—to prove by "his works" that he had repented his scallawag activities. He knew any signs of friendliness toward the Negro might cause his sincerity to be questioned.

The last Greene county Negro in public office came down in 1868. He was Abe Colby, sent to the legislature on the Republican ticket in an election held under martial law. He took his seat in the legislature only to leave it shortly after when the Supreme Court held that Negroes had not yet been granted the right of citizenship. James B. Park, Sr., Colby's opponent on the Democratic ticket, took the seat. No Negro in Greene county held office after this. But ex-slaves continued to vote. The Negroes voted the Republican ticket, and, as the leading white people early foresaw, nearly all the local Whites, rich and poor and ex-scallawags, were Democrats.

The political situation gradually settled down as the controls slipped back into the hands of the Whites, even though the Negro voters far outnumbered them. Under the very eyes of Federal troops, Whites under 21 years voted, Negro ballots were displaced—sometimes chewed up and swallowed—and counts were so conducted that a Democratic minority regularly won over a Republican majority.

Early in 1870 the *Herald* asked wearily: "When will our colored friends learn that their specialty is anything else than politics? In the cotton field, Sambo has no peer. Here he rules supreme." Not so in politics, "he will be repelled to the lobby, and find 'Othello's occupation' still in the *Kitchen* cabinet."

The troops must have threatened to be more alert in their supervision of Greenesboro's elections, for on July 7, 1870 the *Herald,* in large type, asked, "Shall Greenesboro remain a city?" The real question was: Can Greenesboro afford to remain incorporated with 382 Whites and 531 Negroes, with the ballot box guarded by Federal troops?

Greenesboro remained a city, with a Democratic mayor and council.

Neither Federal soldier nor Negro was wholly unappreciated in Greene at this time. John A. Miller, of Greenesboro, put this "Card of Thanks" in the *Herald,* October 14, 1869: "I tender my most sincere thanks to the citizens of Greenesboro, both white and colored. Also to the Federal soldiers, who assisted in preventing my house from being destroyed during the late burning of our (Presbyterian) church."

The one Yankee who left a report of Greenesboro in this period, said the people were very hospitable to him, and that the town itself would compare well with the small towns of New York and New England. He stopped at a house where "the subtle mysteries of thrift and cleanly house-keeping" were practiced, where good food was attractively served by a Negro cook, and where the whole house was as "neat and tastefully and as appropriately furnished as any house" he had ever seen in Massachusetts. Such were the words of praise from Sidney Andrews, a newspaperman of New England who spent a few days in Greenesboro just after the war. It is thought he was entertained at the Mapp home, on West Broad Street.

THE KU KLUX KLAN IN GREENE

As an added precaution against Negro "unruliness," the Ku Klux Klan was active here. The wives of some plantation owners made long white robes for their husbands. In the dark of night white-robed figures warned and threatened.

The Negroes' fear of the KKK caused a bit of excitement in Union Point when an Episcopal clergyman donned his clerics. Nearly all the white people of the town were either Baptist or Methodist, but they turned out at the Methodist Church when it was announced that an Episcopal service would be conducted there. On the outer edge of the crowd were several Negroes. When they saw the fully regaled minister approach the church, they whispered "Ku Klux" and left.

The KKK activities gradually subsided. "After a while," according to Charles Jenkins Thornton, "the necessity for the Klan passed, and so many unreliable men had become members, some using their membership for personal reasons, that it was dissolved."

The March grand jury of 1870 advised that "the time in our opinion has come when reason should resume her sway and the maintenance of law and order should be the watchword of every good citizen. If the law is insufficient let us purify it and make it effective."

"GOOD ORDER" RESTORED

"Good order, kind feelings, peace and quiet now pervades every class of our citizens," said the grand jury presentments of September, 1870. "All are diligently pursuing their respective avocations, and a kind Providence has given us a bountiful harvest as a reward for our diligence."

The state government, still dominated by carpetbaggers, was for a little while longer a source of distress to the county leaders. The March, 1871 grand jury felt it to be "the duty of the Grand Inquest of this ancient and once prosperous county to notice the wasteful expenditures of the public money, and the abuse of the public credit by the present state executive . . . We therefore present the administration of the present Executive as wicked and useless."

The following year, James M. Smith, a Confederate Colonel, became governor of Georgia, and Greene county helped elect him. The next governor after Colonel Smith was General John B. Gordon, and after him Alexander H. Stephens, the vice-president of the late Confederacy. John Collier Hart of Union Point and Hal Lewis of Greenesboro were elected to the state legislature from Greene. Hart served as Judge of the Circuit Court, and later State Tax Assessor. Lewis, too, remained active in Democratic politics for many years. In county and state affairs, the old line Democrats were in full control.

But agriculture, not politics, was the mudsill of Greene's life. So the local paper and the people began to give more thought to farm conditions, to the land, and to the relations between landlord and tenant, creditor and debtor, black man and white.

IX

FREEDOM'S BONDAGE

By the early 1870's the wage hand plantation was well established. But the price of cotton kept dropping from one year to the next, and the debts incurred on the last crop were that much harder to pay. This always necessitated new borrowings. Cotton was relied upon more and more to repay loans each fall.

The planters were now not nearly so independent as they had been before the war, but they were equally in control of the landless workers, White and Negro. It was they who borrowed, they who gave their lands as security, they who used the money to support their workers while growing a crop. Each year they tried to sell enough cotton to repay borrowings and interest, and make a living for themselves. The workers sensed their lot was little better because of freedom. They were restive and unsettled. Or as the planters saw it, they were hard to manage, and not to be depended upon.

Planters were "never to employ a laborer who has contracted with another, until he is legally discharged, and put under the public ban any man who will entice away the labor of another." So ran an editorial in the *Greenesboro Herald* in mid-March of 1870. The second way for planters to hold their labor was "to enforce rigorously the existing law for the special protection of employers."

Some of the large landowners in Greene had been so discouraged by their difficulties that in January, 1870 they offered to give the use of their plantations for the next year to anyone who would agree to pay the taxes. But spring came, and some of winter's pessimism faded. The planters began to work out ways and means of farming another year.

THEY SHARE IN THE RISK

The solution on most plantations to the problem of low cotton prices was the use of "sharecroppers" in the place of wage hands. Small houses were built out in the fields, as one propertyless family after another left the old slave quarters back of the big house, and went to live on the tract of land it was to cultivate that year.

There were few or no written contracts now between plantation owners and those who cultivated their land. The contracts had been long and intricate. The worker, commonly unable to read and always without a lawyer, found no protection in them. The landlords were glad to let the matter drop. Landowner and landless worker orally agreed upon the land to be cultivated and the amount and method of the "furnish"—that is, the food and clothes to be advanced to the worker's family for use while growing the crop.

Tenant or sharecropper farming made it possible for the landlord to dispense with the overseers who had stayed out in the field all day with the wage hands to be sure they put in a full day's work. It provided a means of letting each family get out on a piece of land about the size of that suggested by the "Acre-Right Law."

But though maybe he was one step nearer a farm of his own, the sharecropper soon found that he was sharing in the risk without sharing in the control of the crop. The vast majority of the tenants owned no livestock or farm implements, had no credit, had to be furnished everything by the landlord. Since he was always in debt, even the crop the tenant had not yet harvested belonged to the landowner. The tenant got some money of his own only when his debts had been paid in full. Most years the debts of many families exceeded their part of the crop; when crops were bad, nearly all the families owed more than they made.

To protect their collective interests, the planters continued the "chimney-corner ethic" of hiring a worker or taking a tenant only when agreeable to his last landlord. Wanting more protection, they and the planters in the other parts of the state had the crop lien statutes enacted. These laws made the landowners rent the first claim on the tenant's crop. A supplemental crop lien law was passed to secure payment for advances and supplies. The landowner could terminate at will the services of his croppers, who by law and practice had only the status of wage hands.

The landless families in turn made few improvements on their farms. They did not feel like fixing up a place they might leave at the end of the crop year, or before. Their attitude toward the care of the land was equally short ranged. Each year they got all they could out of the land. Each year more of the new commercial fertilizer, "guano," had to be applied to maintain the yield. Debts mounted while the basic capital, the fertility of the soil, dwindled.

As the years passed the plantation owners left the old homesteads and moved into Greenesboro and the other towns, leaving the sharecroppers to shift for themselves, or work under the management of an overseer.

After a few years, the absentee owners preferred to have on their land, when they could get them, families who could provide their own supplies and pay a fixed cash or crop rent. The great majority of workers remained dependent, however, because it was hard for a cropper family to get even a little ahead.

Landowning and landless ones alike operated on a yearly basis, each trying to get as much as he could out of the other, and out of the land. Every year stood on its own bottom. No plan for the decade or for the century.

TIME-MERCHANT PROSPERITY

To finance the tenant and sharecropper families, the landowners continued to borrow money each season. They gave their land as security for the loans. The state's leading bankers flourished, as did also the leading local merchants.

As the plantation smokehouse stocks dwindled, the merchants did a thriving credit business. More and more it was the time-merchants instead of the landowners who advanced supplies to the tenants and sharecroppers. They held a second lien on the tenant's crop, and through agreement with the landlord sometimes held the first lien, too. To meet these cash demands on farm operation, the whole countyside was planted in cotton. It was the only sure way to get the money needed to pay that year's debts.

By the middle of the 1870's there were at least a dozen time-merchants operating in the county, half of them in Greenesboro. The principal merchandiser was Charles A. Davis, whose small store in Greenesboro had remained open even in those difficult months before and after Appomattox. The fine brick house which Davis built in 1875 created a sensation in town. The *Herald* printed a detailed description of the mantelpieces, the chandeliers, and the staircase.

As early as 1869, one of the plantation owners, J. B. Hart of Union Point, had been able to build a big new house on the knoll overlooking Union Point. It was later christened Hawthorne Heights.

James B. Park, Sr., of Park's Mill had enough influence with the state legislature, of which he had been a member, to get it to change the boundaries of the county in 1872. The county line was extended across the Oconee, so Park's home site would be in Greene with the rest of his land.

Greenesboro had a population of nearly a thousand people. Fines from the town's court kept up the streets, and the marshal's salary came from saloon licenses. Greenesboro had seven lawyers, Union Point one. In the county were fifteen physicians, one dentist—the dentist and four of the physicians in Greenesboro. The Greenesboro Tan Yard was advertising for 100 cords of tan-bark and 1,000 hides. In 1874 kerosene street lamps were put up, and a volunteer fire department was organized, "Anchor Hook and Ladder Company, No. 1."

But Greenesboro was still a country town, for, said the grand jury, "We most respectfully call the attention of the city council to cattle and loose stock running at large in the streets, which has been a great nuisance to members of this body and others in attendance at this court."

Hangings were still public affairs in 1873, as shown by a news story in the *Greenesboro Herald*. A Negro, George Copeland, was placed on the trap, and the trap was sprung. The rope broke, and the victim sat dazed upon the ground. A few minutes later he was led back up the scaffold, and a second noose was put around his neck. The trap sprung, he died. The better-dressed men at the hanging wore paper collars, pegged gaiters, Sing Sing Balmoral shoes, and the ladies wore pegged shoes and hoop skirts. The brass cap-tips on the children's shoes shone in the sun. The poorer folk still got along with coarse jeans and heavy brogans.

The north pillar of the courthouse was repaired, the inside walls plastered, and the broken panes replaced. A fence which "reflected credit upon the builders" now surrounded the public square.

The Greene County Agricultural and Mechanical Association was a booster club. Its officers included such well known names as Janes, Willis, Armour, Carlton, Branch, Brown, and Hart.

In 1872 to 1875, elaborate fairs were set up at Union Point by the County Mechanical and Agricultural Society. Prizes were offered for the best exhibits of livestock, crops, flowers, and clothes. Some pure-bred cattle was shown by Dr. Thomas P. Janes of Penfield, James B. Hart of Union Point, and others. Among the prizes for clothing was one for home-spun men's suits. Large crowds attended.

In 1874, the Third Georgia Regiment, C. S. A., convened at Union Point, and was the first Regimental reunion of Confederate soldiers in the South.

Greene county was once more on the upgrade. Cotton was called white gold; it had again been crowned king in Greene. But now it was debt-ridden and produced with expensive commercial fertilizer.

The smaller white farmowners and tenants may have wondered about their relationship to the big planters in the 1850's, but not in the 1860's. For then they were encouraged to bear their full share, heaped up and pressed down, of the privations and death of the war. War over, they became identified with the Democratic Party which was the South's white party. But they were still far from its leadership, far from a sense of the power of their numerical majority. They remained inarticulate. Their world was now governed, economically and politically, by the flourishing time-merchants and by the big planters who had owned the slaves and who of late had pushed the crop lien laws through the legislature. Those who controlled farm finances controlled the community.

STRAINING TOWARD FREEDOM

A legal marriage was one of the slave's earliest responses to freedom. An awareness of the use of the law is shown by a few early requests for divorce. The first divorce sought by Negroes occurred in March, 1870, when Levi Thornton and his wife Mary Ann appeared in court. Said the local *Herald:* "This is a step in the right direction. Our colored population should be made to understand that their privileges of citizenship are accompanied with the same obligations to observe the law in these respects as upon their white neighbors."

There was always the question of what place the ex-slaves could and should occupy in the county. Were they fitted for freedom, once the marks of slavery were gone? If so, how could "the marks of slavery" be erased? Who would do it? How long would it take? Or were the Negroes foredoomed to servitude by the very nature of their bodies, minds, and spirits? Their bodies were strong and their stamina great. Did not the Whites brag on each other's industry by saying, "That fellow works like a 'nigger'!" Look, too, at the arduous tasks that the Whites had always depended upon them to do. Strong bodies they had, all agreed, but what of their minds and spirits?

The Negroes were not all alike. In slavery some of them did the skilled tasks while others worked in the fields. A few slaves had been taught to read and write.

Alfred Parrott was taught to read and spell by the Reverend Peek's children when they came home from school in the evening. For several years after Appomattox, the Reverend Peek continued to preach to both the Whites and the Negroes in the Smyrna Baptist Church. When the church finally divided, and the Negroes built a log church for themselves at Mount Pleasant, "Preacher" Parrott became their first pastor.

J. H. Kilpatrick, white preacher at White Plains at the end of the war, preached two sermons a day—one to the white members of his church, and one to the Negroes. Also in White Plains, a few years later, a white man conducted a school for Negro children. Another white man opened a school for Negroes at St. Paul's, near Greenesboro. A few "educated" Negroes from outside the county came in to teach and preach, especially from Haines' Institute, at Augusta.

Some of the ex-slaves, who had grown up without learning to write and read, taught themselves, or went to white friends and got them to teach them. Sid Woodfin, who had belonged to Professor Woodfin of Mercer University, decided he would like to read the Bible after he "got religion." The white man for whom he worked after the war helped him by spelling out sentences for him during the noon rest period. He learned to write, too, after he caught another fellow passing notes to his girl.

As important as the right to learn, was the right to own property. A few Negro landowners appeared soon after the war. They were ex-slaves of the larger planters, and secured their land from their ex-masters. The Stocks, Sanders, Ellingtons, Fambroughs, Murdens, Rowlands, and Watts were the first to own land. The ownership of even small tracts anchored them to one locality, and they became the leaders of the Negro churches, which had become the Negro's main organization. This meant that for the most part the leadership of the Negroes was conservative and beholden to the leading white families.

Negro landownership was made possible by the kindly interest of ex-masters. It could continue only as the colored owners behaved in ways which pleased their sponsors, could expand only as desired by the landlords.

The cordial relation which obtained between many ex-masters and their ex-slaves is shown by the prominent part the plantation Negroes took at the funeral of Thomas Stocks, in 1876. They bore him to his grave, as they had succored him in life. Many another planter was lowered into the red sub-soil of Greene county with more tears on black cheeks than on white.

There were a few exceptional Negroes to whom even the white newspapers gave recognition. "Old Kelly King," according to an article in the county paper, "was a natural poet." He could not read or write, and back in slavery "would ask his master's family to write down his rhymes." Then there was blind Thomas Greene Bethune, the prodigy pianist, whose mother had belonged to John Bethune of Greene. In the latter 1860's he appeared in concerts throughout America and Europe. At the age of seventeen, he could repeat after one hearing the most complicated musical numbers. It is believed that "Blind Tom's" mother, taken from the county by her master when he left in the 1830's, put the "Greene" in her son's name in memory of her former home.

The general assumption of the Whites was that the black man was a lower type of being than the white man. Negroes of proved intelligence were considered exceptions, and their ability commonly explained as due to "white blood."

WHEELS WITHIN WHEELS

Freedom had come to the black folk. But inside their new freedom, they kept feeling old pressures. Some of them were exercised by plantation owners, more of them through new laws, new ways of effecting old controls. Wheels within wheels.

When slavery was first challenged, the planters asked, "What then will become of 'old Aunt Fannie'?" As the people found their places in the new plantation system, there were old men and women with no means of support. They could not become renters, share-croppers, or wage hands. Nor could their tenant or wage-hand children and grandchildren take care of them; they could hardly provide for themselves. They soon appeared along with the elderly dependent Whites in the county treasurer's report as the "indigent poor" or "paupers," for whom around $800 a year was spent. But every time one was given aid, two more seemed to show up in need of help.

The "paupers" remained costly. In 1874 the county spent $3,000 on 78 dependent old people. This was an average of less than four dollars per person, per month. Even so, the sum spent on paupers that year in Greene was more than double the amount spent for public education.

One grand jury after another asked that a "pauper farm" be established; $2,500 in bonds were recommended to set it up. By 1875 the "pauper farm" was open. The next year the jury found it had "materially reduced the expenses of the county." So, too, said the next and the next, as they praised the county authorities for giving aid only to those paupers who went to live on the "farm."

But at the farm there were only four paupers, "two old men and two old ladies, all white and well provided for." The "pauper farm" was saving the county money, but it was not taking care of the paupers, so by the end of its fifth year the grand jury asked that it be sold. Two years later a presentment ran: "Eleven paupers, one white and ten blacks—we find that the superintendent has not given board as required by law." Four years later there were but three paupers on the farm and the well had caved in. Two years after, the "pauper farm" was sold for $906, and the county was giving aid to 55 elderly people, at an average rate of $2.12 per person per month, a total annual expenditure of $1,500, half of what was spent before the pauper farm was started. It had served its purpose after all.

In the same fourteen years, school expenditures had doubled.

All of the pauper fund came from Greene's taxes; almost all of the school funds from the state.

During this period, the grand jury asked that the $200 tax exemption be repealed "as we consider the enactment of this sprang from, and is nurtured by a species of Demagogerism and is unjust to the tax payers of the state."

Another change designed to shift an increasing part of the tax load to the smallest property holders was the jury's recommendation "that a tax of $1.00 be imposed on every dog, gun, pistol, or fire arm of any kind owned or kept in this county."

In March of 1874 the presentments hailed the proved success of the newly established county court, which "during the last six months . . . paid into the hands of the county treasurer $945.50, which exceeds the salary of the county judge $455.50" for that period. The money came largely from fines for such petty offenses as vagrancy, loitering, disturbing the peace, simple assault, crap-shooting, and so on through the "sins" of the poorer folk. The judge's salary remained at $1,000 a year for a time, then dropped to $800. Almost regularly the fines from this court were far more than it cost, and almost regularly the grand jury asked for its continuance. The county court also lessened the work of the Superior Court, which was more expensive to the county because it afforded trial by jury and an attorney—sometimes court-appointed—for the accused.

One grand jury asked that the county judge appoint a man in each district "to look after all the vagrants."

———————

The Bluecoats had gone. The scallawags had repented. The slaves were free and had the ballot. But they had no economic resources, no way to escape chronic dependency, no reasonable hope for the coveted 40 acres and a mule. And so as wage hands and sharecroppers, they could not prevent the use of political power to regulate their economic and social condition.

The time-merchants with their high carrying charges were another expense to the already debt-ridden tenants and sharecroppers, another threat to the small owner who might lose his land on a single poor crop.

The basic questions of the small farmers, black and white, remained. Unanswered, too, were many of the problems which were bearing down on the plantation owners. They controlled labor, but they were hard pressed with debts to distant money lenders. Landed and landless, the men of Greene kept seeking a way out.

PART THREE

IN SEARCH OF ANSWERS

X

GUANO AND NEW SETTLERS

THE PRODUCTION of crops on the sharecropper plantations was financed with borrowed money. The few remaining patches of virgin soil in the big plantation areas were put to cotton and corn. The tired land leached and washed. The gullies gnawed deeper into the red lands of Greene. More mud poured into the creeks and the rivers.

GUANO FOR TIRED FIELDS

Each year guano from Chile was hauled to the fields of Greene from the railroad stations. The neighbors knew when a farmer carried home a bag of guano. With the wind it could be smelled a mile, and on warm damp days the stench of it spread out in all directions like an opening fan. Pinches of it were scattered in the furrow with fertilizer horns. Forty or fifty pounds to the acre, rarely a hundred. And that fall more bolls and larger ears were gathered from the enriched rows. The next spring more farmers hauled home sacks of fertilizer. They had larger debts to pay in the fall. The townsfolk met the afternoon train, sniffed the "stinking guano" in the freight warehouse close by; the farm folk sniffed it, too, said, "There must be a hundred dollars' worth in there."

Into Greene also came carloads of salt bacon and flour and corn from the meat houses and granaries of the West. Mules proved especially well suited to sharecropper farming; most of them were imported from Tennessee and Missouri.

To his old line of food and feed and clothes, the time-merchant now added fertilizer and mules. His business flourished.

Between 1870 and 1880, the county's population increased by over a third, with Negroes making up three fourths of the gain. The plantation sections of Greene swarmed with wage hands and share-croppers, all of them dependent upon the planters and merchants. Only a degree less dependent were the small owners.

There were wealthy families as before the war, but they were fewer in number now. Most were merchant-planters. To them fell one tract of land after another as customers failed to pay their debts.

A STATE DEPARTMENT OF AGRICULTURE

Mounting fertilizer bills and wasting fields convinced the more alert farmers that there was great need for better farm practices.

The Georgia Agricultural Society was revived in 1868, with an office in the State House in Atlanta, and a library of about 3,500 volumes. State fairs were held again. In 1870 the Society adopted a resolution calling upon the legislature to establish a State Department of Agriculture. In response to a similar resolution four years later, the legislature created the Department, and appropriated $10,000 a year for its use.

The act authorized the Commissioner of Agriculture to analyze and inspect fertilizers, to discover and recommend ways of controlling insects and plant diseases, to import and distribute seeds, to study the geology of the state, and to report on dairying, sheep and wool raising, fencing, irrigation, and "any subject he may deem of interest to the agriculture of the state."

The Governor appointed as first Commissioner of Agriculture Dr. Thomas P. Janes, large planter of the Penfield community, who was known as a practical and successful farmer. He had demonstrated the rotation of crops, the value of raising pure-bred livestock, and the use of cotton seed for fertilizer.

Commissioner Janes had neighbors who shared his interest in the farm conditions of that day. Said the Greene grand jury of March, 1876: "The cause of our present embarrassments is the almost exclusive cultivation of a crop, expensive in details, and the market value . . . subject to great and sudden fluctuations. We believe that any system of agriculture to be successful with us must be more diversified and self sustaining and must embrace a gradual but constant improvement of the soil." The jury recommended sheep husbandry as a step toward diversification.

In 1879 Commissioner Janes wrote a report for the Georgia Department of Agriculture. It was entitled, *Handbook of Georgia Department of Agriculture.* Dr. Janes stated that the soil of Georgia had "shared the fate of that of all new countries." The system of farming "seemed to be based upon the impression that the fertility of the soil was inexhaustible." He saw developing a new interest in soil conservation: "The scale has now turned in Georgia from the exhausting to the restoring process. Here farmers are now building up their wasted places by an improved system of agriculture, guided by the light of applied science. Both natural and artificial fertilizers are now brought into requisition by the prudent farmer."

As proof of the capacity of Georgia's soil to produce crops under improved culture, he listed several phenomenal yields, some of them from Greene: L. B. Willis, 20 bushels of wheat on 1½ acres of land, and on the following year 27,130 pounds of corn forage; Dr. W. Moody, in one cutting on one acre of Oconee River bottom, 13,953 pounds of Bermuda grass hay; the Commissioner reported from his own farm, a few miles northwest of Penfield, five tons of clover hay per acre in one season—two cuttings.

He warned, however, against the extravagant use of commercial fertilizer, advised that it be used along with barnyard manure or cotton seeds. He insisted that if the seed and plant of the cotton crop be returned to the soil, cotton culture "is less injurious to the soil than any other hoe crop."

Commissioner Janes said the analysis and inspection of fertilizers was the most important thing his Department had done for the farmers. "This supervision has in one single season saved for the farmers of Georgia in actual cash not less than $1,500,000 as demonstrated by the increased actual value of the fertilizers sold . . . and the decreased price at which they were sold . . . this saving amounts to $1.27 per annum for every individual in Georgia; while the entire expense to the state of the 'Department' is only 1-1/6¢ per annum for each individual."

The Commissioner was realistic about the war and its effects. "We went foot," he said, "we are now spelling up slowly . . . Georgia's career lies in the future. Her great hope is in her people." He saw the white people as "given to hospitality; and a foreigner with ordinary prudence will not find them otherwise." He prophesied the ex-slaves would make commendable progress. He wanted to attract immigrants to Georgia's vast spaces of thinly populated land and prodigal soil and seasons.

Dr. Janes concluded his report by pointing out that agriculture "is now generally recognized in Georgia as an applied science. The old prejudice against 'book farming' . . . is rapidly giving way to enlightened programs."

NEW WHITE SETTLERS

A new plantation system had supplanted the old, and there were still twice as many Negroes in the county as Whites. The efforts to get new white settlers continued, and a few families came here to live.

A Land Agency was opened in Greenesboro in 1870 by E. W. Miller "from the North" himself, and personally known to many who desired to "locate in a warmer climate." In mid-March this advertisement appeared in the *Greenesboro Herald*: "*Particular notice* to the people of Greene and adjoining counties. Within the past few weeks I have received a great number of letters from parties North who desire to come here to locate, not as carpet-baggers, but as actual honest settlers."

By early November, as shown by a news item, 3,170 acres had been sold for $29,400 to seven Northerners, many of whom came here to live. Among the tracts was the Joel Early place of 2,200 acres, sold for $20,000 to J. B. Y. Warner of Rochester, New York, who came here with his family. An eighth Northerner bought a city lot for $1,000, and a ninth, the hotel property for $5,000.

A tract of 657 acres, just north of Greenesboro and near the Joel Early place, was bought by Herman Geissler of Frankfort-on-the-Main, Prussia, for $5,000. He left Germany to escape compulsory military service, and came here with his family.

Two years later, the *Greenesboro Herald* was hoping for more European migrants. It advised that some local men "would do well" to join with the "intelligent and enterprising capitalists of Atlanta" who are planning to finance an agent to Europe to secure immigrants "to settle in Georgia, buy up lands, manufacture, and till the soil."

No other Europeans came to Greene, and after a few years the Warners moved back North where "Yankees" were not subjects for community censure.

The proportion of people in Greene who owned no productive property remained about the same as before the Northern families came here to live, about the same in fact as before the war. For only a few ex-slaves had acquired any land, and most of the poorer Whites remained landless.

THE PRIVATE SCHOOLS GO

The academies were closed during the war, and most of them never opened again. The Female College at Greenesboro reopened soon after the war, with a Northern man in charge. He accepted young men as well as women students, and arranged a few scholarships. But he remained unpopular, and was dismissed in the early fall of 1872. On the night following his dismissal the college building burned. The college was abandoned.

Mercer had reopened after the war, and was doing the work of an academy. It hoped to get the resources with which to resume its university work. The Georgia Baptist Association met in Greenesboro in 1869. There was talk of Mercer's being moved. Atlanta and Macon were making attractive offers. Thomas Stocks, the only surviving founder of Mercer, then in his eighty-fourth year, rose and pleaded for the continuation of the school at Penfield or for remuneration to the heirs of its other founders. The Association voted a resolution: "The most efficient means of advancing the prosperity of Mercer University is to forever discountenance the suggestion of its removal from its present location."

It was soon clear that Penfield, stronghold of the wrecked slave economy, could no longer hold Mercer. Local Baptists then tried to locate it at Greenesboro, which time-merchant prosperity had restored to its old preeminence over Penfield. Further offers from Atlanta and Macon soon killed Greene's last hopes, and in 1872 the school was moved to Macon where the representatives of Eastern bankers and insurance companies were establishing their offices. Mercer was near the heart of the new economy as it had been near the heart of the old. Her place on the map shifted as the center of power shifted from the slave plantation to the money lenders and time-merchants.

When the university moved, Penfield lost many of her leading families—especially the college faculty members. Several of the larger houses were left vacant; some of them were torn down and moved to fast-growing Atlanta.

Even with the Female College and Mercer University out of the picture, and with most of the pre-war academies abandoned, pay schools remained in Greene for a time. The Baptist Association maintained a high school at Penfield to care for the families who had bought four- and eight-acre tracts in the town and moved there to educate their children.

By 1873 a Male and Female Academy had been started in Greenesboro. The tuition ranged from $12 to $20 per term.

THE GWYNN ALLISON SCHOOL FUND

The death of Gwynn Allison, President Andrew Jackson's cousin, occurred in 1865. A paragraph in his will read:

I give and bequeath to the Inferior Court of Greene County twenty thousand dollars, the interest of which is to be used for the Education of poor children in Greene County; but no part of the principal is to be used for that purpose.

Throughout his lifetime, Allison had steadfastly refused to accept the $105.25 damages granted him for the railroad right-of-way in 1835. His executors accepted the principal and accrued interest— $300—and added it to his Poor School Fund.

Allison's bequest was challenged. The grand jury of March, 1871 asked the Ordinary to retain two outstanding attorneys, Linton Stephens of Hancock county and Augustus Reese of Morgan county, to represent the county's interests. The September presentments advised that "in the event the Gwynn Allison will is sustained the whole Fund be invested in the Georgia Railroad or other safe bonds." The will was sustained. Nearly half of Allison's bequest was in Confederate Treasury notes and certificates. The payment of lawyers' fees further reduced the amount. The sum of $8,800 was turned over to the Inferior Court of Greene.

PUBLIC SCHOOLS—NOT WANTED

About the time the Gwynn Allison Fund became available for the poor schools in Greene, the legislature of 1871 authorized the establishment of public schools for all the children of the state, white and colored. The school legislation specified that the children of both races were to be educated at public expense, in separate schools, and suggested that a school commissioner be named in each county.

The public school system was not readily accepted here. One grand jury after another questioned its value. The jury of September,

1875 recommended that the office of the county school commissioner be abolished, and that the county treasurer pay the teachers. The presentments of the following March acknowledged that "a diversity of sentiment exists among the members of this body as to the wisdom and policy of the present free school system, and . . . grave doubts are entertained . . . of the practicality of adjusting any system of free and public schools to the requirements of a community not homogeneous."

In March, 1877 the grand jury found that "after a careful investigation of the practical workings of the system of public schools . . . we find that the educational interest of the county has not been advanced. In view of this fact, and in view of the present indebtedness of the county, we deem it unwise, impolitic and inexpedient to levy a tax for the support of these schools during the present year."

The county's indebtedness was less than $7,000 at this time, and the county's annual taxes were approximately $11,000. It will be remembered that it was during the decade of the 1870's that the county's population increased over one third and that some merchants built fine new homes.

PUBLIC SCHOOLS—ACCEPTED

By the middle 1880's the public school system was firmly established, with a school commissioner and county board of education. White teachers were furnished for white children, and Negro teachers for Negro children. Each white school had a board of white trustees, each Negro school a board of Negro trustees.

In 1884 there were 28 white schools with 993 pupils enrolled, 25 colored schools with 1,864. Total expenditures were $4,664.

Most of the funds with which to build rural white schoolhouses and Negro churches, too, were raised by subscription; the merchants were the largest givers. Nine tenths of all school expenditures were for teachers' salaries. The white teachers, with 35 percent of the enrollment, received 56 percent of the money for salaries.

The County Board of Education allocated the money to the schools. The largest sum set up to any school in 1884 was the $380 for the newly established Stocks Institute, in Greenesboro. Five other white schools received sums of over $210.

The Greenesboro "Baptist" colored school received $180, the largest amount given to a Negro school; seven others were given $100 or more. The total money allocated by the county board to white schools was $3,020, to colored schools, $2,805.

Greenesboro and White Plains each had a "Baptist" and a "Methodist" public school for Negroes. Throughout the county most of the colored schools convened in Negro churches, and were looked upon by the Negroes as church schools. The rural white schools early convened in schoolhouses, and many of them were fast by the most popular churches.

THE OLD ROCK JAIL

Greene county was 100 years old by the time the public school system got under way. For three quarters of that century the county's rock jail had stood unchanged—had received into its four dungeon-like cells drunken Red Men reared here, rowdy White Men born in Europe, unruly Black Men born in Africa. Before the war a few white debtors, now and then a white overseer, and since the war a steady flow of crap shooters and chicken stealers, small peddlers of whisky, vagrants and loiterers, and now and again a man accused of burglary or murder—some of them White, most of them Black.

The old jail had long since been unsatisfactory. 'Way back in the 1830's, grand juries had called attention to its unsanitary condition, had repeatedly asked for a new jail. Then came the growing tension between the South and the North, war and reconstruction, and the grand jury made no further mention of the jail until 1875, when it was recommended that the jail be furnished with bedsteads. Three years later the grand jury reported, "Jail safe, but poorly ventilated and in a crowded, filthy condition," and asked that "suitable vessels be provided for carrying the waste matter from prisoners." A sink was asked for a few years later.

"Humanity and Justice alike," said the jury of March, 1887, "demand that some arrangements should be made for heating the jail." The next jury, and the next, asked for heat in the jail, and for those "general sanitary requirements, looking to better and more humane treatment of prisoners." Then successive presentments: remodel the jail, tear down the jail and build a new one "for the comfort and safekeeping of prisoners. We look upon the jail as being a disgrace to our county."

Owing to the stringency of the times, the jury of August, 1893 recommended that "the building of a new jail be put off for a time," though it asked that a sewer be installed. That same year, the county court received $1,195.73 "from fines and hire of convicts," and the jury requested that hat racks and spittoons be placed in the grand jury room, and that $300 be given the Greene Rifles, the local national guard unit.

A new brick jail was built in 1897, and included an apartment for the sheriff's residence.

The County Convict Camp during this period was housed in movable four-wheel iron cages. In February of 1894, Louise Barnhart, Negro, was awarded $750 when her husband was killed on the chain-gang. After 1895, the convicts were used to work the public roads of the county. Mercer Reynolds, then convict warden, reports that he thinks that Greene county was the first county in the state to use convict labor to work public roads.

THE BIG WORLD PUSHES IN

The big world kept pushing in on Greene. Ice was shipped in from Atlanta, with express charges of $1.00 per hundred pounds. Lemon, strawberry, and sarsaparilla were then the standard drinks. The folks of Greenesboro had their first taste of Coca-Cola when on

Memorial Day 1890 local druggist T. B. Rice dispensed ten gallons of "Candler's coffee."

The first phonograph, as reported by the *Herald-Journal*,* appeared on the streets of Greenesboro in 1892; the man exhibiting it "reaped a harvest of nickles from those who wanted to hear the songs, speeches, etc., from this mysterious contrivance." The first embalming was done this same year. Five years later telephones were installed, and druggist Rice soon became the local "telephone man."

It was about this time that the spelling of the county seat was changed from Greenesboro to Greensboro—supposedly by a postal clerk in Washington, who must have known more about the green in turnipgreens than about the great Revolutionary hero, Nathaniel Greene, for whom the county and county-seat were named. Again and again the mistaken spelling was called to the attention of the postal authorities. Each time they took the matter "under advisement." But the spelling in the postal guide was never corrected.

Bethany Presbyterian Church was 100 years old in 1886. It was at the six-day centennial celebration that many a farmer and his wife and children first heard of evolution. Dr. Thomas Woodrow was tried for heresy by the Augusta Presbytery, in which he was a leading divine. He had discussed Darwin's theory too favorably to suit some of his fellow churchmen. The trial, which is locally referred to as the first "monkey trial" on record, lasted for two days. Dr. Woodrow was acquitted. He was the grandfather of a promising young attorney, Thomas Woodrow Wilson.

First among the local Presbyterians, and then throughout this section, the heresy trial was the occasion for much discussion. Some people resented the idea of unending change and adaptation. They looked into their children's faces and saw the image of their God; they looked out of their kitchen windows at their plants and animals, which were as they had always been. Others looked into their

---

* The *Greensboro Herald* was organized in 1866; the *Georgia Home Journal* of Greensboro, 1872. The two papers were merged in 1887 to form the *Herald-Journal*.

children's faces and saw the image of their God, and looked at their gardens and barnyards, fields and woodlots, and saw change everywhere. The corn stalks were shorter and the ears longer than they were a decade ago. The thin shelled pecans were larger than the old ones. The Berkshire and the Poland China pigs would make more and better meat. The new tomatoes were the best variety they had ever had. And some people had seen and eaten Elberta peaches, originated scarcely a decade earlier by Samuel H. Rumph of Marshallville, Georgia.

But most of the argument turned upon whether men had "descended from monkeys." An emotional religious "no" was a common answer. But the matter would not rest. Some people were fascinated by the very excitement that the subject aroused, if not by the theory of evolution itself. The white men talked and the colored men listened. Then some of the colored people went down to their church, talked about man's origin, and "Resolved: First, that God made all Negroes; Second, that God made all White Folks except them that think they come from monkeys."

But cleverly worded resolutions do not resolve great theoretical questions. The Negro still wondered where his forebears had come from, where his children would get to. But he wondered more about the cold hard facts of his everyday life. White people, too, were aware that adequate answers had not been found to the man and land troubles of Greene. New organized efforts were beginning to be made. Some of them local, others were South-wide and national.

XI

WHITE LANDS IN BOOM

PLANTATION FARMING with borrowed money and commercial fertilizer was at best a gamble. By the early 1880's the sharecropper plantation system had reached its peak.

RED LANDS IN DECLINE

Retrenchments and adjustments began to take place throughout the old red land plantations as the land grew poor, the yields smaller.

The first serious agricultural slump occurred in the late 1880's and early 1890's. The area most affected was "prosperity ridge," lying between Richland Creek and the Oconee, and reaching from Long Shoals to northwest of Greensboro. It was in this area and in this period that the first rural white schools and churches went into decline.

Then followed the decline of the Negro schools and churches, as many of the Negroes moved out. A few became renters, and patch farmed the most fertile spots. They got by with as little cash outlay as possible. Sooner or later some of them moved into the plantation houses, for as the years passed one tenant cabin after another caved in and twisted to the ground.

Other plantation areas, too, began to wane, especially the Oakland section northwest of Greensboro. The Presbyterian Church there was moved to Penfield. In the northeast part of the county, the membership of the Bethesda Baptist Church began to drop off. Over in the Forks, the New Hope Baptist Church was moved to Gresham-ville.

The number of plantation holdings of 2,000 acres or over de-creased. So did the population—241 fewer whites in 1890 than in 1880, 255 fewer Negroes. This downward trend continued for the next decade.

The younger members of the old landed families left the planta-tions. Some moved to Greensboro, and a few to the white-land section of Greene. Many more left for the fast growing cities of the South and North, or for the new agricultural West. Some of the landless Negroes drifted into the larger towns and then off to the cities.

As the plantations slowly disintegrated, a few of the more stable Negro renters became landowners. In the early 1890's Negroes owned 7,500 acres, or about three percent of the lands of the county. Most of the Negro owners followed subsistence farm prac-tices, and with little cash lived better than their landless neighbors. Some few used tenants, put up a plantation bell, and followed farm practices as much like a plantation's as their acreage would permit.

Cotton remained the chief crop for white and colored farmers, and each year a great proportion of the food and feed was brought in from outside the state. The railroads hauled the cotton out and the provisions in.

PLANTATION BELLS ON SANDY LAND

Farming activities on the coarse grey lands around White Plains and Siloam took on new life as the old plantation sections of the county declined. With a heavy application of bagged guano, the white lands would yield good crops.

The remaining forests in this section were soon felled for fields, as they had been cut down decades earlier in the red-land areas. Many a family-size farmer added one Negro tenant family, and then another. A few families came to operate plantation-size tracts. Even the larger farmers in this area maintained for themselves the traditional live-at-home program of the white land. But they used tenants and wage hands on the same cash-outlay-basis as did the red-land planters.

Scores of wagons from the White Plains and Siloam areas went regularly to the depot at Union Point. The wagons were heavy with cotton and cotton seed as they went to the station, with food and feed and fertilizer as they returned. By the middle of the 1880's between 4,000 and 5,000 bales of cotton were hauled each year from White Plains to Union Point, over 1,000 from Siloam.

White Plains had been incorporated in 1867. Reverend J. H. Kilpatrick, popular Baptist minister, was the first mayor. One of the town's first ordinances outlawed the sale of intoxicating drinks. Young George W. Tappan came to White Plains from Oak Tree, New Jersey in 1871. Already here and fully identified with the community were Randolph and Alexander Tappan—both active in behalf of the Confederate cause, Alexander as a soldier.

By the early 1880's the town was bustling with activity. New houses were going up every year. The Baptist and Methodist churches, organized in 1806 and 1817, had erected new buildings only a few years back. Dawson Academy was recognized as an excellent school. Farming activity was on the increase.

Negroes became more and more numerous in the white land section as plantation farming expanded. News items from White Plains in the *Georgia Home Journal* contained statements about "too many idle negroes;" "vagrant law ought to be enforced;" "colored men piled up on our streets as thick as bees, but just want one, and . . . like the flea 'he ain't thar.'" County School Commissioner, J. M. Howell, who lived at White Plains, said the local Negro school was the largest in the county.

Unstinted praise in these news items went to the few local farmers who compounded their fertilizer out of compost at home, and who grew their own supplies and so freed themselves "from the shackles" of the "corn and meat houses in the west." Subsistence farming was regularly praised, seldom applied.

HARRY HILL'S SPUR LINE

As the wagon trains rolled heavier and heavier from Union Point to Siloam and White Plains, people became more hopeful of getting a railroad. They all wanted a railroad: first the businessmen at White Plains and Siloam, and then to the last farmowner and share-cropper on the white land. And why shouldn't it come? Just look at the freight in both directions. Railroads were being built here and there throughout Georgia. Northern capital was building them. Most reassuring of all, the new railroads were being promoted by General John B. Gordon, and other Georgia leaders.

The first effort to build a railroad to White Plains was made by Harry Hill, popular conductor on the Georgia Railroad. Son of a prominent Wilkes county planter who owned stock in the Georgia line, Hill was a colorful railroad man of his day. When he took off his conductor's uniform at the end of his runs, he dressed up, spats and all, and moved in the best social circles. Once he put a man off the train for refusing to wear a coat. The offended passenger, a drummer who had boarded the train at Greensboro "just wanted to be comfortable," but he sued in vain to collect damages.

Hill secured the right-of-way for a spur line to leave the Georgia Railroad just west of Union Point. The grading of the survey was pushed four miles toward Siloam. Conductor Hill would look out of the train windows with his passengers to read the sign "Harry Hill's Railroad." Hill's efforts were unequal to the building of the railroad. His spur line was abandoned. And a keen disappointment it was to Harry Hill, and to the white land farmers.

$40,000 SUBSCRIBED

By the middle 1880's tentative plans for a road from Union Point to White Plains had been agreed upon with officials of the Georgia Railroad. But again nothing happened. Shortly an effort was made to effect another connection with Augusta through the Middle of

Georgia Railroad Association. Months wore into years, and no rail-road. Then there was talk of a line from White Plains through San-dersville to Savannah. Again White Plains was in a "full moon" railroad boom, to quote young A. S. Parker, local correspondent for the *Georgia Home Journal.*

White Plains was on the map, but it forgot not its sober youth, for its permanent charter of 1887 included a provision outlawing the sale of intoxicating drinks. The Reverend J. H. Kilpatrick, the town's first mayor, remained the town's leading citizen. His son, William Heard Kilpatrick, was a keen young man in his teens.

Time after time during the late 1880's the people of White Plains confidently hoped to hear soon the "music of the locomotive." At one time there was talk of two railroads for White Plains. Local correspondent Parker imagined new homes, more stores, a thriving business center, an "inland city." Did not the meeting of the rail-roads change the hamlet of Marthasville into the fast-growing Atlanta?

But a railroad doesn't come of its own accord to a town of five hundred just thirteen miles from a main line. The people soon realized it; they realized, too, that a connection with the Georgia Railroad at Union Point was their only hope, and that if they wanted a railroad they would have "to shell out the required amount" to get it.

Up and down the route of the survey went a committee looking for the $40,000 President Mitchell of the Georgia Railroad said they must get before the road could be built. After several months the sum was in hand.

The heaviest subscribers to the railroad were the White Plains merchants who were feeling the competition of the merchants at Greensboro and Union Point. The firms in the railroad towns had begun to figure out ways to get the trade of the larger white land farmers.

The Jones-Greene Company of Greensboro got young A. S. Parker of White Plains to work for them. He was the local newspaper correspondent, son of a leading farmer and direct descendant of one of White Plains' earliest settlers. It is said that he sold for Jones-Greene the largest bill of general merchandise ever sold in one day in the county. This sale was to a White Plains planter, Samuel Lary. The bill totaled $3,500, and consisted of large lots of meat, corn, hay, and other farm supplies. Planter Lary took the money out of his pocket and paid the bill in full. The W. M. Tappan and Son Company at White Plains, which the year before had done a $100,000 business, might well wish they still had A. S. Parker as their clerk.

One of young Parker's selling points to planters was that they could buy wholesale from the Greensboro firm, and haul carload lots home with their own teams and labor. The more the White Plains people saw of Greensboro's competitive tactics, the more determined they were to have a depot of their own. Then Lary and the other planters could afford to trade only at White Plains.

THE U. P. AND W. P. RAILROAD

With the $40,000 worth of stock fully subscribed, the grading of the Union Point and White Plains Railroad was begun early in 1889, on a survey near the fading Harry Hill sign.

The officials of the U. P. and W. P. were chosen from among the larger stockholders. Judge John Collier Hart, of Union Point, was president. Among the directors was a dirt farmer, J. S. "Pete" O'Neal of near Siloam, and an expert mechanic, Alex B. Tappan of White Plains, who had made most of his money building wagons.

By late fall everybody was glad "to see 'er roll." Virginia "Jennie" Sibley, President Hart's niece and belle of Union Point, drove the last spike. A dedication celebration was held at White Plains. General John B. Gordon, then Governor, was the principal speaker. A free barbecue was "served to all," first to the Whites and then to the Negroes. And the town saw its largest crowd.

Men from the white land of Greene held the offices of the new railroad, and made up the board of directors. In their pockets they carried official passes to ride this and other roads at any time they were of a mind to. But all of them together owned less than half of the stock; the controlling share was retained by the Georgia Railroad Company.

With the trains coming and going, the white lands of Greene came into full flower. More cotton was shipped out—7,000 to 8,000 bales—and more food, feed, and fertilizer was shipped in.

As the Tappan and Grant wagon works at White Plains went out of business, the White Plains Manufacturing Company came into prominence. Here in one establishment was a blacksmith shop, wheelwright shop, grist mill, and cotton gin.

At Siloam when the railroad came was the Smyrna Baptist Church, a couple of small stores, a cotton gin, and a half dozen homes. Four years later the Hastings Methodist Church, two miles to the north, put up a new building in town and became the Siloam Methodist Church. The old church at Hastings was then used by the Presbyterians until they, too, built in Siloam a few years later. The newly organized Wesleyan Methodists used the old building a while, but soon erected a church of their own on the Siloam-Greensboro road.

In 1904 the Bank of Siloam was chartered. Three years later a bank was opened at White Plains.

Time was when a man might have apologized for living on the coarse white lands of Greene, but not now as they rode through expanding fields, looked at their new buildings and banks, and listened out for their own train.

"LAND POOR" STILL

But by the time fertilizer bills and supplies had been paid for, there was little or no profit in cotton production. A few planters were prospering, but the farmers as a whole were upon hard times, on white land and red land.

An editorial, "Land Poor," in the *Herald-Journal* on March 24, 1894, declared, "One of our most serious drawbacks to prosperity is the fact that our farmers own more land than they can cultivate . . . the soil is yearly becoming thinner . . . yearly sapping the wealth and prosperity of our people." The editorial then suggested that prosperity comes only to those who tend well smaller acreages, that more white farmers are needed. Not long afterwards: "No sensible man will neglect feed crops to raise cotton at a loss. If you have bread and meat at home, you can afford to raise cotton; otherwise, you cannot."

That fall a public meeting was called to discuss the use of Bermuda grass, and ways of attracting home-seekers here. At this meeting Herman Geissler "doubted whether at present price of cotton our large rural population of colored people are self-supporting—it is certain they will not be with a further decline." In late November of that year the editor of the *Herald-Journal* gloomily predicted: "The talk now is less cotton next year, but we are afraid it will end in talk."

"The Woes of the Cotton Grower" was the name of an editorial reprinted in the *Herald-Journal* of September 9, 1898, from a Macon paper. Endorsing the editorial, the local paper said: "Friends, we must make a change, or the woes of the cotton farmer will increase tenfold. By our all-cotton system of farming, we of the South have killed the goose that layed the golden egg. It will be little short of criminal neglect for the welfare of those dependent upon us, if we keep this thing up." The paper pleaded for a real farmers club that would "subscribe to the best farm, dairy, and fruit publications; learn what is most profitable to raise . . . syndicate and buy fruit trees, evaporators, or whatever is necessary." "The question that now comes closest to our firesides," said the editorial, "is how shall we be fed and how shall we be clothed?"

XII

THIRD PARTY AND TEXTILES

THE HARD times throughout the nation in the early 1890's had blurred the city's bright lights for the farm folk of Greene. Not so many were moving off to the urban centers as a few years earlier. A surplus population was piling up in the county, for local farming activities were on the wane and the natural increase of births over deaths continued. The taxable property on the county digest was dropping from year to year. Times were hard, especially for the small farmowners and landless families. Why should this be so in a nation rich in natural resources, factories, banks, railroads, and wealthy corporations?

POPULIST THOMAS E. WATSON

Fifty miles east of Greensboro, at Thomson, a spokesman for the small owners and farm tenants was gaining a following. He was Thomas E. Watson, an ardent Populist. The people listened to him as he went up and down Georgia, the South, and the nation pointing to the "plutocrats" who controlled the big banks, the big corporations, and especially the railroads, as enemies of the small farmer. Many people in Greene thought they at last had "treed the varmints that had been carrying off our chickens."

In 1894 the Populists saw their first chance to win in the state elections. Watson came to Greensboro to speak. He was among friends, for most of the county offices had been held by Populists for the past two years. His supporters met him at the train and bore him on their shoulders to his carriage. When he reached the courthouse square, he was carried with cheers to the speaker's platform.

Watson urged his followers to be law abiding, said law is the nature of the universe and a thief should be punished "even if he had stolen to satisfy his hunger." To which he forthwith added that railroad men Calhoun and Inman "who stole $10,000,000 should not have been allowed to go scot free in their private car . . . the law should be framed to reach them also." He spoke of President Grover Cleveland as the "Stuffed Prophet of Buzzard Roost."

Watson appealed to the Negroes throughout the crowd before him "to investigate as best they might public questions." He suggested that they vote with the Democrats or with the Republicans if they wished, but to be sure to vote with the Populists if they found they were right. In any event, the Negroes' votes ought to be counted, Watson said. He stated that he did want the Negro vote, and he was going to get it, if he could do it by honorable means. The Democrats, too, he said were doing their best to get the colored vote.

In response to the accusation that he was in favor of Negro social equality, he denied it "by every drop of blood which flows in my veins," condemned Cleveland for signing a bill authorizing mixed schools when he was Governor of New York. Watson assured his audience that the Populists were not going to break down the relation between the races, but the Populists did want "laws which would give all classes, the rich and the poor, the white and the black man, equal justice."

The Populists were not making war on capital, said their leader. They rather wanted "to redeem the government of the people from the power of the money lenders, who were absorbing the wealth of the nation and reducing the people to serfdom . . . the people are begging for bread while the cod fish aristocracy are holding high revel at the White House." Watson pleaded with the dissatisfied Democrats to vote with him.

He closed his speech by asking his followers "to work to educate the masses. Education is the first step toward good government."

He sat down amid great applause and was carried to his hotel on the shoulders of his admirers.

There were many predictions that the Populists would win all of the fall elections. Even so, local leaders advised Watson to stay off the streets during his sojourn in Greensboro.* He had conferences at his hotel during the remainder of the day.

Some weeks later, Watson spoke at White Plains. The *Herald-Journal* found no criticism with his plea for getting rid of "oppressive class legislation," but stated that Democrats will disagree with his statement that Negroes have no reason to vote the Democratic ticket and "hence the negro must be paid to be a Democrat." He had said the Negroes might logically vote Republican because the Republicans "freed" them, or they might more logically vote with the Populists "for without bread and meat their freedom was not worth anything to them." He stated again that white and black were "two distinct races, and that they would ever remain so, having their own churches and schools, and whoever said he was in favor of social equality lied."

THE POLITICAL TEMPERATURE RISES

The political temperature of Greene continued to rise during the spring and summer of 1894, as one candidate after another pleaded for votes. W. Y. Atkinson of Coweta county was Democratic candidate for governor; Judge James K. Hines, of Atlanta, was the Populist candidate. Atkinson spoke here, pointed out that he had helped raise pensions to Confederate soldiers and widows from $23,000 to $450,000 a year. Hines, who spoke in August, accused Atkinson of saying he had "rather see yellow fever and cholera in Georgia than for the Populists to carry the state." Candidate Hines' "reference to the plank in the Populist platform calling for primary

---

* On another visit of Watson's to Greensboro, he had dinner at the Branch home on the Eatonton road with Judge James B. Park and others. While they were eating the turkey, smoke burst into the room. They got out safely, saw the house burn to the ground.

schoolbooks free to public schools," according to the *Herald-Journal,* "seemed to please the large crowd of colored people present very much."

The *Herald-Journal* acknowledged that it had "a hard constituency to satisfy," and formally declared that its columns were "open to both parties, provided courteous language is used." "Narrowing Down" was the title of a September editorial predicting that the forthcoming election would be "the bitterest political contest that has been waged in Georgia since the days of Reconstruction. The Populist movement is a revolt against both old parties. The colored vote is badly divided, and the white Populists are actively canvassing it, as are the Democrats. But how will this agitation end? Neighbor against neighbor, brother against brother, and father against son! . . . We greatly fear bitterness is being engendered which will never heal . . . After the election, there is work plenty for the ministers and Christians to do."

The outcome of the primary was announced in the next issue of the *Herald-Journal* (Oct. 6, 1894): "A Waterloo, for Democracy in this county." A record vote of 2,396 ballots had been cast in the primary, and all Populist candidates were well in the lead. The Democrats had worked hard "among the colored people to stem their stampede into the ranks of the enemy; but the present low price of cotton was used to keep them from voting with the Democrats. That and the 'free schoolbook' plank in the Populist platform." The November election showed a sweeping victory for the Populists in Greene, and in most other counties in central Georgia.

It appears that the *Herald-Journal* during this period sympathized with the Democrats, and wanted to be acceptable to the Populists. Back in January 1892, the paper had said: "Farmers should be careful before they use this Third Party post in the construction of their political fences." A few weeks later it had this Populist-flavored statement: "Jay Gould is coming South. Let's capture him and make him divide his ill gotten gains." Then a little later: "Oh, Liberty, what do those names of negroes on the Third Party committee mean?" By 1894, with Populists in all county offices, there were many Populist statements: "Time for wealth to begin to bear its share of the public expenses." "The country is not willing to surrender body and soul to the plutocrats." The paper persistently advocated the enactment of an income tax law.

PITHY PARAGRAPHS FOR POPULISTS

With the Third Party in office in Greene, the *Augusta Tribune,* the state's leading Populist daily, was widely read here. The following paragraphs were culled from a Greene county scrapbook of that day:

About money and banks:

The greatest trust in the country is the money trust.

Cheap money and dear men, should be the working men's platform.

Let the banks give security or receive no deposits.

Money is not a mere measure of value; it is an instrument of tyranny.

Interest has cost more dollars and human suffering than war, pestilence and famine.

About taxes and money lenders:

Let the law say that non-payment of taxes works forfeiture of the right to vote (as in Georgia) and you have the dollar acting as political boss, and becoming the test of political liberty.

The people should never cease their efforts until a graduated income tax is placed on the statute books if it requires a new constitution to do it.

If it is unconstitutional to tax the rich then we should have a system that would make it impossible for a man to become rich.

Who makes landlords on the one side and tenants on the other? The money lender.

Who holds the majority of the mortgages? The money lender.

Who must the people get rid of in order that they may gain their complete independence? The money lender.

About men and machines:

Unless man owns the machine the machine will displace man.

Improved production should shorten hours of labor rather than cause unemployment.

Changing men will do little good unless we change the system.

About plutocrats and Justice:

Plutocrat's tenet—the man who does the work shall receive the least for it.

The plutocrats must "come off" or there will be trouble in this country.

The idle are a standing menace to society.

The poor have to work so hard to support the rich that they have no time for mischief.

Charity covers up no sins when the gift has been stolen from the poor.

Deny men justice and they become listless slaves or dangerous fiends.

About men and land:

Property in land has ceased to be a right and become a crying evil when one man, or a number of men, can hold a million acres against the natural desire and right of a million men to occupy and use it.

The Populists had a program to correct the evils they saw. Tom Watson himself, as a member of the United States House of Representatives, introduced in 1893 the R. F. D. legislation that put mail boxes fast by the lonely farm homes on the back roads of the nation. He carried on an earnest fight in Congress against the strike-breaking services of the Pinkerton Detective Agency, asked that the convict lease system be investigated, and that the farm tenant's position be legally strengthened so he could protect his crop against seizure when in litigation with his landlord. Populist Watson was a free trader, against all tariffs.

The Populists advocated a graduated income tax, postal banks, insurance on bank deposits, and that currency be issued only by the federal government. They proclaimed that "Government ownership of natural monopolies will go a long way toward killing trusts and combines." "Railroad corporations have done more to corrupt our courts and legislatures than all other things combined," the Populists declared. "Government ownership will avoid all this as well as be a great saving to the people."

As evidence of the need for the reforms they advocated, the Populists pointed to the collapse of banks across the country, to the worsening condition of the farmers. They found "McKinley prosperity" little better than "Cleveland panic," suggested that when the Republicans fail the Democrats help give the Populists a chance. Said the *Augusta Tribune:* "A few more years of this kind of prosperity will settle the hash of both old parties; all the Populists have to do is 'grin and bear it,' and bide their time." But the Democrats, shaken as were their ranks, did not turn to the "people's party."

Called Socialists by their opponents in both old parties, the Populists whipped back: "The government part of our government is Socialism—when it is not favoritism." And they pointed out that "the dangerous person in politics is the one who persists in calling things by their right names."

Such were the public writings and utterances of Populist spokesmen which the Populists of Greene heard and read, believed in and worked for.

PARTY LINES FOLLOW PROPERTY LINES

Tom Watson had a tremendous personal following, and he corralled it by pointing out and attacking "the enemies" of the poorer people. For a little while the South's dislike for outsiders was turned against wealthy "plutocrats" close by, as well as far away.

The party lines followed fairly close along property lines. With a few exceptions, well-to-do townspeople and the larger planters remained within the Democratic Party, and ardently defended it. The smaller landowners, concentrated in and around the white-land section of the county at Siloam and White Plains, Veazy and Liberty were generally active in the Populist Party. The Negro vote was with the Democrats in the big plantation areas, and with the Populists where they were in the ascendency. Scattered here and there in the Populist part of Greene were a dozen large landholders who braved the Populist sentiments of their neighbors and remained Democrats, and were usually successful in controlling the votes of their Negro tenants.

With the Populists and Democrats bidding for all the votes they could get, the Negroes were literally herded to the polls. Members of their own race, upon the wish of leading whites, commonly corralled the Negro voters on the evening before an election, and kept them all night at some central place. Jugs, even barrels of liquor were often used to hold them together until they were marched off to the polls next morning. Negro preachers sometimes proved most effective in getting their flocks to the polls with the right ballots in their hands.

The Populists did not originate the practice of herding Negroes to the polls, they merely tried to use it more effectively than the Democrats and Republicans. As early as 1877, the grand jury had condemned the practice of "treating" prospective voters, especially the "freedmen," to drinks on election day.

There were threats and name-calling. "This Third party," moaned the Democrats, "is made up of bad creditors and Watson-worshippers." They want to put the "bottom rail on top" because they're on the bottom. The Populists answered, told of their plans for "40 acres and a mule" for every farmer, higher taxes, public ownership of natural monopolies, a wider ownership of property. "There's plenty of prosperity," they said, "for the fellows who don't need it." The Democrats called the Populists "wildeyed anarchists," wondered what they would say or do next, cringed to read the Populist statement that "The police seem to be an organization for the protection of criminals that have a pull."

From the outset the local Democrats reminded the local Populists that the Third Party was not safe. They pointed especially to the race question. Had not the Populist paragrapher maintained that "as long as laboring men are divided against themselves capital will take undue advantage of them?" Did this mean that white and colored workers were asked to stand *together?* Was not the general position of the Populists a dangerous one to take in Greene? The Democrats were specific in their questions involving Tom Watson and the Negro. They asked for "yes" and "no" answers. Had not Watson on numerous occasions openly defended the Negro? Pleaded their cases at murder trials? Kept one from being lynched at Thomson? Shaken hands with them? Courted their votes, and got them? When Watson himself was confronted with those accusations, he astutely escaped serious censure. When his followers faced them, they were often apologetic or embarrassed, or just dismissed the whole inquiry as a "scheming lie."

POPULISM WANES—NEGRO DISFRANCHISED

Populism in Greene county, as elsewhere, suffered a severe blow when the Southern and Western wings of the national Populist movement split. Only the Populist candidates for sheriff and clerk in Greene were reelected in 1898. Each had a bare majority, each was personally popular and had been elected in spite of his Populist affiliation.

Even before the 1898 election, the *Augusta Tribune* had accepted with cordiality the suggestion of the *Atlanta Journal* and other Democratic dailies "that the Populists rejoin the Democrats, take their old seats in the Democratic household." "How shall the Populists receive this invitation?" asked the *Tribune.* "If the Populist Party is dead nationally, it would be useless to keep up a state organization. The reforms for which the Populists contend can only be accomplished through national legislation." The *Herald-Journal* reproduced these editorials, and expressed the hope that the Populists would accept the invitation of the Democrats.

Watson's attitude was that if either old party is right "we ought to join without money and without price, without conditions and without reservations. If neither . . . is right, then we ought not to join hands with it, by fusion or otherwise. We ought to glory in being right—no matter how great a minority we are in." The "voice" of the "People's Party" had spoken, but no directions had been given. The Democrats merely welcomed them back, with the burden on the Populists to prove they wanted to be Democrats again.

In returning to the Democratic fold, the Populists were put in much the same position as the few scallawags had been at the end of Reconstruction. They, too, needed to prove their repentance by their works. The Populists, as the scallawags, had found themselves unacceptable to the "leading people" of the community.

The efforts of the small farmers had been frustrated, but economic conditions remained bad. Political rivals in Greene began to cast about for a means to reconcile their differences. The white people had never liked the Negro's participation in politics, and Populists and Democrats were ready to stand together to rid themselves of his vote. Both groups, too, knew how cheap had been their use of the Negro vote, how popular the disfranchisement program would be.

James B. Park, Jr., in the spring of 1900 was asked by the Democrats to run again for the state legislature. He had campaigned for votes in 1898, and was elected, but he was not willing to campaign again in an electorate that included colored as well as white voters. Early in the summer, he and Judge Henry T. Lewis drew up a resolution asking that the Populists join with the Democrats to form "a white man's party." Together they could work for state legislation which would set up a "white primary" and so keep the Negroes from voting. A meeting of the white voters of the county was called at the courthouse. The resolution—the first of its kind in the state, Park thinks—was read and unanimously adopted. Park was re-elected to the legislature without asking for Negro votes. Though unsolicited, some Negroes voted for him.

The white voters in other counties soon held mass meetings, and adopted resolutions similar to the resolution adopted in Greene county.

In 1905 Hoke Smith, a Democrat with a Populist background, was elected governor on the platform of Negro disfranchisement. And so, without anything being done about the issues which gave rise to the Populist movement, it was dissipated in Georgia through a clever maneuver which capitalized on the planters' and small white farmers' recognition that the unassimilated Negro was still in their midst. From newspaper clippings it would appear that the routed Populists got some satisfaction out of Evangelist Sam Jones' attacks on the "drinking 400."

The Populist movement had made the poorer white group politically articulate, and for a little while had put their leaders into positions of control. But it had wrought little if any real change in their thinking and feeling. The poorer Whites wanted to be in political control, but more than that they wanted recognition from the well-to-do Whites. Political harmony among the Whites of Greene was achieved in the early 1900's by depriving the Negro of political participation, as it had been achieved just after the war by the re-establishment of White supremacy, and before the war by the defense of slavery.

The Populist Party was dead by the end of the century. Populist Watson, now known as the sage of Hickory Hill, buried himself in Napoleonic history. A few years later he himself emerged to play on all the strings of intrigue and prejudice and hate which had been used to crush his "People's Party."

THE WHIR OF TEXTILE MACHINERY

The economic dislocation of the 1890's had given rise to the Third Party; it also gave rise to renewed efforts to secure additional payrolls in the county. Said the *Herald-Journal,* June 24, 1894: "The slaves are free, agriculture is prostrate and no longer profitable; therefore, it is to manufacturing we must now look for future greatness and development . . . at the same time guarding against trusts and combines . . . for they build production and thereby reap inordinate profits without employing our surplus labor." The Populist quality of this statement is obvious.

In the middle 1890's, E. R. Boswell and A. J. Boswell had a dozen knitting machines in operation at Penfield. Each year they added equipment, hired more workers.

In early March, 1897 the local editor was pleading for Greene to get more manufacturers so as to keep up with Elbert, Hall, Putnam, Baldwin and other counties. He said the Carolinas were going ahead of Georgia because they were getting cotton mills. He wanted Greene's leaders to "Get a move on you! The little folks will help all they can. Let's get out of the rut of listlessness and laziness we are in." A month later, "Our people can almost hear the whirr of the cotton factory machinery," followed by this warning: "Don't put fancy prices on your property when investors appear. It might scare them clear away."

Early in the next year, the *Herald-Journal* confidently said, "Good fortune again is knocking at our gates." E. A. Copeland and W. R. Jackson of Greensboro had just agreed to furnish at least $40,000 capital for the erection of a $100,000 cotton factory. W. P. "King" McWorter of Woodville also took a leading part in the enterprise. "The offer," according to the local paper, "bristles with importance and magnificent possibilities for our beloved town and county. If we don't embrace it now, let us not resent the charge, when people elsewhere declare we are moribund and doomed to dry rot and finally annihilation." The same paper reported a general textile strike in New England. The building of the cotton mill at Greensboro got under way shortly, for the remainder of the initial capital had been subscribed.

In the late 1890's Samuel H. Sibley, young attorney, at the suggestion of Robert F. Bryan, and in cooperation with other Union Point leaders, got hosiery mill machinery brought to Union Point from Athens. From the beginning white women were employed here, many of them from farms.

The mills at Penfield, Union Point, and Greensboro were financed by local capital. Capital from the outside was wanted, too. The Greene County Development Company was formed to get outside industries to locate here.

In 1899 the Development Company put out a pamphlet showing the industrial advantages of the community. The statement explained that the Company wanted "to attract new industries by offering building sites at cost, donating lots as a bonus, and by other encouragements; above all to promote and safe guard their interests." It continued, "What is, perhaps, of equal importance without special inducements is the fact that New England capital is seeking investment in industries South; ... the natives are well qualified as operatives ... our colored population is well behaved, reasonably contented, and they now realize that the white people are their best friends ... A movement is on foot to exempt all manufacturing industries for a period of years from taxation."

The pamphlet carried commendatory testimonials from three people from the outside who had come to live in the county—Mabel Robinson, an English lady; E. D. Northrup, a Northern gentleman; and Herman Geissler, a German gentleman.

In June, 1900 the Mary-Leila Mill at Greensboro was ready to open. Cloth began to come off its looms. Around 100 people were employed, most of them ex-farmers. Local wood was used for fuel, six to ten cords a day. The farmers who supplied the wood were paid $2.00 a cord for it. Coal was kept on the yard to use when there was no wood on hand.

No outside industries were attracted here, but the three local ones grew. Harold Lamb of Augusta and Charleston took charge of the mill at Union Point in 1900. By 1905 the Boswells at Penfield had erected a three-story brick building to house their growing enterprise, employing over 200 workers.

The Third Party rose to power in Greene in the middle 1890's, faded out of the picture almost in a decade. The textile mills came in the same period. They remained, and were enlarged.

XIII

"PEG-LEG" AND "JIM" DAVISON

THE POPULIST movement and the cotton mills afforded to the poorer white people of Greene some opportunities for expression and added income. In the meantime R. A. Williams, known as "Peg-Leg," was taking Negroes from central Georgia to the new plantation sections of the Mississippi Delta and Texas. He had an office in Atlanta, and centered his activities in Greene, Morgan, and Putnam counties, where there was a surplus Negro population.

FARM HANDS FOR THE DELTA

Williams was asked by leading citizens of Greensboro to relieve the county of 1,000 "surplus" Negroes. He came to Greensboro, discussed his emigration plans with the city and county authorities, promised to cease activities upon request. Commenting on "Peg-Leg's" work in the winter of 1899–1900, the *Augusta Chronicle* of January 14, 1900 said: "It is clear that fully 2,500 Negroes have gone from Morgan and 1,500 to 2,000 from Greene."

Greensboro businessmen, in getting rid of "surplus" Negroes, were not speaking for the planters, who soon found that when the Negroes left their plantations, the cost of farm labor tended to rise.

Luther Boswell, one of the county's largest planters, swore out a warrant for "Peg-Leg." The charge against him was failure to pay the emigrant agent's license, which the state legislature in 1877 had fixed at $500 per county. The sheriff arrested "Peg-Leg;" his bond was fixed at one thousand dollars and T. B. Rice signed bond.

Williams took a roll from his pocket, counted out a thousand dollars, left it with Rice. Within a few days Williams paid the $500 fee in Greene county, and continued his operations here and in surrounding counties.

A couple of weeks later, Williams boarded the west-bound night train out of Greensboro, with a large number of Negro migrants he had corralled. Just across the Greene county line, the Morgan county sheriff boarded the train, took him into custody, and rode with him to Madison. There they left the train, and Williams was lodged in the county jail—where one of his co-workers had already been placed.

While the train was in the Madison station, angry Whites strode through the crowded "For Colored" cars. When the emigrants learned that their "Moses" had been arrested, they left the train pell mell. For a mile out of town the railroad right-of-way was strewn with cardboard valises and bundles. Williams and his agent remained in the jail during the day; men were there from all over the county threatening them with lynch law.

Except in Greene county, Williams refused to pay the $500 emigrant agent's license. Charges were then pending against him in four counties. One court after another had upheld the law. Williams refused to concede its constitutionality, took the case to the United States Supreme Court.

During the summer of 1900 he did public relations work in Memphis and Atlanta. He played both ends against the middle: gave the Memphis papers interviews in which he assured the delta cotton growers that he would bring into that area thousands of good workers; told the Georgia papers that taking the Negroes out of the state would leave room for the white families ex-Governor Northern and other leaders were then trying to attract here. "I bet you never thought of the question in that light before," he said to a reporter of the *Atlanta Constitution* in July. "Peg-Leg" then stated that he already had requests for 5,000 workers the coming winter, but would probably double that number. Most of the emigrants were

Negroes, though he reported in Mississippi that "a lot of white people" were getting interested.

MIGRATION "BUSINESS" STOPPED

Williams confidently opened an office in Atlanta in the early fall of 1900. With an able lawyer, James Davison of Greensboro, in charge of his case before the Supreme Court, he repeatedly refused to pay the licenses in Fulton and the other counties. Attorney "Jim" Davison contended that a license fee of $500 per county was prohibitory, that this high fee amounted to class legislation aimed entirely at laborers, that it precluded freedom of movement and thereby impaired the right of personal liberty. He argued further that the $500 fee was in contradiction to the laws of the Interstate Commerce Commission, and that it was not a legitimate exercise of police power.

Most important of all was the possibility that the law might be interpreted, according to the *Atlanta Journal,* as "in the teeth of the 14th Amendment of the Constitution which clothes the negro with the liberty of the citizen."

The case excited great interest, particularly among the larger farmers of central Georgia. Cotton farmers in Morgan county estimated that their growing crop would be 1,000 bales off because of the loss of the Negro workers; planters readily said that if the $500 fee were declared unconstitutional, some sections of the state would be virtually depopulated of workers and that agriculture would be ruined. Then there was the possibility that the decision in the case might affect the legal status of the Negro as a citizen.

In early fall the Supreme Court heard the evidence. An equal number of justices voted for and against the constitutionality of the Georgia law under which Williams had been convicted in the state courts. The tie automatically upheld the decision of the lower courts. Williams was liable for a $500 license in each county in which he operated. He paid the license in Fulton county, and forthwith notified the tax collector that he was filing suit to recover it. But once the U. S. Supreme Court had spoken, even if in a split voice, "Peg-Leg" Williams' activities in Georgia were done.

NEW WHITE FAMILIES—BOOSTER SPIRIT

The section of Greene most thoroughly depopulated by Williams' activities was the "Lower Forks." Into this area came white families, most of them from north Georgia—first Geiger, Hard, Tingle, Hoard, Statham, and a little later Phelps and Center. Here and there throughout the old plantation areas, new white families came in and took up residence as farm tenants or small owners. With a background of home ownership of family-size farms and a tradition of work, these newcomers soon demonstrated that a family could raise its food and feed on the red lands of Greene. Said the grand jury of March, 1902:

We are receiving accessions to our white population from the upper part of the state . . . a class of energetic, live, and thorough going farmers who are casting their lots with us and materially aiding our sturdy rural population to build up the waste places.

We are pleased to note the fact that . . . our county is now on the upgrade, and rapidly recovering from the depression, and stagnation which has prevailed for the past few years among our farming class.

The booster spirit had reached Greene. "County in good condition," ran the presentments of February, 1903. "People reasonably prosperous and gradually becoming imbued with the spirit of progress." Mention was made of the "great possibilities of our county," of the "many acres of good arable land as yet unimproved," and of the "recognized need and value of immigrants of a desirable class." In view of these considerations the jury urgently recommended that the county commissioners "appropriate the sum of $100 to be used in connection with that appropriated by the Atlanta Chamber of Commerce and other Georgia communities for the purpose of placing before the people of Georgia and other sections of this country the advantages and resources of Greene county."

The jury then proposed that the roads and public buildings of the county be improved, and that the county authorities look into the advisability of issuing bonds for that purpose.

The following August grand jury noted "with a great deal of pride the enterprising spirit which is being manifested in almost every section. Good churches, well equipped schoolhouses, and first class roads will always be the best index to civilization." The steel bridge over the Oconee on the Greensboro-Madison road was completed in 1903. The Oconee in Greene had had no bridge since Sherman's March through Georgia in the 1860's.

The desire for good roads led the county commissioners to take the county's "proportional share of 5-year convicts in lieu of a certain portion of the state school fund." The grand jury approved this step.

In 1898 the county spent $3,337 on roads, two years later over ten thousand. In the county there were nearly 1,000 miles of road and 700 bridges to maintain. One grand jury after another recommended a bond issue for roads. The largest amount, $75,000, was suggested in 1911.

STATE SUPPORTED PUBLIC SCHOOLS

Only on the public schools was more money spent than on the roads. All the road money came from local taxes, and almost all the school money from the state school fund—$12,200 out of $13,316. The grand jury of 1901 recommended a one mill tax for better schools. This was the day of the school committeemen who could "boss the teachers!" Each year teacher institutes were conducted, with penalties of $2.00 for each absent white teacher and $1.00 for each absent colored teacher.

Separate institutes were conducted for the teachers of each race, and the children of each race were taught by teachers of their own race. But accidents will happen: early in 1904 the county·school commissioner, Captain R. B. Smith, was accused of assigning a Negro teacher to a white school. Patrons brought the charge before the county board. The board heard the evidence and found "that he behaved under a mistake in regard to the color of the teacher and meant no disrespect to any individual, or school in the county. With such lights before us we now exonerate him from all censure and blame."

The money for the county schools continued to come from the state. In 1912 nearly $25,000 was spent, and county school commissioner, W. A. Purks, reported to the grand jury that the $440 interest on the Allison Fund was practically the only money "coming into his hands from the county."

INNOVATIONS IN EDUCATION

New things were happening in Greene's public schools. The county board ordered the school commissioner to put a paper blackboard in each school. Some pupils were hauled in wagons at public expense. In 1900 the county board bought a one-horse wagon and harness and a two-horse wagon and harness for use at Greshamville.

In February of 1904 the County Board of Education was host to two of the nation's greatest apostles of public schools, George Buttrick and Charles McIver. McIver spoke to a mass meeting in the courthouse on "Public Schools and How to Get Them." The minutes of the board said he separated those who oppose the schools into those who "Don't want to be taxed to educate my neighbors' children;" those who say "I'm too poor;" those who contend that "The schools are poor;" and others who are not in favor of educating the Negro.

Consolidation of rural white schools was beginning to be mentioned, but only in the most guarded ways. In September 1904 the county board authorized the school commissioner "to consolidate schools of Liberty and Cawthon, provided it can be done without too much opposition."

Shortly after this local school districts began to levy special taxes for their schools, the first to do so being Harmony Grove, in "the Forks" where the north Georgians had settled. By 1907 three school districts had local taxes to extend terms. That same year a brick school building was erected in Greensboro, and a year later a similar one at Union Point.

In 1911 the Presbyterian Church in the United States of America opened the Union Point Normal School, to train Negro workers for rural churches and schools. A substantial two-story frame building was erected. Italia Leconte founded the school. Under his direction, a staff of a half dozen teachers did creditable work.

Philanthropy for education again reached Greene in 1912, when N. O. Nelson, of New Orleans, who had furnished a domestic science teacher for the white schools of Putnam county, extended his interests to include Greene. The grand jury and the *Herald-Journal* commended Nelson and the teacher.

RACIAL DIFFERENTIALS WIDEN

At least three Negro schoolhouses—Woodville, Public Square, and Randolph—were built before 1910 by closing down the schools for three months and applying the teachers' salaries to the purchase of building materials. The patrons did the work themselves. More than three fourths of the colored schools still convened in churches and privately owned houses.

Shortly before 1900 a Greensboro Negro teacher, F. A. Curtright, became an habitual visitor at the meetings of the county school board. He knew something of manual training, and wanted to establish a school in Greensboro where students could be taught trades. He got $600 "from the North" to buy a piece of land on the southwest edge of town and to put up a building. Curtright called his school the Georgia Normal and Industrial School. He induced three prominent white men—T. B. Rice, Conklin Brown, and J. B. Park—to serve as a board of trustees.

Year after year Curtright worked, got his school recognized as a public school, received $260 a year from the county, had 100 pupils and two assistant teachers. But he could not get the money he needed to develop the school. After a year or two the enrollment dropped to 72, and the county board allowed Curtright but one assistant teacher. In the meantime an unsuccessful attempt had been made to close the other colored school in Greensboro. Curtright's dream did not materialize; the trustees retained title to the small acreage; the Negro children remained without a high school, or a manual training school.

Negro disfranchisement was an accomplished legal fact by 1907. Even greater racial differentials in education now appeared. In 1899 the cost of schools per enrolled child had been $4.85 for the whites and $1.81 for the Negroes. In 1907 the outlay was $6.64 per enrolled white child, $1.34 per Negro child. The total school expenditures for the county were up to $20,000. The enrollment was 3,851 pupils, 2,683 of whom were colored. The attendance of the white children was 85 percent of the enrollment, of the colored children 53 percent. More than three fourths of all the colored children were in the first grade.

MORE FOLKS—MORE TAXES

The county as a whole showed an increase of population between 1900 and 1915 only because of the cotton mills at Greensboro, Penfield, and Union Point. Around 200 workers were employed by them in 1900, over 600 in 1915.

The movement here of white farmers, most of them from north Georgia, continued for several years. In the forks were newcomers Austin, House, Malcolm, Greason, Flanigan, Duvall, Dawes, Oaks, Thurmond, Miller, Thomas, Cook, and others; in the Liberty community, Welchel, Strickland, Morehead, Bullock, Williams, and

Kinner; at White Plains, the Taylors, and on throughout the county the Powells, Ellards, Miles, and others. But the newcomers were less numerous than the farm families who had left for the factories.

The Negro population of the county remained about stationary, would have decreased except for the farm tenant houses left vacant by local Whites as they moved into the mill villages in Greene and near by counties.

One grand jury after another during this period recommended things which would increase taxes: a permanent convict camp for the county, State Juvenile Reformatory, State Board of Health to stamp out smallpox, a game warden, a railroad bridge at Cemetery Hill. Each of these grand jury recommendations came in the spring, before cotton was planted.

The total tax valuation of the county rose a million dollars between 1906 and 1912; land values on the tax digest averaged $3.90 per acre in 1906, were up to $5.00 six years later.

The number of grants to Confederate soldiers and their widows in Greene had risen to 172, a total of over $10,000 a year. Paupers remained solely the wards of the county, and 50 of them received an average of slightly less than $1.50 per month.

The county court and convict camp remained self-supporting, and more. In 1907, the judge of this court, S. H. Sibley of Union Point, turned over to the county $3,000 in fines. The grand jury of September 1906 had found an alarming amount of crime among the younger Negroes, appealed to the older Negroes "to cooperate with the officers" in their efforts to cope with them.

Four years later the jury ordered: "Arrange the seats in the courthouse so as to provide separate seats for whites and colored." For years, colored women had been allowed in the courtroom only on business.

In 1912 the dog tax was being collected to the amount of $1,415, and Negroes paid more than half of it. The only other item of taxation in which the Negroes of Greene had ever surpassed the Whites was in payment of poll taxes before they were disfranchised. And then a considerable proportion of their poll taxes was paid by white politicians in order to control their votes.

RAILROAD STRIKE AND RURAL BATHTUBS

The cotton mills whirred away with most of the machines tended by ex-farmers. But something new was stirring on the eighty-year-old Georgia Railroad. The train conductors were out on a strike. Most people utterly condemned the striking conductors, but not Attorney James Davison, of Greensboro, who had earlier taken the "Peg-Leg" Williams cases to the Supreme Court.

For the *Herald-Journal* of October 5, 1912, Davison wrote: "These conductors had a right to strike. They have the right to use all lawful means in their power to prevent others from taking their places. To this end it is not improper to dissuade them from filling their places. Thus far, good citizens can go with them." But when striking trainmen use force to keep away from their jobs the men called in by the railroad company "that very minute they ought to be punished as any other law breaker." The conductors' strike was ironed out, and union labor on the railroads gained strength.

Two roundtrips were now made each day by the combination freight-passenger train on the Union Point and White Plains Railroad. The banks at Siloam and White Plains flourished, and so did the merchants, schools, and churches. The white-land farmers continued to ship out cotton and bring in food, feed, and fertilizer.

Some of the large plantation owners in various sections of the county were getting city conveniences. The J. B. Dolvins, on the edge of the white lands near Siloam, had a bathtub and telephone installed about 1906. The Wrays of Wrayswood, who had owned several thousand acres of the red-lands for over 100 years, had acetylene gas lights and running water by 1910. They also had a post-office and maintained their own telephone line to Maxeys and Madison, and were petitioning the county to put a bridge over the Oconee at Watson Springs.

DAIRY FARMS DEVELOP

The expansion of farming in the grey lands had not offset the red-land losses. The plantations underwent further change. Fewer wage hands were used, overseers thinned, independent renters increased.

The disintegration of plantation farming was now most marked in the Oakland and Penfield sections, as twenty years earlier it had been in the Old Salem, Richland, and Ridge Grove areas. And away to the cities of the South and nation went many members of planter families; stranded landless workers drifted off to towns and cities of Georgia. There was some increase of farming around Woodville, with W. P. "King" McWhorter financing much of it through the Bank of Woodville, organized by him prior to 1910.

The annual cotton production in Greene county rose jumpily for the first fifteen years of the century, from an average of around 11,000 bales to better than 18,000. With the price below ten cents a pound more than half the seasons, the relatively good yields did not make the cotton farmers prosperous. Soil resources were being used up, fertilizer costs were mounting.

Though cotton remained the main crop of most farmers, some were developing dairies. The dairy and cattle business here was continuously threatened by the Texas Cattle Tick. By 1910 the county had employed a man to work for tick eradication. The grand jury of January, 1911 asked that the program be continued and the salary of the worker raised from $50 to $75 a month. The next two semi-annual juries were doubtless dominated by old line cotton farmers, for the first recommended that "no additional appropriation be made for the purpose of eradication of the cattle tick fever"; the second, that "the tick eradication law so far as it applies to Greene County be abolished."

Then for four years the tick eradication work was endorsed by the grand juries. But there was always the possibility that it would be discontinued, for only the largest farmers were in the dairy or beef business, and most farmers were as dependent on cotton as ever, and as opposed to "unnecessary expenditures." Why not just let the men with cattle do whatever they like about the ticks? Why ask the county to help them? Hasn't the cotton farmer always taken care of himself?

A few farmers refused to let the tick fighters come in their barn-yards, even got their guns, and dared them "to fool with" their cows.

TICK ERADICATION DEFENDED

Attorney James Davison of Greensboro addressed a letter to the January, 1911 grand jury pleading for the continuation of the tick eradication program. "Are Farm Conditions Worse in Greene County Than Thirty Years Ago?" * he asked. "They are," he said. "In truth, we have no prosperity . . . what percent of the actual tillers of our soil own their farms, what proportion live in painted houses or give other evidences of possessing those small comforts that change a struggle for existence to a satisfied living? The condition of the man on the farm is worse than it was thirty years ago . . ."

Davison said that he was not speaking of all farms in the county, but that what he was saying "applies to the great majority." Thirty years ago many more farmers were living on their own land, he said; now many of these families had "moved to Atlanta or to the nearest town . . . The houses are deserted or occupied by negro tenants. Blinds are off, hinges are loose, windowpanes out. The whole a grim ruin of former grandeur. The garden has a row of collards, maybe, but more likely cotton or weeds hold sway . . ."

What brought about this condition, he asked—and answered, "All cotton and the tenant system." He told of the rich soils the first

---

* *Herald-Journal*, January 30, 1911.

settlers in the county found, how the trees were chopped down, "piled into heaps and burned." This was done to clear the ground so that its "sole remaining wealth—a pitiful inch of top soil—might be exploited, wasted, and washed away." He emphasized then that the farmer here who tries to grow cotton on already exhausted soil in competition with the Texas farmer who never saw a sack of guano "is foredoomed to failure." The remedy for the situation lies in diversified farming, and "the tenant system must go."

Davison lamented that the people of Georgia sent out more money for foods and feeds each year than they received for the entire cotton crop. "This," he added, "spells bankruptcy. The time is coming when it will be a dishonor for a farmer to buy corn from Kansas City, meat from Chicago, and mules from Missouri." He pleaded for more livestock, an increase of feed and foodstuffs. He saw how "exhausted and weary uplands can be redeemed to productivity," how the "red nakedness and gullied furrows" of the hills along the Oconee and in the headwaters of the Ogeechee can become "a picture of peaceful valleys and green hills covered with a thousand cattle."

In closing he asked, "Gentlemen of the Grand Jury, will you help get rid of the tick by enforcing the law and pressing the work, or will you refuse and set back the wheels of progress? It is a mistake to get in the way of progress."

The grand jury asked the county authorities "to continue to cooperate with and support the state and federal authorities in the eradication of the Texas Fever Tick," asked those authorities to continue their work in the county. This presentment is the first one since the War of the 1860's to mention the Federal Government as a benefactor. One year later the grand jury again recommended continuing the eradication program until "our county is entirely free from ticks."

One by one the farmers who had opposed the tick control realized that a new disease was abroad and that the·only way to protect the small farmer's milk cow and calf was to protect the big farmer's herd. Greene was commonly referred to as the rising dairy and beef cattle county in Georgia.

About the time the last ticks were being disposed of in Greene, World War I broke out in Europe and nothing was stable anywhere.

XIV

PREFACE TO DISASTER

WHEN THE war began in Europe, Greene county was responding to many progressive forces. A grand jury in 1915 recommended "that the public drinking cup in the courthouse be done away with, and each individual be required to furnish his own drinking cup." Shortly after this, there was a presentment on the insanitation of leaking cuspidors in the courthouse, and further: "We find that tobacco spit is all over the walls and floors, and some steps should be taken to stop this in the future."

The courthouse, built in 1849, was no longer adequate. Enlargement was recommended.

The new convict camp was at last reported complete, quarters comfortable and sanitary. The grand jury soon asked for hot water in the county jail in order that the prisoners might "take a bath at least once a week." Farmers were cautioned against overloading their mules in a *Herald-Journal* item about cruelty to animals.

The war brought a rise in farm prices. With money in their pockets, the farmers bought automobiles, many second-hand and a few new. The jury of January, 1916 ordered that a split-log drag "be run over all main roads to fill up holes and washouts." A steel bridge had been recommended at Reid's ferry. County authorities asked that road bonds of $100,000 be voted to secure the cooperation of the Federal Government.

The schools, too, were responding to the times. A county-wide school tax was recommended in January 1917. Ten local white districts had already voted school taxes. As expenditures for white schools increased, racial differentials widened still further. In 1916, the white teachers received annual salaries of nearly $500, the colored teachers less than $100. Less than one fourth of the white enrollment was in the first grade; nearly half of the colored. Two years later, a little over $400 was spent to transport white children to school in busses.

As the war in Europe went into its second year, farm prices continued to advance. Hundreds of acres which had been used for pasture were plowed for cotton. The majority of the people, plantation owners and landless farmers, felt comfortable at last—they could hope for a good cotton crop, higher prices. Merchants increased their stocks; the banks loaned larger sums; more automobiles were bought; houses were painted; old roads were widened and straightened as more land was planted in cotton. Greene county was headed toward a boom.

WORLD WAR I

Then came word that America had declared war on Germany. Some young white men volunteered at once. A little later, Whites and Negroes were conscripted. Giant headlines in the dailies told about the movement of the AEF across the seas, and of American soldiers under fire.

There were 533 young men from Greene in military service during World War I—503 in the Army, 30 in the Navy. Local farm youths saw foreign soil—114 Whites and 122 Negroes—crossed the Atlantic, beheld strange sights, listened to strange languages, yearned for home.

During the war there were "meatless days" in the home, and "fuelless days" in the factory; sugar was scarce, and most of the people gladly ate cornbread to save wheat for the soldiers. At the Mary-Leila Mill the boilers were kept at work on Mondays without the use of coal by burning planing mill shavings. Government officials had thought the idea impracticable, but it worked well and full-time operations were maintained in the mill.

Many more white boys than Negroes were taken out of the county by the first draft, and some Whites feared that racial trouble might arise. As the war lengthened more Negroes were taken until the numbers were almost equal.

There were 280 white boys in service. Among them there were five deaths: Captain Macon C. Overton, Estes Durham, Robert L. Hubbard, Jonnie Chapman, and Carl Mathews. The first three of these were killed in action overseas. The Greene County American Legion Post, formed some years later, was named in honor of Captain Overton of Union Point. His posthumous awards, with citations, were: "Distinguished Service Cross, Oak Leaf Cluster to be worn with DSC, and Croix de Guerre with two Palms and Gilt Star."

Of the 253 Negro soldiers, eight died in service. Aaron Butts and Nathaniel Favors died in the homeland, and six at sea or overseas— Burk Evans, Sherman Hillsman, Clarence Hurt, Alex Morris, Sheppard Sears, and Green Ward. Negroes who had never been out of Greene county, and who had never voted in it, went across an ocean to help "make the world safe for democracy."

When the war was over, the uniformed soldiers began coming home. For a time there were tense moments, lest the Negro soldier not fit back into the community after his experiences abroad. Well over half of the colored soldiers soon moved off to distant cities. Each of the Negro ex-soldiers who remained here became "just a nigger" again. The months passed relatively uneventful, fear gradually subsided.

The returning soldiers found the county more prosperous than when they went away. There was work aplenty, and most of those who stayed here—white and colored—settled down to it. Some were restless. A few could hardly make a go of it at home, or elsewhere, for bombs and poison gas had left them with frayed nerves and injured lungs.

40¢ COTTON!

The boll weevil, which came up out of Mexico in the early 1890's, had already crossed Texas, Mississippi, Alabama, and was well into southwest Georgia. In 1916, some farmers here saw weevils in their fields, a few fallen squares on the ground, but the crop was not injured. Cotton was selling at nearly twenty cents a pound. Then came 1917 and 1918 with almost no weevils. Crops were good, price almost thirty cents.*

By 1919 the price had climbed to thirty-five cents and forty cents a pound, and that year Greene's farmers ginned a little over 20,000 bales. Everything was in boom! And not without real reason, for the county had a $4,000,000 cotton crop—an average of over $1,300 for every farm family in the county. The average for the last two decades had been about $250. Dwelling houses and stores, churches and schools were repaired, enlarged, painted; bright new tin roofs appeared across the countryside; new cotton planters and fertilizer distributors were bought. Trace chains and mule collars, axes and hoes, bull-tongue plows and scooters, overalls and brogans, meal and molasses, fatback and salmon moved off the shelves faster than ever before. There were more sales for bedsteads and split bottom chairs, for guitars and phonographs, and for moonshine liquor too.

Middle-aged men who had never owned land nor mule, paid cash for second-hand automobiles. Young men who had regularly worn denim shirts and overalls from one week to the next, now donned pressed breeches and broadcloth or silk shirts on Saturday afternoon and Sunday. Women came forth with the vari-colored frocks they had been hungering for, and bright socks shone above the new shoes of the children.

The merchants throughout the county were busy and happy. Their goods, whether muslin or mules, could commonly be sold well above the price they had planned to ask. Every community in the county saw its most prosperous time: three big stores and three little

---

* See Appendix No. 7 for Cotton Crops from 1899 to 1942.

ones at Woodville, four stores at Greshamville, a thriving business at Veazy. Penfield was recuperating from the shock of 1916 when the bank and the hosiery mill closed following the burning of the dye plant; White Plains and Siloam, Greensboro and Union Point came to full bloom, and the men and women and children of Greene dressed and schemed as never before.

The Board of Tax Receivers called in one man after another to make certain that the new wealth did not go tax free. The Board found some large new items to tax, and numerous small ones, was pleased with its work. After W. P. "King" McWhorter, of Wood-ville, had recalled additional lands and other properties to be re-turned for taxes, he went home, called to his wife: "Sally, those folks at Greensboro have convinced me I'm a rich man. Let's have fried chicken every day."

Many a farm family for the first time climbed into their own auto-mobile and rode off to Atlanta or Athens, toward the mountains or the sea for their first vacation day. Sunday school picnics were popu-lar outings for old and young. The people saw new sights, new faces, a bigger world. With money in their pockets and a way to go places, they bought the same things at new stores, and they saw new things for sale at the old stores.

Though some Negro families had automobiles, most of them did not. Even those could usually catch a ride, and could join the new lodge and attend its meetings at the near-by church. They helped build lodge halls so the mysteries of initiation could be conducted on the second floor. The first floor could be used by their children for a schoolroom.

All over Greene, when cotton was selling high, Negro lodges and burial societies mushroomed up and flourished: Masons, Knights of Pythias, United Gospel Aid, Builders of the Walls of Jerusalem, Brothers and Sisters of Charity, Good Samaritan of Golden Heart, Improved Good Samaritan, Young Shepherd of Pleasant Home, Sons and Daughters of Peace. The Negroes, like the whites, were in an expansive mood.

LAND PRICES SOAR

Cotton was the basis of this new prosperity, and cotton land was the pearl of great price. While the weevil riddled the crops in southwest Georgia and all across the lower South to Texas, the farmers of Greene heard their land called "weevil proof." Cotton farmers from southwest Georgia and Alabama came in from their weevil-infested sections to look at Greene county land. They bid against each other for acreage.

Farmers here saw lands which they had bought for $5 to $10 an acre priced at four, five, ten times that amount. Some of the very best land went at over $200 an acre. Many farmers sold their lands. Others decided to hold on until tomorrow, or next week, for certainly there would be more purchasers. And indeed there were.

Many a farmer who owned his land free of debt put a mortgage on it to buy additional acreage. Land speculation went wild.

The tenants, white and colored, were ill at ease. Many had been offered work in the North and East. The planters could hold them only by offering larger advances to tenants, higher wages to day laborers. The crop was made still more expensive by the high costs of fertilizers and farm supplies.

THE WEEVIL RETURNS—AND STAYS

As the summer of 1920 wore on, the farmers saw the weevils in their fields, saw the fallen squares along the cotton rows, worried some about what the crop would be. They soon hated to see a cloud, lest there be rain. A shower was all right, but two or three cloudy days would mean additional young cotton squares on the ground.

Autumn came, and a crop of 13,400 bales. And this was not the worst, for the price of cotton had dropped to around fifteen cents—not half what it had sold for the year before. Some borrowings could not be paid back, but perhaps with better production next year Greene could maintain something of its newly-won recognition as a "weevil proof" area. For a 13,400-bale crop compared well enough with the average for the ten-year period preceding the outbreak of the World War; and so the farmers reasoned that although the yield was smaller than they had expected and hoped for, it proved nothing. Had not cotton farmers always operated under a fluctuating yield and an uncertain price? They had a chance so long as the price remained even reasonably good.

A few farmers decided to be careful about their expenditures for the next season. But most of them determined to have a bumper crop. So they called in their tenants early and assured them that rations and fertilizer would be available, and poison for the weevils, too, if they wanted it. The fertilizer agents again did a flourishing business, as did the merchants who sold meat and flour and molasses, trace chains and plow points. The cotton was planted well, came up to a good stand, was chopped clean. An expensive crop must be taken care of. The plows were in the fields after each rain. Hot nights in June and early July made dark green stalks and flowers aplenty.

With the summer rains came the weevils. The squares fell off the little stalks. The sun came out; the stalks grew and new flowers came. Then more rain, and more weevils. All during the summer the stalks grew, the cotton blossomed, and the weevils dropped the little squares to the ground.

By September the planters knew they had taken a licking: when they counted up their ginning tickets they found they had less than 1,400 bales. The tenants were unable to pay back what they had consumed to grow the crop. The renters could not pay their bills nor the rent on the land. The smaller owners were grateful for food and feed at home, would put off taxes until next year. The plantation owners could not take care of their fertilizer bills or their notes at the bank.

In the fall of '21, Greene county's cotton bubble burst. The landless cotton growers looked out across the fields and wondered. How were they to live over the winter? They couldn't even get an extra dollar at Christmas! But they didn't blame the planters, for they knew they had put real money into the crop. And the planters didn't blame them—the weevil had run over the landowner and the landless man alike. The little weevil, powerful little weevil—cross between a termite and a tank.

Some planters went to their tenants, told them what their situation was, agreed to let them farm next year if they could arrange their own credits. This was attempted by a few. But the great majority of them, without food for the winter and with no credit for fertilizer and seed, were in a daze. Some hoped to find farms in adjoining counties. Maybe they could go over in Oglethorpe county, where old Uncle Jim lived, or back to Hancock, or down toward Warrenton. As the weeks passed, they learned that the other counties had been hit too. More than one tenant hopefully remembered an aunt in Atlanta, a brother in Jacksonville, a cousin in New York, a former neighbor now in Pittsburgh.

Many a planter told his tenants to stay in their houses, use wood and water as they always had, get any work they could for cash or rations. He would try to see what could be done about next year's cotton crop. With the tradition of cotton deep in Greene, and with the price going up again, some money was available at planting time. Fertilizer was bought again, but not so much as usual.

Creditors and debtors grimly faced each other at crossroad stores and on the streets of Greensboro, Union Point, and the smaller towns as the crop was planted.

The little stalks came to a stand, were thinned out. Then came hot nights. The stalks grew. Early in the week a bloom was on the stalk, by week's end a small square was on the ground. That fall the farmers of Greene harvested fewer than 350 bales, owed a $600 fertilizer bill alone for every bale of cotton they took away from the gins. The thing which some of the farmers feared in '20 and in '21 was common knowledge by the fall of 1922—Greene county's cotton back was broken.

PART FOUR

HARD YEARS

XV

BOLL WEEVIL DEPRESSION

AND NOW came hard years, made harder by the good yields when prices were high.

THE FATES TRICKED GREENE

The fateful three years between the appearance of the weevil here and the weevil's first sweeping destruction of Greene county cotton fields were years of bumper crops and of soaring prices, driven up and up by short crops elsewhere and the cotton needs of a world just returning to peace. Three years, when the cotton squares of Greene seemed protected in some mysterious way from the snout of the boll weevil. Three years during which weevil-wrecked farmers from other counties sought to buy the "weevil-proof" land. Three years while investment and insurance firms, hungry for interest, were glad to finance land purchases even at boom prices. Years when the long poverty could be forgotten, and cherished desires fulfilled.

High prices, high wages quickly spent, costly fertilizer to make another heavy crop and big down payments on farm land. These carried off the good hard cash, leaving behind big, cheerful debts that worried nobody because another crop was on the way.

And then the weevil came—and stayed. The utter collapse of cotton in the early 1920's left the county economically prostrate.

The farmers who had sold their lands at peak prices were no better off than those who had held on to them, for now they could not collect. Deep defeat settled on landed aristocrat and landless farmer alike.

"If I had took out in '20 and never hit another lick of work," says one farmer, "I would have been sitting pretty all my life. But I got out at 4 o'clock in the morning and made everybody else get up and get at it before sun-up. I hustled about all day long and worked myself out of a fortune and into debt."

Scores of white tenants whose fathers had farmed their own land thought they at last had arranged to become owners, too. They had bargained for acreage, made down payments with their boom-time savings, still owed one fourth, one half, or more of the purchase price. But what was the sense, they would say, of paying the fourth or the half you still owed on a farm, when that fourth or half was two or three times more than the farm was now worth.

The hope of becoming owners was knocked out at one fell blow, and not soon again would it be easy for any newspaper, or local organization, or government agency to argue the advantages of small farm ownership.

The big landowners were in almost as bad plight. They had their lands, but the lands were not equal to their debts; and they had no credit with which to plant the next crop. They knew only cotton, labor knew only cotton, and what reason was there to believe the weevil would not eat it up again?

THOUSANDS LEAVE THE FARMS

The trains began to make longer stops in the stations at Greensboro and Union Point, Woodville and Carey. The Negro farm folk were climbing aboard with their cumbersome bundles. Many left in the fall of 1922, more in 1923, and still more in 1924 and 1925 as cash and credit resources further dwindled. The Whites, a little less dependent, could weather the depression a little longer. So their migration was smaller and its peak was two years later.

Between 1920 and 1930 Greene's colored population decreased by

43 percent, white by 23 percent. Letters came back to Greene from all over the nation, and soon in front of most of the occupied tenant cabins were mail boxes, some of shiny new tin, a few of pine slabs.

The number of farmers in Greene dropped from 3,000 in 1920 to 1,557 in 1930. The number of children of school age shrank by nearly a thousand, reducing the state educational funds sent to the county by almost $5,000 a year.

Nearly seven thousand people left here. They were usually headed for distant cities—Birmingham or Detroit, Chicago or Philadelphia, Cincinnati or Washington—to look for work. But most of them stopped in Atlanta or Athens or Augusta, for they had no money to go farther. Farm people left Greene in the middle 1920's as virtual refugees.* They left with the pinch of hunger upon them.

Reports of the Family Welfare Society in Atlanta showed that most of their clients were recent migrants from the old plantation section between Atlanta and Augusta, and many were from Greene. The assistance that was then available further disrupted the migrant families, for it was much easier for a mother to get relief if she had no able-bodied husband. This policy increased desertion among a group already plagued by it. The women could find work as domestics because they were willing to underbid the women already on the jobs at about $5 a week. Four dollars a week, or even three, is real money when the "relief" you get is not enough to feed your family.

In the late 1920's nearly one third of Greene's migrants were still living in Atlanta, over half in Georgia. Only one fourth lived outside the South, but as the rural refugees pressed into Southern cities many Negroes already there moved off to the North and East.

The migration had taken from Greene a disproportionate number of the most able-bodied men and women, and had left behind practically all the aged and infirm. The better educated tended to leave first.

---

* See *Preface to Peasantry*, U. N. C. Press (1936), pp. 191 ff.

A MILLION MILLION LITTLE PINES

The boll weevil put Greene through many a change. A thousand farm houses, one out of every three, had been abandoned in a decade. The number of farmers, as reported by the U. S. Census, dropped to half. The value of farm lands and buildings fell from about ten million down to two million dollars, the value of land alone from eight million to a little over one million, the value of all crops from almost six million to one million, the land planted to cotton from over 55,000 acres down to 11,000 acres.

Migration was much greater in some parts of the county than in others. Five red-land plantation militia districts lost 67 percent of their colored population, 44 percent of their white. Three small-owner, white-land districts lost but 12 percent of their colored and 4 percent of their white. The live-at-home farmers demonstrated superior ability to stay-out deflation and depression. But a bitter dose it was: land prices down to one fourth or one sixth what they had been, and seldom a purchaser; mules bought at $300 apiece offered for $60; and $100 cows begging buyers at $20.

No new tin roofs were put on the tenant cabins still occupied, no new paint on planter houses; no new fields were plowed, and no new fences built. The whole countryside seemed to be waiting . . .

All around were abandoned fields. Much of the land was spent, too tired to cover itself with grass or weeds during the summer. Dead cotton and corn stalks weathered one winter and came to the next, ground frost spewed loose their dead roots, March winds blew them over, and that year the heavy rains, which always come, washed more loose dirt than ever before into the creeks and rivers of Greene. The next winter and summer, and the next and the next, saw more dirt leave from the least fertile parts of once active fields.

Where the soil was better, the abandoned fields clothed themselves. A few handfuls of Bermuda roots, which a farmer had tried in vain to get out of his cotton fields in 1920, had sodded them down within three years. Other portions of good soil were covered with deep blankets of crab grass and weeds. By the second winter, among the Bermuda and weeds stood scattered sedge grass, more the next. In scarcely half a decade, the waving brown broom sedge had become the county's greatest crop. And it did its work well— up through the matted sedge came a million million little pines, silent and green.

Little pines are not choosy. They are among Earth's greatest commoners. They grow in good soil, and they grow in the poorest—if only it will stand still for the winged seed to put down its first year tap root. Many an abandoned field, too depleted to grow a cover of weeds, supports a good stand of pines after a few years. Little pines spurn upland soil in Greene only when it is moving—only when it is on its death march down to the salt sea.

Winter and summer, and pines grew tall; winter and summer and hillside galls became gullies. Disheartened and defeated farm folk of Greene kept boarding the trains in search of city wages for food and clothing.

FORECLOSED FOR DEBTS AND TAXES

During the hard years taxes were a burden. In 1923 over $33,000 in taxes were uncollected, more in 1924. The county's debt had risen to $120,000, nearly twice its annual income. Difficult indeed was it to pay taxes, especially on idle lands.

One grand jury after another noted the heavy tax burden on farm property, requested that efforts be made to increase income from other sources. "Under the present system," ran a *Herald-Journal* comment in 1923, "the man with a milk cow or a bull calf pays taxes, but the man with the income doesn't pay any taxes."

For several years the grand juries pointed out that to sell the land of small holders for non-payment of taxes would be folly, would merely force many a farmer "to become a dependent on his family or on the county, mean another vacant farm and the loss of a self sustaining citizen."

Down among the sedge and growing pines and around the abandoned houses, rabbit and quail found haven, multiplied. A few people said the land would soon be valuable for hunting preserves, could perhaps be sold or leased to millionaire sportsmen.

The monied sportsmen never came, but the creditors did. By 1927 over 12,000 acres of land had been forfeited to loan companies, by 1934 over 17,000 acres. Practically all this land was in the old plantation sections of the county, and was in tracts of 500 acres or more. The largest holders were the John Hancock and Metropolitan Life Insurance companies, Atlanta Joint Stock Land Bank, the Scottish American Mortgage Company of Scotland and the Federal Land Bank.

Loss of acreage for non-payment of taxes by 1927 totaled 15,785 acres. This too was in the red-land section of the county, three fourths of it in the districts along the Oconee River, nearly all the rest around Penfield and Woodville. Altogether, about one eighth of the county's acreage was forfeited for taxes or to creditors.

Absentee ownership increased as landowners left the county and as acreage was forfeited. Roads and schools and all other public services suffered from reduced taxes. Even so, the tax on the land was still immeasurably higher than during the inflation period. Land prices had decreased about 80 percent, tax costs only around 20 percent.

The farmowners would have lost more land than they did if anybody had wanted it. The state didn't want it for taxes, and the loan companies didn't want it for debts. By 1927, public officials and financiers were wondering what they could do with the acreage they had already let fall into their hands, were ready to defer taxes and reduce loan payments.

BOSWELL'S "DEBT-FREE" BARBECUE

The debts of Greene's people were heavy and long, but humor will out. Early in the weevil depression, October, 1923, A. J. Boswell of Penfield held a barbecue, invited all "debt-free" white men of the county to be his guests. "If you don't owe a single cent to anybody, drop . . . a post card at Penfield . . . to put your name in the pot." The "Richland Philosopher," John E. Finch, then in his eighty-fourth year, wrote for his local column: "In the Great Judgment day if Saint Peter applies the test that our friend A. J. Boswell did at his debt-free feast, we think Heaven will be widely laid off and thinly inhabited." "The most novel barbecue ever proposed, and our guess is, it will be the smallest," said the *Macon News*.

Then came the day for the debt-free feast. Thirteen men were at the head table. Boswell did not sit with his honor guests that day.

Some men were not impressed with the debt-free standard: "It is out of the question for a real live active business man to operate without debts." All agreed with one of the honor guests who said: "It is easy to be debt-free when a man has no credit."

The *New York Sun* and the *New York Globe* wired down for five-hundred-word stories about the barbecue. R. H. Macy and Company ran an advertisement in the *New York Herald:* "What a pity Georgia is so far from Macy's, for buying here costs less, and after buying it you are not in debt." The *Washington Post* noted that a Georgia gentleman was feeding a barbecued rabbit to the people of his county who were absolutely free of debt, suggested that "what is left of the rabbit can be eaten cold the next day for lunch."

To "A. J." the publicity was expensive—he hired a school teacher, for a whole month, to answer his letters.

The Boswell dinner came and went. The heavy debts remained. Home-town merchants begged the people to spend what cash they got with them: "Why murder Greene county dollars buying things elsewhere you can buy here?"

Within five years after the Boswell barbecue, both banks in Greensboro closed, as did the one at Woodville and at White Plains. Only the two banks at Union Point, and the Bank of Siloam, in the heart of the white-land, live-at-home farm area, weathered the boll weevil depression.

U. P. AND W. P. COLLAPSES

At the time when the red-land farmers were losing their lands and the banks were failing, the White Plains merchants lost their railroad.

Around 1920, when crops and prices were good, the Union Point and White Plains Railroad had done a thriving business. The directors were leading merchants and planters in the white-land section. They had no patience with the Populist philosophy of "putting the bottom rail on top," had great respect for money lenders and railroads. They had put their surplus money into the railroad. Why then, when they attended the annual meetings, were they always told there would be no dividends?

The Georgia Railroad owned over 50 percent of the stock, and therefore made the decisions. Some of the directors thought the Georgia Railroad's charges for rolling stock were too high, had been put high to escape payment of dividends. Some wanted to buy the rest of U. P. and W. P. stock and operate the railroad themselves. But even in boom times they could not arrange the purchase. As they fretted in their impotence, the boll weevil came. Then they knew that the money they had put into the U. P. and W. P. would never bring any returns, would never be paid back.

The officials of the U. P. and W. P. had not gone wholly unremunerated. They had used their passes on the local road freely, and their courtesy passes on many other roads too. President Tappan got a pass on the B. & O. by pointing out to its officials that "even if my railroad is much shorter than yours, it is just as wide." Other officials arranged trips on passes to Cuba, Canada, and to points throughout eastern America. An older local attorney was offered complimentary passes to serve the road; he already had passes from the Georgia Railroad, so a younger attorney accepted the post.

By the early summer of 1926, the Georgia Railroad had petitioned the Public Service Commission to discontinue the U. P. and W. P. trains. The Commission looked into the losses during the past four years and granted the request. On December 31 of that year, the last train chugged across its rough track. W. R. Jackson, of Greensboro, bought the track for junk, expected later to extend it to his granite deposit, Flat Rock, near Mosquito Crossing.

That same year the Georgia Railroad discontinued its two fastest trains through Greensboro, and five years later two more passenger trains.

FIGHTING WEEVILS WITH FIRE AND POISON

Hard hit as was Greene by boll weevil and deflation, disheartened as were many of her people, there were those who would not take it lying down. They fought every inch.

The businessmen of Greensboro closed their shops every Thursday at noon to help fight the boll weevil. Prizes were offered in the summer of 1921 to boys and girls under seventeen who would bring the most weevils to the office of County Agent Wade H. West. In early August, Mary Lou Ashley brought in 6,896 weevils, won the $50 first prize. The second prize of $25 and the third of $5 went to Burnie Thurmond and Robert Shelton, each of whom also had over 6,000.

Early the next year calcium arsenate was demonstrated at White Plains as a weevil killer. Some people used it that fall, others picked up squares to burn them. A few farmers, particularly some of the smaller ones, would not bother the weevil lest they interfere with the Lord's plan. "If He didn't want 'em here," inquired one Negro farmer, "why did He send 'em here? Naw, sir, not me, I ain't killin' a single one!"

But even if you are determined to destroy the weevil, how shall you do it? Spraying calcium arsenate on the fruiting plant is expensive, and picking up the squares is tedious. Weevils hibernate the winter, multiply rapidly in mid-summer. A dozen weevils destroyed in winter or spring is a thousand or so not in the fields in late July and August. Weevils winter in cotton stalks, corn stalks, grass and weeds, on terraces, in abandoned fields and in the woods.

On the first warm days of spring, farmers prepared the seed bed—plow handles in their hands, matches in their pockets. And as they plowed, their children, and often their womenfolk piled up the cotton stalks and burned them, set fire to the terraces and to the hedgerows and sometimes to near-by sedgefield and pine woods.

Smoke rose from ten thousand places across the county. Just look at the fires in the fields, and at the glow on the faces of the farm folk making war on the weevil.

The fires in the open fields were bright and brief, the fluffy warm ashes soon plowed under. The fires on the terraces would be smoking next morning. The fire in an abandoned field might march for days and nights through sedgefields of baby pines, through woods full of rich pine knots and fallen boughs—on across hills and hollows to a big creek, a wide road, or a plantation still in cultivation. March winds often spread the fires; spring rains sometimes put them out. Year in and year out during the 1920's, fire seared more uncultivated acres in Greene than were cultivated.

Vacant houses caught on fire, and bare chimneys became common sights. So many farm houses burned in the 1920's that for a time insurance companies stopped writing fire policies on rural property in the county.

Each spring there was plow and smoke, and the chance that this year's crop would be better. Maybe cotton could still be grown in Greene. Many farm families had left, but there remained more than could be used. So year after year cotton was planted, but without much hope and without much fertilizer.

The New Year's letter from the "Big Store" (McCommons-Thompson-Boswell Company) early in 1924 said:

Let's . . . forget our hard luck and losses and go to farming.

The Big Store stands for everything progressive and is anxious to assist and pull with the farmers to get the county back firmly on solid prosperity . . .

Yours for ten thousand bales of cotton in Greene County during 1924.

A carload of calcium arsenate was brought here in April, 1925 and sold at 8½ cents a pound. A month later, the banks and merchants paid for a full page advertisement in the *Herald-Journal* pleading with the farmers to poison the weevils.

But boost as they would, and poison as they could, the cotton crop staged a poor comeback at best. About 1,500 bales were harvested in 1923, a little over 4,000 the next year, and then up to around 5,000 for the next five years. And during this period the price declined, averaged scarcely ten cents. Some farmers blamed the cotton buyers, called them "bale weevils." A favorite saying was: "The 'bale weevil' has hurt me more than the boll weevil!"

The boll weevil wrought a major disaster here, and people who lived through it use it as disaster dates are used everywhere. The people at Johnstown say "before the flood," the people at Charleston, "before the earthquake," the older people who lived through the War of the 1860's say "before the War." Just so with another generation whose lives were cut across by the boll weevil. A farmer speaks of an aging mule as a "before-the-weevil mule." He sleeps in a "before-the-war bed" under "before-the-boll-weevil quilts."

Such a date is often used to preface a description of how the country looked before it grew up in sedge and pines. "Where all that woods is, it used to be pretty rows of cotton. You could stand on this rise and see clear to Union Point," they tell you along some parts of the Bethany Road. And down in the lower part of the county, you can drive for miles between dark pines and hardly see a house or an open field. A lone farmer will tell you: "Once you could get out and holler and have three dozen darkies here in ten minutes. A hundred pupils went to school at Liberty. You could stand on that knoll at night and see the lights in a dozen houses. But—all that was before the boll weevil."

XVI

THEY TRIED EVERYTHING

Now THAT cotton yields were low and the price down, the farmers who remained in Greene tried to find a substitute crop. Money was badly needed, and efforts of all kinds were made to get it. The town folks encouraged and cooperated, for they knew their only chance to stay in business was for the farmers to find new sources of income.

GOOBERS AND RABBITS

The first crop tried on a large scale was the peanut. Local leaders boosted peanuts. The *Herald-Journal* explained that they could be "grown and sold just like cotton."

Several large planters hopefully shifted to the new crop the next spring after the weevil first ruined cotton. Some of the bankers and merchants had no faith in the peanut business, others promoted it lamely, a few enthusiastically. Most active was banker W. C. Davison at White Plains, who sensed the farmer's need of banking assistance for new cash crops.

From the beginning, overproduction was feared. In an effort to stabilize the price, the larger planters affiliated with the Georgia Peanut Growers Association. Well-attended meetings were held at the courthouse, with representatives of the Association here to assure them of ready markets and good prices. The 1923 crop sold for around $100,000, and that was not bad. A larger crop the next year sold for less money, and that was bad. After a year or two even the Association was uncertain what prices would be, so peanuts dropped out as a substitute crop, and the bankers who had financed them took their losses.

There were those who had thought all along that "goobers were fitten only for hogs and small boys at circuses."

Many people turned to the abandoned fields of sedge and young pines for something to eat: berries and muscadines were there for the picking; rabbits and quail were plentiful, 'possum and even wild turkeys more abundant than before. Shotgun shells cost money, and to get more shells to kill more rabbits, hunters were offering for sale more cotton tails than they could find buyers for.

Enterprising A. J. Boswell, at Penfield, began to ship rabbits. The farmers shot hundreds, and the farmers' boys trapped thousands, brought them in—20 cents for a trapped rabbit, 10 to 15 cents for a shot one. Five years after the weevil first ate up Greene's cotton crop, Penfield considered itself the nation's biggest producer of old field rabbits—around 20,000 were shipped out each year. Within a half decade, the rabbit business was no more. Tularemia had appeared and most of the rabbits died in the fields.

SAWMILLS AND COTTON MILLS

Along with the new peanut and rabbit industries came the expansion of sawmilling. The landowners turned to their trees—their long-time crop—when their one-season crops had failed. There was a little of the century-old oak left, there was much half-century pine fully mature, and still younger pine that could be sawed and sold. Farmers started sawmills, scores of them. Sawed their own trees, big and little, and then moved their mills to saw for their neighbors— making impromptu roads through abandoned fields dotted with the infant "boll-weevil" pines.

At first the sawmills were looked upon as a way to survive the boll-weevil depression. Let's get enough money to pay our creditors something. Let's hold on to this land. Fortunes have been made here. Hard times have come before. We will weather it. We won't be beaten. Except for the sawmills, more hundreds of working people would have left the county, and more thousands of acres would have been forfeited for non-payment of taxes or for unpaid debts.

Throughout the old plantation areas, where cultivation had been abandoned between 1880 and 1895, sawable pine trees now stood ready for logging. During the middle 1920's the mills puffed away. The sale of timber was Greene's most important source of income. You could ride across the county on the Georgia Railroad and count 25 new piles of sawdust.

As the 1920's wore to a close, most of the available timber had been sawed, and sold, and spent. The lumber industry was nearing its end. In less than ten years it had cashed in on the timber growth of over half a century. Most of the sawmills went out of business, but a few "coffee-pot" mills were always running. And the pines kept growing—those left behind by the loggers and the big fields of "boll-weevil" pines already waist high.

Stabilizing the economy of Greene during the hard years were the wages paid textile mill workers at Greensboro and Union Point, a weekly payroll of about $4,000 at the former, a little less at the latter. Both mills continued in operation and piled up goods rather than close down when the orders on hand had been filled.

Around 750 people were employed in the mills at this time, and received an annual payroll of nearly $350,000—not a high wage for the mill workers, but more than they could earn at farming or saw-milling. The mills' payrolls were almost four times the value of Greene's best peanut crop, and nearly equal to her best cotton crops during the middle and late 1920's.

"LEGGER LICKER"

An uncertain, but not unimportant, business in Greene and adjoining counties during the hard years was the illegal manufacture and sale of liquor, called "moonshine," "bootleg," or just "legger licker."

The county had always been "dry." The slaveholders had objected to liquor being sold or given to the slaves; the early charters of Penfield, White Plains, Woodville, Union Point, and Siloam expressly prohibited the sale of intoxicating liquors, as did also the Greensboro Charter of 1906. The state prohibition law and later the 18th Amendment were appreciated by the county officials. County policemen were employed to assure local enforcement.

But there were people here and elsewhere who still wanted to drink. And they were willing to pay for it. "Moonshining" began to develop as a big business in rural Georgia soon after the passage of the 18th Amendment. When the weevil came, more people found it attractive.

During the early and middle 1920's Georgia had the reputation of having had more stills confiscated than any other state in the Union. Greene had its share, and to spare. "World's largest still captured in old Greene when a negro made a slip, and they were making enough joy-juice to float a battleship," ran a story in Dudley Glass' column in the *Atlanta Constitution* in late September, 1921. Copper stills, with boilers and worms punctured, were piled high in a room in the courthouse in Greensboro, so high that the grand jury asked that all "confiscated stills in the courthouse be destroyed."

Negroes and Whites, separate and together, worked at the stills. Local and federal enforcement officers caught them in the act, if they could; cruised along back roads looking for smoke down by the little creeks. Now and then they would pick up a man on the road who, as thanks for his ride, would tell them about where they might locate a still or two. Such reports could not always be relied upon, for sometimes the informant was a "legger" himself and might send the officers off on a wild chase, or more dangerously send them on a round about way to his own still where he would go armed to meet them.

Some people who made and sold liquor needed the money, wondered why it should be a crime. Didn't the people who buy it want it? As American citizens, didn't they have some rights? And who were these revenue officers? Didn't many of them drink themselves? Good whiskey sold at a reasonable price, made on your own land and out of your own corn, and with your own wood and water. Well, what was so wrong with that?

More than one crossroad in Greene became a center of the trade. On each Wednesday night, between eleven o'clock and two in the morning, old Fords and Chevrolets with full fruit jars and bottles would stop at an abandoned tenant house on a back road until a truck had been loaded down for Atlanta. Monday or Friday night was "hot" at other points. There was always the possibility that someone would tip off the officers, and certainly a lot of the non-participating local people knew what was going on.

As the raids continued, officers and "leggers" got shot, killed now and then. After a time the liquor-making business became almost solely limited to the lawless element. Once this had happened, much of the liquor itself was no longer "good whiskey." Some of it was "doped," with caustic lye—caused severe sickness, even death.

Greene had numerous bone dry advocates, particularly among the leadership of the Methodist and Baptist denominations. Greene's most prominent prohibitionist was Mary Harris Armour, born in Penfield, known throughout the state and nation for her unceasing fight on the liquor traffic. She spoke often in Greensboro, was referred to as the "Georgia Cyclone," and "Our Matchless Mary."

SWEET MILK AND SOUR CREAM

As soon as the hard years came upon Greene, the people wondered if they had not been a little hasty in letting high cotton prices wipe out their dairy and cattle industry. Could they turn back now to milk and beef? A few of the larger planters made the shift. Others could have changed, had they not depleted their credit resources with the peanuts venture just after having failed with cotton. As the months passed, more milk was shipped.

Some source of cash income was needed by the small farm operators. The shipment of sweet milk was out of the question for them. The weekly sale of sour cream was hit upon. By late 1923 it was hailed a "wonderful success." Showing the small farmers how readily more of them could sell sour cream, County Agent Wade H. West said: "All you need to do is to set your milk aside and let the cream rise. Then put it into a fruit jar or crock, or anything that you have and bring it in here on sales days." It was as simple as that.

In a few months the county's weekly sales rose from 400 pounds to 1,200 pounds. The hope was expressed that at least $1,000 worth could soon be sold each week.

In two years the weekly sales were slightly over a thousand dollars a week, in four years up to nearly $1,300 a week, with sour cream stations at Greensboro, Union Point, White Plains, Siloam, and Penfield.

Shipments of sweet milk, too, continued to increase. By the end of 1927 over 1,300 gallons were shipped from Greene daily. At 30 cents a gallon, the weekly income was around $2,850. The income from sweet milk and sour cream together amounted to almost a quarter of a million dollars a year, a lot of money. Yes, but only half the value of a "measly little 5,000 bales of cotton at 20 cents a pound." There would have to be much more sour cream and sweet milk before it could become a substitute for cotton. "If we do not go heavier into dairies," said the *Herald-Journal,* "we had just as well put out the fire, call the dogs, and go home."

But shipments of dairy products became smaller rather than larger. The dairymen had problems: pastures and feed, "hollow horn" and milk leg, Bang's Disease and TB, and on through the list to low butter fat, high bacteria count, and milk sour when it reached Atlanta. The farmers were overcoming their handicaps one by one. Dairyman Ed. L. Lewis had learned how to get his milk to market sweet. He put a small container of ice down in each can. But learn as much as they might about keeping their herds in good health and the milk sweet, it availed nothing when the price of milk fell to 15 cents a gallon and remained there.

The farmers wondered why their milk, which was sold to Atlanta retailers for over 60 cents a gallon should bring them only 15 cents. They asked why. Were told there was a surplus of milk, and if they didn't like the price they need not take it.

The sour cream business had problems of its own. The creamery at Atlanta was no longer anxious to make purchases here. Arrangements were made with one in Macon, and later in Albany. Prices continued to drop, and after awhile there was a question as to whether anyone would buy sour cream at any price.

The farmers saw their unprotected position, and in October, 1925 formed a dairymen's association, with A. S. Moseley as president. Said Joseph P. Brown at this first meeting: "Man for man we should stand together if we expect to live." Once the price of dairy products had slumped, however, no way was found to boost them.

As early as 1923, an editorial in the *Herald-Journal* had said that cooperatives should be the "watchword of the farmers." Some time after the dairymen's association was organized, a small cooperative creamery was set up. But it was too little and too poorly managed to compete with the larger creameries, and so went out of business after a few months. Its failure did not make the local paper despair of cooperatives as a way out.

Cooperatives can scarcely be developed overnight to function in one lone field of a community's activities. The abandonment of the creamery helped demonstrate that more cooperation was needed, and that the cooperative here should have been effectively related to cooperatives elsewhere. Developing cooperatives among farm tenants and wage hands is most difficult, not easy among large landowners who are accustomed to having farm tenants and wage hands do as they say.

Some people continued to ship milk, and others sold sour cream as long as there was any sale for it. With a ready market for beef, milkers were now and then sold off, and so were most of the calves. But as long as any cows are left, a calf will drop every year or two. And after a couple of summers, even the most neglected heifer becomes some kind of a cow. If there is a sale for either sweet milk or sour cream, butter or beef, a cow is not wholly without value. Toward the late 1920's, the cattle business in Greene had settled down, along with cotton, as an uncertain way to make at least something of a living.

Other means employed across the county to increase farm incomes during the hard years included the planting of peach orchards, particularly on the white lands around Siloam and White Plains. Some good fruit was produced, but it was seldom marketed profitably. Strawberries also proved financially unsuccessful, though since they were first experimented with, a few families have had all they wanted for home use, and for neighbors.

For a couple of years, beginning in 1926, some farmers talked about tobacco. Meetings were held at the courthouse. A few families planted a crop and built curing barns. No market was near, labor knew nothing about its culture, and soon tobacco growing was abandoned.

Even tame rabbits were produced for a time. In September, 1928 the rabbit producers organized, with Mamie Tuggle Mitchell president.

Everything was tried, many things on a large scale. The County Agent ordered clover seed by the carload in the middle 1920's, and a few years later carloads of hairy vetch.

After all their casting about, the farmers of Greene knew they had not found a substitute crop for cotton. They also knew they were still dependent on cotton even though they could never again grow it as they had in pre-weevil days. King Cotton is dead, they said . . . Long Live King Cotton!

BOOSTER CLUBS COME AND GO

The businessmen in the larger towns were interested in the farmers' experiments with new crops. They knew how dependent they were on the money the farmers spent with them.

The roster of booster organizations which were formed during the hard years speaks for itself. The earliest on record was the Greene County Farm Bureau, which in the fall of 1921 sent a committee to Atlanta to try to arrange for the sale there of Greene county farm products. The Greensboro Board of Trade was formed in April, 1924, with W. R. Jackson as president. The Board talked about new crops, and considered the establishment of a modern tourist camp. By September of that year the Board's activities were on the wane. "This city had been the graveyard of Boards of Trade," said the *Herald-Journal*. "None of them lived to be a year old." Late that fall, the Greensboro Board of Trade was transformed into a county-wide Board of Trade, with representative people from the various communities named on its committees. The County Board remained active for a few months.

In September of 1925 a county-wide Booster's Club was organized, with T. H. McGibony, hardware merchant, chairman. The Club's goals were new settlers, new industries, better roads. There were a few enthusiastic meetings. Early in November of that same year the Chamber of Commerce was organized with druggist T. B. Rice president.

Early in 1927 the Greensboro Exchange Club was set up, and proclaimed the need for new settlers. The Club asked the Georgia Association for a list of prospects and got in touch with them by mail, believing that "people usually go where they are invited and wanted." New industries were still needed, and the Club encouraged the grand jury and local paper to recommend that the community offer a five-year tax exemption to induce Northern industry to come here.

After a few meetings, leading citizens from other parts of the county were invited to attend. Harold Lamb of Union Point was a guest, agreed to lend up to $5,000 for the purchase of dairy cows provided an equal amount would be made available from other sources for this purpose. He pointed out that the one-gallon milkers, so common in the county, should be sold for beef, that it took three-gallon cows to make a success of dairying. The conditions of Lamb's offer were never met.

The M. C. Overton Post of the American Legion was organized in April, 1927.

Within the next few years many other clubs were formed. The Exchange Club was reorganized and became the Greene County Civic Club. There was also a Young Men's Democratic Association, a Roosevelt for President Club, a Greene County Agricultural Board, Greene County Livestock Association, a number of Parent-Teachers Associations, and finally the Greensboro and Union Point Lions Clubs. Effectively affiliated with a national organization, the Lions fell heir to the booster tradition, and became the promoters of progressive movements in the county.

The Negroes organized the Greene County Colored Farmers' Association in 1932, with Reverend W. M. Jackson president. Their goal was to make a living, and then sell all the cotton they could.

Such were the organizations which sprang up in Greene during the hard years when the farmers sought to find a cash crop to take the place of cotton.

XVII

COUNTRY EDITORS

A FEW people in Greene realized that the boll weevil had thrown the cotton growers into a new world. But no one seemed to understand what it all meant quite so well as James Cranston Williams, editor and publisher of the *Herald-Journal* since 1906. Courageous and keen, and with a sense of humor, loved by many people and respected by all, editor Williams had come to be known as "Uncle Jim."

UNCLE JIM SPEAKS TO THE FARMERS

As soon as the Negroes began to leave in great numbers, Williams wrote (on March 2, 1923): "The farmer in the future will be forced to give more thought to detail . . . do more work and not depend upon the black man to help him make a living out of the earth." In an analytical mood, he continued, "Even had the boll weevil never come, the laborers would have left the farm . . . black men taking the place of foreigners, who once came in droves to our shores."

Some planters at this time were having to pay laborers $20 per month and board. "This looks very high to the man who is forced to pay it," said the local paper, "but it does look as if an able-bodied man is worth this amount if he is handled intelligently . . . The day of cheap labor is past. And the sooner the farmer realizes this the better it will be for him."

But it is a strain even for a big-souled editor to live under changed conditions. With obvious relief, two months later a five-column headline reported, "Negroes Living in Northern States Dissatisfied."

The editor said it was "Pleasing to hear that, after all, the black brother appreciates his home in Dixie land . . . Really the Southern man is the best friend that the black people will ever have. We understand him and he understands us."

By the time the boll-weevil depression was upon Greene, many of the people on the streets conceded Williams' insight, when on February 8, 1924, he prophesied: "The big farms must go. The future farmer must be the small one who owns his own land." They nodded affirmatively again a month later when they read, "The many large farms in Greene county have retarded the progress of the county since the Civil War. We will never have a great county, good roads, better rural schools and better churches until the large farms are cut up and owned and tilled by energetic white owners."

"Yes, feed the soil. It will feed you," wrote Williams in June of that year. "The one crop system of farming has depleted the soil of its fertility, enslaved the farming classes, and brought our people face to face with stagnation and bankruptcy."

Editor Williams wanted the people to stop complaining of hard times, boosted the cow, hog, and hen program, said, "The hen is the only living critter that can set still and produce dividends." He advocated cooperative marketing, and reminded his readers that it could not accomplish everything; suggested the New Year's slogan of "Owe as little as possible, and pay as you go;" worked for new industrial payrolls, wanted them to be tax exempt for five years. He pointed out that gullies and hillsides should have pine trees set out on them, urged the consolidation of schools, saw the Manley banks crashing and advocated compulsory insurance of bank accounts. All of these things J. C. Williams was talking about before the end of the 1920's.

He worked with others to get the services of a County Farm Agent, and was proud of the program carried on. When the grand jury recommended that this work be abolished in 1925, he wrote sternly: "The *Herald-Journal* has done its part toward helping Greene county come back, but if the county is too damn poor to

pay one half of the salary of a county demonstrator, we are ready
to call in the dogs and quit."

UNCLE JIM ATTACKS HOODED EMPIRE

The Ku Klux Klan, powerful in Georgia in the early 1920's, made
little headway in Greene. J. C. Williams was anti-Klan to the core:
"A civilization that is at the mercy of violence and lawlessness is no
civilization."

He repeatedly went after the hooded empire in his pithy paragraphs and his news columns. Sometimes in direct attack: "An
invisible Government in the shape of a secret order is undermining
the foundations of American Government." Sometimes with ironi-
cal thrusts—wondered if the proposed Klan University "would establish a department of hazing," thought the long white robes
"ought to boost the price of cotton," said the Klan was "to a large
extent taking the place of the church in this country."

Ku Kluxers in high places were not overlooked. Governor Clif-
ford Walker of Georgia was called "Kautious Kleagle Kliff." As
reported by the national press services in October, 1924, Governor
Walker addressed the National Klonvocation of the Klan at Kansas
City, and made "an eloquent plea for Klansmen to get a clear vision
of Christ and Christ's teachings and to make Him their leader in the
battle for Klan supremacy." The Governor then lamented at some
length the "threatened destruction of America and Americanism by
the encroachment of Jewish, Celtic and Mediterranean races." Williams groaned, said that he was "of as pure American blood as any
man that is a member of the order." "For generations," he continued, "Protestant fires have burned on the hearth stones of our ancestors. Yet, we have no faith in the Klan or any other secret political
order that teaches religious bigotry and intolerance. Our conception
of a hundred percent American youth is one that fought and bled
for America—be he Gentile, Catholic, Jew or Negro."

J. C. Williams was one of the three editors in Georgia who stood steadfastly against the Klan during the heyday of its power. Masked men were sometimes seen in Greene, but the Klan was never active here. Along with anti-Klan Editor Williams stood anti-Klan James B. Park, judge of the Superior Court of the Ocmulgee Circuit for 28 years. No prisoner in his circuit—made up of about a dozen counties—was taken from officers and lynched while he was judge. Throughout his judgeship, James B. Park regularly asked grand juries to indict, and petty juries to convict floggers.

"IF YOU WANT TO BE MISSED"

In late October, 1923, Williams said, "Jack (John) Slaton is coming back . . . he did the right thing when he commuted Leo Frank's death sentence to life. The *Herald-Journal,* at the time of the trial, believed in Frank's innocence." He also defended the pamphlet against peonage and lynching sent out in 1921 by Governor Hugh M. Dorsey. "It has borne good fruit," wrote Williams, "and better conditions has been the result."

One of the subjects upon which Uncle Jim felt strongest was that of capital punishment, which he thought should be abolished: "No state should take away from any person or persons something if needed they can't restore." Of similar opinion was Richland Philosopher John E. Finch: "Hanging folks don't stop crime."

Side by side with Uncle Jim's attacks on the Klan, mob violence, and capital punishment, came orthodox black-belt defense of the poll tax requirement for voting, the White Primary, and the use of the lash in the convict camps of the state. "Prison reformers will make convict camps a regular pleasure resort," Williams wrote on January 23, 1923. A week earlier he said most prisoners were good, but there is no way "to handle an unruly negro or white man . . . except . . . a complete thrashing . . . When the lash is discarded wardens can't control the convicts."

Week after week, on the editorial page, came paragraphs heavy with solid sense and high character:

If you want to be missed when you are gone, you had better get busy and do something for humanity.

I would rather be a sore-toed boy in patched trousers at the final roll call, and be honest in the sight of men and angels, than a bloated bond holder who has chiseled his wealth from the poor and needy.

I don't believe the world is going to Hell. In fact, we believe it gets better and better every day. But, if you do believe it is on the down-road to Hell, what are you doing to stop it?

An admirable spirit was Uncle Jim in the depth of Greene's depression, and he never lost his humor: "Oh, yes, Greene County is coming back. There isn't anything else for it to do."

MORE SENSE THAN NONSENSE

Uncle Jim Williams' younger son, Carey, showed when yet a high school boy that he was a paragrapher of ability. His column of pungent short items started in the early 1920's, was first called "Jim Jams," then "Georgia Sunshine," and from 1931 to date "Sense and Nonsense."

Humor and philosophy have been packed into them, and a quick sense of what is happening. In 1921 the college boy wrote: "The old time girl that said, 'You'll have to ask father,' now chirps, 'Step on the gas, dear, dad's gaining ground on us.'"

On the streets, in his printing shop, anywhere, he saw and jotted down a line:

A mud hole in Greensboro is of more interest to a citizen of Greensboro than the digging of the Panama Canal.

Some people make the same mistake so much that it becomes a habit.

A lot of men think it is Christlike to forgive a man they can't whip.

The dice are now rolling for the cotton country's annual gamble with old nature and world consumption.

The two chief troubles of today are the high cost of living and the cheapness of life.

Presidents were not immune. Remembering the Tea Pot Dome Scandal of the Harding Administration, he wrote, "Coolidge is slowly finding out what will take oil stains out of a second-hand cabinet."

Many readers outside of the county first saw Carey Williams' paragraphs in the *Literary Digest's* "Topics in Brief." For over a decade his "Sense and Nonsense" has been syndicated to a score of papers, many of them leading dailies, one in Canada—the *Toronto Telegraph*.

In 1932, when Henry Ford was advocating the reelection of Hoover, Carey Williams and J. B. Winslett of Greensboro offered him "a friendly wager" of a 201-acre farm against a model V-8 Ford that President Hoover would not be reelected. Heavy with prickly political arguments, the "wager" ran:

In 1919, under the last Democratic administration, this 201-acre tract of land was valued at $10,000. There is today approximately 250,000 feet of pine timber, and 50,000 feet of hard wood on the place. The tenant house is in fair condition.

In the event of President Hoover's reelection we feel that we will lose the place anyway and would much prefer you owning it than it being sold by the sheriff.

Uncle Jim quoted the letter in an Associated Press release. The folks at home and far away read the banter, and chuckled.

Political polls might guess badly and go out of business, and Henry Ford might not even answer the letter from Greensboro, but "Sense and Nonsense" kept acomin'. The national depression found Carey Williams a political supporter of Eugene Talmadge, and in 1940 he became a member of the State Board of Education. Throughout the hard times, Carey's pencil was finely pointed:

Now that Uncle Sam shows a deficit, we feel more like the old gentleman is really a relative.

An old-timer is one who can recall when map makers didn't specify that the map was subject to change without notice.

In late 1941 when the mounting differences between the Dies Committee and the Federal Bureau of Investigation was summarily reconciled, Carey said they had "hissed and made up." A few months later, ever alert to current news, he piped, "Another good way to gain the ear of Congress is to make a noise like a labor union," and, "Gas rationing has certainly put many a man on his feet." In his "Tokyo Edition" of the *Herald-Journal* March 14, 1942, he would tolerate no "fifth column," left blank the fifth column on each page of the paper. Greene Countians told Carey it was a clever idea. Again the big dailies took notice—again people asked, "Well, where is this Greensboro, Georgia?"

"Furriners" might not know where Greensboro is, but now for many years no one in Georgia would dare say he knew the state without claiming personal acquaintance with Uncle Jim, who is gone,* and Carey, who carries on.

Cranston Williams, Uncle Jim's older son, has long been outstanding in newspaper circles, is now general manager of the American Newspaper Publishers' Association, lives in New York. Both brothers are listed in *Who's Who in America,* as was their father before them.

---

* Died in 1936.

XVIII

THE OLD ORDER PASSES

Country Editor James Cranston Williams was a transition figure
—he was of the old Greene county, and at the same time a herald
of the new.

BEATING THE "BILLION DOLLAR BANDIT"

Within a decade after the weevil ruined Greene's cotton crop,
Uncle Jim had found a few white and colored farmers who were
growing their own food and feed, and making a fairly good living.
He wrote news stories about them, hoped that others would learn
to do likewise.

But the farmers wanted more than subsistence, they wanted cash
—cash for automobiles, radios, and a trip now and then. Wanted
some new furniture for the living room and a range in the kitchen.
So cotton was relied on again, simply because it was the most certain
crop with which to get some money to spend. By planting the earliest varieties and by heavy use of fertilizer, and sometimes poison,
the bolls could be grown ahead of the weevil. New ways of growing
cotton, neither easy nor cheap, enabled Greene's best farmers to out-
wit the "Billion Dollar Bandit."

In early 1930, the first prize for highest cotton yield in Georgia
went to L. E. Harris of Union Point, who grew 4,955 pounds of lint
cotton on five acres; second prize to E. T. Boswell of Siloam for
4,073 pounds on five acres. Two other prizes went to J. B. Dolvin
and R. S. Underwood, also of near Siloam. The next year A. S.

Moseley, dairy farmer on the outskirts of Greensboro, was chosen as a Master Farmer, one of the ten best farmers in the state.

ILLITERATES AND HARD-SURFACED ROADS

Illiteracy in Greene was first given grand-jury consideration in January, 1930:

Judge Park called our attention to the illiteracy among adults in our state and county. We understand that there are 182 illiterate white adults and about 2,000 illiterate negro adults in our county, which is deplored.

The convict camp was a source of saving to the county. A grand jury of 1932 pointed out that food costs and pay for the guards was but 25 cents a day, and this could be reduced to 15 by raising meats and vegetables on the county farm. Five advantages of convict labor were listed: easy control, work from sun to sun, everybody there ready to go to work on Monday morning, retention of skills learned, convict labor costs only one fourth to one fifth as much as free labor. One grand jury after another recommended screens, lights, and running water for the convict camps. They were finally installed in 1935. An old four-wheeled iron cage which would accommodate up to eighteen men had been enclosed in a shed built alongside the main building. Modern plumbing with hot water and an enclosed iron cage—there they were together, the old and the new.

By operating the county with the greatest possible economy for eleven years, Commissioners Harold Lamb, C. C. King, and H. D. Goodwin announced in 1932 that the county's indebtedness of over $100,000 had been paid off, and that a further reduction of the tax rate could be considered. But it was still difficult to collect taxes on much of the land.

Despite the hard times, new roads were being built in the early 1930's. Eugene Talmadge was Governor. The people here liked his $3.00 automobile tag, and Greene's need for improved roads was at last recognized. The first to be hard-surfaced was the Madison-

Greensboro highway, with concrete bridges over the Appalachee and the Oconee. The old steel bridge across the Oconee was moved down the river to Reid's ferry. A steel bridge had also been built across the Oconee at Watson Springs. At long last, Greene again had three bridges across the Oconee, the number she had in the 1860's when they were destroyed by the outreaches of Sherman's army.

At fifty miles an hour new automobiles sped across the county on new roads. Along the new roads were abandoned farm sites and gullies, sedge and growing pines, and a few successful farmers. Many more worked on and hoped for better times.

GREENE'S NEGROES EVERYWHERE

The ancestors of the Negroes of Greene came from many parts of Africa, saw many parts of eastern America before they were brought here. Now for decades their descendants have been going everywhere. Flournoy Shannon, a successful physician in Kansas, was born and reared in Greensboro. Over washtubs his mother earned the money for him to get an education. During the Harding administration, Salley Inez McWhorter of Greensboro was employed at the White House as personal maid to the nation's First Lady.

Numerous stories were told about the boll weevil exodus. How Negroes went North, got sick, wanted to come home; how it was the dying request of many a migrant that his body be sent back to Greene for burial. Public officials here received inquiries from Family Welfare Associations of distant cities about stranded Negroes who gave this county as their former home, and reported kinsfolk here with whom they might live. City welfare workers usually thought it a good bargain to pay a railroad fare and be rid of a client.

Comparatively few of the total number of migrants have been sent back though, and not many have arranged their own passage, except to visit kinsfolk and friends. Most of them have remained in the cities. Wages there were better when they worked; relief there was better when they didn't.

Migrants found jobs in Ford's River Rouge plant, worked in the steel mills of Pittsburgh or Youngstown, the coal fields of southern Illinois and West Virginia, the packing houses of Chicago and St. Louis. They became ward politicians in a few places, number racket runners in others. They pressed clothes and shined shoes in Atlanta and Philadelphia, sold life insurance in Richmond and Cincinnati, were stevedores at Jacksonville and New Orleans. Most of them were hard working and respectable. Some were thieves and deadbeats, tasted the hot black coffee of rescue homes, felt the "billy" of the night watchman, saw the inside of flophouses and jails. A few bought big automobiles, or homes, or sent their children to college. Most merely eked out a living. All were away from home, and often lonesome and blue.

With others like them, they have supported little storefront chapels in the cheap-rent sections of the big cities. Here they could get together, be priest and potentate, sing and talk as they did back in the cotton South, and pay the monthly rent on their "chapel" with the better wages of the city. With no background of full participation in anything except the church, many migrants have become devotees of Father Divine or Bishop Grace, or of some other dramatic religious cult. Folks back in Greene, educated and illiterate, white and colored, heard of the stories of "peace," "unending feasts," "angels," "heavens"—how far away and strange, and unfathomable. Another world.

WONDERFUL LOVE AT PEACE

Then one day a local merchant opened his mail, and there in his hands was a new kind of letter. The handwriting was typical enough, and so too was the New York address and the "Dear Sir" salutation. But the letter's the thing:

This is to inform you of a small account that I owes you. I made this bill around 8 or 9 years ago. I paid you all but 3 or 4 dollars I declaried that I never would pay you, but I have found God. And he says I must pay you, so I want to pay you   plase send me a statement of it at once. This bill was made in the name of ———— it is on your old record. And I also stole a dipper it was 25¢ I want to pay you for that and I am asking you to forgive me. Let me here from you at once   I thank you very much.

The letter was signed "Miss Wonderful Love," her symbolic name. The merchant put it down, picked it up again, saw the word "Peace" written boldly in the top center of the page. He showed the letter to his associates, looked up the account, and found it to be $2.25 for a suitcase and an umbrella; probably the ones she carried with her when she left.

Within the week a letter went back to Wonderful Love, with a statement of her indebtedness—$2.50 including the dipper—and the acknowledgment that "your letter is so unusual it has made a great impression . . . we assure you we forgive all, and hope your Faith will increase . . ."

But would Wonderful Love pay the bill? Two weeks passed, and three, and then came a letter:

I received your letter   was very glad to here from you, and also received the statement   I am so happy to pay you. Father Divine God Almighty in Bodyly form is here now   he has come to save all mankind and he is causing all men to righting their wrongs and he has caused me to get right with everyone and his spirit is the cause that I am sending you this money. All the credit goes to him so please send the receipt to him so he will see that I have paid you . . . if you send it in with my letter I will give it to him

Write soon and let me know if you received the money.

YoursTruly,

Wonderful Love

In the letter was a money order for $2.50.

Wonderful Love settled an account at another local store, and also sent a money order for ten dollars to a county official, from whom she had borrowed it just before she went North. In repaying the loan, she explained that her religion caused her to do it, and that her religion did not allow her to pay interest. The official was glad enough to get the principal.

The passing of the old order pushed thousands of black folks out of Greene, put them in the kitchens and factories and alleys of America, into the coal mines and slaughter-houses. Away from home they have become sinners and saints and college graduates, "bad niggers," religious fanatics, and substantial citizens. Everything has happened to the Negroes of Greene—in Greene and far away.

PEOPLE—OUR GREATEST EXPORT

Everything has happened to the Whites, too, and much of it has been far away.

Besides the Bowens, other missionaries went from Greene county to foreign fields during the nineteenth century. Rev. J. A. Preston and his wife worked in Indian Territory. Anna Safford, Presbyterian of Greensboro, went to China in 1873. Shortly before 1900 Ella Leveritt, Methodist, of the Greshamville area, also went to China.

About the time of World War I, James G. Boswell of Penfield, retired army officer, stopped farming in the Shiloh neighborhood and went to Kings County, California, to grow and gin cotton. His business prospered, and other people from Greene soon joined him as they felt the "Go West" pull. Dr. John R. McGibony, head of the medical service for the American Indians, and the nationally-known temperance worker, Mary Harris Armour are from Greensboro. The late John Roach Stratton, pastor of New York's Calvary Baptist Church, lived in Greensboro as a boy.

From the Woodville area have gone Davisons, Durhams, McWhorters and others. Best known include R. E. Davison, long-time head of Georgia's Prison Commission; Dr. Hal Davison, who spent three years in Russia during and after World War I, and later became head of the medical staff of the Georgia Baptist Hospital in Atlanta. Asked recently about the origin of "po' white trash" he answered: "Any white family with two generations of malaria and hookworm."

Union Point's leading citizens away from home include Samuel H. Sibley, Federal Judge; A. L. "Fontz" Ivy, son of the town's first mayor, who since 1930 has been president of the Virginia-Carolina Chemical Company; J. Dillard Battle, now secretary of the coal producers' National Coal Association; and Laura M. Smith, personnel representative for women on the general staff of the American Telephone and Telegraph Company.

White Plains' most illustrious away-from-homer is the liberal educator, William Heard Kilpatrick, Professor Emeritus of Teachers College, Columbia University, New York.

Beyond these few, whose names we have mentioned, are thousands of other white people from Greene who have helped swell the population of America's cities.

Try a few experiments: get an ordinary white audience along Peachtree Street or in the cotton mill sections of Atlanta, or a colored audience around Atlanta University or in the slums of the Fourth Ward, and ask for a show of hands of the people born in Greene county. Or look up the home county of the relief clients of the 1930's in a score of cities, or jot down the birthplace of the enlisted men throughout the nation—see how many came from Greene county and other deep South counties like it.

Visit the Bonus Marchers' camp in Washington, D. C., in the early 1930's, and meet Greene county's first volunteer, Edgar D. Wright, and enjoy with him the publicity he got when he propped a dummy in a chair with these words over it: "No food at home— why go 'til 1945."

During its history, Greene county has exported cotton—over a million bales of it. But Greene's greatest export has been people, mostly

Whites from 1800 to 1865; individual Whites and Negroes until near the end of the century; Negroes by the hundreds until World War I. In the post war period whole families by the trainload were pushed out by weevil and deflation, nearly three fourths of them colored. During the 1930's, the migration resumed its individual character —with the able-bodied young men and women the more likely to leave.

Greene's people across the map have made far away dramatic incidents real here. "Why, that's where Sister Mary lives," or "Uncle Joe is out there somewhere," you would hear someone say when the papers headlined a train wreck or a sit-down strike, a hurricane or a race riot.

One of the Boswells who formerly lived here inquired of M. Weinstein, local Jewish merchant, when he was going back to Jerusalem. Weinstein replied, "When all the Boswells go back to Penfield."

ANNO DOMINI 1938

Greene county was no longer young. Greensboro had celebrated its one hundred and fiftieth anniversary, as had also three churches: Bethany, Bethesda, and Liberty. The White Plains Academy and Mercer University had passed their hundredth year. The abandoned cotton factory at Long Shoals stood by the Oconee, with trees inside its weathered brick walls almost as tall as those on the outside. The rock foundations and the last brick arch of the old factory at Scull Shoals appeared to be sinking into the mud of the Oconee bottoms, as one overflow after another deposited its silt.

By 1938 the store buildings at Public Square and Grantville and Jefferson Hall had all burned or rotted down. So had the once-proud plantation homes of many a planter, while others were crumbling and passing from the scene. Well-cared-for and erect stood a few: Jonas Fauche's and Nicholas Lewis' at Greensboro and Joel Early's and Benjamin Weaver's close by, Thomas Wray's at Wrayswood, Redmond Thornton's and Thomas Hart's near Union Point, James

W. Jackson's at Mosquito Crossing, James B. Park's across the Oconee, the pastorium at Penfield, the Judge Tuggle place near Bethesda Church and Bethesda Church itself, the Mercer University buildings at Penfield, the courthouse and other before-the-war brick buildings in Greensboro.

For every one of the old landmarks that were still standing, a half dozen were gone. Most of the free-flowing springs had been buried in sand; giant oaks, pines, and chestnuts in their original forest settings were real only in the minds of such elderly men—white and black—as Judge James B. Park and Alfred "Preacher" Parrott, who seem to have been here always.

The old order was passing. But a few Davis and Barber clocks, made in the Greenesborough of the long ago, still stood on Greene county mantels flawlessly ticking off the time, turning the tomorrows into yesterdays. The county historian, T. B. Rice, in cooperation with the D.A.R. and the U.D.C., had put up historic markers here and there, hoped to put up more.

With the waning of the old order, the grand jury recommended the adoption of the Australian system of balloting, and the installation in the courthouse of a "drinking fountain, electrically cooled." The jury also asked that the County Commissioners "exercise their best efforts toward getting Morgan county to accept as a gracious gift all the land lying on the west side of the Oconee River." The tract of land involved was the acreage J. B. Park, Sr., had had transferred to Greene in 1872. Morgan county was not interested, so the maintenance of the ferryboat at Park's Ferry remained the sole responsibility of Greene.

The cotton seed oil mills at Greensboro, Union Point, and Woodville had gone out of business years before, as had also the fertilizer mixing plants at White Plains and Greensboro. Scheduled busses were transporting more of Greene's people than the trains, and on back country roads and on paved highways more cotton and lumber was carried by motor trucks than by mule-drawn wagons. The textile mills at Union Point and Greensboro had already had their first strike, the National Textile Strike of 1934. The consolidation of the white schools continued—14 in 1930 to 8 in 1938—and the money spent for the transportation of white children had come to be the largest single item in the county's public school expenditures. Negro schools remained much as they had been, with shorter terms than for the Whites, and teachers receiving less than one third the annual salary of the white teachers.

Most of the old-timers were passing on: W. H. Purks and Helen Kilpatrick of White Plains; J. T. Bryson, Judge Gray Lewis, and W. C. Merritt, of Siloam; W. P. "King" McWhorter, of Woodville; B. P. Kimbrough, A. S. Moseley, "Richland Philosopher" John E. Finch, and C. C. Vincent, of Greensboro, who spoke of the Republican tariff as the North's way of "levying tribute" upon the South.

Before the end of the 1930's Thomas and Will Wray of Wrayswood, J. B. "Punch" Dolvin of Siloam, and A. A. "Gus" Kimbrough of Liberty had died. Their plantations had weathered the weevil deflation better than any others in the county, soon showed signs of neglect. Their deaths marked the passing of the last of the old plantations. Said a plantation Negro of Kimbrough: "That man could reach out and ketch people up who nobody else could tetch. Ever since he died, everything around here has been going down. You know how it is when the heart dies, the body is got to perish."

As the plantations declined, Mercer Reynolds bought pine-land by the thousands of acres around old Long Shoals, in late years known as Linger Longer.

The old heads of the big plantations died. Only an occasional young man stepped into their shoes. What was to become of the landless dependent families? Some people were saying they would have to get on work relief. Leading citizens began to discuss the chances of getting the federal government to develop land-use programs in Greene.

As the old went out, the new came in. And down underneath were the land and the people, the seasons and the pines and gullies, new forces and old ideas, pleasure, pain, politics.

XIX

THE NEW DEAL COMES THIS WAY

AFTER THE stock market crash of 1929, the farmers of Greene knew some more years almost as hard as the early Twenties had been. Cotton was cheap and credit was tight.

THERE WAS JUST TOO MUCH COTTON

"Tariff," "Wall Street manipulations," "differential freight rates" were common explanations of the cotton farmer's predicament. The cotton-selling South was chronically in debt to the cotton-buying North and East. And all were agreed that the price of cotton wouldn't go up so long as millions of bales were piled in warehouses.

Gerald K. Smith of Louisiana came to Greene county in early September, 1931. He explained Huey P. Long's plan for making cotton planting illegal for a year. The farmers listened, voted for the plan, did nothing about it.

A month later J. W. Whitley of the near-by town of Warrenton had an article in the *Herald-Journal*. He said the cotton tenant farmer was nearing "the open door to hunger, bankruptcy and slavery":

The Negro race in 1860 were no more in slavery than our white tenant cotton farmers are today . . . They can find no work, no homes to rent and positively not a dime in their pockets for support. They are forced to beg and if you do not feed them they will steal, and if they cannot steal it, they will take it by force, and your jails will not hold those helpless men, women, and children.

In the early 1930's the County Farm Agent of Greene was serving a new function. He was accepting applications for the feed, seed, and fertilizer loans started by the Hoover Administration for farmers who otherwise would be unable to plant a crop. By the spring of 1932 nearly 200 loans, averaging $130 each, had been made. The next years saw the number increase.

For farmers with credit resources, the Piedmont Agricultural Credit Corporation was set up. Then came the RFC loans, which by 1931 were making $55,000 available for the farmers.

In the spring of 1933, the New Deal was reaching Greene. In May of that year twenty-six boys, all white, went away to Civilian Conservation Camps. In June came word that 3,000 acres of cotton must be plowed up. For it that fall and winter, Greene's farmers received over $40,000 in checks ranging from $8 to $700.

The businesses of the county were under the NRA blanket code. In late July, Blue Eagles were in every store window. Many a businessman was, as it were, up a tree—he was a Democrat and wanted to be loyal to the program of the Democratic Administration in Washington; but he was also a deep South Southerner, little accustomed to regulation and emotionally averse to being told what wage to pay his workers, especially the colored ones.

By early winter of 1933, the emergency relief office here had put to work forty white men and sixty-four colored. The rate of pay was thirty cents an hour, the highest wage rate in the county. Over 1,200 people registered when the CWA work-program was launched. Less than one tenth of these were given work.

Money might be ever so scarce in Greene County, but there was money by the millions somewhere, for in early March, 1934, Davis and Jack Pittard, sons of a Greensboro garage man, expected to share in a $12,000,000 fortune. They hoped for about a million dollars each. They didn't get it.

That spring, cotton acreage was cut from 20,000 acres to 16,500. The government rent for each unplanted acre brought to the county nearly $45,000 that fall and winter. Four hundred feed, seed, and fertilizer loans were made. Fifteen farm families—twelve white and three colored—were on the Rural Rehabilitation program of the Resettlement Administration. This agency made loans to farmers unable to secure credit from any other source for the production of a crop, and provided year-round supervision for its borrowers.

By the middle of that year, 140 families were on relief. The local relief administrator asked for five hundred cattle from the drought-seared West, and some months later a cannery was set up at Siloam to process the meat.

WORK RELIEF AND SUBMARGINAL LAND

In the fall of 1934 relief projects had been started throughout the county. School grounds were improved, ditches were cleaned out, sidewalks straightened up, and Ciceronian Hall of old Mercer University renovated and presented to the public school at Penfield. Of the $43,633 spent on federal relief projects through March, 1935, more than half of it was for projects, such as schools, that served white people only, and less than one twentieth that served Negroes only. The other projects, such as drainage, were of a general nature and served both races.

In August, 1934, W. A. Hartman of the U. S. Department of Agriculture opened an office at Eatonton, with plans to study the development of an extensive submarginal land project that was to extend beyond Putnam county to Greene, Morgan, and Jasper. The Greene county grand jury that fall requested Senator Richard B. Russell and Congressman Paul Brown "to use their influence in securing an allotment to establish a national park in Greene county."

In late 1934 the Child Health and Welfare Association was organized, with T. B. Rice as chairman. A county-wide plan was launched to give free immunization to all children against diphtheria and typhoid. Dr. Rice reported that the plan evolved here was soon adopted widely by the Red Cross. Tuberculosis clinics were later organized.

The government program raised the price of cotton from $37.50 a bale in 1932 to $80 in 1934, including seed and government payments. For many of the smaller farmers this rise in price made little difference in income, for they still had small yields on now few acres, and the government payments did not always reach them. Late in 1936 the Soil Conservation Association was organized. Nearly $100,000 was paid to the farmers of Greene that year for cooperation in the federal farm programs.

The need to control forest fires had led to the organization in 1933 of the Woodville Timber Protective Association, and in 1935 to the Greene County Timber Fire Protective Association.

Early in 1937 the NYA appeared in Greene, helped twenty-one high school and eighteen college students to the amount of $331 per month. Not half of the applicants could be served.

For poll tax defaulting, as reported in the *Herald-Journal,* May 21, 1937, over 1,700 voters were stricken from the county lists. Practically all these were Whites, for even before this there had been but thirty-five Negroes on the registration lists.

Efforts had first been made to get a CCC camp in 1934. Two years later the Greensboro Lions Club began to agitate for a camp, and in early June, 1937 a committee from the Club went to Washington to see CCC officials there. In the meantime, the Rural Electrification Association had begun its program, putting electric wires into areas heretofore not reached.

By the middle of 1937, the courthouse was being renovated and enlarged. A bond election for $15,000 was voted down. The county was in relatively good financial condition, and so arranged with pride to pay the whole cost.

The Bankhead-Jones farm tenant purchase bill was then before the U. S. Congress, and on July 2, 1937, the *Herald-Journal* pointed out that Greene might benefit from it, for "It is understood that federal officials have Greene county in mind in regard to a resettlement project if the bill passes." The bill did pass, and Greene county was listed for five to ten loans to tenant farmers who wanted to buy farms of their own.

Greene then had 412 people totally unemployed, 102 on federal emergency relief projects, 395 partly employed who desired full-time work. About seventy-five farm families—one third of them colored —were being financed and supervised in 1937 by the Rural Rehabilitation program of the Farm Security Administration. There were 146 the next year. The families on this program were commonly referred to as "government farmers" or "Rehabs," sometimes as "A-rabs."

UNSCHOOLED IN DECEPTION

Greene was bearing its share, and more, of the national depression, but its people were not without hope. Unschooled in deception, they listened to a stranger's searching questions, and answered them as best they could. Only a few people saw the questioner, and some of them did not remember his name when he was gone—until in *Collier's* of January 1, 1938, appeared "Devil in de Cotton," by Owen P. White. The *Herald-Journal* censured *Collier's* for "parading our poverty." The grand jury condemned "in strongest terms, the scurrilous, unwarranted, and most unnecessary article." Judge James B. Park answered the piece in the *Atlanta Constitution* on January 9, 1938, by citing the performances of some of the county's most successful farmers; County Historian Rice wrote a defense of Greene county, which Congressman Paul Brown read into the *Congressional Record* of January 16, 1938.

One year after another the farmers of Greene had voted on crop limitation. In the spring of 1938 a total of 996 votes were cast, and all but thirty-eight favored the program. In the soil district election that year, only thirteen out of 239 landowners voted against it. The farm folk of the county were cooperating in the federal program.

E. H. Downs of the Georgia Farm Security Administration office came into the county about this time to observe the farm program then under way, and to make recommendations for its further development.

The towns, too, were cooperating in the government programs. All of them had had their streets, sidewalks and schoolgrounds improved by the relief projects. Then, in mid-1938, Greensboro received $15,750 assistance from the PWA with which to erect an auditorium-gymnasium.

NO MORE PAUPERS

The county no longer doled out checks of $1.50 or $2.00 a month to about 75 paupers. The County Welfare Board had been organized, and was giving Old-Age Assistance to 119 Whites and 111 Negroes, aid to 11 dependent white children, to 2 blind Whites and 1 blind Negro. The Old-Age Assistance clients were receiving a little over $7 a month. Dr. Rice, chairman of the Board, appeared before the grand jury in July, 1938 and stated that the government would not permit a smaller monthly amount, and that there was no truth in the report that Negroes were getting more than their share of the old-age benefits. Altogether nearly $2,000 was being spent each month, with but one half the white and one fourth the colored applicants served. The county's tenth for this new program was about equal to the cost of the pauper fund it replaced. But now over three times as many people were helped, and each received more than three times as much as a pauper had received.

The Welfare office's other duties were to select relief clients, CCC boys, WPA workers, and persons to get Surplus Commodities.

The grand jury of January, 1938 asked that the County Commissioners consider the purchase of terracing machinery "to be used at cost . . . for the benefit of the landowner as our best means of correcting the eroded condition of our lands." This jury also asked the county authorities to cooperate "in establishing a state and federal soil conservation district," the adoption of the Ellis Health Law, the use of county police to ferret out forest fire starters and "to hire help when necessary in fighting such fires." This jury also recommended that the County Commissioners "look into the advisability of using all the lands bought in for taxes, as a forestry investment project, to give homes and employment as care-takers to the needy who do not come under the state welfare aid."

FARM PROGRAMS EXPAND

In late 1938 the Extension Service had two white employees and one colored. They urged the farmers to grow and preserve foods, and plant soil-building crops. The Soil Conservation Service had six supervisors at work, and funds on hand to purchase during the next year 8,500 acres of submarginal land for pastures and woodlands. The AAA was distributing benefits of around $100,000 a year.

The Farm Security Administration had a staff of five to administer the Rural Rehabilitation Program, and to help selected tenants become landowners through Tenant-Purchase. E. H. Downs of the FSA talked with leading people throughout the county, asked how they thought the farm programs could be improved. A great deal of interest developed out of the trip with Downs to Coffee County, Alabama, where the FSA had a county-wide program. The visitors came home enthusiastic, talked about getting a county-wide program started here.

Hamp McGibony, chairman of the Board of County Commissioners, expressed the hope that the local, state, and federal agencies would work out a more intensive program for this county. The Commissioners agreed to put up the county funds necessary for the Ellis Health Law when the third grand jury, as provided by law, had recommended it. The physicians of the county wanted to develop a county-wide public health program.

Greene's school officials became interested in having agriculture and home economics taught in the schools. Robert Vansant of the state FSA office spoke to the Greensboro Lions in early November, 1938. Shortly afterwards it was announced that the FSA would cooperate with the County Board of Education and the WPA in the erection of five vocational buildings at the white schools and two four-room colored schools.

In the fall of 1938, representatives of the Extension Service and of the Bureau of Agricultural Economics discussed the setting up of a county planning organization. For lack of funds, this was deferred until early the next year.

STANDING SIDE BY SIDE

By this time the old and the new were standing together in Greene. Tenant-Purchase homes of the new government program were alongside slave plantation houses. Relief clients were paid more than farm wage hands. Surplus Commodities, distributed free to needy people, were often carried past plantation stores. Land-owners who had always taken care of their labor during the slack-work seasons now helped them get on relief over the winter. Hundreds of men, white and colored, ineligible to vote because of the poll tax requirement and the White Primary, stood shoulder to shoulder and cast their ballots in the cotton allotment elections, with more than one landless man reporting that he had been told to vote for control if he wanted to farm next year.

Some of the county politicians feared the precedent of letting all the cotton farmers vote, but feared more to take a stand against the government program, with its crop-reduction payments, rehabilitation loans to stranded farmers, cash wages to the unemployed, checks to the old people and Surplus Commodities for the needy.

The new order had come; the old order remained. Some people liked the new, hoped it could last; others liked the old, hoped it would not pass.

Perhaps above all else, the people of Greene had learned that things are not always just what they seem. By 1938 they knew that the prosperity of their best years—1914 to 1920—was far from adequate, and that their hardest years—1921 to 1933—had not been so barren as they had thought. They knew at last that when cotton prices were high their lands were growing thinner. They knew, too, that the million million little pines that came after the weevil deflation would soon be big enough to saw and sell. Most important of all, the people had tried different crops and formed new organizations. True enough, most of these efforts had failed, but enough of them had succeeded for hopes to rise again in late 1938, when plans were discussed for developing a Unified Farm Program in Greene.

PART FIVE

WORKING TOGETHER

XX

A NEW DAY

THE SPOTLIGHT was on Greene county by the end of 1938. It was being talked of in the U. S. Department of Agriculture as a demonstration area in which county, state, and federal agencies would work together in a new way. A county-wide Unified Farm Program was under consideration. The agricultural agencies here and the county leaders liked the idea. So, too, did Senator Richard B. Russell and Congressman Paul Brown of the Tenth District.

THE FARMERS MAKE A PLAN

When it had been determined in early 1939 that a Unified Farm Program would be developed in Greene, the first step was to plan the program. Twenty-one local people from various sections of the county were asked by the State Land-Use Planning Committee to serve as a County Program Planning Committee. R. B. Weil, a farmer of Greshamville, was chairman. Representatives of the agencies already at work here served as advisors. This committee thought it needed first to find out the best uses for the county's 266,000 acres. It created a Land-Use Planning Committee of twelve farmers, D. B. Taylor, of near Greensboro, chairman.

Taylor's committee spent two days making a hurried inspection of the county. It then decided that in each community a committee of local farmers would be asked to determine the best use of the land. When these local committees had finished their work, a map of the county was made showing the areas that should be cultivated and those that should be retired to permanent pastures or forests.

The committee recommended that intensive erosion control be used in about two thirds of the county. Most of the county's uplands had already been terraced, but only one tenth of it had been done correctly. Erosion was worse in the red-land sections of the county, but the committee warned that the newer white lands are naturally more susceptible to erosion and, without proper treatment, would soon be in as bad a condition as the red lands.

With these facts before them, the farmers and their technical assistants recommended tested methods of erosion control, the fertilizing of present pastures, and development of pastures on additional open lands and certain types of woodlands.

The family-type farm was recommended. About 150 acres was thought to be the best size, though a smaller acreage might in some instances be adequate; 300-acre units would be needed if farm machinery was to be used effectively.

Looking squarely at the farm people and their past experience, the committee reported that "only about 20 percent of the white tenants and sharecroppers, and 10 percent of the colored are now qualified to operate successfully as owners."

The Land-Use Committee felt that any farm program worked out for the sharecroppers and tenants would need to provide year-round supervision along with financial assistance. A major part of the program, the committee thought, should deal with the improvement of landlord-tenant relations.

SOMETHING TO SEE

By early 1939 the program was developing rapidly. Nearly $50,000 was being spent for the purchase of submarginal lands. The number of families on FSA was upped from 146 to over 530. The grand jury recommended, for the third time, the passage of the Ellis Health Law, and the Commissioners appropriated the county's share of the funds to begin work. Arrangements had been made for the hiring of a dozen agricultural and home economics teachers, and the school building program was getting under way. Word came that the Negro CCC camp at Monticello would be transferred to Greene, and that it would be used in the county's soil conservation work.

In early spring the Georgia Academy of Social Sciences made a visit to Greene to see the program at first hand. Dr. Cullen B. Gosnell of Emory University, president of the Academy, and some fifty members motored down, were met in Greensboro by representatives of the agencies at work here. Members of the Academy were interested to hear that county leaders had helped make the plans for the county program; that they were taking an active part in the development of the health service, the improvement of the schools, and the efforts to lengthen the tenure of farm tenants and make their houses and diets more adequate. After making a brief excursion through the county, the motorcade proceeded to Augusta to hear a speech that night by Dr. W. W. Alexander, head of the Farm Security Administration.

Alexander spoke of his recent visit to Denmark, and about the progress the Danish farmers had made. Less than one hundred years ago the great bulk of Denmark's farm people had been in much the same situation as the tenants and wage hands in the Southeast. The Danish farmers themselves, through cooperative programs, had multiplied the number of farmowners, eliminated illiteracy, improved their health, and developed an international market for their high-grade farm products. In short, the Danes had made a garden of their little country. He expressed the belief that the same kind of advancement could be made in the Southeast, and that the program being developed in Greene county was an effort to move in that direction.

THE FSA ADMINISTRATOR KNEW GREENE

Alexander's interest in Greene county went back several years. In 1927, as director of the Commission on Interracial Cooperation, in Atlanta, he was wondering why Georgia should be losing its rural population more rapidly than any other state. He asked Arthur Raper, an assistant, to determine which county or counties had lost most heavily. Raper found that the area with greatest losses lay midway between Atlanta and Augusta and that Greene and Putnam counties had lost most. Greene was chosen for an intensive study. For purposes of comparison, a county which had lost practically no population was also to be studied. Macon county, 150 miles to the southwest, was selected.

For a period of two years, Raper spent at least two thirds of his time in these counties, visited all the schools, collected records at the courthouse, filled in questionnaires for hundreds of families, talked with people, white and colored, in the fields and in their homes, at the stores and churches, and on hunting and fishing trips.

The facts showed that the great population losses in Greene were caused by the breaking up of the cotton plantation system. The study also revealed the need for better houses and health, improved educational facilities, and above all else an increase of family incomes and the conservation of the soil.

Soon after the coming of the New Deal, Alexander again sent Raper to Greene and Macon counties to see what was happening. Several more months were spent collecting information. In 1936 the findings were published in *Preface to Peasantry*. Alexander wrote the Foreword, emphasized the meaning of the breakdown of the plantation, pleaded for the restoration of the soil and the rehabilitation of the people.

In the meantime, Alexander had had other trained people collecting detailed information about Southern agricultural conditions. Among them were Rupert B. Vance, of the University of North Carolina, and Charles S. Johnson, of Fisk University, Nashville. In late 1935, a summary of these wider studies was published, *The Collapse of Cotton Tenancy*.

Alexander knew the basic problems of the rural South, had ideas about what might be done. Rexford G. Tugwell asked him to come to Washington to assist in the development of the work of the Resettlement Administration. He went to Washington in the fall of 1935. When the Resettlement Administration was reorganized, Alexander was put in charge of the Farm Security Administration.

As FSA Administrator, Alexander remembered the counties in the Southeast which had been hardest hit by the single cash crop of cotton, by boll weevil and deflation, and later by national depression. He knew the potentialities of the farm people in the deep South could be developed only when counties like Greene had programs which met their real needs. So back of Ed Downs' coming to Greene in mid-1938, and back of the common sense approach which Downs followed here was Alexander, who had made it clear that he wanted the FSA to cooperate with all agencies—county, state, and federal—in developing programs best suited to Greene county.

THE BRIGHT NEW WAGONS ROLL

Things began to happen in Greene county when the Unified Farm Program was begun early in 1939. Government experts looked at the land and suggested what ought to be done, looked at the landowners and farm tenants, and made more recommendations. The farmers, too, made suggestions; some were addressed to themselves, others to the county authorities, still others to state and federal agencies. The programs of well-established agencies were revitalized, new programs were launched. The farmers and their wives and children had more meetings to attend, more programs to follow, more records to keep—more things to do and think about, less time to sit.

Under the Unified County Program there was an increase of soil-building crops, terraced fields, strip farming. Kudzu and sericea were planted in waterways and on spent hillsides, and eroded lands were retired to forests. New farm dwellings were built, old ones repaired, sanitary privies installed. Screens were put at windows and doors, pumps in wells. There were new barns, too, and permanent fences, pastures cleared and fertilized for additional cows and calves. More brood sows and fattening hogs, brooders for baby chicks, and crates full of eggs for the market. Bigger sweet potato hills, larger gardens, pressure cookers by the hundreds and glass jars by the hundred thousands. New schoolhouses and vocational buildings, better-trained teachers, hot lunch programs, a county library and a bookmobile. School children examined, lined up for "shots" by public nurses. Public clinics for expectant mothers, and for well babies; clinics to get rid of syphilis; clinics to keep from having diphtheria and typhoid.

When the new wagons of the farm program began to roll on dirt roads and on paved highways, new paint began to appear on town houses, especially on those of the general merchants and mule dealers. The leading lawyers and the Clerk of Court were more active than before, new Venetian blinds hung in the windows at the bank, beauticians were added at the beauty shops, and larger stocks were ordered by the hardware and furniture dealers. Doctors and druggists and dentists were busier after the Health and Dental Care Associations had been organized; and with the launching of the Veterinary Association, the veterinarian went to farm yards he had never visited before.

There was more activity everywhere. An air of accomplishment could be seen in the faces of the townsfolk as sale of farm equipment and supplies rose. There was hope, too, on the face of many a farmer—white or black—as he turned toward the county seat to qualify for AAA payments, for an FSA Rehabilitation Loan or Tenant-Purchase contract, for TVA lime and phosphate for his land or for a new CCC fence around his cow pasture. A farmer might have eroded land for sale that one government agency would buy, or better land that would be appraised and purchased by another agency. Without land or a farm, many a man and woman looked to the county welfare office in Greensboro for an Old-Age Assistance check and Surplus Commodities. Many made inquiries about the

CCC and NYA for their willing but idle maturing children. Some desired only that they be certified to WPA.

The new farm dwellings and barns, schoolhouses and vocational buildings, fences and pastures meant more jobs in the county, more chances for the people of Greene to work and live here. A world of things have been done in the past four years. A larger world of things still remain to be done.

FROM JOEL EARLY'S ORCHARDS TO WASHINGTON, D. C.

The things which have been done are not new. The roots of the Unified Farm Program go far back into the checkered history of Greene. In 1800 Joel Early left specific instructions in his will for the care of his orchards and fields. Thomas Stocks was first president of the Southeastern Agricultural Society in the 1840's, and in the 1850's Judge Garnett Andrews spoke of the severe erosion of the soil. Dr. Thomas P. Janes, in the 1870's, was the first head of Georgia's Department of Agriculture, the first in the nation. The Populists agitated for more landowners and lower interest rates on small loans; shortly after 1900, G. C. Torbet laid off bench-terraces on over 1,000 acres, spoke of soil erosion as "the cancer of agriculture."

The first cooperation of local, state, and federal agencies came a little later in the effort to get rid of the Texas tick fever. In the early 1910's, the county cooperated with the U. S. Department of Agriculture in the employment of its first County Farm Agent, J. L. Brown, and then Edward Odum and Jack Hart. A little later philanthropist N. O. Nelson, of New Orleans, provided the funds for the first home demonstration work in the county, carried on by Flora Brown, then by Ruth Williams, and Estelle Colclough. Ruby Thompson, employed cooperatively by the county board of education and the Extension Service, was the first to wear the title of Home Demonstration Agent of Greene County. In 1919 a detailed soil survey was made by the U. S. Department of Agriculture and the State College of Agriculture at Athens. And across these years Uncle Jim Williams in his *Herald-Journal* kept on advocating family-size farms and soil conservation.

We have noted the many evidences of deep and right thinking about agriculture by the men of Greene in recent years, and in the long ago. But the good ideas expressed usually failed to become prevailing practices.

Most farmers felt that prices were against them, and that they had little choice but to get what money they could at the end of the year, even if they did keep on exploiting the soil, even if they did fail again to make the repairs on buildings and fences which they knew were needed.

Involved, too, has been the fact of the two races—most of the Whites never quite willing to do all the work for themselves, and never quite able to get the Negro to do it for them in a profitable way.

In thin soil and gullies the land records its neglect; in weakened bodies and dwarfed hopes, society records its own inhumanities. Here and there were acres as rich as they ever were, and everybody knew it would be better if there were more good acres. People there were with good health, energy to spare, and unfailing honesty and hope. And there might be more of them if more families had bigger gardens, more cows, better schools, and medical care.

The job of planning for the decade was too big for the local leaders. So they, the rightful heirs of earlier leaders, assisted the federal government in developing a program to meet the needs of Greene.

Nowadays we look back on the right things that have been advocated by the men of Greene, realize we have in the county the land and people for good farm homes. And so the Unified Farm Program is the logical next step. It marks a new day—in an old calendar.

XXI

COUNTY AGENTS AND FARM SUBSIDIES

GREENE's Unified Farm Program has been made possible by the working together of many local, state, and federal agencies. Some, like the Extension Service of the Department of Agriculture, are quite old. Some, such as the Federal Land Bank and the Land Bank Commission, the RFC, and emergency crop loans, date back to pre-New Deal days. Many others came only when Roosevelt agreed to remember the "forgotten man": the CCC, PWA, WPA, NYA, Social Security and Surplus Commodities. Through all of these channels, Greene has received help with her program.

Most important of all have been the various agencies of the Department of Agriculture: besides the Extension Service, the Agricultural Adjustment Administration, Farm Security Administration, the Bureau of Agricultural Economics, the Soil Conservation Service, Forestry Service, the Farm Credit Administration, and the Office of Land-Use Coordination.

These federal services, with their long high-sounding names, are becoming as much a part of the history of Greene as the first bridge across the Oconee, or the first cotton gins, or the cotton mills. Anyone who wants to understand the Unified Farm Program as a whole must know what is being done, agency by agency.*

LIVESTOCK LOANS AND 4-H CLUBS

As he made the emergency crop loans year after year, County Agent Francis Bowen had faced the plight of the poorer farmers.**

* See Appendix, No. 16, for Lee Coleman's study of Community Organization and Agricultural Plowing in Greene County, Georgia.
** See Appendix, No. 17, for facts about Emergency Crop Loans in 1941–1942.

He administered the AAA program up until 1938, and so knew all the farmers of the county. For the last several years he and the Home Demonstration Agent have carried on their programs under the supervision of county committees. Their experiences with committee work made them useful in setting up the county-wide program, and especially in the work of the planning committee.

The work of the County Agent has been expanded with the development of the Program. In the very next year more soil-building legumes were distributed to the farmers. Austrian peas, for example, were increased from 15 tons in 1939 to nearly 25 tons in 1940, vetch from 2½ tons to 20 tons. The amount of fertilizer distributed through his office was also greatly increased—limestone from 80 to 120 tons, phosphates from none to 40 tons, basic slag by the carload.

In the fall of 1939, Bowen began to arrange livestock loans through the Twin-State Livestock Association of Augusta. About 150 loans have been made, ranging from $40 to $1,000. The borrowers have made money on their livestock. Only one small loan has not been collected when due.

Another activity of the County Agent has been the development of a forest fire program in cooperation with E. V. Brender and George Powers of the Soil Conservation Service. This project is an example of how agencies that are doing related but different tasks can handle together a job they are all interested in but could not handle alone.

One of the oldest phases of the Extension program in the county is the 4-H Club work, conducted by the two agents jointly for boys and girls in each of the county's eight white schools. The membership is around 425, nearly two thirds of them sons and daughters of tenant farmers. The Clubs meet monthly during school hours. Student officers preside, games are played and a demonstration is given related to the projects the children are carrying on at home.

Victory gardens are most popular with the boys, pigs second, then poultry. Clothing projects take first place among the girls, then gardening, poultry, and food preservation. A poultry project involves the hatching or buying and raising of twenty-five or more chickens. Records are kept of the feeds consumed, and of the friers and eggs used or sold. Poultry projects will perhaps become even more popular, for the Agents now supervise the Club members in grading and marketing high class fresh eggs. It is with pride that the 4-H Clubber learns from a kinsman in Atlanta that his eggs are attractively marked "4-H Club, Greene County," and that they sell at a premium price.

THE SCIENCE OF HOMEMAKING

The Home Demonstration Agent has clubs for women at ten points in the county, with a total membership of over 400. Once a month they meet and discuss gardens, poultry, cooking, canning, sewing or other things of interest to housekeepers. The Clubs serve in a double way: they provide helpful instruction, and an opportunity for pleasant social contacts for women who spend nearly all of their time at work in the home.

Nelle Thrash, the present Agent, reports that twenty-six women are now keeping home account books, and a score are improving their kitchens. The prize winner in canning this year had put up over a thousand quarts. The prize for the best scrap book went to Josie Maddox Graham, who handed in a 300 page book.

On the rolls of the Clubs are represented one half of the white farm families of the county, including over fifty women from families on the FSA. About half of all Club members are from farm tenant families.

Even before the tire and gas shortage, it was impossible for many isolated farm men and women to attend meetings they might be interested in. Now the need is still greater for some form of cheap transportation at least monthly into the community centers.

PROGRAMS FOR NEGRO MEN AND CHILDREN

In 1935, a Negro County Agent, C. L. Tapley, began work in Greene and two nearby counties.

Agent Tapley has cooperated in the annual meetings of the State Negro Farmers Conference. In 1937 he assisted Miles Hackney, Negro landowner, to organize at his farm the Conference's first field meeting. Officials of some of the federal farm programs participated in this meeting, explained the work of their agencies, answered questions, ate the barbecue prepared for them. But that was not all. The officials listened to the colored farmers as they told of their hard lot, or as they related the successes they had had. Soon after this meeting, Agent Tapley began to give his full time to Greene county. And Hackney later served as collaborator to the AAA, with travel account but no salary, to explain the program to Negro farmers. Hackney attributes his success as an explainer to the fact that he understands the AAA. Says Hackney: "You can't teach people what you don't know, any more than you can come back from where you ain't been."

Negro 4-H Clubs are now organized in 17 of the larger Negro schools, with over 700 boys and girls enrolled. About half of the colored members do not have bona fide projects. Agent Tapley feels there is an advantage, however, in getting youths into the Clubs even if they can do no more than claim as their own one or two of the family's dozen hens, or a row of beans across the garden.

Gardens are the most popular project among the colored boys and girls. Several boys have calves, fourteen have pure bred pigs, and many have poultry projects. Melvin and Milton Stephens of Woodville made the headlines at the Augusta Fat Cattle Show in 1940, and again in 1941 by winning prizes with their white-face steers. Cattleman Smith, operator of the Fat Cattle Show, said Melvin's prize winner was about as fine a calf as he had ever seen.

Last year Agent Tapley arranged through County Agent Bowen for twenty-six livestock loans for 4-H Club members from the Twin-State Livestock Association. All livestock loans to Negroes have been collected when due.

Farm Agent Tapley serves the adult Negro farmers in much the same way that Agent Bowen does the white farmers. Robert E.

Lewis, Negro farmowner near White Plains, heads up Tapley's advisory board. The Negro women are without a program, for the county has no Negro Home Demonstration Agent.

In the spring of 1942 all three Extension Service workers, in cooperation with other agencies, held "Food for Victory" meetings throughout the county. A little later the Agents were setting up Neighborhood Leadership Organizations, white and colored, to reach everyone quickly with information that farmers might need in war time.

The Technical Workers' Group, of which Bowen is president, and the County War Board discussed the county production goals. The farmers planted more than usual, and have hopes of better prices than in many years.

SUBSIDIES OF OVER $700,000

The farmers of Greene have needed better prices, and have been willing to limit production and to cooperate in soil building programs to secure the AAA benefit checks. The program has brought nearly three quarters of a million dollars to the farmers since 1933. The largest amount distributed in any one year was $126,000 in 1938.

Since 1939, the AAA program has been administered by W. M. Jernigan, a White Plains farmer, with the help of three county committeemen and twelve community committeemen, elected by the farmers. Over $88,600 was distributed in 1940.*

A CHANCE TO BUILD THE SOIL—OR JUST TO SIT

The AAA has been a life-saver to many producers, large and small. It made it easy for them to increase subsistence farming and thus reduce cash expenditures. They could give more attention to soil-building crops and practices, and could use their rental and

---

* For numbers of participating farmers, and size of payments, see Appendix No. 18.

parity payments to buy farm equipment. With more soil-building crops and better equipment, yields could be upped enough to compensate for part, or all, of the reduced acreage in cotton.

"You can take a little land," said one farmer, "and work it as much as you would a whole lot of land, and make just about as much."

To other farmers the AAA program has been worth little, for they have not turned their released land or time to the production of food and feed, or to the conservation of the soil. They remain all-cotton farmers, and still secure their same low yields. Most of these are tenant farmers who have no tradition of self-support, and who feel little security in their tenure situation. They are not interested in soil improvement, for they may move at the end of the year. They are uninterested, too, in growing their own food and feed, because they have always lived from hand to mouth, and the cotton they produced has almost regularly gone to their creditors for debts they incurred while growing the crop. The chief difference the AAA program has made to these farmers is that they have had more time to sit, and sit.

Is it not likely though that the AAA, if it had the personnel, could get some of these families to take advantage of the program? Long-time leases alone might suffice in some instances; in others, practical demonstrations would do; while for others, nothing short of constant supervision will be of value.

The distribution of the benefits of the AAA program has been no small job in itself. There has been much tedious detail in determining the exact acreage which each farmer would be allowed to plant to cotton. The farmers regularly voted for the program, and understood the necessity of restricted planting. Yet, some farmers have continued to feel that their own acreages are too small.

The County AAA Committee as time has passed, however, has convinced most cotton growers that, farm to farm, a fair allotment has been made. Aerial photographs have proved helpful in locating all fields and in determining acreages.

The farmers generally feel that the cotton allotment for Greene as a whole has been altogether too low, that the county has been unjustly penalized because of her poor cotton record during the late 1920's and early 1930's. Repeated efforts have been made to increase the county's allotment, but to no avail—"rules is rules."

ALL CHECKS ACCEPTED, BUT TWO

Many farmers in the county have fretted under the AAA's crop control measures. When the government checks came, such objections as there have been were dropped. Only two farmers, the late Sam Turner and his son J. N. Turner, of Liberty, have refused to accept the AAA checks. They thought it was wrong for a farmer to be paid for doing his duty—wrong to accept from the government money for soil-building programs and crop control which the farmer ought to do of his own accord. Mercer Reynolds, who lives in Chattanooga and owns more land in this county than any other man, lets his AAA checks go to the families who live on his extensive acreage—most of it in pines.

The farmers of Greene got from the AAA in 1940 not only parity and rental checks amounting to over $88,000, but large quantities of soil-building legumes and fertilizers—45 tons of Austrian peas, 361 tons of limestone, 53 tons of superphosphate, and 68½ tons of basic slag. To make these soil-building items the more attractive to the farmers, the AAA allowed the farmer, for example, $4 a ton to put out the limestone that it had sold to him at $2.60 a ton. Superphosphates and basic slag cost the farmer almost no money, for the subsidy paid to him for spreading them on his fields is almost equal to their price.

EVERY FARMER HAS A VOTE

Although the AAA program does not reach the farm wage hands, and some tenants have never thought they received their full share, it has helped many a farmer in Greene increase his income and improve his land. It has also afforded farmers—little and big, white and black—an opportunity to express their choices in elections, and to ask questions in the community meetings which are held to explain the year's program. And there is meaning in this participation, even if tenant farmers have sometimes been warned by landlords to vote for the program if they wanted to farm the next year; even if on a chilly morning the white farmers stand close about the stove while the Negro farmers sit around the outer edges of the room.

The important thing is this: the propertyless and voteless cotton farmers, white and black, are voting—often uninstructed—along with the landowners. Landlords and tenants are meeting to discuss the farm program, and all are encouraged to ask questions and state their points of view. Now that we are in war, the experience the farmers have had in AAA elections and meetings assumes added meaning. By reason of having taken part in the AAA program, the farmers can now be more articulate and responsible participants in the "food for victory" campaigns.

XXII

TO PROTECT THIS LAND AND THESE TREES

MATT WRIGHT, JR., and E. H. Armour, Jr., scions of two old Greene county families stood on the Oconee bridge when the river was in flood. Said Wright to Armour: "See, there goes Greene county under the bridge." "Yes," nodded E. H., "and it's too thick to drink and too thin to plow!"

Greene county land continues to wash, but real beginnings have been made to stop it. Thousands of acres have been terraced already by the Soil Conservation Service, and plans have been made for many more terraces. Strip-farming and soil-building crops have been increased.

Some of the land is too spent to respond to soil-building crops. It is being retired from cultivation.

"SOCIAL SECURITY" FOR WORN-OUT LANDS

Cotton has been the nation's greatest export crop and the nation's greatest consumer of soil fertility. The red-lands of Greene are old in the service of cotton. Now the eroded acres are being "retired" by the government—a sort of "social security" for worn-out lands to sit down and rest for a century or two.

To buy up this tired land and develop permanent forests and pastures on it, the North Central Georgia Land-Utilization Project Number 22 was set up. The land is called "submarginal"—below the margin of cultivation. The Project embraces the severely eroded lands along the Oconee and Appalachee rivers in Greene, Morgan, Oconee, and Oglethorpe counties. Priorities of land purchases in the

Project have been given Greene, because of the Unified Farm Program, and 85 percent of the land purchased thus far is here. Nearly 30,000 acres, in eighty-five tracts, have been bought. Most of this acreage is in the northwest section of the county, and includes about one fourth of all the land in this severely eroded area.

The people in Greene seem well pleased with the Land-Use Project. First of all, it brought to the owners of these eighty-five tracts a total of $164,574. Over two thirds of the land sold to the government was owned by people who lived in Greene or adjoining counties; of the remaining owners, two were in New York, three in Edinburgh, Scotland, and one in South America.

Most of the Project land is in second-growth pines, and had been cut over in recent years. The people who owned it could get no further timber income from it now, and seldom had an opportunity to sell it. Much of the land was under mortgage; on seven of the larger plantation tracts there were debts of almost $25,000. The average price paid was $6.17 an acre, just a little below the government appraisers' price.

The county authorities look with favor on the Project. The various owners paid well over $5,000 in back taxes to qualify their lands for purchase. Then, too, the government's payment to the county for one fourth the income from the Project will likely exceed the tax revenue which the county could have got off the land.

As planned, the income will increase from year to year, for when the timber matures it will be sold on a sustained-yield basis. Pastures will also be developed. Already there have been 116 acres planted in kudzu, 23 in sericea, 36 in lespedeza, 150 acres of pasture have been developed, and 250 acres have been planted in trees, mostly pine seedlings. Additional acreage will be developed until all the land in the Project—except a few small acreages especially adapted to cultivation—is either growing timber or is in perennial vegetation.

After a few seasons, large quantities of sericea and lespedeza seed can be made available to the farmers of the Piedmont Soil Conservation District on much the same basis that pine and kudzu seedlings are now.

In the fall of 1942 local representatives of the SCS, Extension Service, and Vocational Agriculture were planning to develop a wild life camp, with cabin and lake, on the Project land. Future Farmers of America members and 4-H Clubbers can use the camp for outings, and to carry on some experimental farming.

THE DAVIS GRESHAM TOWER

Project Conservationist E. V. Brender knows fire is his greatest hazard. An eighty-foot steel observation tower has been built near the middle of the purchased land on the knoll where Davis Gresham, nearly one hundred and fifty years ago, built his Indian Fort. The lookout is glassed in and equipped with a fire finder which rotates over a stationary map that shows each tract of land owned by the Project. A man is on lookout-duty at least part of each day during fire hazard seasons.

The value of the tower was demonstrated shortly after its completion when a fire was sighted to the west. The instrument showed that it was on acreage then under option for purchase. When Brender went to the optioned property the next day, he found that an abandoned house valued at $300 had burned. He told the owner that the lost property would have to be made good before the purchase could be completed. Thus, the $800 tower yielded an immediate saving of $300.

There is urgent need for one or more towers in other parts of the county. When the Unified Program started, the FSA hoped to build one, and the county another. If these towers were built, manned, and connected by telephone, it would be possible to locate to the acre any fire that occurs. One fire tower is at best but a beginning. Forest fires, even on the Project lands, can be kept down only when the rural people of the county are determined that there shall be no forest fires.

A FIRE'LL OPEN UP THINGS AROUND HERE

The difficulties of keeping fire out of the woods are many. Some farmowners still like to see last year's cotton and corn stalks piled and burned, and many of them let fire sweep the hedges and land-lines—keeps down the briars, and may kill some weevils, too. The landless farm folk use fire a great deal, especially scattered renters in the abandoned plantation sections of the county.

During the winter a farm tenant is out hunting rabbits in an old field with young pines head high. He notices how deep the bed of broom sedge is on the ridge. He knows cotton or corn will grow there. In early spring, when the land begins to dry out, he puts a plow in his wagon and rides off through the young pines to the patch of thick sedge. Why not use the best land one can find, even if it is in the middle of a hundred acres, or a thousand, that have not been cultivated for a dozen years? His plow is small and his mule is light. He must get rid of the sedge and brambles, so he strikes a match. As the fire crackles and smokes, he mounts the wagon, sees a place where the blaze is low and drives the mule into the widening charred area, always growing fastest on the side with the wind.

In the burnt-over patch small pines, stripped of most of their limbs and all of their needle-leaves, can readily be chopped off at the ground and piled out of the way. The fire burns on, and the farmer notes with a sense of satisfaction that in a half hour or less it has cleaned away more trash than he could in a week; in an hour it will have done more work than he could do in a month.

He runs a furrow, and another and another. The light turnplow moves through sodded grass roots. The mouldboard is often unequal to its task. The man between the handles looks back, groans to see the furrow open scarcely half of the way. He slaps the slow-going mule with the plowline, and off to work again, to have the stubborn sod flop back into the furrow right behind him, with the plow now and then thrown out of the ground by the tap root of one of the little pines he has just chopped off. He walks on, shoes covered with new soot and fresh dirt, nostrils full of fire's many smells, shoulders and back a bit tired already. He comes to the end, pleads, "Gee 'round, bonehead."

He turns back up the furrow, face full to a spring breeze. The smoke ahead of him swings low to the ground. Off to his right and left the fire is burning fast now. As he turns to look behind him, he grabs his hat and yells, "Woah!" Black smoke billows up, a flame here and there reaches above the tops of the low green pines. The farmer looks at the fire but a second, turns back around, calls "Gid-up" to his mule and goes on plowing. He knows he couldn't stop it now even if he tried.

When he goes home at noon his wife 'lows as how the fire must have got away from him. He nods it did, but guesses by late afternoon it will burn on out the ridge and down to the creek and over to the old Greensboro road. It can't spread out much on account of the galls and gullies on the sides of the ridge.

You know, that fire'll open up things over there like the one did here below the house last year. Why, you couldn't hardly see out if it wasn't for fires, and heaven only knows how thick the snakes would get if the woods didn't burn off every now and then. Ain't nothin' back in there nohow, 'cept thickets and more thickets and a few empty tenant houses. Well, that's not quite right, for Seab Johnson does live out there on the ridge. It'll do him no hurt though, for his house and barn have plowed fields all around them.

But did the fire stop at creek and road and galls, or did it "jump" them? Or did the wind change in the night and sweep the flames along in a new direction? Was anything done about it? Or did farmers and their wives and children in the windward merely say, "There's a fire in the woods around here somewhere."

From a half to two thirds of the woodlands of the county are burned over each year. Some of this burning is done to get "new" grass for the cows, or to keep down the trash and so prevent the inferno of a forest fire in dry weather. But most of it is wholly unplanned. It is the result of carelessness.

VOLUNTEER FOREST FIRE CONTROL

It was in the face of such facts that County Agent Bowen and Conservationists Brender and George F. Powers launched their Volunteer Forest Fire Control Program in the spring of 1942. They advised with representatives of other agencies and divided the county up into 25 small districts, with a tool chest of fire-fighting equipment in each, in charge of a local farmer. They sent out a four-page statement of facts about forests: three fourths of all the land in the county is growing trees, practically every landowner has woodlands, fire kills young trees, slows down the growth of older trees, causes the land to wash, kills birds and game. Timber has helped the people through many a hard place, is now the county's greatest single source of income, can be of more help in the future if properly cared for. "The absence of forest fires alone," said the statement, "will permit at least 30 percent more timber to grow from the same acreage." *

The cooperative nature of the volunteer fire-fighting venture is suggested by the way in which the tools and boxes were secured. Lumber for half of them was given by the Greensboro Lumber Company and the other half by the Knox Lumber Company; nails, hinges, and locks were furnished by the County Commissioners; the CCC boys built the boxes and painted them red; the paint was bought by the Board of Education. The equipment for the boxes, including Indian-back fire pumps, was provided by the Land-Use Project and by the local office of the Piedmont Soil Conservation District.

All the agencies participating in the Unified Farm Program agreed to help: the FSA would encourage their clients to work with the captain in their district whenever a fire broke out; the vocational teachers would continue to emphasize the danger of forest fires;

---

* Larger increases of timber values can be expected when woodlands are also protected from over-grazing, and when trees are cut in accordance with approved practices; so state Brender and C. R. Sayre of the Bureau of Agricultural Economics in an unpublished study of Greene county's woodlands.

the school officials would call it to the attention of the teachers; the CCC camp (until discontinued) would provide fire fighters if a fire got beyond the control of the district fire fighters.

The County Commissioners are offering a standing reward of $25 for evidence leading to the conviction of any person setting a forest fire. They have authorized the county police to make arrests of fire starters, and have instructed all county employees to report any forest fire they see. Large absentee landowners are asked to help buy equipment for the district tool boxes.

It is clear that the major responsibility for forest fire prevention lies at the door of the farmers themselves. But will they think it worth while to put out fires in woodlands that can be bought for two to ten dollars an acre? If they do want to keep down fires, will owners send their tenants, and will they go themselves? And in the wooded decadent plantation areas, who will put out the fires of hunters who drop cigarette stubs as they follow the dogs, or of "fire bugs" who set off the woods just to see them burn? Are not families most scattered in the very districts with most woodlands to protect?

No special program is needed in some sections of the county where tree-loving landowners live. Forest fires do not run through elderly "Dutch" Caldwell's woods, or through those of the Underwood brothers close by. For decades they have kept an eye out for fires, and quit everything to stop the ones that got started. At least one large absentee owner has succeeded in keeping fire out of his woods—Fire protection is the first obligation of the families living on Mercer Reynolds' extensive woodlands at Linger Longer.

INDIAN-BACK AND POWER PUMPS

Two big fires occurred the week the Volunteer Program was being set up, and two farm tenants from different parts of the county were arrested and put in jail. They were amazed when a request for help to their leading white acquaintances did not get them out.

Neither of them meant to set fires in the woods, and neither of them wanted the woods to burn. They were merely cleaning back the edges of the fields they were plowing, and the fire got beyond their control. Both of these fires were stopped after they had been reported by the lookout in the fire tower.

Many a smaller fire, too, has been seen early, reported, and put out. The watcher sees smoke, turns the fire-finder to see if the smoke is on Project acreage or on land dangerously near. The smoke may remain small and disappear—just a farmer burning a hedgerow or stalks in the field. If it comes up steady and black for ten minutes or so, subsides, and then fades out—a brush pile or flimsy tenant house. A steady black column of smoke high in the air for half an hour or more marks the burning of a substantial dwelling or barn.

The beginnings of a forest fire are readily detected by the man in the tower: uncertain smoke on the horizon fades out whitish. In the direction that the breeze is blowing, a dark column of smoke rises, later another beyond, and then another beyond it. Each column rises black and puffy, then fades out to low white smoke, and a new black column rises on the advancing edge of the fire. Such is the general design of a forest fire, though wind and weather never permit monotonous repetition of detail.

On their way to the fire, the work crew or the tower man may pick up any farmers who are willing to help. If it turns out to be impossible to get the 250-gallon power pump or the smaller one within reach of the blaze, and the men on the scene with Indian-back pumps cannot put it out, someone drives off to notify County Agent Bowen that Volunteer Fire Fighters from other parts of the county are needed.

CCC—FENCES PUT UP AND FIRES PUT DOWN

Up until July, 1942, when the CCC was discontinued by an act of Congress, the CCC camp at Greensboro regularly put out the large forest fires. George F. Powers, Work Unit Conservationist of the Piedmont Soil Conservation District and Roy C. Hart, Camp Superintendent, estimated that from the time the CCC was set up in May, 1939, until it was abolished, not less than 4,000 man-days were spent fighting fires in the county.

Many times the CCC boys looked up from the pine seedlings, which they planted on over 400 acres of the county's land, to see the distant smoke of a forest fire that might be destroying voluntary seedlings a thousand times faster than they could plant them. They would keep an eye out for a car, ready to check their tools onto their trucks and go put out another fire.

Before the CCC work was stopped, Powers and Hart had begun to feel that the readiness with which the boys had been sent to put out fires may have made local farmers less inclined to do their part in fire-fighting.

In harmony with the policy of helping those who needed help, the boys from the CCC camp went immediately to the aid of farm families when a tornado hit the county in the late winter of 1941. In less than an hour after the twister struck, the Camp boys were clearing away the debris of shattered farm buildings. They followed the path of the storm from one farm to the next, picking up and piling up planks and plows, sidemeat and featherbeds, cook pots and hoes, burlap bags and corn in the shuck, glass bottles, churns, mule collars, and crinkled pieces of galvanized iron roofing off a neighbor's barn a half mile away. Altogether, they devoted 735 man-hours to tornado relief.

Just before the CCC camp was discontinued, the boys helped to clean off and grade the Penfield Cemetery preparatory to its permanent upkeep by a bequest recently made for that purpose by James G. Boswell, former Greene county man now living in California.

TERRACED FIELDS AND IMPROVED PASTURES

And the CCC boys had plenty of work to do in the county besides fighting forest fires, cleaning up after tornadoes, planting pine seedlings, and cleaning off cemeteries. The soil conservation work done by them is evident throughout the county: over a hundred pastures averaging 40 acres each were developed, with 30,000 rods of new fences built.

With the cooperation of the CCC camp, the SCS had terraced 7,500 acres of land; planted 17,000 acres of kudzu and 173 acres of sericea; had built 718 meadow outlets, and seeded, resodded, and made pasture improvements—other than fences and clearings—on over 2,000 more acres. Three thousand acres had approved rotation of crops, or rotation in strips. The complete conservation program recommended by the SCS had been developed on over 8,000 acres. In all, around four hundred farms had been served through March, 1942.

To get the terraces and pastures, the farmer agrees to follow the recommendations of the Soil Conservation District in the use of all his acreage, including the application of fertilizer (through AAA grants), the rotation of crops, strip rotation on slopes, kudzu on steep hillsides and on severely eroded areas, sericea or kudzu in water draws, meadow and pasture strips along small streams, pasture improvements, and the planting of seedlings if needed.

A common-sense farmer may have groaned when one of the caterpillar tractors and scrapers first tore winding gashes in his field to make wide terraces that could be cultivated over. After two years, if he followed directions for making outlets and keeping up his terraces, he is satisfied that the wide terraces are superior to the old narrow ones. Neighboring farmers look on, are convinced and apply for new terraces themselves. They like the looks of the pastures, too.

In order to get new pastures and terraces, now that the CCC boys are gone, farmers will have to do much more of the work themselves. The terracing machinery is still available. The farmers will have to take the next step, perhaps learn to work together to make the best use of it.

GULLIES AND SUNKEN GARDENS

There was other work done by the CCC that the farmers will now need to do. The SCS, for example, had brought into the county upward of 1,500,000 kudzu crowns. The CCC boys planted most of them. From now on an abundant supply of crowns, with many to spare, will be available in the county. The farmers will have to plant them themselves.

Long before the SCS program was begun, the Underwood brothers of Siloam and A. J. Steward of Union Point had already demonstrated that kudzu would make good hay or a good dry weather pasture in late summer.

Other farmers had used kudzu as a porch vine. J. E. Moncrief and Will Colclough, both of Penfield, had seen cast-off seedlings from their porches spread across nearby gullies and begin the difficult job of covering them. On a summer day now, you look out over a sea of bold green leaves and vines. "That very place was a gully some years ago," Moncrief will say, "worth less than nothing, ugly and dangerous, too." Now he is proud of it for it is beautiful and valuable. Then he tells how he sold enough crows from "that old gully" to buy the new roof he put on his house a few months ago. The Underwood brothers, too, have sold crows.

The story of kudzu in Greene county is one of the clearest illustrations of a basic truth about the whole Unified Program. Kudzu had long been used successfully by a few progressive farmers; the Unified Program is making it available to farmers throughout the county, and also to those thousands of tired acres recently purchased by the government for forest and pasture development.

Ride over the county today and look at the kudzu, sericea, lespedeza, strip farming, wide terraces, permanent fences, and improved pastures. Not one of these things was first introduced in the county by the Unified Program, but as you go along the roads from one farm to the next, ask yourself two questions: First, "How many of these things would be out here where they are now if there had been no Unified Program?" Second, "How will the county look ten years from now if the conservation program goes on?"

At the rate the work was being done by the CCC boys, if they could have stayed here ten years more, Powers estimates that practically all the land in the county could have been developed in accordance with the recommendations of the Piedmont Soil Conservation District. To what extent the discontinuation of the CCC camp, and the war, will slow up the soil improvement work remains to be seen.

"THE GREATEST PATRIOT"

Financiers may measure their patriotism by the number of bonds they buy. Farmers in an eroded county, who haven't much ready cash, may best measure theirs by the fires they put out, the terraces they built, and the kudzu they planted. Remember what Patrick Henry said when an old man: "Since Independence, he is the greatest patriot who has stopped the most gullies."

The war situation also faces farmers with the necessity of producing most of their fertilizers at home. They will have to turn to their barnyard and to the legumes in their fields for nitrogen, phosphates, and other plant foodstuffs. They will be grateful for every improved pasture, every rod of permanent fence, every correctly terraced field, every acre in a soil-building crop, and for every strip of row crop with a strip of small grain below it to catch the plant food in the run-off. The unnecessary loss of plant food is tragically expensive when commercial fertilizer is plentiful; it will be fatal when none is available.

The creeks of the county still carry off unmeasured riches from our fields. The waters of the Oconee and the Ogeechee remain sluiceways to the sea for the living soils of Greene and other counties. But in the five years since SCS has been here, much less dirt is leaving from the farms where its program has been started.

The soil of Greene can be kept in the fields, and can be enriched. Look at the garden patches near the resident farmowners' houses throughout the county, and at whole fields here and there across the county—Dock and Faris Taylor's toward Carey Station, R. K. Smith's of Greensboro, John Malcolm's beyond Greshamville, J. G. Price's of Macedonia, the Underwood brothers near Siloam, Arthur Stewart's and Floyd Thompson's of White Plains, and some of C. L. Harris' fields on the old Wray plantation at Wrayswood.

Wise planning and constant attention account for every good acre of land in the county now. Nature gave us a thin layer of good soil here. Our past farm practices have mined much of the fertility out of it. Part of the explanation lies in such physical factors as soil composition and depth, topography, torrential rainfall; part in such national and international forces as world markets, tariffs, and the rapid rise of Western cotton; part in the burdensome credit arrangements inherent in the remnants of the plantation system, rooted as it is upon the slave plantation. Landless farmers seldom love the land they work, seldom have a standard of living which makes them proud of the houses they live in, seldom lead a life they would want their children to follow.

THE MAN SIDE OF LAND

To make Greene county's farms flower again as they did when the soil was first plowed, the farmers will have to retire most of the hillsides to permanent woodland or pasture, cover the galls and gullies with kudzu, enrich and cultivate only the more level fields. To replenish the humus, nitrogen, lime, phosphate and potash that these fields have lost, the farmers will have to plow under hundreds of thousands of tons of legumes, haul onto them tens of thousands of tons of barnyard manure and compost. Farmers will do these things effectively only when they own the land, or have a long-term tenure. But just owning the land or having long-term tenure will not suffice. The farm people themselves must be afforded the opportunity to realize higher levels of living, to take more pride in being dirt farmers.

Man and land are all tied up together in a farm community, and the likelihood of the soil being conserved and restored turns upon such concrete facts as whether the farm people are finding answers to their needs for higher incomes, better houses, good food, improved health and school facilities, and responsible participation in the affairs of the local community and the nation.

If the farmer does not receive a fair price for the products he has to sell as compared with the things he buys, he is likely to put less back into his land than he takes out of it. Such a procedure in a few years depletes the fertility in his fields; a few years more and galled places appear, followed by gullies that get larger from year to year.

Many a gully in the county is the earthy receipt for cotton that sold too cheaply and plowpoints and trace chains, seed and feed that were purchased too dearly. Unbalanced diets, inadequate medical care, just plain lack of hope—low physical vitality for whatever reason—may, after a decade or two, also issue in the form of eroded fields.

Just as there is a human side to soil conservation, there is a soil side to the rehabilitation of farmers. And so the Soil Conservation Service and the Farm Security Administration worked in close cooperation. When the Rural Rehabilitation program of the FSA puts more livestock on farms and more hope in farmers' lives, it is making a basic contribution toward the conservation of our soil.

XXIII

GOOD GARDENS AND "PRECIOUS" COOKERS

THERE IS deep satisfaction in a good garden close to the house. On this patch of earth a farmer and his wife perform nobly. Here they stir the land most hopefully, for here they conserve and replenish the soil gladly. Here they deal justly with the Almighty, and here they reap abundantly.

The young mother on the arm of her husband walks first to the garden. Here little feet first make tracks in loose soil. Here the child first sees seed planted, waits for the rows of new sprouts, sees the spaces between filled with other sprouts—learns that beans and beets have to be protected from weeds and grass. A farm child learns to keep the garden gate shut against the chickens and pigs long before he knows anything about war or politics.

Year after year, the garden yields up its dishes for those who tend it. Then one afternoon an old man, too feeble to reach the fields or even the barn, hobbles out of the garden and closes the gate behind him. In a few days the neighbors gather, their faces sad, their voices low. The old man's last tracks are in the garden.

That garden could have been across the road, or on the other side of the house. The real meaning of a good garden anywhere is that we could make gardens almost everywhere.

BEGIN THE WEEK RIGHT

The making of good gardens has been an essential part of the Farm Security Administration's work in Greene county. Ride along with an FSA supervisor on a spring day, observe the gardens of the "government farmers," gardens not yet four years old. Look at them now. See with what pride the family takes you through the garden gate.

When the Unified Farm Program was launched early in 1939, the number of families on FSA was increased from 146 to 535, the staff from one supervisor to twelve supervisors, two engineers, two nurses, and four clerical assistants.

The county was divided into five districts, with a farm and home supervisor in each, and administrative farm and home supervisors in charge of the whole. Four districts were served by white supervisors, one by Negro supervisors. About one fourth of the families are white, three fourths colored. Since 1939 over five hundred families have been on the program. This is a little more than a third of the farm families in the county, and they operate just less than one third of the plows.

The expanded FSA program in Greene was designed to include approved soil building farm practices, balanced diets and better health, improved schools, and community participation. A more adequate diet was early acknowledged as a basic need.

Each FSA family is required to have a garden. Practically all these gardens are fenced against pigs and chickens, and many are a half acre or larger. The farm and home supervisors stress the importance of the garden, point to it as the family's most valuable piece of land, advise the menfolks to begin the week right by plowing it the first thing Monday morning. In 1942 the families averaged three acres in gardens and truck patches together.

Much discussion has gone on about what ought to be planted in the garden. Irish potatoes are new for some FSA borrowers; clients often distinguish them from sweet potatoes by referring to "Irish 'taters" and "eatin' 'taters." When the program began many families had no taste for carrots, beets, lettuce, English peas, and spinach. Every family is asked to plant at least one new vegetable in the garden each year. Recipes are distributed, cooking and serving demonstrations are held. Children sometimes ask their mothers to prepare dishes they have learned to like at the school lunchroom.

In this climate it is possible to have a year-round garden. The FSA supervisors first got their clients to make good spring gardens. Now, more of the families are learning to plant at least three gardens a year—a spring garden, a fall garden, and a winter garden, with extra plantings of beans and tomatoes as they are needed during the summer.

A low-income rural family is making economic and spiritual progress when they plant new vegetables, eat a wider range of home-grown foods. An enlarged garden contributes to a balanced diet and a keen appetite, and also to love of place and pride of achievement.

GLASS JARS BY THE HUNDRED THOUSANDS

During the first year of the expanded FSA program, 1939, the families canned an average of over 225 quarts of fruit and vegetables. Four fifths of the clients were new on the program, had averaged scarcely a dozen quarts each the year before. In 1940 the average per family was upped to above 350 quarts. In spite of the extremes of wet and dry weather in 1941 and the general crop failure of that year, 507 of the families on the program put up an average of 386 quarts. The 1942 average was 499 quarts per family.

The quality of the canned goods has improved from year to year. At first there were stories of hundreds of jars filled with cabbages, half-ripe cowpeas, and sweet potatoes. This was partly in response to the limited canning experiences of the families before they got on the program, and perhaps even more to the efforts of the families to reach their canning quotas. By 1941 the canned goods were limited largely to the things which the supervisors said should be canned.

There are farm women who still can some turnip greens, green cowpeas, and sweet potatoes. These women know why they want them, too. They point out how difficult it is to have good sweet potatoes in a hill in late March and April, and how their menfolks want food with real strength in it when they are breaking land for corn and ridging rows for cotton. Canned green peas, too, will stick to your ribs when you are working long hours in the dusty fields at planting time. And a few cans of turnip greens and cabbages always come in handy to farm families who live far from the town stores and have little ready cash in their pockets. Build a fire in the stove, open a jar of turnip greens and a jar of sweet potatoes—why, you can serve a good hot meal in no time.

In many instances the largest amounts of canning have been done by families who live in the shabbiest houses.* "I'm tellin' my folks," said one big canner, "we gwine have to git under the house, we have so much canned stuff in it."

Rivalry between families may become very keen. Last summer one Negro mother kept half of her filled jars in the house for her neighbors to see, the other half she hid under hay in the barn, not to be brought to light until late fall when the home supervisors came around to count.

In another Negro woman's case the number of jars said to have been filled far transcended local credulity. Merchants in Greensboro heard the report, just knew it couldn't be true, for they had known the family for years. But the reports kept coming. So a representative from the Negro church was sent down to count the canned goods. She reported back to the church that Julia Miller really had 1,202 quarts. This performance was a welcome surprise to all, even to District Home Supervisor Pearl Wheeler Tappan, who has tried to help all five of the home supervisors realize that any of their families may be led to do well any part of their home and farm program. The encouragement of the supervisor may mean much. Even a little bragging, yes, or a lot of it, is sometimes needed.

"A GARDEN IN THE KITCHEN"

The canning quotas have been possible of attainment because of the loans the FSA made to its borrowers for family-size pressure

---

* See Appendix No. 19 for names of largest canners and range of goods canned.

cookers and jars, and because of the supervision provided. In a client's home or at some central point, the supervisor demonstrated the use of the home canner. One demonstration usually sufficed. Even the supervisors were surprised how readily the mothers and daughters, grandmothers and great-grandmothers learned to operate the pressure cookers. When you see a thing done, you don't have to know how to read to do it.

All sorts of foods have been put in glass jars which a few years ago these same families thought could not be canned—squash, English peas, sweet corn, string beans, okra, spinach, soup mixture, and especially veal and beef. Over 350 calves and cows were killed and canned by FSA farmers in 1941, still more in 1942.

The women worked hard, were delighted with the bright colors of the fruits and vegetables in the glass jars. They could store them for the winter in the same pasteboard boxes that the empty jars had come in. Almost none of it spoiled, and when they opened it in cold weather, it tasted good.

Most of the borrower families got pressure cookers the first year, and commonly called them "precious" cookers in prophetic mispronunciation. A bushel or two of snap beans a day and a wheelbarrow of squash besides do not cause panic when the use of the home cooker has been mastered. In the peak of the canning season the father and older boys are not very busy with field work. "The biggest of the canning," observed one mother, "comes in the spare we used to visit around in the summer."

The traditional subservience of the woman on the cotton farm is gone when the mother presides at the "precious" cooker. Rather she becomes the commander-in-chief of the household. "It set women free," said a man who had been helping his wife can all week.

But don't think for a minute that men can't operate the cookers, for Roy Lee Smith, Negro widower near Bairdstown, with the help of his seven children, has put up the canned goods for his motherless family the past two years. In another family an 18-year-old son did the canning when his mother was confined in childbirth.

At first it was often easier to get families to fill their jars in the summer than to get them to empty them that winter. They seemed to think they had finished an assignment when the jars had been filled and stacked away. "I don't keer about the cans myself, but I want to do what they say," you would hear sometimes. So the home supervisors began to encourage them to use their canned goods daily, demonstrated whole meals from jars on their shelves, explained that all empty jars could be refilled with fresh fruits and vegetables. By early summer most of the jars were empty, and many a child's face, and parent's too, had new life in it. And what if at first some of them did put it in jars just for the supervisors, and then take it out and eat it just for the supervisors! The families now realize that they are doing the canning for their own use. Within three years, most of the women have come to prize their canned goods. Said one mother looking at her hundreds of jars, "It's the same as having a garden in your house all winter."

NOW THEY CHURN AT HOME

The increased production and use of eggs and milk on the FSA farms has made it easier for housewives to prepare vegetables in tasty ways. Some vegetables are good when boiled with fatback, but a larger variety can be made palatable only when there are milk and eggs in the kitchen. Read the menus in yesterday's daily, or eat the best meal of your life at a family-size farmer's table. Then figure up the milk and butter and eggs that went into the eggplant soufflé, the potato salad, the buttered beets, the frozen custard. Count, too, how many hot biscuits you buttered and ate. Even the fried chicken was buttermilk fed, and the bright green spinach was made more appetizing by the slices of hard-boiled egg on top.

The farmers liked chicken and eggs, and would eat beef when it was available, though usually they had only pork. But many of the families have had to learn to like sweet milk, for they rarely had any under the old cotton economy. Buttermilk was an old friend—it was often received as payment for churning at the plantation owner's house.

From the beginning of the FSA program, each family was provided with at least one cow. By the fall of 1941, each family had two milk cows, or one and a heifer. Sweet milk is already more popular among the children.

A few of the cows are well fed and are good milkers, most are not. There is need for better breeds. The cows in the county now average less than a gallon a day, though one finds here and there a four- or five-gallon cow. The great majority of them even with the best feed treatment would still produce less than two gallons a day. Feed for many of these cows is still inadequate, and it may be wise to rely on local poor milkers until more feed is available. Efforts are now being made to get extra hay and grain produced.

It may just be, on the other hand, that one of the best ways to get more cow feed produced would be to supply the families with milkers they would be proud of. Some years ago there was a good sprinkling of dairy cows in the county, and there are now a few pure-bred dairy bulls. But for the most part, the quality of milk cow here remains inferior, and no real improvement can be made until some plan is worked out to make pedigreed bulls available to the smaller farmers throughout the county.

When word came in the spring of 1941 that each family should have at least two cows—as their part of the "Food for Defense" program—there were not enough local cows to supply the demand. The price rose sharply. A loan of around fifty dollars was set up, and there was a tendency for almost any kind of a cow to be priced at or near $50. A few farmers and traders in the county did a lucrative business. They went here and there buying up cows at $20 to $35, resold them to the "government farmers" at $40 or $50. "If I'd had to take that $40 out of my own pocket," said a borrower, "I'd thought a long time before I bought that last cow."

It was unfortunate, but natural, that a sudden demand for a relatively large number of cows should step up the price. Some were brought in from outside the county, but by the time they were delivered they were little if any cheaper than those on the locally inflated market. The additional cow, even if in many instances bought too dearly, may not be a bad investment for farm families who need milk every day of the year for their own use, and more of it than they have ever had. Any surplus dairy products can be sold as sour cream or butter, or used as feed for pigs and chickens.

40,000 BABY CHICKS

At the outset each family was provided with porkers and at least a dozen laying hens. Then the National Defense program called for a larger production of meat and eggs as well as milk. "Food for Defense" loans were also made for either a brood sow or additional chickens. Since pigs are usually plentiful enough here, nearly all the families increased their poultry.

Week after week in the spring of 1941, baby chicks were shipped in by the thousands. The supervisors met the noon train from Atlanta, loaded the chicks in their cars, rushed off with them to the FSA farmers. Altogether, thirty-three thousand baby chicks and over three thousand pullets were distributed.

The loans for the chickens included feed with which to grow them off, and the cost of a kerosene lamp brooder. Most of the brooders, some four hundred, were built in the vocational shops at the schools.

The baby chicks were distributed in May. The fatalities were only a fraction of what local people expected. Well over 90 percent lived, largely because starting mash was delivered with the chicks, and brooders were used to keep the biddies off the ground.

In 1942 over forty thousand baby chicks were ordered and delivered a month earlier than last year. Some of the chicks were in bad condition when they arrived, and were replaced with good ones.

Beginning in March of 1942, eggs were gathered each Wednesday by FSA supervisors, who candled and crated them, and put them on the market at an expense of two cents a dozen. From three to four hundred dozen eggs were shipped each week during the spring and early summer.

Most families usually let their pullets scratch for food. They did not mature properly, did not produce many eggs during the winter and early spring. With the egg marketing well under way, and the demand for poultry products, especially eggs, on the increase, there is reason to believe that many families will use egg money to buy feed and so grow a superior hen and have eggs regularly for sale during the late fall and winter when prices are best.

The grading and shipping of eggs by the FSA, and by the Extension Service for 4-H Club members as mentioned above, may well mark the beginning of an enlarged poultry activity here. It was simply impossible to get small farmers to do the work necessary to secure quality egg production, when they had seen eggs drop to fifteen cents or below every spring, the only time of year they ever had any to sell.

The farmers got twenty-five cents and more per dozen for the eggs shipped out in the spring of 1942. The local market rose above fifteen cents. Some town housewives frowned upon the grading and shipping of eggs, wanted them "nice and cheap" like they had always been in the spring. A few merchants, too, wondered if the "government" wasn't interfering a little too much with private business. Most merchants and housewives, however, were quick to admit that eggs usually got too cheap around Easter. The farmers felt that the shipping price was still too low in view of the high cost of laying mash and chicken wire.

HOME-GROWN MEAT AND BREAD

The FSA families were encouraged to raise their own meat and bread at home. By the fall of 1942, a good number of families had enough porkers to carry them till next hog-killing time came around, and enough wheat to last through the year for flour. "Ain't bought a sack of flour since we got on the government," is a common saying. "Ain't nothing but foolishness going to the store for flour." Some families with almost no tradition of subsistence farming have made real gains when they can report half enough meat and bread to do them.

To produce eggs and milk and pork cheaper than heretofore, the FSA families are now being urged to grow more of their feed. Much of the work in growing the needed small grains and in developing hog and cow pastures can be done when the farmers are not busy with corn and cotton and canning. The program to increase small grains and improve pastures fits well into the soil conservation program, which each farm family in the county—"government farmer" and otherwise—is urged to follow.

As one rode over the county in the spring of 1942 he saw more wheat, oats, and barley than ever before. Some of it was dark green, more was not. Nitrate of soda was already scarce, bagged fertilizers, too. The increase of livestock by FSA families will help supply barnyard fertilizers in larger quantities. Even should no nitrate of soda be available, it is now believed that within a few years by judicious livestock farming greater yields can be secured without soda than have heretofore been secured with it. When we are prepared to get yields without soda, we will have reached another milestone. The compost pens which the FSA is now advocating for each family is a small but important step toward putting more humus back in the soil.

XXIV

MEETING BASIC HUMAN NEEDS

IF YOU want to have a healthy farm family, you need home-grown food, and plenty of it. But that isn't all. You need a roof that turns the water, some window lights and screens, too, if you can possibly get them. A good stove is worth a lot, and your folks will sleep better if they have mattresses. Then there's this business of water to drink, and dry shelter space for your stock in cold weather. And everybody knows there come times when you've just got to have a doctor, or die.

The improvement of rural housing soon became a regular part of the FSA program in Greene.

The houses and barns of all twelve Tenant-Purchase families— eight white and four colored—are either new or have been repaired and enlarged. It was rather simple to arrange for adequate farm buildings under the forty-year repayment plan of the TP contract.

THE ADVANCE-RENT PLAN OF DOWNS AND THOMAS

But what of the FSA families who do not live on land they own or are buying? After a time, a method to improve these farm buildings was worked out on an advance-rent basis. The landlord signed over to the FSA a part of his rent from the land for from five to seven years. The advance-rent was then used by the FSA, or the renter, to make improvements on the house and other farm buildings. The landlord was glad to get his buildings improved without having to put out cash. The tenant liked it because he had a better house and barn. The FSA found it a good way to secure five- or seven-year leases on the land for their borrowers.

The advance-rent agreements have made it easier for farmers to remain at the same place year after year. Families who moved every year or so had little interest in permanent gardens and fruit trees—many of them never even planted annual flowers.

Before they got on the program, about 40 percent of the families moved each year, since then less than 4 percent. Gardens, fruit trees, terraces, flowers, and many another vital need could be had only when these families were anchored to a patch of earth.

Through late March, 1942, about $50,000 worth of future rent on 265 farms had been signed over to the FSA. With these advanced rents, 90 new barns have been built, 15 more repaired; 5 new houses erected, 105 repaired. Most noticeable of all, white creosote has been sprayed on over 200 unpainted dwellings throughout the county.

The houses and barns of borrower families on whole plantations have been repaired. Riding across the county, one will readily spot the large number of improved houses on the Jackson plantation near Mosquito Crossing and the Jones plantation above Wrayswood. On each of these places, as elsewhere, the repairs are modest though substantial. Anyone looking for a great gap between the typical tenant house and these will be disappointed; anyone looking for basic improvements that can be made at relatively low cost will probably be satisfied.

About three fifths of the advance-rent money has been used to improve farm buildings, the other two fifths to terrace land. Over 5,000 acres of land on FSA farms have already been terraced, and agreements have been made for terracing several thousand more. The SCS has cooperated with the FSA in this work, which represents two thirds of the SCS's terracing in the county.

Associated with Ed Downs in the development of the advance-rent plan, which was originated in Greene county, was Joel Thomas, full of common sense and love for rural people.

KEEPING THE FLIES OUT

The families on the FSA program also needed safe water, and sanitary facilities. Wells on 220 farms have been protected against surface water by concrete curbing, and new pumps have been put in. Two hundred and thirty-five dwellings have been screened, and 325 sanitary pit privies have been placed on FSA farms.

Some of the screened doors on these houses are seldom shut, and some of the window screens commonly swing in the breeze. Screens don't do much good in warped doors and windows. One family usually keeps the screens propped open "to let the flies go out."

A large family in a small house is a tax on even the best screens, and holes in the lower part of the screen doors are ready for mending at some houses every few days, and the mending is not always done. For the most part though the families like their screens and make good use of them.

If anyone wants to know what a third-grade mother of a landless family thinks about screens, let him read what she wrote to the local FSA office when her family moved, and so lived again in a house without screens and panes:

We are one of the FSA families we use scream door and windows for three years i gess we will have to for get about them but i would like mighty well to have mines. You said they was mine and i know they was i has to nail up the shetters now, caint see out them i keep doors shut long as i could it is hot tho and all kind of flies and ensect is here i goes to the field and fan flies come home to cook and fan flies and eats and fan flies just any kind of screams will do, and i needs some old lights in the windows too

The protected wells and pumps are appreciated, as are also the fly-proof privies which a little over two thirds of the families now have. Many a family has regretted to leave the new privy behind when they moved. Now and then a farmer loaded the privy on a wagon or truck and took it along. In at least one case, the landlord made the farmer bring it back.

NEW FARMHOUSES AND BARNS

The new farm buildings on the Greene County Farms, Incorporated, are the latest and most striking phase of the FSA's housing program in Greene. Eighty-two new farm units are now being developed on lands which the FSA has bought. On eight tracts farm dwellings have been repaired, on the 74 others new houses have just been built. Each unit has a new barn, smokehouse, fifty-bird poultry house, and sanitary privy. Plans for thirty-three more new farm units on FSA-owned lands have been postponed because of the war.

These new units are on land bought by the FSA in those parts of the county where the Land-Use Planning Committee recommended that farming be done. Over half of the acreage is in the white-land section, centering around White Plains and Siloam. A total of over 19,000 acres was bought at an average price of a little over $10 per acre.

The land purchases of the FSA, like the even larger ones of the SCS already mentioned, have been a big help to the landowners. Several of the largest and most successful farmers found it desirable to sell part of their acreage. Large and small, seventy-nine plats of land have been bought by the FSA. Some lie adjacent to each other, more do not.

The cost of these new farm units, buildings and land, is around $3,500. Most of them have about 140 acres, as recommended by the County Land-Use Planning Committee. Roughly one third of the acreage is devoted to cultivated crops, one third to pasture, and one third to woodland. The local SCS cooperated with the FSA in laying out some of these farms.

The common-sense thing is done: the direction of a boundary line fence is run to halve or third a low lying meadow, so two or three farm families may have some good pasture in dry weather. Within reason, the same principle is followed in dividing up the best crop lands, and the worst eroded areas. Though these farm units are of irregular shape, it is believed that they will prove superior to the traditional gridiron landlines, which recognize neither hill nor hollow, rain nor drought.

The new houses and barns and outbuildings of the Greene County Farms, Incorporated, serve as a sort of diploma for the families on the FSA program with the best records. Unfortunately, the elderly couples—and there are many who have done well—cannot occupy the new houses on a long-tenure basis, though some are now in them with one-year leases.

The plan is to locate an eligible, long-tenure family on each farm, charge maintenance and depreciation rent of a little more than $100 a year, and encourage the family when able to begin to buy the farm. Here in Greene county we see in operation a common-sense plan, designed to train dependent landless families, step by step, for home ownership.

"PIECY" HOUSES ARE DISCOURAGING

Impressive as are the housing improvements which the FSA has made in Greene, it is well to remember that roughly two fifths of the FSA families have had nothing done to their houses. Some of these were in good condition when the families got on the program, but about one fourth of the FSA families still live in houses badly in need of repair. The list of complaints is long: "Get tired of moving my bed every night to keep it out of the wet;" "You can catch a dishpan of water over the stove any time it rains hard;" "We're just walking in water;" "Holes in the roof big enough for a turkey to fly through." At one farm the smokehouse where the canned fruit is locked was the only roof on the place that would turn water. Unceiled rooms and sashless windows are common even among the houses that have been worked on.

Scores of families are still without sanitary facilities and without screens. Some have no water, spring or well—"Not a livin' stream of water on the place." On nearly a hundred farms where there are wells, precautions have not been taken against surface water.

To live in a "piecy" house without a pump or privy is very discouraging to a family who may feel that they have done the things the Program expected of them. Many a borrower still hopes that the FSA will be able to make their dwelling livable within at least modest limits.

Beyond the homes of the FSA farmers are the many houses of the sawmill hands, farm laborers, and other wage workers. The worst FSA houses are not worse than most of them, and no plan is in sight to make them any better. These shabby unscreened houses stick out like sore thumbs because of the good work which the FSA has already done in improving farm homes.

MEDICAL CARE FOR 500 FAMILIES

A man with lumbago makes a poor farmer, and a woman with pellagra can hardly wash, iron, cook, can, churn, and take care of the baby. An abscessed tooth may make a strong man weak, and a little insulin make a sick man well.

An important part of the FSA work in the county is its medical care program. In May, 1938 a Health Association was organized, with 130 borrower families as members. Each family paid an annual fee, depending on the number in the family. All the physicians in the county, except one, participated in the Association, and the member families could choose any doctor they wished.

In 1939, when the number of borrowers was increased to 535, the Association served 515 families. Since then around 500 families, over 2,500 persons, have belonged to this voluntary Association. The basic fee in 1941 and 1942 was $12 per family, plus $1 for each individual in the family, up to $20. This coming year, as now planned, the fee will be from $20 to $25 per family.

The total amount paid in by the families for the year ending

March, 1942 was $8,647. These funds were disbursed as follows: $5,150 for doctors, $2,086 for drugs, $658 for hospitalization, $62 for ambulances, $559 for surgeons and other specialists outside the county, $105 for midwives, and $20 for administrative expenses.

By pooling their payments, the families have had services they could hardly have hoped for before. The doctors make their charges to the Association on the basis of mileage to the patient. In this way the families who live near a doctor help to pay the bills of those who live farther away, just as families with little or no illness help pay the bills where there is much illness.

Many FSA families, even without the Association, would have called doctors. But if a serious protracted illness had occurred, a big doctor's bill would have resulted. The physician then would have had to donate most of his services, or the family, even to pay him in part, might have had to sell everything—down to the last pig.

LEARNING WHEN TO CALL THE DOCTOR

Within the Health Association, all has not been smooth sailing. Some families called the doctor needlessly. They seemed to feel that when they had paid their annual dues they could call the doctor any time they were of a mind to. Families who had never called the doctor as much as they had wanted to, now had the opportunity of their lives. If he came and found them sick, nothing could be more comforting than his advice and medicines. If he found they were not really sick, then they would have the consolation of knowing it, could the better throw off their puny feelings. There's something of body and something of mind in how a fellow feels, and many farm people want a doctor to deal with both.

In a few instances, families without automobiles in remote parts of the county had the doctor come to avoid the personal expense of sending a slightly ailing member of the family to his office. Such abuses soon came to light, and a form letter was sent to the members of the Association asking that they call a doctor only when really necessary. This resulted in the doctor's not being called sometimes when he should have been. As time has passed, the supervisors have had to encourage some families to use the medical service enough, and others not to make unnecessary demands upon it.

The members of the Association like the feeling that is theirs when they send for a doctor, like knowing they have some claim on his services. The doctor is from that prosperous world of colleges, "educated" talk, grapefruit for breakfast and Sunday clothes all week long. In some of the poorer homes he and the FSA supervisors are the only persons from that world who ever come inside the house and sit down and talk.

It is an exciting decision for a rural family to send for the doctor. The ailing one is encouraged to repeat his aches and pains. They are compared with this and that former illness in the household or at a neighbor's. Not uncommonly an elderly man or woman from near by is called in. If the sickness appears to be similar to a serious one, or if it has strange angles, someone goes off to the nearest telephone. The best possible news he can bring back is that the doctor will come at once.

The doctor's visit is an occasion. The sick person's bed must be clean, the room straightened up, the hall and front porch swept, the children's faces washed and maybe better clothes slipped on some of them. After a time, all is ready. Waiting for the doctor, the farm home stands on its tiptoes—even the sick one often feels better than before the doctor was called. And what can leave a farm home more thoroughly let down than for the doctor not to come the hour he is expected, or the next hour, or the next?

Negro family members of the Association pay at the same rate as the white, are entitled to the same services except at childbirth. The physicians deliver the white babies, and midwives deliver the colored ones if the observations at the prenatal clinic give assurance of a normal delivery. Should the nurse have reason to believe the delivery will not be normal, a doctor is called and the bill is paid by the Association. And in all cases, the clients know the midwife is supposed to call a doctor if she needs him. The Association allows midwives $5 for each delivery; the family may supplement this by another $5. The doctor's charge is $25. In the first six months of 1942 fourteen babies were born to members of the Association; five of the mothers were attended by physicians, nine by midwives.

During a recent six-months' period, a little over four fifths of the white families and a little less than four fifths of the colored used the medical service. Within this half year, slightly over one fourth of the white families and a little less than one eighth of the colored incurred bills in excess of their annual dues to the Association. Over a tenth of the white families and under a twentieth of the colored used the medical service every month. With a better diet and a doctor when needed, many FSA families report the best health ever.

THE SERVICE BEGINS WITH FATHER

During this six-months' period, physicians charged 659 home visits and 1,452 office visits to the Association. The parents were the recipients of over nine tenths of all these medical services, the fathers alone received over three fourths of them. The office visits reported by the physicians are most numerous on Saturday, and especially from noon on through the afternoon. The records show unmistakably that Whites use the service more than Negroes, that parents use it more than children, and that men use it more than women.

Clearly enough, the participating physicians do not want to have unnecessary calls made by the clients, for there is available each month only a stipulated amount of money. During the last year the doctors submitted bills of $11,453, of which the Association paid a little less than half. A little over three fourths of the year's $2,730 drug bill was paid. The druggists bill each prescription at a flat rate of sixty cents.

The doctors and druggists would be glad enough to collect 100 percent of their charges, but they know that the amount they are now paid by the Association far exceeds the amount they would otherwise secure from these same families.

If a doctor lives in a community where practically all of the families have incomes sufficient to pay doctor bills, it is simple enough for him never to turn down a call, and never to ask whether the money is available. But here a large number of families have annual cash incomes of under $200 a year, and there are around 3,000 people to each doctor. It would be financially and physically impossible for the doctors to accept all calls, if the poorer families called the doctors for the same ailments that their paying patients now call them for. The doctors still do a great deal of free work, but are glad that the Health Association can pay a large part of the bills for 500 families.

To supplement the services of the Medical Association, a "special medical" fund for corrective work may be set up in the family's loan. The FSA clients have also received a number of services, along with the other people of the county, from the local health office, the State Department of Health, and other agencies. Last year three crippled children were treated, one colored child had a defective eye removed and a glass eye put in, treatment was provided for one white and three colored persons suffering with cancer, 31 tubercular suspects were x-rayed and the positive cases encouraged to go to the state sanitarium or to use one of the portable fresh-air houses which the FSA made available to the county health office.

CURING THE TOOTHACHE

Encouraged by the success of the Health Association, the FSA organized a Dental Care Association. Four hundred and seventy-four families are members, paying an annual family fee of $3.00. The dental services of 1942 were 722 extractions, and five sixths of these were for parents; 142 fillings; 30 cleanings; 10 gum treatments; and 10 x-rays.

"I have been hearin' of late that my rheumatiz might get better if I'd have 'em pulled out," said a farmer to his wife, "and I think I will. Teeth that don't hit hain't worth nothin' nohow." Said another: "I got most of mine still, but I'd just as well have 'em all yanked out, for some of 'em been loose for years, and every few months one of my back teethies gits long and hurts so I can't even sleep. Then that one gits better, and then another one gits long and hurts. I'll have 'em pulled and gum it 'til I can git some store teeth."

On a per family basis, the white clients made nearly twice as much use of the dental service as the colored. The difference was even greater for non-extraction services, over three fourths of which were for the Whites. Only a half dozen white families and two colored used all the dental services available. A number of white children came in for the first time when Alla Mayze Bailey, the FSA social worker, devoted some time to encouraging white FSA families to go to the dentist.

The FSA supervisors hope that a preventive dental health program can be developed for their borrowers through membership in the dental care program. There is every reason to believe that preventive dental service will increase as the families themselves learn that the dentist can prevent toothache by conserving teeth as well as "cure" toothache by pulling them out.

A Veterinary Association, too, has been organized: 477 families participate, and the annual fee is $3.00. It is a real economy when a low-income family can call the veterinarian for a sick cow or mule. Then there is hog cholera, which without his care may leave a family with no meat for the winter. Chickens, too, are subject to diseases. The veterinarian in the county likes the program well enough. It affords him the opportunity to secure some income from the FSA families, makes it possible for him to render them needed services.

The FSA farmers are coming to realize that there are ways of helping themselves and their neighbors and their county at the same time.

PART SIX

TOWARD SELF-SUPPORT

XXV

GROWING PAINS

BEFORE THEY got on the FSA program, some of the families had owned mules and some had owned farms, but a big majority had worked for landlords all their lives. Inheritors of the broken plantation system, they had lived on cotton, without any plan, chronically in debt and dependent.

It was a help for the FSA to make loans to these families at a lower rate of interest than they had had before. But just money was not enough. The borrowers would need someone to help them plan how to use their loans to the best advantage. If cotton farmers were to become subsistence farmers and if they were to build up the land, they would have to learn how to do a lot of things. They would have to work harder, and do more work throughout the year.

Many onlookers thought the FSA had undertaken an impossible job. In the Reconstruction Period, hadn't some people tried to make a clean break with slavery, and hadn't the effort failed? Hadn't the sharecropper plantation been the best compromise they could work out? Could the dependent, the illiterate, the landless among the clients ever be taught to work "on their own?"

THE SLOW MARCH TOWARD INDEPENDENCE

Trained in agriculture and home economics, the FSA supervisors help the families budget their money and plan their work, teach them new skills of home-making and farming, and encourage the families to stay at the job. They are the guides of the ex-share-croppers and tenants in their slow march toward independence.

Upon securing a loan, the farmer and his wife agree to accept the supervision of the FSA staff. The farm supervisor works out a farm plan with the husband, who agrees to make his own feed if he can, care for his livestock, cooperate in the planting of soil-building crops, take good care of his cotton.

The home supervisor sits down with the mother and goes over her plan of work for the year, including the size of the garden to be planted, the amount of canning to be done, the baby chicks to be raised, clothes to be made. From time to time the supervisors drop by to see how things are going.

The nature of the FSA program makes it unnatural for the supervisor to put direct pressure on the client. Speaking of one home supervisor, a client said, "She doesn't *tell* you, she *asks* you."

Most families are put on their own. They are told that they are not the kind of people who have to be watched, that they know how to farm and carry out their part of the agreement. The assumption is that the family will make most progress when given as much responsibility as it can take. An increased measure of self-direction for the client is the essence of his contract with the government.

After the farmer signs up, he may feel that close supervision is a reflection on him, and resent it, especially if he does not have a plantation background. Encouragement and suggestions, therefore, are the supervisor's most ready approaches.

On the other side of the picture, the supervisors, with around one hundred families each, do not have time to do their required office work and provide as much detailed supervision as some families need. The clients may even feel hurt if the supervisors do not come often enough. They are anxious that they come and go over the crop now and then to see that they are "trying." Then if the crop fails, they will know why, and not have "to draw conclusions," as one borrower put it.

Group meetings have proved to be a good way for the supervisors to give general instructions to a score or more clients at one time, and for the clients to get supervision in a friendly group discussion. Twenty-one local clubs for the colored FSA farm operators and home-makers have been formed. They meet at a schoolhouse, in a church, or a home. Each club has a president, a secretary, and a treasurer. The meetings are opened with songs, Bible reading or prayer, and sometimes a club member "speaks a piece." The farm and home supervisors are usually present and are duly called upon for any matters they would like to bring up.

AROUND THE CALENDAR

When one attends such a meeting for the first time, he is impressed with how commonplace are all the things the supervisors say. A simple affirmative is the correct answer to nearly every question they ask. Wouldn't it be well to do this? Had you thought about that?

In January the supervisors talk about fixing the fences, getting up stovewood for the summer, keeping the cows and mules sheltered, killing the last porkers and curing the meat. In February they check on fences, feed and shelter for animals, point out it is time to break land if the rain halts, and agree to wait until the next meeting to ask how many have stovewood enough to last out the summer.

The March meeting comes. The supervisors ask for a show of hands on the stovewood business, brag on the few hands that are raised, ask about gardens, express the hope that all will have them planted by the next meeting, time now to begin ridging land for cotton and breaking it for corn, put soda on wheat and oats and barley. Time for the women to get most of their last year's jars empty, and remember that you and your menfolk need good food when you are working hard, so open up two or three or four jars a day if you have them—why in another six weeks there'll be fresh stuff in your gardens.

And so it goes, month after month around the calendar, through hatching and caring for baby chicks, planting crops, poisoning the potato bugs and bean beetles and boll weevils, keeping the mouths of the terraces open, plowing regularly in dry weather to conserve moisture, chopping grass in wet spells, saving the heifer calves for cows, fattening the bull calves for canning. On and on go the supervisors' suggestions about the never-ending jobs of ex-tenant farmers learning subsistence farming and self-reliance.

WE HAVE LEARNED A LOT WE DIDN'T KNOW

At most of the meetings a "demonstration" is given. One client is asked to assist the supervisor. From helping and watching, the clients really learn a new skill. To be sure that everyone has a chance to see and learn, extra demonstrations are arranged—in the white homes for the white clients, and in the colored homes for the colored clients.

The adult education program of the FSA has been practical and thorough-going.

In the early summer of 1939 came the demonstrations to show how vegetables should be canned with the pressure cooker. That fall, because of the chronic low consumption of lean meat, the program featured the canning of calves and beeves. People who hardly knew how to begin except to kill the calf, looked on attentively as a specialist dressed the animal, cut it for cans, cooked and sealed it. After a single exhibition, in which some of the onlookers took part, the families successfully canned their own veal and beef.

To make peanut butter, chicken feed, and whole wheat flour at home, 375 hand mills were distributed; to kill insects on garden vegetables, 452 spray guns; to make sausage, over 300 sausage mills.

Other types of demonstrations include: making cotton mattresses, comforts, plowing and planting gardens, making carpets and scarfs of fertilizer sacks, mats of corn shucks, dressmaking, kitchen arrangement, hot frames, poultry culling, egg candling, balanced meals, getting hens to set, coloring materials with natural dyes.

One mother said: "I enjoy being on a government farm, because we have learnt a lot we didn't know. We are learning to take care of ourselves." Another appreciated the fact that "We had food before, but we didn't know how to get the best use out of it."

Through the group meetings and demonstrations, the families on the program have become aware of the advantages in the wholesale purchase of baby chicks and feed for them, of cabbage plants and sweet potato slips, fertilizer, garden seeds, furniture, stoves, refrigerators, and other household equipment. The collection and sale of graded eggs, begun in the spring of 1942, have shown them the sense of group marketing of standardized products.

HOW THEY GOT ON THE FSA

The readiness with which the client accepts supervision is not unrelated to whether he at first wanted to get on the program, later decided it was a good thing and made application, or was put on it by his landlord. Many farmers signed up for rehabilitation loans as soon as they were available, because "Ev'ybody claimed that was the thing." Others hesitated.

Many prospects wanted to see how the program would work out before signing up. Most reassuring to these wait-and-see families were the mules and wagons, cows and pigs, pressure cookers and jars which early came to the farmers with rehabilitation loans. One farm woman said she made up her mind when she saw folks hauling bed ticks: "I said to myself I wish I could get on that thing that give them those bed ticks." Soon the families on the program were also looking forward to better houses, new pumps, terraced fields. In the face of those attractions, many another farmer put in his application even if it did strain or break his old credit arrangements.

The majority of the families, however, were "put on the government" by their landlords, who decided to lease to them the land they were living on for a period of five to seven years. The FSA helped

arrange these leases so it could make and supervise long-term rehabilitation loans to these farm tenants.

Generally speaking, the tenants on such a place liked the change
well enough. But there was not much they could do even if they did
not. For should they reject the FSA loans they would at the same
time be forfeiting any claim on their landlord whose advice they had
refused to follow. In the spring of 1939 there was but little private
capital in the county to finance even the most cooperative tenant
farmers.

LANDOWNERS AND TENANTS LIKED THE LOANS

The late 1930's was a likely time for plantation owners in Greene
to shift their farming risks to any agency that would finance farm
operations. At the end of 1938, when the FSA program was being
expanded, the landowners and tenants alike were upon hard times:
the cotton crop of 3,800 bales was far below the post-weevil average;
only the three severest weevil years of the early 1920's had been
worse. Planters wondered whether they could finance the next crop;
tenants wondered whether they could secure food and supplies to
farm at all the next year. People remember back: "The banks had
done stopped helping . . ." "The landlords had done dropped us
down where they couldn't save us. If the Government hadn't took
hold of us, it would have been a tough time in this land."

FSA's advance-rent plan to terrace land and improve farm buildings looked good to the plantation owner; a five- to seven-year lease
looked good to the tenant families. So the landlords signed up, advised their tenants to accept FSA loans and supervision. "The gov'-
ment do for the colored folks what our white folks couldn't do,"
explained a Negro landowner. Said a white landowner who let his
tenants go on FSA: "Got to where I couldn't manage 'em myself.
So I sez to the gov'ment if it could, to go to it."

The small farmowners and independent renters, too, were near
the end of their row by the fall of 1938. They had been borrowing
from the banks, or had been furnished by the merchants, or secured

federal emergency feed, seed, and fertilizer loans. These sources of credit had vanished for many, for they had let unpaid debts accrue on the livestock and farm equipment which they commonly used as security. By the early spring of 1939, the bankers, merchants and representatives of the federal emergency loans were asking that FSA loans be made available to many of their former clients.

The rehabilitation loans, designed to aid farmers who could not finance farm operations from any other source, were available here at a most opportune time. A few planters may have qualified their tenants for these loans by merely telling them they would not be financed further. But the vast majority of the FSA clients, tenants and small independent operators alike, were qualified by their economic plight. They were like the one who said: "I wanted help, and I didn't have no help."

SPENDING THE MONEY AS PLANNED

How well pleased the farmer remained after he got on "that thing" which would lend him money—at a low rate of interest—to buy a mule of his own, and a cow, and give him a bed tick, has depended on many factors. One was whether he got what he wanted most, or simply got what the supervisors thought he ought to have.

There were those clients who seemed to need direct supervision in all their expenditures. The supervisor's choice in such cases was not an easy one. If the client did not use his borrowings as planned, he failed to get full advantage of them, and the program itself often got a bad name in the community. On the other hand, if purchases were supervised too closely, the client smarted under the limitations placed upon him, deeply resented the implication that he was unable to spend his own borrowings wisely.

Prior to 1938, report followed report that loans were not being used as intended. So when the program was expanded, it was decided that the things to be purchased must be itemized on each check. The more independent clients were truthfully told that this rule, which applied to all families, was made to regulate those who had not yet learned to spend their borrowings for purposes agreed upon.

Misunderstandings still arose about the spending of "grant checks." Looking realistically at the low incomes of the poorer farmers in the county, the FSA had made grants to most of the borrowers beyond the loans which are to be paid back. These grants, which averaged from $65 to $75 each, were given in the winter to families who had not made enough cotton to carry them through the year on a wholesome plane of living.

Some people were against the grant checks from the beginning—better to give a bonus to the best five than supplement the poorest ninety-five. The FSA held though that a farm family must not be allowed to fall below a certain food and shelter level, for fear it would become less and less capable of responding to the program.

But then it was found that there were some families who were not using their grant money for food and clothes for the winter as planned. The client's point of view might be most reasonable: the check had come to him through the mail, was made out to him, and had to be cashed by him. He needed feed to keep the livestock he had from starving, a creditor was pressing him for settlement of a debt overdue, or the mother prevailed on the father to spend practically all of the money for clothes. Money gone, the client showed up at the office in need of food. The supervisor felt that such a client had not cooperated. He had not only spent the money for a purpose other than what it had been secured for, but he defended the expenditure, and still needed the things the money had been given him to get. If the client didn't want to play by the rules, let him leave the program.

Several cases more or less like this occurred in the winter of 1939–1940, almost none since then. The clients have learned that the grants are for specific purposes, and the checks are subject to expenditure only for purchases agreed upon, and only when countersigned by the supervisor. "The gov'ment ain't furnishin' you no money to spree wid."

THE GRANTS BECOME WORK GRANTS

In the last two years, instead of receiving the grant as a gift, the father of the family has worked for it—at the rate of twenty-five or thirty cents an hour. He works on some project approved by the FSA. He may, for example, cut posts on his own farm for a fence. Or he may work on one of the tracts recently purchased by the FSA: clear land for fields or pasture, or prepare green pines for fence posts by peeling them and seasoning them with preservative chemicals.

One looks at the treated pine posts and hopes they prove practical. Native hardwoods are scarce here, and posts are often made of small white oaks that should be allowed to grow. Even young black walnut is cut that should be saved for veneer lumber or for solid walnut bedsteads and bureaus, which the families could make themselves at the vocational shops. If the pine post experiment is successful, as now seems likely, the FSA farmers, while earning a little additional income during the winter months, will have lessened the continuous pressure upon hardwoods for fence posts.

SOMETHING OF THEIR VERY OWN

With the work grant check for specific purposes and every loan for specific things, the families sometimes groan that they have nothing for themselves, nothing of their very own. The FSA representatives reason that to help them have something of their very own is the central purpose of the program. And they point to the client's wagon, canned fruit, screens, pump, milk, eggs, medical service. Well and good, say many of them, but my debts are many and my ways of paying them are few, and sometimes I'm not so certain my situation is very different from what it would be if there had been no government program.

Many a family in the spring of 1941 was sure that no workable plan had yet been made for securing clothes. The families wanted more money for clothes, or the right to buy clothes with a larger part of their work grant checks. "Clothes is needed bad. You can't work barefooted in winter," said one woman whose family had got no shoes and no winter clothes. Another said: "The government's way is to let you go naked with a full stomach."

The families on the program must, of course, have substantial clothes, and the FSA hopes to help them secure them. The cotton stamps, which many families received in the fall of '41, helped out.

But beyond what the clients need for physical comfort may lie what they want for personal satisfaction. Maybe a colorful dress even if shoddy. Maybe a pair of patent leather shoes that will shine convincingly if not long. Ride along the roads of Greene county any warm Sunday afternoon and enjoy the colorful clothes worn by the men and women, particularly the Negroes, who work in the fields and live in the little houses.

A white mother frankly admitted that she did not have the heart to make her girls go regularly to high school. "You can't blame them for not wanting to go to school poorly dressed," she explained, "because the town children shun them and even laugh at them."

Local FSA officials realize that rehabilitation involves an awareness of the traditional wants of their clients as well as helping them secure the minimum physical subsistence needs defined by government experts. More eggs and milk and canned goods are essential, but the best of food can serve its purpose only when the people eating it are glad to be alive.

It is a hopeful sign that the FSA families are agitating for more money for clothes. For people want more and better clothes when they eat more wholesome food, feel better in general, go to church regularly, and take part in more social activities. Clothes do not make the man—or the woman or the child—but they do suggest his position in the community, and often something of his estimate of himself.

THE LOCAL STOREKEEPERS FROWN

In getting a new source of farm finance and supervision, the FSA families broke many of their old ties to landlord and storekeeper.

Itemizing the expenditures of each check placed no direct limitation on where the check might be used. Quite naturally, however, most of the expenditures were in Greensboro, and at the larger stores. The mere fact that the check had to be drawn for the exact amount of a specific purchase, or purchases, meant that in most instances the purchases would be made from the same store where the price information had been secured. Then, too, the loans were administered from the FSA office in Greensboro. The clients often went in for their checks, and made their purchases before leaving town. It early developed that while the larger merchants—particularly in Greensboro—looked at their cash registers and were satisfied, the scattered country storekeepers were often skeptical about the loans.

The rural storekeepers disliked most of all for the clients to be told to make a purchase at some specific store in Greensboro, White Plains, Union Point, Siloam, or Woodville. Such instructions, while not common, were given whenever the FSA had bought pressure cookers, glass jars, sugar, or other supplies in bulk through the lowest bidder. When jars were to be used by the tens of thousands a week, and when sugar for canning had to be available in hundred pound lots for several hundred families, it was essential that these supplies be on hand when needed.

Such a service to the clients, while generally appreciated, was resented by some. They wanted the money so they could buy at the local store where lay their traditional security against a rainy day. Not certain but that the government program would stop in a year or so, they were anxious to keep themselves in good standing at the store down the road. Further complicating the matter, the local storekeeper might have sold fewer jars or a hundred or so pounds of sugar less than he had expected, and so have had a "good price" to offer. In the face of his local "good price," the borrower received a notice that his jars or sugar were at a certain store in Greensboro, or elsewhere. He did not like it, felt that his rights were not being respected, that he ought to be allowed to buy where he pleased, especially when he could get a better price than the one arranged for him by the FSA. When the client stopped to realize that plans for large orders have to be made ahead of time, his feelings about the matter may have been somewhat allayed.

THE URGE TO GO TO TOWN

The county FSA office became the center of activities for some clients. They turned to it often. So often, in fact, that some non-FSA farmers early reflected that the clients were spending too much time on the road to Greensboro. At first the supervisors commonly asked the clients to come to town when a check needed to be signed, a pressure cooker delivered, a loan agreement made, or for any one of a dozen other reasons. People began to talk. One FSA farmer, it was said, had bought a bicycle to ride to Greensboro. He could make a quicker trip on the bicycle, and have a rested mule to plow when he got home. Another client complained that every time it got dry enough to plow that spring, he had a notice to come to the county office. Still another, used to the verbal contracts of plantation days, said: " 'Tain't no use for us to run in to see a little piece of paper."

Other government workers teased the FSA supervisors about their "office farmers." At a meeting of the County Program Planning Committee an FSA supervisor lamented that too many farmers tried to live off too little work, the county had too many "three-months farmers." A listener expressed surprise that he should be against "three-months farming" for, he said, "I've been hearing that the FSA keeps its clients on the road to and from Greensboro about nine months in the year." Everybody laughed heartily, for everybody there knew what the FSA program was doing to fill the year with meaningful farm work—cows to milk, chickens to tend, terraces to keep up, pasture fences to mend, and in more families than ever before enough stovewood by March to last out the summer.

Some of the FSA clients came to the county office more often than they were called by the supervisors. They wanted to know about an item of their indebtedness, or whether the new wagon had come.

Truth is, there are farm men and women who like so well to get into town every day or two that they will go upon the most flimsy excuse. When one of these families got on the program, there was always some relatively plausible reason for going to Greensboro. The urge to go to town is not limited to FSA farmers, as everybody knows.

When supervision from the office had been tried for a few months, clients and supervisors were agreed it could better be done at home, and in group meetings. For the past year now, the clients drop the supervisor a card when they want to see him.

Some families need more supervision than others. The clients are divided into four groups, and the supervisors call on some of them at least three times as often as others.

A VOICE IN HIS OWN AFFAIRS

Tradition is a powerful thing. And even if the farmers have had more time to work since the supervisors come by to see them, they may sometimes have had less will to work than when they got off to town more often. Discerning people raised an eyebrow when they first saw trucks deliver fertilizer to FSA clients, and in the fall saw trucks pick up their cotton. A way needs to be found for a farmer to get the advantages of mass purchasing and wholesale marketing, and still have his finger in the buying of his fertilizer and disposing of his cotton.

It would be hard to determine how much of the work that goes into the production of a cotton crop turns upon the expectations, not only of the father but the mother and the children, of getting into town when the crop is sold. Settlement time is an old institution in these parts. And though crops have not always been good for any of the farmers and seldom good for some of them, the end of the year is a time to celebrate with something good t'eat, at least some new clothes and, if there is money enough left, a new bed or radio or even an automobile.

The spring of the year is a time of hope. The buying of fertilizer and the contracting of debts to grow a crop is the essence of the season to most farmers. You are on the market for fertilizer, and the men who have it to sell treat you with deference, as do the merchants when you go in to talk about supplies. When these arrangements have been made you know where you stand in terms of your obligations. And in spring there is always the possibility that the seasons will strike right this year, that the market will rise, that this fall at settlement time you can pay your debts and have some money all your own.

Is there any way for the small farmer to profit by the economies of mass purchases and marketing and at the same time retain a sense of control over his own affairs? The further development of cooperative buying and selling would seem to be the best answer. But it is not an easy answer here, where propertyless Whites have little tradition of participation, propertyless Negroes almost none.

Hopeful beginnings have been made. Last year 9 mowing machines and hay rakes were made available to a half hundred FSA clients through master and cooperative loans. In working out schedules for using these machines, the farmers are learning to work together. As they develop further in self-reliance, perhaps they can take a larger part in the decisions of the Marketing and Purchasing Association. When the members of the governing board of the Association are chosen by all the farmers, they will have a sense of control built on actual fact. And this likely will be more satisfying than ever was the spring-time deference of creditors in the old plantation days.

There has been strain, but it is the strain of growth. The backgrounds of the borrowers are not alike. They are in different stages of development. Some remember their old sharecropper days, see they are now being asked to perform on a different level; all know they must work more and keep their eyes open. Neither they nor their supervisors deny the difficulty of what they have undertaken. Prayed the farmer-preacher who opened an FSA club meeting at Jones' Central High: "Lord, prop us up on every leaning side."

XXVI

SLOW PAYING

WHAT OVER a million dollars of FSA money has done to Greene's land and houses has seemed like a miracle to many people, who all their lives had lived with hard luck—"on the pig end of the hog, 'way back on the tail."

"GOD AND THE GOVERNMENT"

Often the new "government houses" stand next to the old tenant cabins. Many a family is now moving out of a two- or three-room tenant cabin that cost less than $300 into a five- or six-room house that is painted, has inside ceiling, window sash, electric wire sockets and a sink and water faucets in the kitchen. The REA program was cut short by the war, so current is available to only a few families and no power pumps have been installed. But some day there may be water and electric light in the house.

And beyond the modest little white houses are red barns that do not leak, cow pastures with cows in them, fenced hog lots. "God must have had something to do with it," said an elderly Negro near Carey Station. "You know, President Roosevelt in Washington must be aworkin' along with God, and the President must have had somebody who understood him to bring his plans down here to Greene county and work 'em out." His eyes full of yesterdays, he looked at the cabins which stand in the fields near the new houses: "I'll tell you, I don't know what would have come of us by now if it hadn't been for God and the Government."

In interviews all over the county, the question was asked: "What do you suppose would have happened if the government program hadn't come to Greene county?" Over and over God and Washington were linked together. "There would have been some po' hongry folks," was a typical answer. Others said: "Wouldn't have had no farmers by now. Everybody would have gone to the city." "Us po' folks woulda done perished and died out;" "Greene county would have been gone by now." "Glad some nation took pity on us," said an old man. "Glad the white folks' government bought us some mules." It was hoped that God would spare the life of the President: "I hope the Lord 'ranges for that good man to live. I just hope He 'ranges it." And Louisiana Dunn Thomas, a Negro farm tenant mother, wrote a poem: *

> Uncle Sam is my shepherd
> And I shall not want
> He help me to care for my children
> And raise all my food if I don't.
>
> He don't make me lie down in green pastures
> He lead me down to the tin warehouse
> And give me a cotton mattress.
>
> He restoreth my cow and pigs
> And chickens and some eggs
> He leadeth me in the path of sleeping
> When he gave me the cotton beds.
>
> Yea though I walk through the valley
> And shadow of death to stay here
> But as long as Uncle Sam hold everything
> No evil will I fear.
>
> Thou help me prepare my table
> It's a wonderful thing to tell,
> Surely the next few days of my life
> On a government farm I will dwell.

---

* For sketch about Poet Thomas see Appendix No. 15.

NEIGHBORS ARE IMPRESSED

But it isn't just the farmers who are working under the government program who are affected by it. The elderly Negro farmer near Carey Station who thought he could see God's hand in the Unified Farm Program is one of the oldest deacons at Moses Chapel, built soon after the slaves were freed. The church was named for a white plantation owning family, by the name of Moore, who left "prosperity ridge" when the plantations there went into decline. The name of Moore's Chapel was gradually changed to "Moses" Chapel by the local Negroes, who used too few r's to maintain the good old English name. The church was first painted in 1919 when cotton prices were high, and before many weevils had got here. It was never painted again until a few months ago when the church members, looking at the new FSA houses near by, painted it, lest their church —God's house—suffer by comparison.

A number of other Negro churches in the county were painted soon after white creosote had been sprayed on two hundred farm houses with money from FSA advance-rent agreements. Non-FSA farmers saw the creosote brighten up borrower houses, wanted their own sprayed. On a cost basis, the FSA equipment was used to spray 32 dwellings, 6 barns, 13 school buildings, 1 church, and the County Convict Camp.

Many another thing started here by the FSA has spilled over to other families. The people throughout the county have become very conscious of canning. This, of course, has not been solely because of the FSA program, for other agricultural agencies have emphasized it, too. A landlady speaks with pride of her tenant's determination to can as much as the FSA family down the road. The sale of pressure cookers to families off the program has been increased by the popularity of the cookers among the borrowers.

Soon after the FSA had the clients build their first chicken houses of slabs, other families began to build similar ones. When District Supervisor Downs of the FSA stopped by one of these places and asked the farmer why he had built the chicken house, the man was surprised: "You must be a stranger around here. Why, a lot of the families 'on the government' are building these things, and I wanted one, too."

The brooders distributed to care for the chicks have also been widely copied. Here again a specific project of the FSA has increased an activity stressed by other local agricultural agencies.

The home supervisors have emphasized the improvement of even the poorest kitchens by white-washing the walls. Many neighbors have white-washed theirs. Families off the program were so impressed by the hand mills and spray guns of the borrowers that they bought some themselves. Many a non-FSA garden, too, has been enlarged.

The monthly club meetings of FSA patrons attract some men and women not on the program. One of them, a regular attendant, said, "I'm simply not going to let them learn nothin' I don't learn."

There has been imitation, too, of FSA terracing, improved pastures, hot beds. Last year when 350 packages of fruit trees—seven peach, two apple and one pear—were delivered to clients at $1 a package, thirty extra orders were taken upon request of neighboring farm families.

IT WAS DONE WITH BORROWED MONEY

The neighbors like the things the FSA families have. But all these things cost money, and most of them were secured through loans. Of the million dollars plus, which the FSA has brought into Greene county, about one fifth has come in lieu of taxes for education and as work grants for families who needed more income than they could earn on their farms. That fifth does not have to be paid back. Two fifths has been used to buy land and develop farm units on it, and will be repaid over a period of twenty years or more by the families who live on these farms. The other two fifths of the money has been used for rehabilitation loans, and is subject to repayment over a period of five years.

The government naturally takes a considerable risk in the making of rehabilitation loans. When a family is accepted on the FSA program, such a loan is made to secure the livestock and farm equipment which he needs to work effectively, and which he could get from no other source. The family is scheduled to repay the loan in five annual installments, with the privilege of deferring payments when necessary.

TOO DRY, AND THEN TOO WET

Some of the families were feeling pretty blue about all the money they owed even before the weather extremes of spring and summer of 1941 cut short their cotton and feed crops. First it was dry, too dry to get a good stand of row crops or vegetables in the garden. Day after day the sun baked the fields; day after day the farmers hoped for rain.

When a shower did come, it was followed by another and another and another—showers in the afternoon, at night, in mid-morning—rain practically every day for six weeks. Neither hoe nor plow could be put at the roots of the lush growing grass in the fields and gardens. Now and then a farmer waded into his water-soaked land and chopped up weeds and grass, but the next shower set them to growing again. "Ain't never seen so much natural rain in all my life."

The corn stalks greened and grew with the first showers, then yellowed; the cotton stalks kept on growing. Cotton blooms appeared, and with them the weevils. Poison was of little use so long as the rain washed it off every few hours. In the fall of 1941 the farmers of Greene ginned 1,505 bales. Only in 1921, 1922, and 1923 had the cotton crops been smaller. Other crops, too, were far below normal. That fall less than 4 percent of the FSA families made their full payments, only 5 percent put aside all the money needed to produce the next year's crop. Additional loans were made to grow the next crop.

While they were further in debt at the end of 1941, most of the

FSA families were better prepared for the winter because they were on the program. They had pigs, cows, and chickens; and despite weather that was too dry and then too wet, they had more canned fruits, vegetables, and meats than ever before. Except for the FSA program, the farm people of the county would have been in a much worse condition than they were.

REPAYMENTS HAVE BEEN SLOW

All might readily agree that it is a good thing to have the things the FSA families have had, but who is going to pay for them? The families themselves, or the taxpayers of the nation? The facts provide the only satisfactory answer.

The total amount of money loaned to FSA families in the county through October 24, 1942 was $550,763. Of the $192,420 which was due on or before December 31, 1942, $107,970 had been paid by November 13, 1942, and it was estimated that $42,600 more would be paid by the end of 1942. This will leave unpaid $41,800 of the payments due up through 1942, or a little less than $65 for each of the 690 borrowing families.

OVER AGAINST THE COSTS

Since coming on the program, the tangible assets of the families— in livestock and farm equipment, home produced foods and feeds —have increased from an average of $363 to $857, a gain of $494. This suggests that the $65 "loss" on the loan service to date is a sound investment. Moreover, it is estimated by the best informed people of the county that under present farm prices and with average crops, repayments can be made on schedule from now on and at least two thirds of the remaining back payments will be collected.*

The assets of the county have increased, too. Look at the new houses and barns and the old ones brightened up with paint or white

---

* For more detailed facts, see Appendix No. 20.

creosote, at the terraced fields and developed pastures, at the better food on the farmers' tables, at the bank accounts of the leading merchants, professional men, and county officials.

What would have happened if no intensive program had ever been launched here? Without the FSA program would the population in the county have increased 8 percent in the last decade? Or would it have remained practically stationary or showed a decline along with all the surrounding counties? Wherever the additional people from Greene would have gone if there had been no population increase here, many of them would have most likely been on WPA or some other form of government subsidy. During the middle and late 1930's, surplus unskilled farm labor could find little regular employment anywhere in the nation.

When farm people left here they went into other rural areas or more likely into cities where there were already more workers than jobs. Look at the large work relief figures of the urban centers of the nation during this period, and notice how many of these workers were born and reared on Southern farms and left them only because farm operations could no longer be financed. So, the FSA program here must be seen not only in terms of what it is costing the taxpayers of the nation to have it, but how much more it might have cost the taxpayers of the nation to be without it.

Besides the increased assets in dollars-and-cents that have come to the families and the county through the program, there are other values not so easy to measure. People are more productive when they can operate a pressure cooker, develop a garden, keep baby chicks alive, care for cows and work stock.

Over against the cost of the program, too, should be set those less tangible assets of improved health and a more hopeful outlook. What value is to be put on the fact that 11 boys and girls from FSA homes finished high school this year and 17 more finished junior high school? What is it worth for children and their parents to eat a more adequate diet, and eat it in a screened house?

What value, too, is there in the assurance that your livestock and farm equipment, and food and feed for the winter, will not be sold to satisfy debts even if in a wet spell the weevils destroy most of your cotton, as they did in 1941? The farmers will tell you what this assurance means to them: "The government gives you a chance if disaster comes." "They won't take our foodstuffs, they lets us keep that." "Been living better on account we has plenty to eat. The government leave everything except the cotton."

The families on the program have more food and more debts than before they got on it. As yet, however, they have found no sure way of earning the extra money to pay their larger bills.

INCOME FROM LIVESTOCK UNCERTAIN

The new farm units being developed by the Greene County Farms, Incorporated, are set up for subsistence farming, and cash income from livestock and cotton. It is confidently hoped by FSA officials that this dual source of cash income—even without war-time prices —insures the repayment of the rent or purchase price of these 140-acre farm units with their new buildings and fences.

The development of livestock farming has already been achieved with a half dozen FSA families. Other families are well on the way. But it takes time or money—usually both—for a man to set himself up in the cattle business even on a small scale. If he buys the animals, it takes a deal of cash; if he grows them from calves, it takes two or three years at the least.

Livestock farming requires the constant attention of the farmer, every evening and morning of every day of the year. Some families, who still like to declare a holiday from Saturday noon to Monday morning, will have to reorganize their lives to make a success of it. When one looks at the things the FSA has already got its borrowers to do about gardens and canning, this daily care of livestock would not seem too difficult to achieve.

Some real progress has been made already through the placement of mules, cows, pigs, and chickens with each of over 500 farm families, nearly two thirds of whom had had no animals of their own beyond a pig or two and a half dozen chickens.

Some neglect of animals on these farms has occurred and some have starved to death. Here are the figures: During the past three years, a tenth of the clients have had a mule to die. Less than a tenth of the deaths, as shown by the veterinarian's reports, were due primarily to starvation. Altogether 175 cows and calves died, about one fifth directly from such avoidable causes as starvation or failure to provide shelter. These losses are heavy when compared with the farmers in the county who have always had livestock. But the deaths of mules and cows have been but a fraction of what was expected by some plantation owners and many a town dweller who at the beginning of the program predicted: "You can put the mules and cows out there, but they'll let 'em die this winter."

The FSA staff is determined to reduce the livestock mortality rates of their clients, and progress has already been made. Scientific medical care is provided through the Veterinary Association, and the production of feed crops is being increasingly stressed. Within ten years the FSA supervisors believe the record of their clients will stack up well with those of good livestock farmers anywhere.

COTTON CROP REMAINS SMALL AND COSTLY

But what of the FSA farmers' production of cotton? You will hear many people say the "government farmers" are doing a pretty good job of "everything except the main thing—cotton." And that until their cotton crops are better they will remain hopelessly in debt. The only sure way yet found to pay farm debts here is to have cotton to sell, and plenty of it. The cotton records of the county show that the FSA farmers have produced a little more than their proportion of the county's cotton crop. The production per plow in 1940 was 1.9 bales per FSA plow and 1.6 for the remainder of the county. Again in 1941, the production per FSA plow was a little above the county average.

The truth is, as everybody here will point out to you, the cotton crop for the county is small and costly.

The cotton acreage under the crop control program has been low, and will remain low so long as it is figured on the county's post-weevil record, when the cotton acreage was less than one third what it had been in pre-weevil days. "Looks like they don't want a man to pay out, they give us so little cotton to plant."

The cotton crop is costly because good yields can be had only by heavy applications of commercial fertilizers. A farm tenant's fertilizer bill commonly exceeds the annual rent for the farm he puts it on, sometimes costs more per acre than the purchase price of the land. FSA farmers along with the rest of the cotton farmers of Greene find it hard to pay debts with cotton, harder with anything else.

It is important that the FSA client have a sense of security. It is also important that he accept the obligation to repay the money loaned to him for this purpose. The borrower family is making the greatest progress only when its sense of responsibility deepens along with its feeling of security.

XXVII

DEBTS AND WHAT THEY MEAN

A MAN, landed or landless, likes to make a purchase now and then, with only his name standing for its payment.

CREDIT MAY BOLSTER THE SOUL

Men of means get money at the bank on their signature, and are pleased with their own good reputation. A landless man without a dime in his pocket walks out of a store with more than a sack of flour and a slab of meat—he walks home with the satisfaction of knowing that the storekeeper has confidence in him as a man. Credit in a pinch does more than stave off starvation, it bolsters the soul.

The weak position of the propertyless man, however, gives a dishonest creditor an opportunity to exploit him, be he white or black. When people with smaller incomes buy things on credit, receipts may be needed later to prove that the bill was paid. Or perhaps the bill was not paid in full when the purchaser thought it was. Second and third graders are readily confused about payments, are satisfied only when they have the "paid-in-full" slip in their hands.

A creditor may have a propertyless man arrested and put in jail on the technical charge of having gotten "a thing of value under false pretenses." A few months ago a case involving this point was taken before the United States Supreme Court from nearby Hancock County. The Court declared such imprisonment illegal. But it takes time for a Supreme Court decision to get down through the State courts to county officials, and so a propertyless man may still be arrested and put in jail for non-payment of a debt.

With oral contracts only, many a tenant and many a landlord has become convinced that the other was not living up to the agreement. And hundreds are the landless farmers who have felt that their store accounts were too big when they went to settle up. The total is often a shock to any purchaser. He can hardly believe he had bought so much. But if he cannot read the items and add up the figures, he cannot satisfy himself as to whether the storekeeper is right. And so the feeling lingers that he has been cheated—about as poisonous a feeling as a human can have.

Without written records there is no way to prove anything. Just one man's word against another, just a column of figures on a ledger against a fellow's impression of what ought to be there. Debtor and creditor alike are protected when each has a record of his own.

RECORD BOOKS ARE IMPORTANT

The FSA has encouraged its families to keep full records. In this way the family can escape the unprotected position of a recordless debtor.

At their first visit, or soon after, the supervisors show the family the detailed record book in which they are to enter all incomes and expenditures. Over one fourth of the colored parents and one eighth of the white parents are illiterate, and a much larger proportion can barely read and write. It is doubtful whether more than a third of the Negro parents and two thirds of the Whites have had enough education to keep a record book.

One unschooled farmer, when asked about his records, reported that he had them all in order, and to prove it brought out a rusty wire hanging full of letters, contracts, and other printed instructions involved in his "government farm" operations. Even though neither he nor his wife could read, they had no trouble in distinguishing the letters which came from the FSA office. Never before had they received letters without stamps on them. Many a client early noted that the stampless letters that included checks were different from the others, wanted more of them.

It is tedious to keep detailed records of all cash incomes and expenditures, and many families soon tired of it. "Writin' down all that stuff don't make you any money, just helps you know where it went, and you know that anyway if you spend it right."

ONE LOAN AFTER ANOTHER

The simplest part of their record keeping when they went on the FSA in the spring of 1939 was the matter of how much they owed the government. It was a single item of $300 or $500, due in five yearly payments of $60 or $100 each, plus interest. But in most cases, the interest and only a part of this yearly payment was made. The unpaid portion of it was reloaned to the farmer, to be paid back over a period of 5 years. He put aside part of the money to grow the next crop, got the rest he needed through a supplemental loan, to be paid back in five annual installments. That fall he owed the second fifth of his original loan and the interest, the first fifth of the "re-loan" and interest, and the first fifth of his supplemental loan and interest. In the meantime there had been two grant checks to most families, one each in 1939 and another in 1940, and maybe a sanitation grant besides.

By the early spring of 1941, when the difference between what they owed and what they paid on the past year's bill had been re-loaned to them for five years, most of the clients were overwhelmed by the mechanics of bookkeeping. Only a fraction of the borrowers knew how much they owed. They just knew that all their cotton—the only cash crop they had—now went to the government, much as it had formerly gone to landowner Smith or Jones, or to store-keeper Johnson or Brown. "I don't know how much I can pay," said one farmer, "all I know is I makes the cotton and they takes it." Or again: "I'm between the chip and the bark, I'm jest in there."

When they were asked what was the difference in their condition now and before they got on the program they usually answered that they had more milk and eggs and canned goods to live on, and that they got a financial statement from the Montgomery FSA office every six months.

But how were they to understand the statement? Not one of them had ever studied bookkeeping, but few had gone beyond the fourth grade in a one-teacher school. The farm and home supervisors could explain the figures, but with all their office work to do they had little time to sit down with a hundred farmers, one after another, until each of them knew where he stood.

In the late spring of 1941 came the "Food-for-Defense" loans. Most of the families were glad enough to get the additional chickens and cow, but some felt they already had as many debts as they could carry. Nonetheless, the chickens arrived on schedule, and the debts of the families were larger.

WHOSE COCKERELS?

As the chicks lived and grew, a question arose about whose chickens they were. Did they belong to the families, and could some be eaten when they were big enough to fry? Or did they belong to the government because of the loan? All understood from the outset that the pullets were to be kept for layers. But what of the other half of them, the cockerels? After awhile word came that they were to be fed up to two pounds, that the supervisors would get the nicest of them to sell, and that the money they brought would go toward the settlement of the purchase loan.

"We're not going to be able to pay our debts anyway," was the way one woman put it, "and I don't imagine the chickens will go far." The resentment of another was a prolonged wail:

They give me them chickens, and told me I'd be a big nigger. I was so glad I had something that showed me how to raise them many chickens at one time . . .

I had a hard time raisin' 'em. It'd rain, and I'd get up at night wid 'em.

I cleaned out their brooder ev'y day. I'd give 'em corn and wheat and collards to keep 'em nibblin'.

I asked 'em not to give me them chickens 'cause I knew I'd get crazy about 'em. But they said they was mine and I did feel like when a white man told me something it was right.

Now they tell me to cotch up all my roosters 'cause a truck's a-comin' for 'em. If they come here after my roosters, I'll give 'em the pullets and the brooder, too. I don't want none of 'em.

When you've tended somep'n, gettin' up in the night and cleanin' the brooder, it's like chillun.

They said them was my chickens. Now they take 'em off.

The plan to apply the cockerels to a debt was a strange new thing, for families here had always had undisputed ownership of their chickens, and could eat or sell them at will. The cows and hogs, mules and wagons and plows were commonly used as collateral for loans. But the chickens remained unencumbered along with the cats and dogs, not because they were without monetary value like the cats and dogs but because they were likely to be eaten if company came, or to be picked up and sold the next time the family was pressed for cash. And the rolling store comes by every week, and a hen will always buy some snuff and flavoring, candy and chewing gum, or flour and fatback.

The supervisors, on the other hand, had good reasons to apply the sale of the cockerels to the purchase loan. The chicken project had been expensive, and aside from the sale of the cockerels, no income could be secured from it until winter or spring, when the pullets began to lay.

Getting the cockerels up to the standard two-pound size was not easy. Many of the families thought it foolish to feed them in the pen when they could be allowed to forage for themselves.

But when they were turned out, the chickens just ran around after you waiting for something to eat. Many a woman looked at the brooder-raised chickens standing about the yard while her hen-raised chickens were out hunting for food, decided she liked best the ones that would scratch for themselves . . . "I ain't as proud of these brooder chickens as I am of my own. They didn't have no mother to teach 'em to scratch, and they ain't got as much sense."

One Negro woman was mildly reprimanded by her supervisor for speaking of her brooder chickens as "government chickens." Asked the supervisor, a little piqued, "Do you call your mule a 'government mule'?" A polite "No, sir," was the answer; but the woman turned to her neighbor and said, "I'll call 'em 'government chickens' anyway; I got to have some way of tellin' 'em from my real chickens."

Here and there that winter, a family fed their "government pullets" as recommended, and there were eggs by the dozens in kitchens where no eggs had ever been except in high spring when the "real chickens" that scratch for themselves always lay a nestful or two before they begin to set.

The farmer and his wife are right in letting their unimproved breeds scratch for themselves, for they would not produce many eggs even with the best of feed. The supervisors are equally right when they ask that the higher bred laying varieties be kept off the ground for the first several weeks, and fed properly. The supervisors and a few of the farmers know, and other farmers are learning, that a hen's value lies in her ability to lay eggs rather than to scratch, and that good hens are worth having even if one has to give up the cockerels to pay off a part of the purchase loan.

DEBTS NEED TO BE UNDERSTOOD

By mid-summer of 1941, perhaps not more than one farmer in eight or ten knew what his debts were, or what he was supposed to pay that fall. And nothing will demoralize an ex-plantation family so quickly and thoroughly as debts they do not understand.

It was the accepting of credits and the paying of debts that defined the dependent place of the landless man in the old plantation system, which left him under-housed and under-fed. And the creditor landlord, be he ever so honest, was seldom believed by the debtor tenants to be playing the game fairly. Nor is it likely that the families on the FSA program will believe they are being dealt with fairly very long after they have become overwhelmed in debts they do not understand.

Said one farmer in a rebellious mood: "I know I'm stirring all I can, and I want to know how I'm doing. It's not necessary for me to work and pay and not know nothing."

A financial statement is needed which the family can understand, even if as much time is spent in working up such a statement and in explaining it as was required to get the family to put up its first hundred quarts of canned goods. It may be better for the family to have a little less to eat and fewer tools to work with, than to have all it needs except the will to use the things provided for its use. It is not the fact of debts that crushes the family nearly so much as the family's failure to understand them.

"I just loved this 'government farm' business the first two years," one borrower recalled. "Why, I would have skunt a flea for his tallow!" But now—"When you don't know where you are, it sort of makes a fellow mad, and he can't work like he ought to. I'm like a blind dog in a meat house about this program. Good things in it, I know, but I don't know how to turn to them."

Debts, of course, are not paid with understanding. They are paid with money—with money earned by debtors. And debtors pay more debts when they work with a will to repay them. That is why creditors need to help debtors understand the amount they owe, how these obligations were incurred, and what happens when they fail to pay them.

The FSA owes it to itself and to its clients to find ways of helping the clients know what their total debts are, and how much they owe each fall.

SECURITY THROUGH DEBT

Some FSA borrowers do not seem to be very much concerned about their debts. Debts are cherished by some dependent farm families. There are historical causes for this. The slave found his greatest security in being owned by a powerful planter. After Emancipation the farm wage hand or sharecropper soon found that his greatest security lay in the assistance and protection of influential people, and that his best way to be protected by them was to be in debt to them. Creditors everywhere afford some protection to the people who owe them money; otherwise, debts would scarcely ever be collected.

It seems clear that many of the FSA borrowers do not want to get out of debt, but rather want to pay just enough to remain in debt. The truth behind this fact measures the extent to which dependent farm families have found greater security in debts than in whatever efforts they may have made to lead independent lives. This may be because the efforts some have made to become independent have not worked out. Others may never have realized there was any way of life for them except chronic dependency. About this group, some would say, "Well, they're born that way."

The records of families who have tried to become independent are heavy with failures, and for many reasons. First of all, cotton is a hazardous crop. The costs of production here are high. Hundreds of landless families—white and colored—who put the savings of their good years into the purchase of land often found that by the time they had paid a half or two thirds of the purchase price the sale value of the land had dropped to a figure below the amount still owed on it.

"FORTY-ACRES AND A MULE"—ALMOST FORGOTTEN

Race and class values, too, have made it harder for families to become independent. Again there are backgrounds: it was never assumed by the large plantation owners during slavery that their lands would ever be owned by either the slaves or poorer whites. Nor has it been assumed by many of the leading families of more recent years that this was a desirable thing to happen. Consequently, the mass of the poorer people, white and black, disfranchised through the White Primary and the poll tax, have had little encouragement from either the large landowning families or the politicians to become independent through the ownership of farm land.

Some talk of "forty-acres and a mule" was heard here during Reconstruction days. And again in the 1890's when the Third Party was active. Even today the matter has not been wholly forgotten. Said an elderly Negro: "Some of us old folks still talks about it a little, you know, up under our hat; but the young folks don't seem to know nothing about it."

The landless man has remained landless, and has needed the protective security of the landed families. And who is there to blame the man without land and without a vote who likes to be in debt to a man who has land and political influence? How can this landless man be more certain he will have a friend, should he be brought into court? And how else can he be sure he will get something to eat in hard times? Herein lies the situation out of which come those meaningful phrases: "He is a good tenant," or "He is a good nigger."

Some dependent farm tenants like to have more than one creditor, for each additional creditor—wanting his payments, too—makes certain that the debtor's other creditors do not sell the debtor out or make him pay too much.

Out of the landless man's security through debt comes his theory of letting the creditor look out for himself, and paying on his debts not to become an independent man—for he may have no hopes of that—but rather just enough to remain in the good graces of his creditor, or creditors.

The clients well know the traditional cleavages within the local community. They know how the members of each economic and racial group are expected to behave toward the other. The FSA program came, and they soon sensed what was new in it and what was old, and whether the new or the old was the more powerful.

SOME NEED TO BE "HABILITATED"

The fact that a farmer has become a "government farmer" may give him a new slant on his debts and his responsibility for them, or it may not. Much depends on how the client feels about his situation, and especially what he thinks is the attitude of his supervisors. He may think of them as plantation overseers, and of himself as a sharecropper on a government plantation; or in unnumbered ways he may be assured by his supervisors that they expect him to be a thoughtful person, assume responsibility, and exercise his own judgment.

The gulf between a sharecropper and a self-sufficient farmer is wide, and some feel it cannot be crossed. Some critics of the program insist that the FSA is not primarily interested in rehabilitation. They point out that the program seems to stem from social values rather than economic values. The FSA representatives may readily agree with him, if by social he means human, and if by economic he means materialistic. The FSA has tried to put human values first, and the materialistic phases of the program have been geared to the development of more adequate human beings, as persons and as members of communities. These critics of the program further point out that it is impossible to "rehabilitate" a family that has never been "habilitated." The FSA was set up to help hard-pressed farm families to become self-supporting as soon as they can, irrespective of whether in their lives they had ever got very far from slavery. Therefore, for a portion of the families on the program the term "rehabilitation" is more a polite word than a true word.

The fact that the program is something new for some of the people here underscores its possible importance in the light of the democratic concepts upon which the nation is founded, and for the protection of which the nation is now deep in an international war. The FSA program also seems to be contributing to democracy when it helps the sons and daughters of small owners, who have fallen into landlessness along the way, achieve a status more nearly like that of their parents.

Perhaps nothing so well emphasizes the low plane of living of many rural families in the county as the fact that the comparatively modest loans made by the FSA to its borrowers have not been repaid up to schedule. It is not that the families are now living too well. The loans were small, and have been used only for such basic human needs as a more adequate diet, a doctor when sick, a mule or two, a cow or so, and a little farm equipment.

HONORED WITH A WAGON

There are families on the program who still have need of some of the most basic things.

"Lige" Rachel, a Negro farmer, had been on the FSA program six years. He had a pressure cooker, had been sent some chickens, had bought a mule and a cow, but he wanted a wagon. On a bright day in June, 1941, he stood between the plow handles in the midst of his growing cotton, knee high. Elderly and stooped, his face was beaded with sweat. He hadn't minded working all these years, but he never had understood why he hadn't got a wagon. He thought he would get one the first year, then the second, and was sure he would get one the third, but he didn't, nor in the fourth either.

When the fifth year came he had real hopes because the families on the Billups place down the road went on the program, and they all got a wagon. He asked his supervisor about it repeatedly, begged him. What he really had on his mind was a new wagon, but if he couldn't get that he'd be glad to have a second-hand one.

He took the matter to his white friends, talked with Hamp McGibony and Wade West, and priced a wagon at Binns Hardware Store in Greensboro for $39. But he had no way of paying for it. Straightening his stooped shoulders, he said: "It's been six years now, and I done the best I could. Some of the folks around here have automobiles. Now I never wanted one of them, but it does look like they would honor me with a wagon." Another year passed. It was early summer of 1942. "Lige" Rachel signed a check, and his supervisor countersigned it. At last, a wagon.

The borrowers have unpaid debts on a wagon and a mule, a cow and some chickens, a pressure cooker and some glass jars—debts unpaid primarily because cash incomes on farms are chronically low here, and because some families have found more security in debt than out of it. "You can't work with your hands alone. A fellow needs a wagon, plow-gears, good stock . . ."

SOME FAMILY-SIZE FARMS

Some small farmers have always made their way here. Even in a bad crop year like 1941, ten white and six colored FSA borrowers met their payments in full. A goodly number of family-size farmers in the county, on and off the FSA program, are proving to all comers that this is a good section for livestock, small fruits, diversified farming, and healthful wholesome living. Drive off from Greensboro in any direction, and soon you will find a small landowner or independent renter who is making his own meat and bread at home, paying his debts, and slowly raising his plane of living.

Most of the successful family-size farmers grow all the cotton they can, then supplement their cash income with sour cream, eggs, a beef, or the sale of a patch of timber now and then. In many cases one or more members of the family will be working for wages at the sawmill or cotton mill, driving a school bus, or doing some other work to keep ready cash coming in all along.

Among these family-size farmers who pay their debts even in the hard years are young families and old ones, black ones and white ones. You'll find them living on the white lands and on the red, members of the Baptist or Methodist or Presbyterian churches. Some of them never plant until the moon is right. Others pay no attention to the moon, merely watch the soil and the seasons. Ask one of these farmers after another how he does it, and you soon find that back of each there is hard work and planning, and a family pulling together.

The FSA has tried to multiply the number of these farm families who are doing well.

WHERE DO WE GO FROM HERE?

In Greene county the FSA has three big challenges before it: first, to help farmers develop additional sources of cash income; second, to help the more dependent farmers learn that they can find security through the payment of debts; third, to help the farmers and their wives become more active in local affairs.

CHALLENGE I—MORE CASH

Efforts are being made to increase the production of livestock products to supplement the cash income. The growing chickens this year, cockerels and pullets alike, are the undisputed property of the farm families, who will sell, eat, or trade their cockerels as they please. The families are already liking the brooder chickens better than last year. Several clients have agreed to feed off their pullets, and start using laying mash in late fall. It is believed that many farmers here will soon be producing eggs for the market during the winter months when egg prices are best.

Years of supervision will still be required for the typical cotton farmer before he will take good enough care of his cows and chickens to get the best results from them.

CHALLENGE II—MORE HOPE

Advancement is being made toward security through the payment of debts. Each year more families object to further obligations being added to what they owe. This is a good sign. It means that they are hoping to get out of debt and so achieve greater self-reliance. To encourage this attitude, the FSA might arrange for their clients to get acquainted with some farmers about like themselves who have already achieved a good measure of the security they are being encouraged to work toward. The white clients would revel in reports from some members of their own group who might go and see the things being done at Pine Mountain, Georgia, on the Ashwood Farms in South Carolina, or in Coffee county, Alabama.

Even though gasoline and rubber are scarce, representatives of the Negro borrowers might well visit and report back on some project such as the Flint River Farms, in Macon county, where some of them visited two years ago. Real appreciation was expressed by all who went. Louisiana Dunn Thomas did a four stanza poem about the trip. Two of them were:

> Early on one Sunday morning
>   We left on a trip to see
> How life in the lower south
>   Compared to this could be.

> We arrived in the peaceful country,
>   The things we saw would take a prize
> I could hear a little whisper
>   Go back home and do likewise.

The FSA supervisors are coming to understand more of the clients' feelings. The more dependent a client was before he came on the program, the greater his need for a supervisor who has faith in his power to develop, and who takes pride in his every achievement. The supervisors are more willing than ever before to stop their routine tasks and take time to help a family understand their debt situation. They see, too, something of the importance of helping their clients become better performers by reason of the faith they have in them as people, people who are capable of paying their own way while they go forward.

CHALLENGE III—MORE BELONGING

Many an FSA client is already taking a more active part in church and school affairs. How can the FSA help this happen? Mainly by continuing its regular program. Perhaps it would help to try with the Extension Service and the County Board of Education to work out a "parents' bus" once a week or even once a month, with club meetings scheduled on different days for the different communities.

The people of the county can help the FSA program by seeking out farm people who do not take an active part in community affairs, giving them things to do, and making them feel wanted. This is perhaps the point at which the general citizen can make his best contribution to the Unified Farm Program, by rejoicing in the advancement of the government farmers, by being cordial and friendly at the cannery, courthouse, store, school, and church. By welcoming them into the leadership as well as the followship of the county.

The FSA representatives in Greene have cooperated with other agencies in the development of a county-wide program, and in the improvement of the schools. Recreation has been boosted as have also the volunteer forest fire control, school lunchrooms, county library, nutrition programs, and the activities of the County War Board. The FSA staff members have busied themselves with these wider community matters because they are interested in the full development of all the farm people.

PART SEVEN

TO THE LAST MAN

XXVIII

THE FIRST CLINICS

THREE GRAND JURIES showed their interest in the emerging Unified Farm Program by recommending the adoption of the Ellis Health Law. Dr. Goodwin Gheesling was asked to serve as chairman of the County Board of Health. The County Commissioners set aside their share of the funds for the health work, and in June 1939 the program was begun with Dr. J. A. Johnson in charge. Working with him were two registered nurses provided by the FSA, a sanitary engineer, and an office clerk.

A year after the first public clinics in the county were started, Dr. Johnson estimated that because of low incomes less than half the people of the county had had effective medical service before the health program was launched and before the Health Association for FSA clients was organized. With these activities under way, he thought that about one fourth the people were still without medical services, but that the clinics of the health department could meet a part of the needs of this group.

Some public health work had been done in the county before the Ellis Health Law program began. Two nurses from the State Department of Health had been working part-time in the county on tuberculosis, immunization work, and the supervision of midwives. The WPA had installed about two hundred sanitary privies.

Like most of the Unified Program, the new health work represented not a new approach, but the expanding of services already begun on a small scale.

TESTS AND HYPO-NEEDLES

During the first six months of the Ellis Health Law here, the county health office rendered medical and nursing service to 680 persons; immunized 2,167 against smallpox, 222 against diphtheria, 1,901 against typhoid fever; 2,560 white school children were examined. Of the 718 persons tested for hookworm only 5 were infected, and all these had recently moved into the county. There was practically no malaria either. One thousand four hundred and thirteen tests were made for syphilis; 10.8 percent were positive. During that six-months' period, 537 venereal disease treatments were given.

Besides the full roster of clinics at Greensboro and Union Point for each race, pre-natal and well-baby clinics were set up within comparatively easy reach of all sections of the county, except the Greshamville and Wrayswood communities.

At the well-baby clinics the youngsters early learned to appreciate the nurse's interest in them; with the cooperation of the FSA home supervisors, tasty dishes were prepared in the presence of the mothers and served to the mothers and babies.

The work in the county health department of the sanitary engineer has been no less tangible than that of the health commissioner and nurses. Nearly 300 sanitary privies have been installed, 40 of these at public schools, and 200 on FSA farms. The water supply program includes the examination of water samples, the installation of approved individual wells, and the improvement of others. A few septic tanks have been installed, and a number of premises surveyed for rodent control.

The services of the county health office have continued along the lines of its first six months' work.

"COME IN, DOCTOR"

Though no child likes a hypodermic needle poised for his arm, the children who are most distressed are the ones from homes where doctors seldom call. It was late one afternoon at Brown's Chapel, a colored school. Word had gone out among the children that the doctor would probably come around that afternoon to give them typhoid shots. You know nothing of this, drive up to the two-story Negro lodge hall in which the school convenes and find everything unnaturally quiet. The teacher answers your tap at the door, says, "Come in, Doctor." The children, all tiny tots, remain immobile until they learn that you are not the "needle doctor." Only then do you hear noises upstairs where twenty larger children, in equal fear of being vaccinated, had sat speechless until they heard the relieving news come through the planks which separate the two floors. But as the health doctor and nurses make their annual rounds of the schools, Negro and White, the children become less afraid. And as the Unified Farm Program has gone on, as we shall see shortly, the colored school that was held in the lodge hall at Brown's Chapel now convenes in a new schoolhouse just up the road.

Special work has been done in the care of tubercular cases and suspects. Just recently nearly 75 x-rays were made.

The two venereal disease clinics are still held each week. In a single month this past summer over 750 treatments were given, more than in the whole first six months. Seventeen patients were dismissed as no longer infectious. While a few of the syphilitics almost never report for treatment unless threatened with arrest and imprisonment, the majority of them come regularly. Two years ago a man hobbled about on crutches, too crippled to do any work. Now he does his own farm work, even new-ground plowing. A woman, happy to be feeling well again, is glad, too, to know that she "won't disease nobody now."

It is difficult for people without automobiles in remote parts of the county to attend the clinics. There are some patients, however, who let nothing keep them away—one regularly walked over seven miles, each way, for her treatments.

There was urgent need for a relatively inexpensive mode of transportation for the poorer farm folk to the clinics even when tires and gasoline were available. Now that these are restricted, the need for scheduled transportation is all the more acute. The County Health Department might cooperate with other agencies in developing a plan by which weekly transportation could be worked out for families to attend farm meetings, school gatherings, recreational programs, and other community affairs.

THE MIDWIVES COOPERATE

One of the important functions of the County Health Program has been the supervision of Negro midwives, who deliver over half of the babies born in the county.

With the coming of the Ellis Health Law, the oldest midwives were put on old-age pensions and the number allowed to practice was reduced to fifteen, from about twice that number. Supervision was made systematic. The midwives attend monthly meetings for instructions in obstetrics and care of the mothers and babies, and they are given maternity kits which they are taught to keep ready for a call.

To make certain that midwives perform only in normal deliveries, the county health office has tried, with good success, to have the mothers who expect to be delivered by midwives attend the prenatal clinics. Tests made there will reveal almost any abnormality. If the trouble cannot be corrected, the health office refers the case to a physician.

Standards still remain low. A few of the midwives can read and write, most of them cannot. Five cannot even sign their names, and only three can fill out a birth certificate. Superstitions about birthing babies, which have grown up through hundreds of years of folk practice, do not disappear within a fortnight or a decade.

The county health nurse, for example, leaves instructions that the newborn baby sleep by itself. She shows how a comfortable crib can be made of a barrel or apple box, and sometimes to be sure that one is available she takes one with her. But the midwife and the grandmother, who have always felt it was "bad luck" for a baby to sleep away from the mother, may put the baby back in the mother's bed as soon as the nurse is out of sight. Between June, 1939, and June, 1942, at least four babies were killed by mothers rolling over on them during the night.

WITH VISIONS AND VOICES

Midwifery is an avocation for some Negro women. It gives them something important to do, and brings in a few dollars now and then. For others, midwifery is a calling, with visions and voices. Here is how it happened to Ada Mathis:

It was eighteen years ago, the eleventh of November. I had quilted out a quilt that day, all by myself. I finished it late at night and put it in the closet, said to myself, "Now, tomorrow morning I can begin another task." I sat down in front of the fire. Was tired, so tired. I sat there for awhile and rested, and then when I leaned over and started to untie my shoe, the spirit spoke to me. The spirit said, "You'll have to put those shoes back on before day." You understand that the spirit don't talk out loud like I'm talking now, but speaks low, like a deep reasoning in the heart.

I stopped and folded my hands and looked in the fire, and went over the community in my mind to see if anybody was sick. But I didn't find nobody sick. Then I took off my shoes and bowed on my knees, laid my hands out in the chair I was sitting in, and prayed, "Lord, whatsoever my hands find to do, let me do it joyfully, and bless the work of my hands, and bless everything my hands have laid to for good. Lord, my eyes are dim, strengthen my eyes so I can see; my knees are weak, strengthen my knees so I can run on your erruns." Then I got up and went to bed, and right off to sleep.

Way in the night, Jake—who lives a mile down the road—called at my winder, "Mis Ada, get up. I want you to go down home." Through my sleep, I asked him what was the matter. He said Inez was sick, and he wanted me to come and wait on her. So I got up and sponged my body with cold water, like I do every morning, put on my shoes, rushed out of the door, and run all the way to Jake's house.

When I got there, the baby was ready born. I didn't have no medicine bag then like I got now, and I never had cut a cord. So I knelt down on the floor by the mother and baby and kept asayin', "Lord, now help me do this right. Show me how, Lord, show me how." Then I tied and cut the cord, and it didn't bleed a speck. I got the mother and baby up on the bed and scoured the floor. When the other children heard the new baby cry, they came running in. I made up their beds then, and swept the floor and put away things.

All tired out, I went to the kitchen and pushed out the shutter. And there it was a beautiful morning, the sun was rose just above the trees. Then it all came back to me what the spirit had spoke. Before the daylight, I had put on my shoes, I had run, and I had done all that work, and now the sun was just a-coming up. Hadn't I asked the Lord to strengthen my knees? Hadn't I asked Him to bless the work of my hands?

From that day, I've borned seventy-five babies, white and colored, and I ain't lost a one in birth, mother or baby, and I ain't had to call a doctor but six times. But I come near losing the last two babies I borned, twins. They was little babies. You know, the kind that you have to send word to the nurse about. They were so little, just three pounds apiece, and I thought I would never get them to cry. I fought and fought with the first one, and he finally cried. And then the second one, born two hours later, he just wouldn't cry. I slapped it with cold water, and I slapped it with hot water, and I was about to give up—but I didn't. I kept afightin', and got to cryin', "Lord, I have borned seventy-four babies and haven't lost a one, give me this baby, don't let my baby die." And then it squalled out, and I stopped slapping the baby and started slapping my hands. Tears were runnin' down my cheeks, but I laughed through my tears and praised the Lord. He knew all the time what He was going to do, but He wanted to see what I was going to do! If I hadn't called on the Lord to help me, I sure would have lost that last baby I borned.

Even though the "grannies" are not always scientific in their skills, many women, some white as well as colored, prefer midwives to doctors. They can stay at the house before and after the birth. There is no frantic last-minute call, as for the doctor, and none of the rushing back and forth to attend other patients.

Most of the midwives like their work and take pride in it. If the mothers will attend the prenatal clinics regularly, and the midwives can learn when, during a delivery, a doctor needs to be called, they can render a service without endangering the life of any mother or child.

Another agency that contributes to the health needs in the county is the American Red Cross. A chapter was organized here in World War I, and has always oversubscribed its war quotas.

In peacetime it has had an annual roll call of around 150 members, most of them at a dollar a year. The program has been limited largely to assisting veterans, and occasionally helping a needy family. In one instance a boy who had lost his eyesight was taken to a specialist in Athens. In another case, the mother of a large family was carried to a distant hospital for an operation; the surgeon donated his fee, and again the Red Cross paid the remaining expenses.

During the early years of the depression, and before the federal relief agencies were organized, the Red Cross shipped flour and meat and clothes in here each winter by the carload. Plantation owners often encouraged their tenants to apply for the free food and clothes, sometimes sent trucks to carry it home for them. It was at this time that relief first "spoiled" workers in Greene county. The county's monthly pauper allowance of one to three dollars had never caused any trouble, but full-size sacks of flour and meat and clothes—just for the asking—was a different matter.

Red Cross food and clothes helped many a farm tenant family through the hard winter months, and relieved debt-pressed planters of having to provide for their tenants while they were not working. Then, too, practically all of a debtor-tenant's crops could be sold to settle accounts when he could readily get food and clothes free. The Red Cross supplies stopped coming to Greene only when the expanded federal relief program became operative here.

The only natural disaster to occur in the county in recent years was a tornado in February, 1942. The National Red Cross and the local chapter helped more than 20 families after the tornado had gone across the lower part of the county. It had torn down 15 houses, 24 barns, and small farm buildings. The tornado destroyed $75,000 worth of property. No people were killed.

To give the families a place to stay, and the food and clothes they needed, the Red Cross spent $2,243. Five white families were given $1,600 in all; over a dozen Negro families were given altogether about $700. The FSA also helped the families through tornado grants, $865 to 11 of its clients and $2,130 to 28 other families.

UNMET HEALTH NEEDS

There are unmet health needs in the county even after the clinics of the County Health Department and the Health Association of the FSA have done their work. The programs have been in the right direction, but they have not yet reached all of the people. As noted above, scheduled transportation would take care of some.

The preponderance of extractions by FSA's Dental Care Association reveals clearly that as yet almost no dental work is being done for the children of these families, while in non-FSA families even necessary extractions are often neglected.

There is still very poor nutrition in some groups in spite of the good food program of the agricultural agencies and hot lunches in the white schools and many of the Negro schools. The families of most sawmill workers and wage hands still eat unbalanced diets. It is not solely because they do not have enough money, but sometimes the result of the traditional food habits of plantation days. The emphasis on canning is reaching this group noticeably. A few families were influenced by a recent questionnaire from Washington. It included questions about family purchases of lean meat, eggs, citrus fruits. Some of the dependent Negro families realized for the first time that some people thought they might eat the same foods as the landowning white folks.

Most of the people in the county in the fall of 1942 were eating bleached white flour, buying it from stores where enriched flour was not even offered for sale. Where enriched flour could be found, it was regularly in the most expensive brands.

The women of the poorer farm families are in greatest need of additional health care. They are the mothers of large families, and childbirth is consuming, though you will now and then hear a woman who has had ten or a dozen children ignore childbirth and report that she has never been sick a day in her life. They do all of their own work and help the menfolk in rush seasons.

Pellagra is common among these mothers, and their ailment is not always treated. They may be thought of as "puny women," always complaining. More than a few of them have suffered lacerations at childbirth, and have been weakened by protracted slow bleeding. They struggle along, half ashamed of their weakness, half afraid of doctors, and in terror of operations. A few are conscious of their situation: "So many sorry women in the world from being half tended to." Even among families on FSA's Health Association, ill health is sometimes accepted for years as if there were no remedy. Women's troubles may be looked upon as the work of the Lord.

Some of the poorer Negro women eat white clay, particularly during pregnancy. Scattered deposits of this clay, which contains some available calcium and phosphorus, have been found in Greene and adjoining counties. A farm boy near Siloam will dig out a gallon bucket-full for a dime.

Hospitals are faraway and expensive, and ailing tonsils and appendices are often kept too long for safety. Efforts to get a county hospital have been under way for several months.

There is great need that sawmill operators make arrangements so any worker who is severely injured can be taken to the nearest doctor, and secure immediate treatment, without waiting to locate the sawmill operator and get his instructions.

These needs remain—human, vital, and often aching needs. The FSA's Health and Dental Care Associations and the County Health Program have cleared up many health hazards, have thrown into relief the health work yet to be done.

XXIX

"SOME GOOD LEARNING"

"THINGS ARE so enlightened to what they was when I was a chap," said a Greene county farmer about the new schools. "If they had just been helping back then like they are now, I could have got some good learning."

The County Board of Education, M. H. Tappan, Chairman, Floyd T. Corry, Superintendent, have been most cooperative in building up their part of the Unified Farm Program. Better-trained teachers have been employed, 26 new school buildings have been erected.* And all of this shot through with the realization that the public school system renders its fullest service when it helps parents and children understand how they can make best use of the natural and human resources of their community.

VOCATIONAL TRAINING

Though the county has always been predominantly rural, no teachers of agriculture had ever been used until 1939, when five vocational teachers were hired. Home economics teachers were added a little later. By the end of 1941 there were 13 vocational and home economics teachers in the county, 7 white and 6 colored.

They have related their teaching to home situations. O. M. Cates, vocational teacher in the Greensboro High School, serves as sponsor for an active Future Farmers of America chapter, with 31 members. In the spring of 1942, under the war food program, the FFA boys bought 6,000 baby chicks and grew off broilers for the market. The

* For more facts about teachers and schools, see Appendix No. 21.

Club gives an annual father-son banquet. Here one sees boys say they plan to be farmers, and fathers well satisfied with their sons' decisions.

The Negro vocational teachers have New Farmers of America chapters for their older boys. These clubs are similar to the FFA clubs for the Whites.

SCHOOL SHOPS ARE USEFUL

Perhaps the most impressive work done by the vocational teachers, white and colored, is carried on in the vocational shops. Here in a new building, fast by the schoolhouse, the teachers and their pupils and parents have built hundreds of brooders for baby chicks, and children came home and fixed the door-steps or made benches. The farmers throughout the school community are encouraged to bring farm tools that need to be mended. More than a score of pick-up trucks wear frames which the vocational teachers have helped fathers and sons build. The WPA cooperated in the school shop work by providing a full-time shop assistant for each of the vocational teachers.

Now that war has come and new farm tools can hardly be bought, the vocational teachers have announced that repairs can be made on farm equipment in the school shop—plow points can be sharpened, wagon tires tightened, harrows repaired, handles put on hoes. The county vocational building in Greensboro is equipped for electric welding and other more complicated tasks.

The home economics teachers, white and colored, relate their program to the life of the people in the school community.

SUPERVISION HELPS

Life-related programs in the white and colored schools have been developed through the use of supervisors. In the fall of 1940, J. D. Salter of the University of Georgia began a year of supervision in the white schools in the county. At that same time Lucille Stone Welch became the Jeanes Supervisor for the colored schools. They assisted the teachers in improving their classroom techniques, and impressed upon them the need of understanding the family and community situations out of which their pupils came.

In the summer of 1941 workshops to promote life-related teaching were held at Athens and Fort Valley for the white and colored teachers, respectively. Each workshop formulated a plan of work for the year, and they have been carried through much as planned. The present white supervisor, Mary Jernigan Holmes of White Plains, has emphasized more effective teaching methods, and the use of appropriate reading materials. Creative art has also been featured, and displays of students' work have been exhibited at the county-wide teachers' meetings which are held each month.

The Negro supervisor in her quarterly teachers' meetings has featured the community aspects of the school program, such as the planting of gardens, the improvement of health habits and better reading practices. With the outbreak of the war, representatives of the smaller Negro schools decided to make a quilt for the American Red Cross. Nearly two score of these have been made and turned over to the local chapter.

The county board and school superintendent have come to look upon supervision as an important part of the educational system of the county.

MUSIC IS FUN

Glee club work and assembly singing have been featured in several of the white schools.

In 1942 a musical program among the Negro schools of the county was developed by Bruce Welch, principal of the Alexander Community School. Welch also carried on a weekly radio program of fifteen minutes over WMAZ, Macon, during the winter. He had various school groups to participate; most of his performers had never been on the air before.

HOT LUNCHES ARE POPULAR

Hot lunches for school children is another relatively new phase of Greene county's public school system. Through the cooperation of Surplus Commodities, WPA, NYA, the parent-teacher associations and school trustees, hot lunches have been served for the past three years at all of the white schools in the county, except at Greensboro.

About half the county's colored schools, including all the larger ones, have had hot lunches; cold Surplus Commodities were served at the others.

With the war came questions about whether WPA and NYA assistance would be available for the hot lunch program another year. Also disturbing was the possibility that Surplus Commodities, too, might be curtailed or withdrawn. The principals and trustees of the county schools met in county-wide meetings to consider how best they might continue the hot lunches.

A steam cannery has been installed in the county vocational building at Greensboro. It is operated under the supervision of the county vocational teacher and is available to the white people throughout the county. With considerably less equipment, the Negroes are busy canning with an open cooker and retort at the Alexander Community School under the supervision of the Negro vocational teacher here.

The County Board of Education assisted in the purchase of the equipment for both canneries; they were busy in the summer of 1942 piling up canned goods for the winter's school lunches, and serving farm families who wanted to use them.

MOTION PICTURES AND LIBRARIES

A few months ago the County Board of Education purchased a motion picture projector, with sound belt. It has been used a half hundred times at the white schools and at community gatherings in the evening, with a total attendance of nearly 5,000. It has been used a half dozen times for colored audiences, with an attendance of over a thousand. There has been some discussion of buying a set of batteries so the machine can be operated where electrical current is not available.

Another recent educational development in the county is the County Library and bookmobile. From the outset, $55 or more was available each month for the purchase of books. This amount is raised by the County Board of Education, the city councils of Greensboro, Union Point, and White Plains, and occasional small amounts from the other communities, and $5.00 a month from a former resident, Cranston Williams.

The County Library, now located in the County Vocational Building, has 2,300 volumes of its own, over 600 that belong to the WPA, 200 to the State Library Commission. Recently 16 popular magazines were subscribed to.

Since early in 1942, a bookmobile—also a cooperative project of the WPA and the county—began its rounds, soon became a popular part of the county's new program. White teachers, school children and parents flocked around it, returned their last books, picked out new ones. Most of Greene county is rural and the bookmobile has the first call on all books. In a recent month approximately three times as many books were put in circulation by the bookmobile as across the desk in the library. And this was as it should be in a rural county like Greene.

Each of the eight white schools in the county has a library of some type or other. The Greensboro High School Library has 2,800 volumes, and $350 to $400 a year is available for new books. The Union Point school has the second largest library.

The Woman's Club of White Plains, the only federated woman's club in the county, maintains a library. It was organized over 40 years ago, has some 600 volumes and a dozen popular magazines.

Only a few families in the county have private libraries of as many as 100 volumes. Around Penfield a rare old volume may still be found.

Most of the Negro schools were wholly without libraries until some months ago, when a half dozen of the largest schools secured a small collection of books furnished by the Rosenwald Fund and distributed by the State Department of Education. Practically every one of the county's one-teacher schools has a "library corner" where a few bulletins are displayed, and books—commonly less than a dozen, and most of them discarded texts. Except for these beginnings, the Negro schools and the Negro population remain without library books or library service.

MUCH STILL TO DO

Taking the county as a whole, as shown in the 1941 annual report to the State Superintendent of Schools, there were 5,446 library books in the white schools of the county, 394 in the Negro schools. This same report showed that the white teachers in the county system received average annual salaries of $799, and the colored teachers $437. About 750 white school children were transported to school at a yearly cost of $16.80, and 159 colored at $7.15.

The improvement of the schools of the county has been an integral part of the Unified Farm Program. The FSA assisted through its practice of making monetary donations to counties in lieu of taxes. It made around $60,000 available to the County Board of Education for its building program, in which the WPA and NYA cooperated.

Obvious as are the advancements in school equipment and the training of the teachers, there is little room for complacency. The average school attainment for white pupils is the eighth grade, for the Negroes low third grade. In the recent military drafts, one white boy in twenty was turned down because of illiteracy, one colored boy in three.

It should be remembered of course that the educational advancements of the last four years are not old enough to have affected the present draftees. Even with the hot lunch program, the new water-tight buildings and vocational programs, the attendance is still poor, particularly at the smaller Negro schools where these improvements are least in evidence.

With much more cotton to pick in the fall of 1942 than the year before, and with labor scarcer, the county school authorities arranged for the Negro schools to close each day at noon during picking time. The white schools maintained their regular day's schedule during this period, but the children from some of the schools went in a group to the cotton fields on Saturday morning. One such experiment was not successful, another was highly so as when the Siloam school youngsters worked under the supervision of their Principal R. F. Burke, who picked almost as much cotton as any two of his pupils.

As the war goes on and as more men go into the armed forces and to war industries, the farmers will need their children on the farms. The school authorities are aware of this trend, want the parents to keep their children in school as regularly as possible, lest county educational levels decline and illiteracy become even more common than it is now, and the farm children when they grow up have as much trouble as their parents keeping farm records.

One mother with a large brood is proud that her eldest son is in the seventh grade, and that he can do all her writing for her. She keeps the others in school regularly, too. "It's bad when you can't read and write," she says, "so I gets them there."

XXX

TO THE END OF THE ROAD

GREENE COUNTY's Unified Program was designed to deal with the whole county, to develop a program for every kind of situation. It was, in short, to demonstrate that the government's program—local, state, and federal—would reach to the last man.

WPA KEEPS WOLF FROM DOOR

Something has been said already about the cooperation of the WPA in the execution of the school building and hot lunch programs, and in the county library and the bookmobile. The WPA has made other contributions to the county. One of its first projects was to put top soil on the road to Reid's Ferry. By mid-1942 a $75,000 sewer project and a brick auditorium-gymnasium had been completed at Union Point.

WPA's activities in Greensboro included a street and sidewalk improvement project, an underpass at the depot, a sewer line from the mill village, projects on historical records and the tracing of land titles, and sewing rooms. Altogether, the WPA spent around a half million dollars in the county, an average of $35 for every man, woman, and child.

During the past years, the WPA helped to bring these basic improvements to the county; more than that, it made it possible for many a breadwinner to keep the wolf away from his family's door. To some the WPA became a new sort of security.

When a rural white woman walks seven miles a day to work in the WPA sewing room she really needs the work, and she is willing to make a personal sacrifice to get it. So, too, does a white father who supplements his WPA wage with a garden which he plants without fertilizer and cultivates by letting his boys pull the plow.

Negro men secured employment on WPA along with the white men, but in relatively smaller numbers. Only a few WPA jobs, in the school lunchrooms and at the sewing room, were available for Negro women. From 1937 through April of 1942 a total of 1,210 people worked on WPA, 58 percent white and 42 percent colored.

THE YOUNG FOLKS KNEW SOMEBODY CARED

The NYA has assisted about 1,000 Greene county boys and girls. A little less than one tenth of these were high school or college students, the others were out-of-school youths—730 Whites, 176 Negroes.

Last year, the NYA assisted nine white high school students and twelve colored junior high students to attend school in the county. Around $60 a month was available for all of them together. More than this amount in NYA employment was available to Greene county boys and girls away at college.

Out-of-school youths, white and colored, were used in building rural Negro schoolhouses, and as helpers in the school lunchrooms. A number of white youths, and a few colored, attended NYA resident projects. The girls were given training in cooking and housekeeping, the boys in woodwork, pottery, and farming. Ten to fifteen out-of-school white girls did clerical work for NYA's $16.00 a month.

Sixteen dollars for a half-month's work is not important until you find yourself wanting to help out at home and have no money, wanting to buy a new dress or coat or suit for yourself and no way of paying for it, wanting to see a movie or take a trip and no money for the fare.

The NYA had jobs for youths when they needed them. Through the new skills they learned, many youths stepped straight from NYA training schools to regular employment, and in later months to jobs in war industries.

The County Welfare Board has cooperated in the Unified Farm Program by qualifying eligible persons for WPA, CCC, Old Age Assistance, Aid to Dependent Children, Aid to the Blind, and for Surplus Commodities.

From 1937 through April, 1942 the Board certified 312 boys to CCC, 54 percent white, 46 percent colored. Some of them went to camps near by, others to camps over the Rockies. They learned skills, bragged about how many states they had seen, and taught their folks back home the meaning of the word "conservation."

Of 420 certified to Old Age Assistance, 52 percent were white, 48 percent colored. The monthly checks to the Whites averaged a little over $9.00, to the Negroes a little less than $7.00. One elderly man said he didn't like to be accepting money from anybody, but "the government is better able to take care of me than I am to take care of myself." Others feel Old Age assistance is their due. Said an 80-year-old woman: "I gits grits, but I don't git no money. They ought to gimme the money. I'm old enough to git the money."

Of the 1,153 persons certified for Surplus Commodities in the past five years, 58 percent were white, 42 percent colored. Up until the end of 1940 nearly three fifths of all the clients had been colored. Since then 522 have been added, and over three fourths of the additions have been Whites.

Surplus Commodities have introduced many new foods to rural diets. When you walk up to a house and see a child with a handful of raisins, you almost know they are on the "Commodities" list. More oranges and grapefruits, prunes and raisins have been eaten here since the "Commodities" came than in the whole history of the county before.

If you want to know what comes of the Surplus Commodities

and the government checks to WPA workers, CCC boys, Old Age Assistance clients, follow them home to the little houses throughout the county, see the meager furnishings, and the simple fare. Six to ten dollars a month and 50 pounds of "Commodities" make a big difference to people who throughout their lives as cotton farmers have had family incomes of $250 a year or less. The $20 monthly check from a CCC boy has made many a family relatively comfortable, and checks of less than $20 a month have made it possible for widowed mothers to care for their children at home.

THE WAGES AND HOURS LAW

Along with the FSA, WPA, NYA, Old Age Assistance and Surplus Commodities came the federal wage and hour legislation. The legislation reached into the textile mills at Greensboro and Union Point, where more than 800 people work under its minimum provisions. First the minimum wage was 25¢ an hour, then 32½¢, 37½¢, 40¢, and later 46½¢ by order of the War Labor Board.

On the surface, a minimum wage for the whole textile industry seems simple enough. But when the minimum is raised, all of the wages above the old minimum must be dealt with too. Doffers or loom fixers might be willing enough to work for 32½¢ an hour when floor sweepers get 15¢, but not when the minimum is raised to 32½¢ for all employees. They know the greater value of their work. Generally speaking, the better paid workers throughout the industry wanted their wages upped in proportion to each hike in the minimum wage; the management, on the other hand, often felt that the minimum had been raised too much, and it was not reasonable for the above-the-minimum workers to insist on commensurate raises. The workers complained that the minimum wage was about to become the maximum wage, too. Then there was the matter of the speed at which the machinery is run, the tasks each worker is to perform, and the legal right of workers to participate in collective bargaining through the labor union of their choice. Here are many opportunities for differences between workers and management.

The ownership and management of both the Mary-Leila Mill in Greensboro and the Union Manufacturing Company in Union Point is composed of local people, and the controlling stocks of both mills are owned by resident Greene county families. Most of the workers, too, are from the county, many of them born and reared on farms, and some of them still living on farms and commuting daily to their work. The mill managers and workers know each other by their first names, and employer-employee relations have been on a personal basis. Except for the national textile strike in 1934—which was forced on the local operatives and which the management soon forgot—neither mill had ever been closed down because of labor trouble when the federal wage and hour legislation was enacted.

UNION MANUFACTURING COMPANY

Soon after the Wagner Act was passed and the National Labor Relations Board set up, workers from the Union Manufacturing Company at Union Point began to take grievances before it. Union members, it was alleged, had been dismissed without cause, and mill officials had operated credit stores and deducted store bills from employees' checks. These differences were taken before government officials. In the case of one employee, a member of a CIO labor union, the management was ordered to restore him to his job and give him back pay for the period that had elapsed since he was laid off. This decision was appealed by the management, and 'round and 'round through the maze of courts and NLRB hearings have gone the differences of the management and some of the workers.

Strikes were repeatedly threatened, but none materialized until the spring of 1937, when for two weeks the machines went unattended. Then the mill was opened up, and no strike occurred until early in 1942, when the mill was idle for four weeks.

The management invited the workers to return to their jobs. The strike leaders claimed that no workers wanted to go back, and if they did they wouldn't let them. The management asked police protection for workers who wanted to return. Sheriff Wyatt and his deputies were there to see that everything was orderly.

A few minutes before time for the whistle, a group of workers marched down the sidewalk, two abreast, and into the gate amidst the jeering of the "peaceful" pickets. One shift only that day, and not nearly all the machines were manned. The next day and the next saw more workers at their posts—pocketbooks were flat and union leaders had not been able to get the aid they had requested to tide the workers over. The picket line thinned out, and "the law" was always there to keep things quiet. A week passed and two shifts were working at capacity; then the third shift was added, and by the third week cotton socks were again coming off the machines on a 24-hour-day schedule.

Just before the strike was called, the laborers had been given a small raise. The strikers went back in the hope that they could get a CIO Union contract later. The United States was already at war, and the Union Manufacturing Company was making socks for the government. Around 550 operatives were employed on three shifts, and were receiving an annual payroll of over $375,000.

THE MARY-LEILA MILL

The Mary-Leila Mill at Greensboro is now also filling government orders. The operatives are working under a CIO Union contract, which was secured in mid-June, 1941, after the mill had been out of operation four months.

For a third of a year, the mill management and the operatives eyed each other around the mill and the town. The management and the operatives had explanations of everything, but their explanations differed on many a vital point. The doffers struck and the other employees *walked out* in sympathy for them, said the management. The doffers struck and the rest of the employees were *locked out* of the mill, said the employees. We were locked out and ought to get federal unemployment compensation, said the workers. You walked out and therefore should not get unemployment compensation, said the management. And so flew the words month after month while the Mary-Leila looms stood still.

All of these differences and others were taken before the NLRB, with the lawyers for each side sparring or waiting for the advantage.

An election, held by the NLRB in mid-March, recorded a vote of 264 to 3 in favor of the CIO's Textile Workers Union of America to represent the operatives in collective bargaining.

As the strike lengthened the idle workers strained their credits at the stores, and the union leaders had some supplies sent in and kept assuring the workers that they would get unemployment compensation for the time they were idle.

The general sentiment of the community, which seemed at first in favor of the operatives, tended to turn toward the management when it offered a general 10 percent rise in wages and agreed to hire all former workers. The operatives held that a promise outside a union contract could be readily set aside, and therefore did not constitute a serious intention. The management considered this a blow below the belt—since when could a CIO Union talk about what constituted a "serious intention?"

With the payroll of over $4,000 a week stopped, businessmen were feeling it, wanted the mill to open up. Some blamed the CIO; others did not. There was at one time some rough talk, and for a day or two it looked as if a vigilante group might rise up and attempt to run the CIO organizers out of the county.

Shortly after the mill stopped, a representative of the National Labor Conciliation Service came to Greensboro. He was never given an audience by the management. Months later Lucy Randolph Mason, Public Relations Representative of the CIO in the Southern States, came to Greensboro. When she went to the mill building looking for the manager, she was served with a restraining paper which charged her with trespassing upon and damaging private property.

The management and the operatives continued to repeat their old differences and bring out new ones. Then the management announced that the mill would open for any who wanted to come back to work. The strikers said they would not let any workers go in the mill. The Governor's office telephoned Sheriff Wyatt to know whether he needed the assistance of the National Guard, as a spokesman then in the Governor's office claimed. The sheriff's answer was that he and the city police had the situation well in hand and that the Guard was not needed. The management then asked for police protection for employees who wanted to work. The sheriff and the city police stayed on hand to see that the pickets limited their activities to peaceful persuasion. The union members held out for a contract, picketed the mill, carried placards, sang songs, called "scab" at the few workers who went back to their jobs.

Day after day the "loyal" workers went in for a single shift, but not enough of them to operate nearly all the machinery. Most of the people who went back to work lived out in the country, seemed to feel more closely identified with the mill employers than the mill workers. Truth is many of the farm-dwelling mill workers do employ some farm labor, and the employment of a single farm wage hand seems to give a man as deep a dose of employer philosophy as if he hired a hundred.

At any rate in early June the management announced it had signed a contract with the CIO Union, and that full operations would be resumed at once. A few weeks later word came that all operatives except the doffers would get unemployment compensation—a total of $19,000—for the time they had been out of work.

The management and the operatives went back to work in good spirits, and the Mary-Leila Mill was again rolling out cloth as it had been doing for four decades. Nearly 300 operatives worked in three shifts, and were receiving an annual payroll of over $200,000.

THE SAWMILL OPERATORS GROANED

Many a small sawmill operator groaned when the wage and hour legislation came. They said the 8-hour day was too short, that the 25¢ an hour minimum wage would close out the sawmill business in short order. Some operators went ahead as usual, waited to see whether the inspectors would ever get around to their mills. Other mill owners attempted to relieve themselves of the necessity of conforming to the federal law—which applies to products shipped across state lines—by limiting themselves to trade inside Georgia. This could scarcely be done except through some southwide lumber broker who could execute bids in his own name and then sublet them to dealers within each state. The inter-state quality of such intra-state transactions was obvious from the outset.

Within a few months it was clear to all of the 96 sawmill operators in the county that they would have to take account of the wage and hour provisions of the law, or run the risk of being hailed into court.

Some operators saw the inspectors, asked how they could arrange the transportation and board of their logging camps and mill crews in a satisfactory manner. Others evaded the inspectors, sent their workers home to keep them from being questioned, pleaded bankruptcy when faced with violations, did the other things that an employer can readily do when faced with a federal law that does not jibe with local practices.

The wage and hour legislation soon speeded up the rate of work throughout the sawmill business, from loggers to planing mill operatives. Some mill owners looked at their employees and wondered if the shorter faster day would not be even harder on them than the old slow long day had been. "The average man can't last ten years," said one operator, "at the rate we've got to make 'em go under this wage-hour law!"

Then came hearings before the Wage and Hour Administrator, and the wage was upped from 25¢ an hour to 30¢, to 35¢ or $2.80 per day. By then there were comparatively few objections, for the

National Defense Program was well under way, and the price of pine lumber had reached a new high.

Sometimes an employer let it be known that he thought his employees ought to give 30 minutes' or an hour's work each day just to help out a little. And the employees would do it. But the inspectors kept coming, and the 8-hour day is now more firmly established and the full wage goes direct to the employees more than ever before.

AT THE END OF THE ROAD

The way to tell whether the government has reached the last man is to drive out across the county. Don't stop at the house where you see a privy, a fenced garden, and black-framed screens on the windows. Without stopping you know that family is one of the 500 working with the FSA.

Be adventurous. Try to get lost. Keep going until you come to some side road that is a thread through the woods, not even a mailbox to mark it. See what's at the end of that road.

Deep in the pines, an old woman was asked: "Has the government got down here?" She rarely had a chance to talk to anyone, was suspicious of a stranger, and was slow in her answers. "No, sir," was the answer to a number of questions.

"No, sir, we ain't on no government farm."

"Ain't sent off no boy to the CCC camp."

"Nobody around here worked for the WP and A."

"Nothing to do with the Wages and Hours."

"Don't git no pension. Old enough to git it. Like to git it. But they won't gimme it."

Looking around at the rickety old cabin, the field where the corn had come up "so missing," the sorry cotton, the pine woods closing in on three sides, the questioner concluded that this was one place where the government hadn't been.

The old woman said she was "about" seventy years old. She had had "about" fourteen children, "about" five or six of whom were still living—in Atlanta, Chattanooga, somewhere up in Ohio. Living with her were a grandson whose mother's residence she did not know, a grand-son-in-law, and a grand-daughter fifteen years old who had had a baby two weeks before.

All hunched over on the chopping block where she sat, digging in the bare ground with a piece of stick, she said she believed times were worse instead of better. As she remembers it, you used to be able to work hard and make a living. Now she had worked hard all her life, forty years on the same place, and nothing to show for it. Paid enough rent on this land to have bought it.

"It's about time for me to be leaving this world," she said. "I've worked too hard to live to be ninety like my mother. Lord only knows what will happen next."

Gradually the conversation moved back around to the subject of the government. It came out that though she did not get an old-age pension, she got some grits and other things from the Surplus Commodities sometimes. The County Welfare Office had given her two dresses. The boys had typhoid shots from the public nurses. The grand-son is the first child she ever raised who rode to school in a bus and had a hot lunch. The grand-daughter was attended by one of the county supervised midwives when her baby came. The woman did not remember how much but some years they received a check from the government for their cotton.

At most of the other houses, big and little, the families have much more to report. Some are interested in one part of the program. Some in another.

Here is a large farmowner who is a director of FSA's Marketing and Purchasing Association, or on the County Planning Board, or a Member of the County AAA Committee.

"The REA—that's the best thing that ever happened to country folks," says the wife of a farmowner who is enjoying a radio and refrigerator.

"The wages and hours have holp us a whole lot," say the sawmill workers.

"I believe in unions. I belong to the CIO," a cotton-mill worker will tell you.

And here is a family on WPA: "It pulled me too tight the last year we tried to farm," remarked the frail mother of a large family of little children, "so my husband went on public work."

One man generalized: "I can look all around this county and see a big indifference from a few years ago."

What is this new personality of "government" in Greene county? It no longer means just the police or the postman. The people speak of being "on the government" and "off the government." They speak of "government farms," "government chickens," "government men." They say: "We belong to the government;" "The government never turns us down." The phrase "before the government came" is as definite a way of speaking about time as "back in slavery times," and "before the boll weevil." People feel they are in a new era.

And some do not like it.

XXXI

THE FAMILY-SIZE FARMER—
HIS TROUBLES AND HIS STRENGTH

THERE IS a widespread tradition among white people here that the landless Negro will not work unless he has to. If he gets more than a mere subsistence wage, he will sit around until it is all gone. He will work only when he is forced to do so from fear of the rod, or from hunger. Many a well-dressed white man will tell all comers that "Once the colored man can't be whipped on the back or in the stomach, you simply can't get any work out of him!"

MORE MONEY FOR FEWER HOURS

Most of the sawmill operators, and all of the farmers, frowned on the wage and hour law because they felt that $2.00 or $2.80 a day was simply too much money for a Negro man to have.

No sooner had the higher wages begun than their employers began to point to evidence in support of their claim—a man drunk and gambling, and his money gone before he gets home; a man off the job on Monday and Tuesday, and all because he had enough money to stay off; three workers in jail at Athens Monday morning, because they had enough money to go up there Saturday night.

Other workers with the larger pay envelopes bought themselves some clothes on the installment plan, and stepped out dudish enough to satisfy a longing they had felt for years. But not all the sawmill employees spent their larger checks for a "good time" and showy clothes. Some used their very first raise to take home more food and clothes for their families.

The higher wages that some thought would ruin the sawmill workers have only made more workers available. The sawmills run regularly, begin Monday mornings with a full crew.

Some of those who spent their first checks for frills soon began to carry home more food and clothes, take out new sick-benefit and death policies, buy wicker bottom chairs and perhaps a shiny bedstead and bureau—with a mirror on it "the size of the county paper."

Radios and guitars, too, have multiplied in these homes. The women and children dress better, and there have been teeth pulled that would have been left in to hurt and cause stiff joints. Almost any elderly person—man or woman, white or colored—who has had aching teeth over a period of years can tell you when it is going to rain.

Sawmill wages have pulled out abscessed teeth, put in plates of false teeth, and now and then an upper front gold tooth—just to shine. Eyes have been examined, and uncrossed. Goiters have been taken out, tumors removed.

These families live in the same kind of houses they did before their wages were raised. Generally speaking, the increased sawmill wages tend to be used first for a "good time," then for showy clothes for self, and later for food and clothes for the family, furniture and sometimes for dental and medical care.

Sawmill work is hard work, and many sawmills move every few weeks or months and the workers may have to find another place to live. Other workers are carried to the mill in trucks, leaving in early morning and getting back in late evening—8 hours of work, but 14 hours away from home. The wives dislike the long lonesome days, especially if their husbands are among those who run through with most of their wages, bring home only the traditional bread and bacon fare. But the sawmill workers on the whole have more gardens, pigs, and chickens than when wages were lower, more than farm wage hands have now.

Sawmill worker families average 17 chickens each, farm wage hand families, 14; sawmill workers 210 pounds of home-killed meat, wage hands, 175 pounds; the families of each group averaged around 65 quarts of home-canned fruits and vegetables last year. Both of these groups show a marked improvement in the home production of foods in the last few years.

Quite naturally the workers themselves preferred sawmill employment for 8 hours a day at $2.80 to the farmer's 9- to 12-hour day at 75¢. And quite naturally the farmers complained—complained that labor was being ruined—ruined by the wage and hour law, the WPA, the FSA, Old Age Assistance, and Surplus Commodities. Everything seemed to be out of joint to the farmer who still wanted to hire labor at the rate farm labor had always been paid.

Fathers often found it impossible to hold their own children: "You have to let your own boys go off on public work when they want to. You can't whip them and hold them on the farm." These fathers are often irritated when they are unable to find a cheap wage hand to take the place of the departing son.

The landowners with tenant houses have had relatively little trouble getting labor, for they will let only such families live in their houses as agree to work on the place when needed. If the men have spare time, they are usually free to work wherever they like. Some men, in order to get a house for the family, will work a few 65-hour weeks each year on the farm at less than $4.00 a week, and then work at the sawmill the rest of the year at $14.00 for a 40-hour week.

Many of the small farmers who moved in here from north Georgia continued to do their own work. Others drifted more and more into the local practice of depending on hired labor. Hardest hit of all by the farm labor situation were the small farm operators who grew up here, in an old plantation county where everybody who was anybody owned land, and landless men worked it. The desire to be plantation folk outran the ability of the families to accumulate land.

With the coming of commercial fertilizer the live-at-home small white-land farmers around Siloam and White Plains, Veazey and Liberty, continued their own live-at-home farm practices, but began to set up a sharecropper or two, or to plant larger cotton acreages for themselves by the use of a little hired labor in the busy seasons. And so the family-size farmer, called the backbone of democracy by Thomas Jefferson, here took on the quality of a planter, not uncommonly spoke of his 60- or 100-acre farm as a "plantation," came to think and act in many ways like the owners of the big plantations.

They were all Democrats, big landowners and little ones, and the landless men who worked for them were economically dependent, and politically impotent through the poll tax and the White Primary. That's why to understand a farmer's outlook here you note first the color of his skin, and then ask whether he hires labor. You can of course ask how many laborers he hires, but you may often find that the employer point of view is achieved about as thoroughly if he hires a laborer now and then to help on his one-horse farm as if he operates a big plantation.

With the passage of years the relatively low natural fertility of the coarse white land has declined to the point that even with fertilizer the farmers are in about the same condition they were before commercial fertilizer came. That is, they have the land resources for only a subsistence farm, but they have the plantation tradition of using hired labor. They feel they just must have extra labor a few days in spring and a week or two in the fall, and a day or so now and then between times.

FARM HANDS AND COOKS HARD TO FIND

A farmer can cultivate nearly twice as much cotton and corn as he can hoe and harvest. He wants the larger acreage because of the tight squeeze between low yields and high production costs. So when he can find no one to help chop or pick at prevailing farm wages, the labor situation seems intolerable.

"Can't hardly pick up a colored man to do a day's real farm work now for love nor money," he will complain. You then hear how different things are now from what they used to be before the government began all these programs. "Now, don't misunderstand me," is a common expression, "the government has helped some people who deserved it, but it's ruined a lot more than it has helped." You listen and wonder as earnest self-supporting farmers look you straight in the face and say that once a man works for WPA he's worthless as a farm laborer, and once a family gets on the FSA they will never be good tenants again.

The availability of cheap farm labor at the peak work times of the year has been a well-established institution here. Most landless rural Negro families had a house to live in and privileges of gathering wood and a patch to plant by virtue of their willingness to work for the owners of these houses any time they might need them, and at the going wage. Negro farmowners and independent renters, too, often found that a white farmer in the neighborhood would expect some members of their families to work for him in the busy seasons.

Perhaps nothing makes white farmers here feel more kindly toward Negroes than for Negro farm labor to be available when white farmers want it. The presence of this Negro labor did more than increase the farming operations of the white farmers; it afforded them satisfying evidence that they were still in position to command the services of the Negro.

The sawmill wages under the wage and hour law made Negro farm labor and cooks less accessible to the white farmers, and so the relation between the races became a bit strained. The matter was further complicated by WPA, NYA, CCC, Old Age Assistance and Surplus Commodities, though in no case were these administered here without a marked racial differential, as shown above.

One or more members of almost every family in the county was touched by the programs of one or more of these agencies. And they all had disturbing features—WPA's wage was above the farm wage. "Seems like colored people just naturally like to do 'public work' more than they do farm work."

Boys and girls that might have been ready to work on farms when needed in spring and fall enrolled with NYA. "I thought this NYA was going to be one of the best things in the world helping boys and girls to go to school. But the colored boy that we had last year got on NYA where he made $14 a month, and had some time off. So he quit the farm."

Others went off to the CCC. And worse than that they sent money back home and made it less likely that other members of the family would be interested in earning local farm wages.

Old Age Assistance and Surplus Commodities for the needy is well and good. "But," says the farmer looking in vain for labor, "how can you keep the people who should work from lying around and living off the stuff set aside for those needy people?"

The New Deal programs in Greene also thinned out the supply of Negro domestics in the open country. Many farm women accustomed to having a cook, bitterly complain that no one will work for $1.50 a week as heretofore. Some still have their "old faithfuls," and a few have raised wages, while many now have no regular help. Negro farm women, with no protection from wage and hour legislation, find farm wages of 50¢ to 60¢ a day much better than those paid to cooks. Washer women are still available, and get as much for a couple of family washes as the cook could earn in a week.

Domestic wages in Greensboro and the other larger towns range from two to three dollars a week, with a servant now and then paid four. In mill worker families, where the wife also works, a Negro woman will be hired for $1.50 to $3.00 a week to keep house and tend the children.

THEIR FIRST FIVE DEFEATS

Earlier in this story of Greene, it was told how the expanding slave plantations pushed the small white farmers of the frontier out of ownership in the best farming areas of the county, and not infrequently out of the county. And so, the Jeffersonian farmers in

Greene suffered their first defeat long before Sherman's march to the sea. Immediately after the War of the 1860's, in the period when there was talk of "40 acres and a mule" for ex-slaves, the small independent white farmers again rose toward power, but they were soon squelched by the planters and the time-merchants and money lenders that came with the sharecropper system.

In the 1890's the Third Party advocated widespread ownership of land, raised again the old cry "40 acres and a mule," challenged the power of the money lenders and corporations, demanded low rates of interest, public ownership of the railroads, and other measures designed to elevate the dirt farmer along with the common man everywhere. The voters of Greene, white and colored, turned out and elected a full slate of Populist officials. But the national Populist movement split, and the local Populists went back with the Democrats to disfranchise the Negro, and to bury the Third Party platform. And so the small farmers of Greene chalked down against themselves this, their third defeat. Many of them came to rely on cheap Negro labor and so slipped a notch from Jefferson's family-size farmer.

A quarter-century later, Greene county was in boom with cotton crops of from 15,000 to 20,000 bales, selling at 25¢ to 40¢ a pound. Again the small farm operators, many of whom did not now own a farm, moved toward the only light on their horizon, landownership. Their savings were used to make down payments. If they owned a little land, they wanted more. If white and landless, they would own some land as their fathers had before them; if black, they would get some land and shed the last vestiges of slavery. But the land they bargained for was at inflated prices. Then the weevils came and stayed, and the price of cotton dropped to below 12¢ a pound and remained there, and the land they had purchased and put all their savings in could not be sold for anything like the amount they still owed on it. Thus the "Jeffersonian" farmers of Greene went down, way down, to their fourth defeat.

With the bruises of this defeat still heavy upon them, they found themselves the victims of a fifth one, and a continuing defeat it was —a sort of legal robbing of farm people by means of the national tariff, the inequality between farm prices and factory prices, the development of technology, and the handicap of a debtor in a money economy. All of the farmers of Greene were penalized by these things, but the small independent farmer most.

The larger farmers could buy and sell in large quantities and could absorb a part of these handicaps through cheap labor, high charges on advances to their tenants, the sale of timber, and the further exploitation of soil fertility by abandoning the poorer fields and opening up new ones in the lands from which the timber had been cut. The small independent farmer did not have enough acreage to sell timber or to open up new fields. His only way of lightening his load was to get labor cheap during the peak work seasons.

And so the small farmer lived harder. But his situation was not relatively worse than it had been, for the planters were in new danger of losing their lands to their creditors, and the farm tenants had been pushed to lower levels than ever before by the economic plight of the plantation owners and the fact that urban employment opportunities had practically evaporated. The independent farmer had taken a step downward, but the dependent farm tenants and wage hands were still a "safe distance" below him. His proof of this was that he could still command the cheap labor of the Negro.

THE NEW DEAL TOUCHED THEM LIGHTLY

But the end was not yet, for early in the 1930's as conditions grew worse for the three layers of farmers here, there was political talk of the "Forgotten Man." He had in fact become a national hero. When the ballots were counted in Greene county—as in the nation—Franklin D. Roosevelt, the man who had promised to remember the "Forgotten Man," had the most votes. After a few months the New Deal reached Greene, and after a few more months reached the last man in Greene—through parity and rental checks, loans and grants, work relief and direct relief, Old Age Assistance and Surplus Commodities, wage and hour legislation, and the purchase of farm lands and woodlands, mules and wagons, cows and pigs and chickens, screens and pumps and pressure cookers.

Everybody got something, but the small independent farmers got the least. Worst of all, as they saw it, most of the cheap Negro labor was gone off to the sawmills, living on "government farms," or inclined to stay around the house of a relative or friend who was on WPA, or who had a youth on NYA or CCC, or who had qualified for Old Age Assistance or Surplus Commodities. The New Deal had reached the last man at the bottom, and it had steadied the plantation owners and the merchants and professional people at the top. But it had touched lightly the small independent farmers. Said one small farmer: "The gov'ment has helped farmers who were getting along fine in the first place. Just helped them go a little higher. And it's helping farmers who never have had anything anyhow; but it's helped folks like us precious little."

The New Deal had lengthened the distance between the upper layer families and the small independent farmers, shortened the distance between them and the dependent families below.

THEY ARE THE BACKBONE OF DEMOCRACY

It is no accident that the benefits of the New Deal have been spread thinnest among the small independent farmers. Rather, it was by design, for these live-at-home farm families throughout the nation, as in Greene county, have been the most self-sufficient group in our whole economy. Consequently they could weather hard times better than either the large commercial farmers or the landless tenants and wage laborers dependent upon them, better too than either the industrialists with surplus stocks of goods piling up or industrial workers faced with part-time employment and then unemployment.

The live-at-home farmer's neighbors knew he had staying qualities, and so did the government experts. Most of the activities of the

United States Department of Agriculture in Greene county, as throughout the South and the nation, are designed to get all farmers to follow in the well-worn footsteps of the family-size farmowners who have always grown their food and feed at home. Diversified farming was not begun in response to a government program; it was begun by farm families themselves. The solid sense of such a way of life on the land caused the federal and state governments to promote it.

It has not yet been proved that Thomas Jefferson was wrong when he pointed to the small independent farmer as the backbone of a democratic society. Nor do the repeated reverses of the Jeffersonian farmers in Greene, or their present unrest, prove that the family-size farm is not the best possible type of farm organization for this and adjoining counties. There is good reason to believe that the present agricultural programs which are helping make it possible for more families to own family-size farms are following a sound policy. A policy which now flows out of Washington toward Greene, got to Washington from the best judgment distilled from Greene and all the other counties.

It is because they believe in the future of the family-size farm here that government experts have developed the FSA dwellings and red barns, chicken houses, fenced pastures and gardens. If you think the idea is new here, listen back across the years to 1923 and 1924 and hear Uncle Jim Williams say:

> The farmer in the future will be forced to give more thought to detail. And, also, do more work and not depend upon the black man to help him make a living out of the earth.
> The big farms must go. The future farmer must be the small one who owns his own home.

Keep on looking at the new houses and barns on these family-size farms and hear Attorney James Davison in 1914:

> In truth we have no prosperity . . . the growing of clean crops on soil already exhausted cannot continue or ever become profitable . . . The farm-

ers who grow their own food stuffs are better off . . . The tenant system must go. The all-cotton plan must go . . . Diversified farming is the only hope . . . The time is coming when it will be a dishonor for a farmer to buy corn from Kansas City, wheat from Chicago, mules from Missouri.

Behind Uncle Jim was James Davison, and behind him was many another Greene county man—Thomas P. Janes, Thomas Stocks, Garnett Andrews, Joel Early and others—who saw the people on the farms, and yearned for the time when a better stewardship of the land could be given.

THE GOOD HUSBANDMAN

So despite the trials and tribulations of the family-size farmer in Greene, he still stands forth as our best performer here. And well it is that his tribe is being increased by the Unified Farm Program. These farmers will need to develop the habit of doing all of their own work. This need not be burdensome, however, for through the cooperative purchase and use of light farm machinery they can plant, cultivate, and harvest larger crops at less expense than they could when they relied on cheap Negro labor in busy seasons. Such a practice will also make it easier for Negro farm families to make their own way, for then all the labor of the family will be available throughout peak work times. Negro families, too, can secure cooperative machinery for their own use.

The small farmers are now more ready than ever before to develop all sorts of cooperative enterprises, especially if the families on the new FSA units and their old-line live-at-home neighbors learn to work together. The Unified Farm Program in Greene could now well afford to extend to all small farmers many of the self-supporting services which have been developed for their own borrowers. The Marketing and Purchasing Association buys fertilizer, feeds and seeds and sells eggs and other farm produce. Once the old-line live-at-home farmers see how they can make their own way without extra labor, they will bless the day. For then they will at last have escaped the paradox of attempting to operate a plantation on a family-size tract, will have escaped, too, the tedium of being dependent upon the cheap labor of a man not really interested in his work. It's hard to make a living from the land, but harder still to make another man make your living from the land.

Is it not reasonable to hope, and expect, that the same sound earthy judgment that led some families to develop live-at-home farming will now rise up from among their children to point the way for farm people today? Certainly there is no group closer to the earth, no group better qualified to do their share of the world's work, no group better prepared to live and let live. If the small live-at-home farmer will learn to cooperate with his fellow small farmers he can sell his produce at an equitable price, buy his supplies on a fair market, use light labor-saving machinery, pay for the essential community services, live reasonably well without exploiting the labor of any man, be an good husbandman and leave fertile fields to the next generation.

XXXII

IT'S NOT ALL WORK

PEOPLE WILL work one way or another for bread and money. So the best way to tell whether they have made real change is to see what they do when they are having fun.

Some new developments in recreation came with the government farm programs. But for the most part the same people meet together to enjoy themselves in the same ways.

The holiday occasions of the year are Christmas, court week, and county fair. And Saturday afternoon remains an institution.

WATERMELONS AND BARBECUES

A farmer like Frank Hopkins who is a good watermelon-raiser will always be a prince among his neighbors. So is a man who knows how to make good southern barbecue and brunswick stew. The civic enterprises promoted by the Greensboro and Union Point Lions change from year to year, but they and their ladies never fail to pay homage in the best Southern tradition to a roast pig or two during the summer.

Madison and Washington continue the greatest rivals of the Greensboro High School Athletic Association. You would have a hard time stirring up more excitement over a game than last year when Greensboro's Tigers defeated the Washington football team on the newly dedicated athletic field, named for Greensboro's Mayor C. E. Robinson.

The bridge clubs in the towns are made up of the leading women. The one at Siloam has met for years with practically the same membership. So has the White Plains Woman's Club, the only Federated

Woman's Club in the county. And in the country there is much going back and forth "to spend the day" with friends and relatives.

"Just sitting around" at the courthouse, on the bench in front of the bank, at the drugstore, or on front porches in the evenings is the common way neighbors have of getting together.

In winter weather we all sit closer to the fire, in summer we hunt for the deep shade or reach down in our pockets for a ticket to Greensboro's air-conditioned movie. Two other artificially cooled spots are the offices of the Mary-Leila Mills and a portion of W. R. Jackson's residence.

Hunting, fishing, canoeing on the Oconee are favorite sports of the men and boys. And there are poolrooms for men and boys, and here and there an abandoned tenant cabin used by poker players who like to stay at their cards hours on end.

The most popular paid amusements are the moving picture shows at Union Point and Greensboro; and for the Whites one dance hall between Greensboro and Union Point where you can take your partner and a nickel or so and dance to "Don't Sit Under the Apple Tree" and "Deep in the Night." At juke joints for Negroes in Greensboro, Union Point, and Siloam, nickels play the same kind of nickelodeons and Negro youths dance and gyrate to the same tunes.

The country boys and girls sometime come in to the movies, too, but they are more likely to meet at the country stores and churches, and their biggest occasions are the 4-H Club trips. For some adults the Extension Service's annual "Farm and Home Week" has been a cherished outing.

In the country, checkers under a shade-tree in summer and around the stove in winter is a favorite amusement for colored people. And "welcome" is written on every door-step for the banjo or fiddle player.

CHURCHES EVERYWHERE

After the homes in Greene county, there are more churches than any other kind of institution. There are about 30 churches for

Whites, 50 for Negroes. The Baptists are most numerous in each racial group, Methodists next, and then Presbyterians. Many of the churches date back to the county's earliest history, others are rather new, like the Church of God at Union Point and the rural Wesleyan Methodist churches served by the county's only woman minister.

The Negro churches were formed soon after Emancipation, and remain the most powerful organization of the colored people. A Negro farmer who becomes a deacon may be questioned for hours to be certain he will be a good church leader.

Revival meetings are popular. They are usually held during the slack-work season of mid-summer, when watermelons and fried chicken are in their prime, and when neighbors have time to go to church on week days, entertain the preachers and song leaders, visit with each other, and hope that the membership of their churches will be enlarged. With numerous small churches, as in Greene, most of the preachers receive modest salaries.

A goodly number of the Negro preachers are farmers who have answered "the call." And if you want to hear in a Black Belt county present-day parables that have much of the vivid simplicity of the New Testament, listen to the Negro farmer-preacher as he tells how a soul is gullied with sin, and how Jesus heals it with the Kudzu Vine of his Grace.

POLITICIANS GET THE CROWDS

A big political meeting will get more people out than anything else. And a politician would never think of asking for votes who wasn't willing to shake a thousand hands in an afternoon. It's the custom for a preacher to pray for the success of his candidate in an opening prayer.

The women claim they leave politics up to the men, as they always did, and most of them do not vote. But around election time, they are usually wishing they had registered or paid their poll taxes, and some talk politics as big as anybody.

Even the children take sides, and it's popular to have a bright little boy take the microphone on a political occasion to speak for his favorite candidate. The colored folks stand along the fringes of these crowds, often over by the Confederate monument when the meetings are held in front of the courthouse at Greensboro.

EXODUS WITHOUT A MOSES

Town and country, white and black, families and neighbors, about the same people like to be together as always did, but some new ideas are seeping into the field of entertainment.

Greensboro's New Greenland Theatre was opened in late 1940. Two local young men, James M. Reynolds, Jr., and William R. Boswell, had built and equipped a theatre that a town twice the size of Greensboro would brag about. The opening night was a big affair. The downstairs was filled with white people and the balcony with Negroes. Everybody leaned back in the comfortable new seats and enjoyed the feature film.

Then the lights were turned on, and one public official after another went to the stage. Each congratulated the community and the owners on the completion of the beautiful theatre, called attention to the spacious balcony and the traditional good conduct of the colored people in the old Greenland Theatre across the way. At length a speaker arose, complained that what he had planned to say had already been said, and his predicament reminded him of "an old nigger who . . ." And just then there was audible resentment in the balcony—"Callin' us 'niggers' again!" a voice was heard to say. "Let's get out of here, and stay out!" And most of the Negroes moved out, made so much noise that the white people downstairs could hardly hear the conclusion of the typical deep South story. Many white men and women who have lived here all of their lives were amazed. "Since when can't we call them 'nigger?' Why, we've done it all our lives!"

The next show and the next found the balcony almost empty. The colored people were really boycotting the New Greenland. The theatre owners were soon serious, for they had gone to expense to provide a balcony for Negroes, and their patronage was needed to retire its cost. There was talk among some of the Whites about Negroes getting out of their place, fear there would be race trouble if the balcony continued to remain but partially filled.

Old-time residents looked toward the Negro CCC camp and the few Negro supervisors who help administer the Unified Farm Program. But one and all denied leading the Negroes out of the theatre; declared that they did not go out, or if they did, that the people leaving the theatre just pushed them along and they couldn't keep from coming down out of the balcony. Listening to these explanations, one would think everybody had been pushed out by everybody else! An Exodus without a Moses, it was—so far as the white public could learn.

After a few weeks the balcony was again patronized as usual, and talk of race trouble died back down to its low boiling point, and except for slight rises now and then has remained there. The Negroes went back because the movie was their best opportunity for amusement. In the meantime some of the leading Negroes of the community had advised their people to forget the boycott; anyhow, there would be no more opening-night speeches.

But why did the colored people ever walk out? Being referred to as "niggers" certainly was nothing new to them. Some of them did not explain why they left except that they just did; others were more articulate. One man said, "It makes a fellow feel heavy down in his heart to be called that." Most definitive of all was the colored man who said he didn't mind being called a "nigger" by white people when he worked for them, for he figured part of his pay was for that, but he didn't like to be called a "nigger" or otherwise made uncomfortable when he paid out his own money for an evening of relaxation at the movie.

OCONEE TRAIL

With the coming of the Unified Farm Program, there are more occasions on which the townspeople and the country people meet together. "Georgia Songs," a county-wide musical program for white people, was put on in the fall of 1939 by the Greensboro Lions Club, FSA, WPA, Extension Service and the City and County Boards of Education. Each community presented its favorite songs. The programs afforded participation for a goodly number of farm people, many of them FSA clients. The new gymnasium-auditorium in Greensboro could not accommodate the crowd.

Another county-wide program for Whites was staged at the auditorium in the fall of the following year. It was a colorful pageant, "Oconee Trail." It reviewed by dramatic episode and appropriate musical score the history of the county from pioneer days on through slave plantation prosperity, the war, rise of the sharecropper system, soil depletion, boll-weevil deflation, migration, and the launching of the Unified Farm Program.

In the staging of the pageant, the town and country people worked and played together. Again the auditorium was filled to capacity with many on the outside listening through the doors. The county-wide recreational programs proved to be a good approach to adult education. Farm people throughout the county liked them, asked for more.

There is need for the development of similar county-wide programs for the colored people. A Negro community building, with auditorium, would help.

GREENSBORO'S GARDEN CLUB

The Greensboro Garden Club, with 56 members, was organized in 1940. In the following year it was federated with the Garden Clubs of Georgia. It featured horticulture and flower arrangement the first year, beautifying the town the second, and for the next two years will specialize on the care of the cemetery. To assist the Club in this latter project, the City Council is making $30 available each month so a full-time caretaker can be employed.

The Club has had four flower shows, three of them in the city auditorium. In the spring of 1942, six miniature gardens of the United Nations were featured. The niches depicted such outstanding periods of the nation's history as the Indian, English-Colonial, French, Civil War. With well laid plans in their heads, and deft hands willing to work, the members of the Garden Club—with their servants—in a day or so transformed the auditorium into a place of beauty and good taste.

Union Point has had a garden club for several years.

The increasing popularity of the Home Demonstration clubs, FSA group meetings, county-wide pageants, and flower shows is an indication that people are learning to have fun, and do something at the same time.

GREATER GREENE COUNTY WEEK

The County Nutrition Committee held a county-wide meeting in the Greensboro auditorium in July, 1941. A nutrition skit, "Food Is Strength," was presented. Dr. Willis A. Sutton, superintendent of the Atlanta schools, spoke on food and health.

Greater Greene County Week was inaugurated in the fall of 1941, with the churches and other agencies arranging the program. Music was furnished by a county-wide choir, under the leadership of James M. Reynolds. Leading Georgia ministers preached. Senator Richard B. Russell spoke on Patriotic Night. He was introduced by Jones T. Bond, active local Legionnaire, who called attention to Russell's interest in the Unified Farm Program in Greene, said his chief concern in the Senate "has been the restoration of the farmer to his rightful place in our economic system." The Senator explained the relation of the federal farm program to the welfare of the whole country.

The popularity of Greater Greene County Week grew out of its effective mixture of religion and patriotism. The white people were distressed by the increasing signs that America was about to go to war. The speakers of the week—preachers and politicians alike—expressed the hope that the United States could stay out of the war, but that we had better be prepared for whatever comes.

THE WAR CLOUDS DIP LOW

With each passing week, war clouds dipped low over the convoys that carried Lend-Lease shipments across the Atlantic. More enlisted youths were stationed on the fortified islands of the Pacific. Voting to make Greater Greene County Week an annual affair, the people of Greene were glad of whatever new ways of working together they had learned, and of the resources they were developing to meet the national crisis.

The National Defense Program met immediate response in Greene. The farmers agreed to produce and preserve more foodstuffs, especially canned goods and livestock products. Sawmill owners and operatives rushed off carloads of pine lumber to build barracks for the draftees. The textile mills began to make cloth and socks for the army. The school lunchrooms were now thought of as builders of the strong backs and steady nerves needed in wartime. Some people realized for the first time the national importance of the County Health Department's clinics and immunizations. People saved money to buy National Defense Bonds. Young men enrolled in the courses set up to train them for employment in defense industries.

The new county vocational building in Greensboro housed the classes for Whites in auto mechanics, woodwork, elementary electricity, tempering, welding, and machinery repair. The instructors were selected for their practical experience without regard to academic training. In the courses on tempering, welding, and machinery repair, the instructor was Courtney Ingram who had finished only the third grade, but who had completed an advanced course in welding and had had fifteen years of experience.

Three courses in auto mechanics have been conducted at the Alexander Community School for Negro youths. Roy Kimbrough, local Negro mechanic, serves as instructor. He had learned about gasoline engines by keeping old automobiles and farm tractors in operation. Twenty-five Negro boys have taken these courses.

The equipment for the National Defense training was secured by the County Board of Education through the State Board of Vocational Education, and is expanding the activities of the vocational teachers. A farmer breaks a piece of machinery, and he comes to the vocational shop and gets it repaired without cost. The vocational teacher, his students, and the farmer get experience under an expert's supervision and the repaired machinery goes back to work. The shop equipment has been used as planned. The young men have learned skills that are needed now that we are at war.

PART EIGHT

A SMALLER ROUNDER WORLD

XXXIII

IN WAR AGAIN

MANY GREENE COUNTY families were represented in the initial encounters of World War II. Nearly 200 young men, 160 white and 38 colored, had entered the U. S. Army and Navy as enlistees before the United States entered the war. They were in Iceland and on patrol ships in the Atlantic, in Hawaii and the Philippines.

LOCAL BOYS AT PEARL HARBOR

Young Carl Moore of White Plains heard the Japanese bombers at Pearl Harbor on December 7, 1941. He and his wife ran out of the house, felt the jar of exploding bombs, looked helplessly on as an enemy plane flew directly over them with machine guns in action. They counted the bullet holes in the house, flinched to see one had pierced the plaster near the baby's crib.

Other young men from Greene heard those first bombs fall. Ensign Lamar Taylor, of Greensboro, was cited by Admiral Nimitz of the U. S. Navy "For distinguished devotion to duty and extraordinary courage and disregard for your own safety during the attack of the United States Pacific Fleet, in Pearl Harbor, Territory of Hawaii, by Japanese Forces."

A few weeks later, when Manila was taken, Greene county boys retired with General MacArthur to Bataan and to the bravery, deprivations, and capitulation there and at Corregidor and Cebu. Within the first six months of the war, Greene county parents had three times received word that a son was "missing in action . . . No report of his death or injury has been received and he may be a prisoner of war." So came official statements about Thomas Bryan, John Fred Taylor, and William McGibony—since then others.

Americans can well acknowledge their debt of gratitude to the men who had secured training before the war came. They were the first in battle, the first to pay the full price.

ENLISTMENT WAS THEIR BEST OPENING

Most people in Greene county, as in Georgia and the South, are patriotic and they will do all they can to help win the war. But patriotism alone does not account for the relatively large number of enlisted men from this county. A basic reason is that during the depression years local young men often found enlistment in the Army and Navy their best opening. It gave them opportunity to travel, and besides their food, clothes and shelter, more money than they could earn at home as farm laborers. The sawmills and textile mills in the county paid better, but they regularly had all the workers they wanted.

During the late 1930's the enlistment agencies were reporting how much cheaper it was to recruit soldiers and sailors in the Southeastern states than anywhere else in the nation. Georgia was one of the best states in the region for recruiting, and Greene and adjoining counties one of the most prolific sections of Georgia. If white boys had been enlisted in the service from all parts of the nation at the same rate they had from Greene, there would have been almost 3,000,000 men in the service when we declared war on Germany and Japan.

Through June, 1942, nearly three fourths of all the men from Greene in the armed forces were volunteers—195 Whites out of 251, 47 colored out of 75. Most of the Negro volunteers lived in Greensboro, many of them signing up as they left the CCC camp. When the CCC was abolished by Congress, an additional number of the CCC boys enlisted. A larger number of the Negro youths from the towns and farms would have volunteered before the draft if the recruiting agencies had encouraged them to do so.

SOME LISTEN AND WONDER

When the time came for men between 21 and 35 years of age to register at the school-houses for a year's military training, some rural Negroes and an occasional white did not register on the date set. It is natural that people who lived in isolated homes, without a radio or newspaper, might not understand about the registration. When they learned from friends and neighbors that the draft included them, they complied and their delay was overlooked.

Illiterates appeared before the registrars. Many of them did not know when they were born, though in most instances they would tell you how many years old they were, would often mention a month, leaving the date to the discretion of the registering official. In one such case an illiterate mentioned July. The official asked, "Will July 4 be all right?" "Yassuh," was the obliging reply.

Four percent of the 850 Whites who registered in the first draft could not write their names, 30 percent of the 869 Negroes. Some who could write their names, however, could not write anything else, and could not read.

Registrants who met all other requirements for military service have been turned down because of illiteracy at the rate of about 5 percent of the Whites and over 35 percent of the colored. A Negro teacher provided by the WPA conducted classes at Union Point and Greensboro for these and other Negro illiterates. Later instructions from Selective Service permitted the local Draft Board to certify illiterates in each quota.

Now that we are in war, the large families of rural Greene and the South present the greatest challenge to American democracy, and the nation's greatest hope. Hope because they believe in the American ideals of liberty and justice. Challenge because many of them are still little more than human fixtures in the debt-ridden cotton economy. Too often they eat the same inadequate diet they have always eaten, live in the same shabby houses, and remain voteless because of the White Primary and the poll tax requirements for voting. Nowadays these propertyless folk are hearing about America's war to defend herself and the other democracies around the world. They listen and wonder, still inarticulate, defenseless, landless.

A SMALLER ROUNDER WORLD

Many a father and mother with a son or two in the North Atlantic or the islands of the Pacific first heard of Iceland, Pearl Harbor, Wake Island, Midway, and Manila only when death was overtaking their sons at these distant points. Often they could not look them up because they had no map of the world in the house. They would study the first map they saw, and remember the names of these new places, most of them mere dots in blue oceans. Their vocabularies grew larger as the world grew smaller, and rounder—for globes best revealed where the boys were, showed they were less far away through the earth than around it.

Their sons are facing death with Filipinos and Chinese and other dark-complected allies. Many white soldiers and sailors from Greene are finding themselves in a strange world.* And local racial thinking may out. One mother reports that her pilot-son compares the complexion of the pilot in the other plane with his own and brings him down if it doesn't match. "But suppose he is one of our dark-skinned allies?" comes the quick inquiry. "Oh well, he'd rather take a chance on bringing one of our bunch down by mistake than leaving one of theirs up there."

When you get out in the county you will find some people who have collected a lot of scrap iron and rubber and are doing all they

---

* In 1940 there were ten foreign-born people in the county. Best known among the group was Charlie Poulos, operator of the City Café; he owns a farm, takes an active part in civic affairs. Three of the other nine foreign-born residents were from Italy, and one each from England, Irish Free State, Germany, Russia, Poland, and Syria.

can in the war effort, but don't know what nations are our allies. Practically everybody knows England is on our side and that Germany and Japan are our enemies. But they often do not know whether we are fighting with or against China and Russia. Except for the radio, there would be an even greater lack of understanding among the poorer farm families.

"THE RADIO DOES MY READING FOR ME"

The radio at the county-seat or crossroad's store, or across the fields at a neighbor's house had long been recognized as a ready means of amusement. Here were programs at the turn of the dial, hillbilly music and Fibber McGee and Molly, Bob Burns, Amos 'n Andy, and Lum 'n Abner. When the war came the regular news broadcasts became popular over night. Interested in the news and wanting to hear the President's speeches, many another family without electricity made the down payment on a radio and set of batteries.

"After I got the radio I stopped the paper," said one farmer. "I can't read right good and it's better to sit down when I'm tired and listen to the radio. Radio does my reading for me."

Something fundamental may be happening when a landless man, in an unscreened house that leaks when it rains, turns on his battery-radio. He is now interested in world news, and in what people are saying about the conduct of the war, and the prospects for peace. He has a son "somewhere on the Atlantic," nephews in the Pacific, first and second cousins scattered around the world with our armed forces. He hears the President speak on the Four Freedoms, hears the news commentator say what the Vice-President said these Four Freedoms should mean to the common man, particularly the last of the four, "Freedom from Want." Without ever having dipped into the indirect world of books and magazines and newspapers, and not uncommonly without a vote now, he sits there by his own fire-place with his wife and children about him and hears the voices of earth's leading men and women say common-sense things about the most basic human desires and needs.

Better than anything else perhaps, this man knows the spoken word. He has lived in that world. What he has learned of life beyond his own personal experiences, he has got by word of mouth. He has lived on another man's land, with only a verbal contract; year after year he and his family have eaten food and worn clothes in the spring and summer which they paid for that fall when the cotton was sold, and the agreements were all oral.

Will this man, and others like him who are now bearing more than their share of the burdens of the world, remember the things they have heard about "freedom from want" when the war is over? Will they believe more in them than if they had read them?

OCEANS AND CONTINENTS ARE UNKNOWN

The influences of the war are reaching down powerfully to the last man and woman. Men who cannot read and write now need to know their ages and birthdays when they register in the military draft. Need to know them, too, when they apply for work in war industries, or when they work at a sawmill or cotton mill in the county and are eligible for unemployment compensation, and later old-age pensions.

A Negro mother may doubt the value of sending her children to school, may think they will get along with the white folk better without an education. But she wants a birth certificate filled in for her new baby. She thinks it would be a sad oversight for her baby to grow up and be kept out of the army or a good job just because his birth certificate had not been filled in. She couldn't fill it in, nor could her husband or the midwife who was there when the baby was born. A week later the husband, embarrassed as only a proud father can be, asked a neighbor if he would come up to the house and "send in a record of his baby to the government."

These landless and voteless people in the rurals are deeply concerned. "How's the war?" is a common query. "Is it coming this way now?" is another, and clearly harks back to that still most real war in these parts, Sherman's march to the sea. Involved in their questions is a complete ignorance of such primary facts of geography as oceans and continents. Nor do they assume that the most elemental things they know about the pull of gravity and falling bodies apply to the airplanes that regularly pass over their heads. For years now the scheduled mail planes have flown over them, and in recent months more day planes. Great droves of training planes pass over in the dark. Then one night a few planes with searchlights flew over. Next day came reports that the planes had stopped in mid-air, turned on big flashlights and looked around. They asked, "What do you suppose they were looking for?" You ask, "Did you see them? Are you sure they stood still?" You speculate on the probability of autogyro planes having been there. They still want to know whether you know what they were looking for. In self-defense you go out the next night, see the planes come straight overhead, see one now and then cut on a great searchlight, and understand how someone might think they were standing still.

BUT DEATH IS REAL

But being unacquainted with geography and willing to believe miracles of airplanes do not make them unmindful of death from the sky. Soon after Pearl Harbor there was talk of blackouts in New York and Atlanta, in Greensboro and Siloam, and in the sharecropper cabins between. "Better blow out your lamp when you hear a plane at night." "Why?" asks a mother. "Just to be sure no bomb is dropped on your house." She inquires about bombs, hears how they are dropped from airplanes, and faints when she understands how readily her house and family could be blotted out. And who is there to condemn the overwhelming fear of an illiterate landless voteless mother when she first realizes the full measure of defenseless death that modern science may have in store for her and her family.

They still hear about bombings, see planes go over their heads every day, hear them up there almost every night. They sit in houses not worth $200 amid their belongings of less than $500, and wonder if they'll be bombed. At church and at the crossroad's store they exchange the reports they hear. Wonder if one big bomb does really cost more than their house and furnishings, livestock and plows and wagons all put together! Wonder if they are really safe because they are scattered, and poor!

Then came sugar rationing, and they got their part—share and share alike. "All the little folks and the big folks in it together now. One can't git more than another. I ain't got no money and I can't git it. You got money and you can't git it."

The poorer people felt it was their patriotic opportunity to buy their full ration of "table sugar," though it was more sugar than they usually bought. What was left over could be used for jellies and preserves. Then came the sugar for canning, five pounds to a person. "Why, you ought to see how much sugar they've rationed out to me!" And along with the sugar often went reports—that if you get it for canning, you've got to use it for that; men will come around to see your canned fruit and will open the jars to find out if you put your sugar in it. And then reckless reports, that every family had to can a lot of stuff for the army, and if the canned goods wasn't there and properly sweetened—why, right into the chain-gang you'd go.

Not having fast and dependable ways of finding out the truth about a war situation far beyond their comprehension, some people purposefully repeated or made up extravagances just for the fun of it, just to see how the folks would act. Just to see what two ten-year-old boys would do when told that in a few days they would be drafted and sent off to camp to learn how to make bombs. Each of the youngsters had a brother under 20 in the last registration.

Their main hope was that they would be sent to the same camp. Before night they learned this report was not true, heard others, wondered whether they were true.

IN RESPONSE TO THE NATION'S NEEDS

Over against the fears and fumblings of the least schooled folk stands the high number of young men who are already in military service, most of them volunteers. Through September of 1942, over 425 men had gone from Greene county, and the monthly calls for men grew larger. Before the end of the first year of World War II, more men were in the armed forces than at the close of World War I.

Out from the county have also gone scores of young men and women to the basic war industries, and sometimes older men, too, to the construction of cantonments. Some farmers with a knack at hammering and sawing have found good wages helping to build Camp Gordon, near Augusta. Warren Merritt, of Siloam, recent graduate of Georgia Tech, works as an electrical engineer in the Glenn L. Martin Aircraft Corporation in Baltimore. In this same plant are over 50 more white youths from the county, most of them from around Union Point.

It might be expected that the farm labor situation here would be worse now than last year, but it is not. The reason is that the people, under the impetus of the war, are doing more farm work with less hired labor. They are doing more work themselves, and making greater use of the 150 farm tractors in the county. When a farmer knows he can't get labor, he more readily arranges with his tractor-owning neighbor to get his spring and fall plowing done. And the tractor plowing, always better, often turns out to be cheaper, too.

In the summer of 1941 the garden at the Beloved Precious Kimbrough place went unplanted for the first time since this home-site was established over 150 years ago. The next year the garden was planted again, and Gussie Kimbrough—active in all local war efforts—was doing a part of the work. Many another woman of the old landed families is looking after her garden more closely, and doing more canning than ever before.

The farmers, in 1942, in response to war needs, planted around 700 acres of peanuts for sale. The farmers have also increased their egg, milk, and meat production. Much of the increase is in response to the expectation of high prices; more than a little of it from the farmers' desire to help win the war. There is now comparatively little sympathy left here for the old individualistic phrase, common until a few months ago: "I don't like for the government to tell me what I can plant."

The war is affecting the life of the people in other ways. The rubber shortage and rationing of gasoline have caused neighbors to ride together more often than formerly. Gas station operators and auto mechanics are feeling the pinch and are moving off to other work.

Quite aside from the rubber and gas shortages and the fact that many families have no car, it would be good sense for the Unified Farm Program to work out scheduled cheap transportation for the rural areas. Then each family would not feel so deeply the need for a privately owned automobile, could put more of its money to uses in keeping with the war effort and the Unified Farm Program. People do need to get into the community centers now and then, but it is tragic if to do so they spend on an automobile money which they need for such elemental things as food and clothing.

OF DRIVES THERE ARE MANY

Shortly after America entered the war, the local Red Cross took on new activities. The first War Relief quota of $1,750 was soon over-subscribed.

Four months after war was declared, 50 people in Greene county had finished the Red Cross standard and advanced courses in first aid. Later 26 completed the instructors course. Several of them then organized classes for white people at different places in the county.

Plans have been discussed for teaching first aid to Negroes, including the instructors course, which will qualify local Negroes to give the standard first aid course to their own people. If this is done, the Junior Red Cross first aid courses can be taught in the larger Negro schools this fall, as already planned for in the white schools. The Red Cross is now offering courses in home nursing and nutrition.

A county-wide Red Cross work shop was organized some months ago. Under the leadership of Gussie Kimbrough, nearly 200 white women are now working, many of them in missionary societies. Over 1,100 articles have been made for the war relief, and 700 more for the armed forces. Included among the war relief items were 24 quilts and blankets handed in by as many one-teacher rural Negro schools.

The Greene County War Board is made up of selected farmers and representatives of various agencies of the Unified Farm Program. It is headed by H. C. Stewart, of White Plains. The Board is urging farm people to help increase production of peanuts, soy beans, eggs and other livestock products. It boosted the collection of scrap iron and aluminum, old rubber tires and tubes, and other salvage materials. It also put on a campaign for the sale of War Stamps and Bonds to farm families. Wherever the local canvassers have taken the trouble, they have been able to sign up nearly everybody, even though many of the poorer people felt they could promise to buy only a dime or quarter stamp each month. These small monthly purchases count up very slowly, and so far in most rural communities only the leading propertied families have been asked to subscribe.

It is doubtful whether one fourth of the rural families of the county have bought a single bond or stamp. Negro canvassers might well be appointed by the County War Board, two or more to each one-teacher school district.

Through August of 1942, the sale of bonds and stamps has been more than the county's monthly quota of $19,000. Committees have been set up in Greensboro and Union Point. Thus far, the employees in two business enterprises have signed up for the systematic purchase of stamps and bonds.

Of drives there are many—USO and China Relief just now, and before that the TB seal sale, Red Cross Roll Call, Jewish Relief, Greek Relief, Russian Relief—and ahead United War Work Relief and many another.

As the new requests come the people wonder how they are to meet the demands upon them. How can they put money in all these things when the cost of living is rising? Then they remember we are in war, that the price the soldiers and sailors are paying is far beyond anything asked of them, and so—on with the work.

A unit of the Georgia Home Guard, Number 84 in District 4 was organized at Greensboro in the fall of 1940. The unit had sent 60 percent of its members into the armed forces by July of 1942. The unit has a sub-machine gun, four automatic pistols, has given training in scouting and patrolling, riot duty, close- and extended-order drill. E. Lloyd Lewis, County Ordinary, and Earl L. Butler, active American Legionnaire of Union Point have taken leading parts in the Home Guard work.

ONE DAY IT WILL BE OVER

The people are finding a deep satisfaction in the war effort. It gives them something big and important to work on together. It helps overcome petty differences. It defines a real enemy outside our county and country. Now that we are at war, many of the things we need to do something about are not so close home.

When we looked at our depleted land and the houses of many of our people, we were uncomfortable. The refusal to recognize local needs will stifle the soul of any man; to acknowledge them does not make for an easy restful life. And so, many people in Greene, as throughout our nation, found the war a good chance to shed concern for unwholesome conditions around them.

The more obvious of our local problems have been relieved by the war. All during the 1930's men here and elsewhere had said, "A good war is what we need!" Then the government—they would say —could stop the relief work, unemployment would vanish, prices of farm products would rise, wages for labor would go up, the people would again feel closer together. And all these things had happened in Greene before the war was a year old.

There are now more jobs than workers, and there is a place for everybody. The "Forgotten Man" here has disappeared for the time being. But one day the war will end, and wholesale readjustment will have to be made. Some of the middle-aged men who have left here in recent months to take high paying jobs are wondering what they will come back to after the war. The boom period of the last war is remembered, but not so plainly as the depression and unemployment which followed. The people are already a little fearful of what conditions will be for themselves and the returning soldiers when the war is over.

But this is more than a national war, it is a world war. Some of our allies have been fighting hard while we have been getting ready, and some of our leaders have talked about national responsibility to the forgotten people of the United Nations—and then of all the world.

Said one aged farmer: "They tells me we are fighting for justice, but we ain't never had justice." Many people in Greene are coming to realize that we must continue to develop democracy in our local communities while we put down the enemies of democracy abroad.

XXXIV

RECORDED IN FIELDS AND FACES

THERE ARE good reasons why the federal government should continue to cooperate in Green's Unified Farm Program. The people here are citizens of the United States, and are entitled to the normal opportunities afforded the people of the nation. The fact that we are relatively poor does not mean that we are a liability, or that the nation will lose by helping us have better education and health programs than our local taxes will support.

LET'S CARE FOR THESE SEEDBEDS

Men and money are now needed. Greene county has less than its share of money to put into the war effort, but it has more than its share of men to contribute. And who is there to say men are less important than money? All during the depression, and for the past hundred years as pointed out earlier, this county has been exporting people. And the nation, even if only to protect itself, needs to help local agencies maintain reasonably adequate public services in the high birth-rate areas, these seedbeds of population, out of which flow people to the more wealthy portions of the country where there are more deaths than births.

During the ten years before we got in World War II, the population of Greene showed an increase of about 8 percent. Yet the oldest child in school from 895 families reported the migration during this decade of 596 older brothers and sisters, and of 2,300 other relatives. Only about one tenth as many people moved into the county to live as moved out of it.

A spot map of the present residences of these migrants, almost equally divided as to race, shows that roughly three fourths of the Whites and nearly nine tenths of the Negroes now live in urban communities, nearly a third of them in Atlanta alone. These new migrants may swell Atlanta's total population little if any, however, for Atlanta's population moves toward the still larger urban centers of the nation in much the same way that the rural dwellers of Greene move into the Greensboro houses vacated by the people who went to Atlanta. A number of the people who left here since 1930 had already arrived in distant cities before World War II came— 82 in New York City, 58 in Detroit, 38 Cincinnati, 35 Philadelphia, 34 Miami, 32 Cleveland, 27 District of Columbia, 26 Birmingham, and scores of other cities with a dozen or more. *

Most of these migrants to the cities left here as young men and women. Here they lived during their youth; here they ate their meals and got their schooling. Better health, housing, and education in Greene mean better equipped people to work in the distant communities to which they go.

The facts are clear that while Greene county is economically poor, it had made a great contribution to the nation through the manpower it sends out. So, from the national point of view as well as from the local, the money loaned and spent here by the Unified Farm Program represents an investment rather than an expenditure.

AND BECAUSE DEBTS ARE HARD TO PAY

The very fact that farm debts are hard to pay here is all the more reason why the Unified Farm Program should have been launched here. Diets can be improved by an increase of home-grown foods, but it is to cotton and livestock, especially to cotton, we still look for most of our cash. The cotton allotment here has been low, figured as it was on our post-weevil cotton record. But suppose the county's cotton allotment acreage had been figured on our 1916–1920

---

* For more facts about present residence of migrants, see Appendix No. 14.

record rather than for 1926–1932. Under an allotment on the earlier period we could have been planting nearly three times as many acres of cotton. The larger acreage, however, would not have solved our problem of low income, for cotton cannot be grown cheaply here with commercial fertilizer—cannot be grown at all without it.

The good price paid for pine lumber for the last few years has increased the local sawmill business. The present rate of operations can continue for only a few months more, for most of the sawable timber has already been cut. The people will then be all the more dependent upon cotton and the emerging livestock industry, or will leave the county in increasing numbers for work elsewhere.

It is right that the U. S. Department of Agriculture should have launched the Unified Farm Program in Greene to see what could be done in an area with a low cotton allotment. Then there are those who would hold that the federal government—under its public welfare clause—has the responsibility to help equalize the unequal places that occur for whatever reasons.

On a purely monetary basis, Greene county has two claims. First, over a period of decades the national tariff policy has quietly siphoned vastly more money out of Greene county than may ever be put back here by the FSA and all the other agencies of the Unified Farm Program. Second, there is the whole matter of credits and debts, and the tribute money in the form of interest which the farmers of Greene have paid on mortgage loans since the middle 1860's; and also the imbalance between urban and rural economy with the farmers here regularly selling their cotton and other farm produce at relatively low prices and buying their supplies at relatively high prices. Says elderly Judge James B. Park, "The truth of it is this, the farmers have not got as much for their crops as they were worth, and they've had to pay more for their supplies than they were worth. That kind of business will bankrupt any community sooner or later."

Enmeshed in these and other national conditions lie local race and class values which have often hindered the full development of

Greene's human and natural resources. Greene's differentials, along with those of the rest of the South, have been imposed from without, and from within. And it may just be that we Southerners have been the easier exploited economically by outsiders because the great majority of Southern people have often been discounted, and disfranchised, by insiders.

WHAT LIES AHEAD?

Now that we are in war again, and more and more men and supplies will be needed, we wonder what changes be ahead for Greene. Wonder when "finis" will be written to the casualty list, and what it will look like. Wonder whether this county will remain rural with a high birth-rate, and people always moving out of it. What changes will occur in the way the landlords and tenants treat each other, in the way Negroes and Whites deal with members of their own race and with the members of the other race? Will more people be allowed to vote, or fewer, and what differences will that make in political speeches and public policy? Will it be easier or harder for the farmers to pay their debts and make a living? What will happen to the terraces, the spent fields sown down in lespedeza and the galled hillsides planted in kudzu? Will the fire tower on the Land Utilization Project be maintained, and will lumber be correctly harvested from the Project acreage as now planned? What will become of the new family-size farm units which have been so hopefully developed on plantation lands? What will happen to the new gardens, and the canning program? What to the clinics, and to the midwife supervision? Will the shops remain open at the schools to serve the farmers, will the school busses still run, the new county library continue to grow month by month, and the bookmobile still go to rural communities throughout the county? What comes of old age assistance and surplus commodities? Will minimum wage and hour legislation be continued, expanded, or dropped? What will become of county planning, and of the supervision on low-interest loans to

once-stranded farmers? What will happen to the new faith that
many a farmer and factory worker has in himself?

The answers to these questions rest with the future. The outcome
of the war will be a part of the answer, and the kind of peace we
strive for another part of it. If we remember the "forgotten man" on
the other side of the globe at the peace table, the chances are that the
farmers here will fare much better than if that far-off man is ignored. There is no way to do full justice to any man until we are
ready and able to do justice to all men; there is no way to remember
forgotten men anywhere without remembering them everywhere.

There is the chance that we will have the insight and character
to proclaim the "forgotten man" of today "the common man" of
tomorrow, that we will learn that these undeveloped men do not
need things done for them nearly so much as they need the chance
to do things for themselves.

A PART OF THE WHOLE

Greene county is a small patch of the whole earth. What has
happened here records something of mankind's history. What
happens here from now on will doubtless record even more of it.
For here we have the world in miniature—the forest-covered hills
and hollows were here. Then the men came. Indians in the stone age
supplanted by European settlers, who prized personal freedom and
private property, and owned slaves. The slaves were freed when the
white men of the South, slaveowners and non-slaveowners alike, had
been overwhelmed in battle. And the land was already going. Came
sharecroppers and time-merchants, and the best of the land was
gone. Thousands of us left the spent fields, other thousands of us
remained. And we pay for every inch of soil that slipped down the
river to the sea.

And here we are today, white men and black, landed and landless,
with our interests and fears and hopes.

The farmers now live within a county-wide Unified Farm Program which can develop on eroded land a better living for the average farm family than ever was attained when the land was still good. The typical farm family with a plan can now make a better living on eroded land than the slave or sharecropper formerly made on much better land. And now the land itself is being made more productive, whereas the lands tilled by the slaves and sharecroppers were always becoming poorer.

Once we insisted upon the adequacy of our States' Rights way of life. Now we may still defend the choice we made then, and wish it could have continued. But we use Jersey cows, Poland China hogs, Bermuda grass, soy beans from China, lespedeza from Korea, kudzu from Japan. We use all these things from the ends of the earth because they are of service to us in our attempt to live as best we can here in one county. Whether we think of the present war, the backgrounds of our own people, or the farm animals and crops about us, we know we are a small, but representative patch of earth, and that any sensible answers we work out here to our basic problems will be answers to similar problems anywhere. For now we know Greene county is a part of Georgia, and Georgia is a part of the world.

NOW IS FEAR AND FAITH

A world in which bombs fall upon cities from planes four miles high, and out of sight, and piloted by farm boys who but a few months ago walked between the handles of one-horse plows. A world in which the news of earth's greatest battles are heard an hour later over the radio even by people who never learned to read or write. A world in which fear of death and faith in the future are compounded in the most terrifying and hopeful ways. Here in Greene we now hear more about dictators and more about the common man than ever before.

We listen to all the prophecies of doom, and to all the portents of the fuller life. The seasons remind us that time is not disturbed; the waters of the Oconee and Appalachee and Ogeechee go peacefully down their courses; the oaks and sweet gums put on new leaves, the birds sing the same old songs; and with the people are birth and growth and death and love, fear and hope.

There's many a thing out of joint in Greene county and in the world, but there's infinitely more that is not. We shall hold fast to that truth, and work. Men and women and children are we, town and country, white and black, landed and landless. Tenants of the Almighty, all of us, as time writes on the face of the earth our care of the land, and in our own faces our care of each other.

APPENDICES

WHITE AND NEGRO POPULATION IN GREENE COUNTY, GEORGIA

1800 THROUGH 1940 *

YEAR	WHITE		NEGRO	TOTAL
	NUMBER	PER CENT		
1800	7,097	66.0%	3,664	10,761
1810	6,398	54.8	5,281	11,679
1820	6,599	48.6	6,990	13,589
1830	5,026	40.1	7,523	12,549
1840	4,641	39.7	7,049	11,690
1850	4,744	36.3	8,324	13,068
1860	4,229	33.4	8,423	12,652
1870	4,298	34.5	8,156	12,454
1880	5,573	31.7	11,974	17,547
1890	5,332	31.3	11,719	17,051
1900	5,325	32.2	11,217	16,542
1910	6,875	37.2	11,636	18,511
1920	7,771	41.0	11,200	18,971
1930	5,988	47.1	6,628	12,616
1940	6,554	47.5	7,154	13,707

* U. S. Census.

Appendix No. 2
OWNERSHIP OF NEGRO SLAVES BY GREENE COUNTY TAXPAYERS IN 1810 AND 1859 *

NUMBER OF SLAVES OWNED	1810 NUMBER FAMILIES OWNING SLAVES	1859 NUMBER FAMILIES OWNING SLAVES	NUMBER OF SLAVES OWNED	1810 NUMBER FAMILIES OWNING SLAVES	1859 NUMBER FAMILIES OWNING SLAVES
None	684	557	40	1	2
1	127	68	41	..	2
2	76	45	42	..	..
3	67	31	43	..	1
4	54	31	44	..	2
5	64	30	45	..	1
6	50	39	46	..	3
7	37	29	47	..	2
8	24	28	48	..	2
9	28	19	49	1	1
10	26	24	50	..	1
11	18	13	51	..	..
12	21	8	52	..	3
13	18	15	53	..	1
14	17	13	54	..	1
15	16	10	55	..	2
16	14	6	56	..	..
17	13	9	57	..	..
18	8	14	58	..	..
19	5	7	59	..	..
20	3	7	60	..	1
21	2	9	61	..	..
22	1	8	62	..	2
23	1	8	63	..	1
24	3	8	64	..	1
25	2	6	65	..	..
26	2	5	66	..	..
27	1	4	67	..	..
28	2	6	68	..	1
29	1	3	69	..	..
30	4	9	70	..	1
31	2	5	74	..	1
32	..	4	76	..	1
33	..	1	77	..	2
34	..	9	80	..	1
35	2	1	95	..	1
36	..	3	102	..	1
37	..	1	131	..	1
38	2	1		1,398	1,135
39	1	2	Total No. Slaves	5,012	8,006

* Data compiled from Greene County Tax Digests of 1810 and 1859, now on file in Duke University Library.

APPENDIX No. 3

TAXPAYERS IN GREENE COUNTY, GEORGIA, WITH 40 OR MORE SLAVES IN 1822 *

Nicholas Lewis	73	Thomas Mosley	49
Thomas Grimes	68	Reuben Thornton	46
Thomas Winston	64	Thomas Grimes	44
Robert Wright	62	Adiel Sherwood	44
Thomas Terrell	58	James Daniel	41
James Woodruff	55	Armstead Atkinson	41
Richard Asbury	55		
Nancy Andrews	54	James Park	41
		A. W. Todd	40
Thomas Legon	53	Wm. Grimes	40
Thomas W. Cobb	51	Thomas Greenwood	40

* Data from Greene County Tax Digest of 1822, now on file in Duke University Library.

APPENDIX No. 4

TAXPAYERS IN GREENE COUNTY, GEORGIA, WITH 40 OR MORE SLAVES IN 1854 *

T. N. Poullain	133	Frances C. Walker	48
R. J. Willis	102	James B. Nicholson	47
Thomas Wray	90		
J. W. Champion	79	Ambrose Hutchinson	47
O. T. Daniel	76	Joseph Catchings	47
D. J. Foster	75	V. R. Thornton	46
		Wm. H. Sweney	46
R. T. Parks, Estate	70	James Carlton	46
Jas. W. Jackson	64	Wm. Rowland	45
W. D. W. Weaver	64	R. H. Ward	44
John H. Broughton	64		
Joel Early, Estate	63	Thomas Merritt	44
Wm. C. Davison	63	Wm. A. Corry	43
		Thomas M. Hamilton, Agt.	43
Baldwin Copeland	61	Jackson Stephens	42
Absalom Janes, Estate	59	Thomas Stocks	42
Dr. T. P. Janes	54	Thomas Thompson	42
Greene Moore	54		
James Moore	53	John Curtwright	42
Wm. B. Ellington, Estate	52	Thomas C. Williamson	42
		James N. Armour	41
James Devant	52	E. D. Alfriend	41
John Brande	51		
F. B. Daniel, Estate	51	John E. Jackson	40
D. C. Barrow	50	John Colley, Estate	40

* Data from Greene County Tax Digest of 1854, now on file in Duke University Library.

Appendix No. 5

STORY OF THE MARRIAGE OF JENNIE HART, OF UNION POINT, TO SAMUEL HALE SIBLEY, IN MID-NOVEMBER 1865 *

Although my grand parents (the J. B. Harts) had moved from Augusta to Union Point about 1854, my mother (Jennie Hart) had a strong sentiment for the historic First Presbyterian Church in Augusta (where she, as well as my father, Samuel Hale Sibley, had been baptized as infants). Accordingly, their marriage, which was the first large wedding following the Civil War, took place in that building. Unfortunately, it was a rainy evening and to protect the bride's white slippers old "Mammy Rose" enclosed them in a pair of grandpa's white socks. In the confusion of spreading the white silk train and arranging the veil in the vestibule, the socks were overlooked and not thought of until the nuptial knot had been tied and "the socks" were walking down the aisle when the bride's downcast eyes discovered the oversight. Following the church ceremony, a large reception was held in the home of an aunt living in the city. But the unusual feature of the event was the next day's wedding journey.

At that time, November 15, 1865, there was no passenger train service on the Georgia Railroad, so my father chartered a passenger car, and hired a brass band. The entire wedding party got aboard, and the car was attached to a freight train. When the first station was reached the "wedding car" was detached, the band struck up and the ladies and gentlemen danced on the big "cotton platform" while the engine shifted. That program was carried out all day until dark found them at their destination, Union Point, where the grove at the top of the "Big Steps" had been floored over and illuminated by bon-fires. Guests from Greene and adjoining counties were gathered and a dance and wedding feast were enjoyed until the wee small hours.

Receipt for Wedding Cake

20 lbs. of butter	20 nutmegs
20 lbs. of sugar	1 oz. of cinnamons
20 lbs. of raisins	20 glasses of wine
40 lbs. of currants	20 glasses of brandy
12 lbs. of citrons	200 eggs

---

* Quoted, by permission, from a personal letter of November 17, 1942, from Jennie Sibley Lamb, Hawthorne Heights, Union Point, Georgia.

Use flour as needed. Add cloves to your taste. If you wish it richer, add 2 lbs. of currants and 1 lb. of raisins to each pound of flour.

Appendix No. 6

COPY OF THE FIRST CONTRACT MADE BY T. B. THORNTON AND THOSE OF HIS FORMER SLAVES WHO REMAINED WITH HIM AFTER THEY WERE INFORMED OF THEIR FREEDOM *

STATE OF GEORGIA, GREENE COUNTY

This contract made this 3rd day of June 1865 between Thomas R. Thornton of said date and county, of the first part, and his former slaves, to wit, Jim, representing himself, his wife and six children, Aruns for herself and four children, Mary for herself and one child, Kitty Ann for herself and three children, Tom for himself and two children, Chunk, Ned, Violet, and Ophelia, Wiley and Cyrus, all of said state and county. Each one for himself and herself of the second part.

WITNESSETH: The said party of the first part has agreed to retain in his services the said party of the second part on the following terms, to wit: said party of the second part, including all who are able to labor for said party of the first part, as heretofore on the farm or in the house kitchen or elsewhere, and are to do whatever they are told to do that is lawful, and are to be industrial, faithful, honest, sober, truthful, respectful, obedient. And those who represent children are to require children to be respectful and obedient, and to make themselves as useful as possible, and to behave themselves alright in every way.

In return for the services thus rendered, said party of the first part is to feed, clothe and lodge all the parties of the second part, including those whom they represent, and to treat them as kind as he had done heretofore; and at the end of the period for which this contract is made is to give said parties of the second part one sixth of all the corn, wheat, peas, syrup, and sweet potatoes that may be on hand at the time, made from the present growing crop. And if the said party of the first part should sell any of these articles made from the present growing crop before said payment of one sixth, then the portion thus sold is to be considered as being on hand, and said parties of the second part are to divide said produce among themselves as they see proper, it being delivered to said parties of

* Used by permission of J. C. Thornton of Atlanta, formerly of Greene county, Ga.

the second part in bulk. In case medical attention is necessary it will be furnished by said party of the first part, but the expenses of the same will be deducted of the produce which is due to said party of the second part. In case of protracted sickness, a reasonable deduction for loss of time shall be paid from the portion to be paid said party of the second part. And should any or one or more of the said parties of the second part be idle or disobedient or disrespectful or dishonest or unfaithful, or get drunk, or in any way fail to perform their part of this contract, they shall be liable to be instantly dismissed from the service of the party of the first part. And they, and all those they represent shall be at the will and action of the party of the first part, required to leave his premises, and shall receive no wages or other compensation for past labor and shall forfeit every right, and privilege and benefit conferred by this contract, and such forfeiture shall be in favor of said party of the first part. And this contract shall be of force until the 25th day of December next and no longer. In witness whereof the parties have hereunto set their hands, the day and year first above written.

Signed and acknowledged in the presence of H.H. Tucker, A.W. Broom, J.T. Thornton, Wm.A. Overton.

Thos. R. Thornton (Seal) Jim (His mark) (Seal) Anna (Her mark) (Seal) Mary, (Her mark) (Seal) Kitty Ann (Her mark) (Seal) Tom, (His mark) (Seal) Chunk (His mark) (Seal) Violet (Her mark) (Seal) Ophelia (Her mark) (Seal) Wiley (His mark) (Seal) Cyrus (His mark) (Seal)

APPENDIX No. 7

COTTON CROP, GREENE COUNTY, GEORGIA

1899–1942 *

YEAR	BALES	AVERAGE PRICE PER POUND	YEAR	BALES	AVERAGE PRICE PER POUND
1899	11,563	7.2¢	1921	1,420	16.6¢
1900	10,719	9.5	1922	326	23.9¢
1901	12,754	7.2	1923	1,510	32.0¢
1902	14,479	8.0	1924	4,298	22.4¢
1903	12,598	10.7	1925	4,736	19.0¢
1904	16,446	9.4	1926	6,792	11.1¢
1905	16,957	10.9	1927	4,660	19.4¢
1906	14,670	9.8	1928	4,660	18.2¢
1907	18,650	10.6	1929	7,660	15.8¢
1908	19,404	8.7	1930	8,540	9.3¢
1909	16,304	14.2	1931	6,940	5.7¢
1910	14,295	14.2	1932	4,560	5.8¢
1911	25,709	8.9	1933	5,570	9.4¢
1912	14,697	12.4	1934	5,700	12.1¢
1913	18,252	12.8	1935	5,300	11.1¢
1914	20,888	6.9	1936	4,420	12.5¢
1915	15,181	11.4	1937	6,870	8.7¢
1916	12,387	19.9	1938	3,800	8.7¢
1917	16,203	28.8	1939	4,916	9.4¢
1918	22,314	27.5	1940	5,065	10.7¢
1919	21,479	35.8	1941	1,698	17.4¢
1920	14,025	15.3	1942	3,492 (through Dec. 1)	18.0¢

* U. S. Census.

APPENDIX No. 8

NUMBER OF FARM OPERATORS BY RACE AND TENURE CLASS IN GREENE COUNTY, GEORGIA

1900 to 1940 *

YEAR	WHITE		NEGRO		TOTAL
	OWNERS	TENANTS	OWNERS	TENANTS	
1900	376	433	108	1,194	2,111
1910	477	512	147	1,684	2,820
1920	452	589	171	1,788	3,000
1930	278	337	93	849	1,557
1940	326	315	100	596	1,337

* U. S. Census.

Appendix No. 9

NUMBER OF WHITE LANDOWNERS BY SIZE OF HOLDINGS GREENE COUNTY, GEORGIA, 1827–1941 *

ACRES

YEAR	0–19	20–49	50–99	100–249	250–499	500–999	1000–1999	2000 PLUS	TOTAL
1827	4	12	54	272	173	100	18	3	636
1853	19	21	17	135	110	108	62	13	485
1874	21	22	58	185	180	89	45	12	612
1894	21	40	116	291	151	92	35	12	758
1904	34	45	121	318	154	65	34	11	782
1914	29	81	155	318	145	60	32	8	828
1925	42	96	203	352	133	68	37	5	936
1934	53	103	216	421	123	68	29	4	1,017
1941	52	98	225	408	164	64	28	6	1,045

* Data compiled from Greene County Tax Digests.

Appendix No. 10

NUMBER OF NEGRO LANDOWNERS BY SIZE OF HOLDINGS GREENE COUNTY, GEORGIA, 1870 to 1941 *

ACRES

YEAR	LESS THAN 20 ACRES	MORE THAN 20 ACRES	TOTAL ACREAGE
1870	1	3	421
1874	2	27	3,537
1884	9	34	4,722
1894	27	48	7,560
1904	34	119	11,705
1914	41	127	13,672
1925	53	135	12,741
1934	85	126	11,543
1941	71	126	12,957

* Data compiled from Greene County Tax Digests.

APPENDIX No. 11

SOME FACTS ABOUT 895 TOWN AND COUNTRY FAMILIES IN GREENE COUNTY, GEORGIA, IN 1941 *

FAMILIES	WHITE	NEGRO	TOTAL
Number	474	421	895
% with both parents at home	81.4	64.6	73.5
% with painted houses	61.9	13.3	39.0
% with ceiled houses	93.7	57.2	76.5
% with window panes	92.6	56.8	75.7
% with screens	88.2	36.6	63.9
% with electricity	63.6	6.2	36.6
% with radio	78.6	25.2	53.5
% with pressure cooker	24.3	40.4	31.9
% with automobile	84.9	25.7	46.4
% with fenced gardens	62.8	67.5	65.0
% with home-canned goods	84.8	94.3	89.3
% with cows	63.4	62.5	63.0
% with home-grown meat	69.1	83.6	76.0
% with chickens	80.4	91.7	85.2
% with dogs	75.3	75.1	75.2
Average quarts of canned goods per family	132	154	142
Average number of pounds of meat killed	510	371	445

* Data secured from oldest child in school.

APPENDIX No. 12

PERCENTAGE DISTRIBUTION OF STUDENTS BY AGE-GRADE ADVANCEMENT, BY RACE, GREENE COUNTY, GEORGIA

1927 and 1941 [a]

	WHITE		NEGRO	
AGE-GRADE ADVANCEMENT	*1927*	*1941* *	*1927*	*1941* *
Normal advancement	53	49	19	4
Retarded one year	22	23	14	10
Retarded two-three years	21	26	35	50
Retarded four years or more	4	2	32	46

[a] Data compiled from oldest-child blanks filled in for this study.

* The poorer showing for 1941 is accounted for by the standardization of the grades in all white schools, and the trend toward standardization in the Negro schools.

Appendix No. 13

RURAL FAMILY INCOME BY RACE, GREENE COUNTY, GEORGIA, IN 1927, 1934, and 1941 [a]

TENURE	WHITES		NEGROES		
	1934	*1941*	*1927*	*1934*	*1941*
Owners:					
Cash Income	$395	$1,376	$495	$237	$374
Value of H. G. Prov.*	251	412	125	264	372
Total	646	1,788	620	501	746
Renters:					
Cash Income	292	551	290	172	194
Value of H. G. Prov.*	258	310	112	244	346
Total	550	861	402	416	540
FSA Borrowers:					
Cash Income	..	448	..	..	220
Value of H. G. Prov.*	..	403	..	..	385
Total	..	851	..	..	605
Wage and Hour Workers: **					
Cash Income	..	855	..	..	401
Value of H. G. Prov.*	..	233	..	..	27
Total	..	1,088	..	..	428
Others, Farm Wage Hands, Etc.:					
Cash Income	147	495	131	86	291
Value of H. G. Prov.*	69	135	14	25	29
Total	216	630	145	111	320
All Families:					
Cash Income	301	844	302	151	259
Value of H. G. Prov.*	221	344	87	170	257
Total	522	1,188	389	321	516

[a] Data compiled from 13-page schedules filled in for this study.
* Value of home-grown provisions consumed by the family during the year.
** Cotton mill and sawmill workers under the Wage and Hour Law.

Appendix No. 14

RESIDENCE IN 1941 OF 2,844 MIGRANTS FROM 895 GREENE COUNTY FAMILIES *

RESIDENCE	WHITE MIGRANTS	NEGRO MIGRANTS
Georgia:	*Number*	*Number*
Adjoining Counties	94	75
Atlanta	250	529
Other Georgia Cities	169	97
Elsewhere in Georgia	322	116
Total	835	817
Other Southern States:		
South Carolina	88	12
North Carolina	46	36
Washington, D. C.	16	11
Va., W. Va., Md., and Del.	21	14
Florida	132	49
Tennessee	14	62
Kentucky	5	9
Alabama	26	44
Miss., La., Okla., Ark., Texas	37	7
Total	385	244
Middle Atlantic and New England States:		
Pennsylvania	1	48
New Jersey	9	15
New York	16	74
New England States	2	7
Total	28	144
East North Central States:		
Ohio	18	83
Indiana	5	5
Illinois	13	67
Michigan	12	53
Total	48	208
Elsewhere West of Mississippi River	35	15
Outside the United States	10	..
Unknown	56	19
GRAND TOTAL	1,397	1,447

* Data secured from oldest child in school.

Appendix No. 15

POET LOUISIANA DUNN THOMAS, NEGRO FARM TENANT MOTHER OF SILOAM, GEORGIA

Louisiana Dunn was born on a plantation near White Plains, Greene county, Georgia, in 1893. She went to school a few years at a one-room school, finished the fifth grade there. Her father was a sharecropper. She worked in the cotton fields with her brothers and sisters.

Upon reaching maturity she married Josh Thomas, and since that time has been the wife of a farm wage hand and farm tenant. She has given birth to thirteen children, ten of whom are living. The four youngest children are still at home. The six oldest are in Atlanta. The family got an FSA loan four years ago, and since then has been a "government farmer."

For many years Louisiana has read all the books she could get her hands on, and written one poem after another. Sometimes she wrote just for the fun of it, at other times upon request.

Over the years she worked part-time at the J. T. Bryson household as cook, washerwoman, ironer, and nursemaid to the Turner Bryson children. When a grade child, Jean Bryson liked Louisiana's rhymes, would ask her to write on one topic after another. Obligingly enough, Louisiana wrote the requested poems, often looking up something on the subject from a book she carried home from the Brysons. One day she brought in a requested poem and said, "I must be the Poet Laureate of the Bryson family."

We reproduced one of Louisiana's poems, "Uncle Sam Is My Shepherd," in the text of *Tenants of the Almighty* (Bk. III, p. 270) and two stanzas of "Trip to Flint River Project" (Bk. III, p. 292) and two verses of "Miss Ethel" in the picture section (Bk. II, Plate 17).

The title of this book, *Tenants of the Almighty,* is taken from the following poem:

A BRIGHTER DAY HAS DAWNED *

A brighter day has dawned
So bright that we can see
That God has sent a Moses
To lead his people free.

---

* Printed by permission of the author, Louisiana Dunn Thomas, Siloam, Greene county, Georgia.

Every year so many people
Was wondering here and there
Till there came a leader
With ways and plans for human welfare.

The houses was falling down
And barns had long since gone
Now stands in its place
A beautiful little white home.

We are tenants of the Almighty
Entrusted with a portion of His earth
To dress and keep
And pass on to the next generation
When evening comes and we must fall asleep.

Here are three more of Louisiana's poems:

MISS ETHEL *

I see the buggy coming
Come at once will you
What is the matter I pray
I want you to come and help me
Miss Ethel's coming today.

From the kitchen to the parlor
The house must be clean
All I could hear her say
Get this out, hurry about
Miss Ethel is coming today.

Now dress the chickens
I must have my way
To kill so many I thought was mean
But Miss Ethel's coming today.

* Printed by permission of the author, Louisiana Dunn Thomas, Siloam, Greene county, Georgia.

That was long long ago
I can see the train of years behind
Sorrow has played upon my heart
And trouble is weaved there like a vine
But I am here and still can say
Miss Ethel's coming today.

SPINNING WHEEL *

There was an old spinning wheel
Sitting by the fireplace
And upon the mantel
Sat grandmother's vase.

And over in a corner
Sat Grandfather's clock
And the little boy
Sat on a covered block.

The spinning wheel was busy
Humming all day long
To the little children
It was a beautiful song.

But it was spinning thread
Altho strange as it may seem
It wasn't in the parlor
And it wasn't spinning dreams.

The old spinning wheel is silent now
Scarce as the mighty dollar
No wonder we only find them
Sitting in the parlor.

------

* Printed by permission of the author, Louisiana Dunn Thomas, Siloam, Greene county, Georgia.

TOMORROW *

Don't worry about tomorrow
For it is just another day
We never know what it will bring
But we know it is on the way.

We like to think of tomorrow
And things we want to do
Work and plan and study
To make our dreams come true.

As long as time been rolling
And years been stealing away
We never has seen tomorrow
For its just another day.

In early 1942, the author of this book went from Miami to San Juan, Puerto Rico, by clipper. Upon returning to Greene he gave Louisiana a picture of the clipper, and asked her for a poem. Here are a few of her stanzas:

The first flying began a chapter *
that's still being written yet
of air travel Air Mail and freighters
it was a thrill you bet

Sitting by the cabin window
looking out on nothing to See
two miles up from every thing
can eat and have your tea

Just think of leaving Mimia
and spanning the Caribbean sea
all in one short day
is a Mistry to me

* Printed by permission of the author, Louisiana Dunn Thomas, Siloam, Greene county, Georgia.

> I know time is flying fast
> go swift as you can or will
> but someone has found a way
> to make time stand still.

APPENDIX No. 16

COMMUNITY ORGANIZATION AND AGRICULTURAL PLANNING
GREENE COUNTY, GEORGIA *

By

Lee Coleman

*Bureau of Agricultural Economics
United States Department of Agriculture
Southeastern Area
Atlanta, Ga.
January 1942*

SUMMARY OF FINDINGS AND RECOMMENDATIONS

There are five kinds of administrative areas and districts in Greene County, three of them created by agricultural agencies for the local administration of their programs. These various districts do not coincide with each other nor with the natural communities and neighborhoods. The criss-crossing and overlapping of district boundaries is very confusing in certain areas, and the development of strong neighborhoods and communities is retarded by it. Some neighborhoods are divided between ten or twelve districts of various kinds.

The "communities" recognized by the Agricultural Adjustment Administration largely ignore the natural community groupings in some parts of the county. One neighborhood is divided between four "communities" and others are divided between two or three.

Of the five Farm Security Administration districts all but one contain parts of three or four natural communities. Nine white neighborhoods are split between two or more districts, as are eleven Negro neighborhoods.

---

* Reproduced by permission of Lee Coleman, and Bureau of Agr. Economics of the U. S. Dept. of Agr.

The eight local districts created for representation on the Soil Conservation District Priority Committee bear little resemblance to the eight natural communities in the county.

Greene County has twenty-six white neighborhoods and eight communities, and thirty-seven Negro neighborhoods forming eleven or twelve weak communities. The larger number of the Negro communities is accounted for principally by subdivisions of white communities. With this many units, any agency should be able to set up districts which do not divide communities and neighborhoods. A revision of local districts so as to fit in with and utilize the natural associational tendencies would increase the chances of success for a given program and help to build up stronger rural communities.

The persons holding official positions or board memberships are more largely concentrated in towns and villages than are those holding positions on agricultural committees and boards, but the distribution by communities of the two types of positions is not significantly different. On the agricultural committees there is a much greater piling up of positions on certain individuals and families than is the case with the official positions. In general, the persons serving in official positions are a different group from those serving on agricultural committees and boards, for only fourteen out of one hundred and two individuals hold positions of both types.

Natural neighborhood and community boundaries have also been largely ignored in establishing local school districts. The health service could be made more adequate by establishing more clinics. Militia districts do not correspond to the neighborhood and community areas.

Church attendance and trade areas are dominant factors in determining natural neighborhood and community boundaries. A change in the trade center patronized by an individual family is often followed by a shift of community affiliations to the same center. In Greene County, only one white community is without a local trade center, and it is served by several local stores. Church attendance is influential here in determining neighborhoods, but has little effect on the wider community pattern.

Present associational patterns of rural Negroes in Greene County are similar in many ways to those of the white people of forty years ago. Nowhere in the county is there a fully-integrated rural Negro community of the farm-village type. Wherever wider community affiliations of Negroes do exist, they tend to follow the general lines of the white communities, with some further community subdivisions. The boundaries of Negro and white neighborhoods do not correspond.

Suggestions for building up and strengthening rural communities include the following:

1. Revise the various administrative areas and districts so that they will more nearly coincide or fit in with each other and the natural neighborhoods and communities.

2. Give each community adequate representation on planning committees or boards and councils, and each neighborhood a voice in the selection of community representatives.

3. Revise the consolidated school districts so that they will more nearly coincide with the communities.

4. Build up churches and other community institutions. Where open-country churches no longer meet the need, encourage and assist rural people to participate in church activities at their community center.

5. Wherever practicable, decentralize Farm Security and other agency activities to the rural community centers.

6. Encourage local community initiative, planning, and responsibility.

7. Spread membership on the various committees and boards more widely, and among all classes of the population.

Appendix No. 17

EMERGENCY CROP LOANS TO GREENE COUNTY FARMERS IN 1941–42 *

In 1942, the Emergency Crop and Feed Loan Office of the United States Farm Credit Administration made loans to 47 White farmers and 38 colored farmers. The total amount loaned was $11,510. In 1941, 73 percent of the money loaned was collected. It is estimated that 95 percent of 1942's borrowings will be collected.

Appendix No. 18

AAA PAYMENTS TO FARMERS, GREENE COUNTY, GEORGIA 1940 **

The Census of 1940 reported 1,337 farms in Greene. That same year, 1,457 farm families—including dependent tenants on plantations—shared

---

* Data from letter from H. H. Blount, Sparta, Georgia, of Oct. 2, 1942.
** Data from records in Greene County AAA office.

in the benefits. Payments went to 720 single-producer operators, that is, to family-size independent owners or renters and averaged $61.13; 256 payments went to two-or-more producer units, that is, to owners of plantations and the dependent farm tenant families on them, and averaged $174.31 per plantation, or $60.55 for each of the 737 families who shared in these 256 checks.

A little over $88,600 was distributed in 1940, $38,200 in parity payments and $50,400 in rental payments. The size and number of payments, parity and rental combined, were:

Size of Payment	Number
Up to $9.99	21
$10 to 19.99	48
20 to 39.99	278
40 to 79.99	334
80 to 159.99	186
160 to 319.99	66
320 to 639.99	25
640 and over	18

The largest payment in the county was $1,496, the second largest $1,141. There were two other payments of over $1,000. The 72 payments of $200 or more made a total of a little over $42,000, or 47.5 percent of the total. Nearly all of these larger payments were for two-or-more producer farm units, that is, plantations.

APPENDIX No. 19

TYPES OF GOODS CANNED BY FSA CLIENTS IN GREENE COUNTY, GEORGIA, AND NAMES OF LARGEST CANNERS

1940-1941 *

The range of canned goods put up by the 507 families on FSA in 1941 is shown by the following totals: 15,022 quarts of tomatoes, 59,685 vegetables, 78,482 fruits, 1,521 fruit juices, 11,403 sweets, 11,653 pickles, and 18,049 meat.

In 1940 the canning performance of white and colored families was about the same. Nine families put up over 750 quarts. The largest number, 1,100, belonged to Daisy Saggus, Negro woman near Bairdstown; the

---

* Data from records in Greene County FSA office.

second largest number, 927, to William Corry, Negro, near Bethany Church. Earl Swan, white, and Lazelle Stykes, Negro, had 843 each; A. T. Wilkes, white, 838, John Green, colored, 835; E. D. Lewis, colored, 780; Peter Champion, colored, 776; John Robbins, colored, 769; Ed Lewis, colored, 760; Frank Champion, colored, 755.

In 1941, one half of the FSA families surpassed their canning quota of 85 quarts for each member of the family. In four districts—three with white supervisors and one with colored—the white families averaged 345 quarts, the Negroes 416. One district with white supervisors averaged nearly 450. The second highest average, 425, was in the district with Negro supervisors. Eleven families in the county, all of them Negroes and most of them bearing the names of prominent slaveowning families, put up 900 or more quarts each in 1941; Dock Miller, 1,202; Will Lawrence, 1,096; Gus Wright, 993; Thomas Willis, 944; Toombs Brown, 918; John Robbins and Sam Edwards, 909 each; John Greene, 905; Edmond Reid, 901; and Oscar Robbins and Jessie Kimbrough, 900 each. Six of these eleven were in the district where the Negro supervisors work.

In noting the preponderance of colored families with outstanding canning records, it should be remembered that nearly three fourths of the FSA families are colored, and that exceptionally large families are more common among them, and their quota would, therefore, be somewhat higher than for the Whites. The white FSA families throughout the county average 4.2, colored 5.7. There are thirty Negro households with ten or more persons each, and only one White with that number.

In 1942, over 230,000 quarts were put up by 475 families. Over 300 of these families reached or surpassed their quotas.

Appendix No. 20

REPAYMENT OF LOANS BY FSA FARMERS, GREENE COUNTY, GEORGIA, 1939–1942, AND NUMBER OF FAMILIES WHO HAVE LEFT THE PROGRAM DURING THAT PERIOD *

In 1939, 23 percent of the FSA families made full payment of loans due, and most of the others paid in part; 18 percent set aside the money needed to grow the next year's crop, and 75 percent more a part of it. Early in 1940 supplemental loans were made to almost 75 percent of the families because they had not made enough to grow the next crop. This loan, too,

* Data from records in Greene County FSA office.

was to be paid back in five years, the first payment due that fall. At the end of the year, 22 percent of the families met their payments in full, and 17 percent set aside all the money to produce the 1941 crop. A second or third supplemental loan was made to a little over 70 percent of the families during 1941, many of them for "Food-for-Defense" chickens and cows.

By the end of 1941, 113 families—48 white and 65 colored—had left the program, and almost as many new families had been added. Twenty-two of the farmers had voluntarily withdrawn from the program; 67 went off for lack of cooperation, death of wife, physical disability, spending too much money on an automobile, or conviction of a crime; 16 families left the program because of death of husband, and 8 for all other causes. Members of most of these families made other arrangements to farm, found employment at sawmills or cotton mills, got on WPA, became casual laborers, or were eligible for public welfare assistance. Three of those who left the program had paid up their obligations in full. Several others could have if the 1941 crop had been an average one.

In 1942, over $73,000 was repaid on FSA loans, and a sum one third as large set aside to produce the next crop.

Appendix No. 21

SCHOOL BUILDINGS AND SCHOOL TEACHERS, GREENE COUNTY, GEORGIA, 1934–1942 *

Since the Unified Program was launched in early 1939, twenty-six new buildings have been erected. Twelve of these were built through the combined efforts of the FSA, WPA, and the County Board of Education: 1 brick eight-room county vocational building in Greensboro, 5 four-room vocational buildings and 2 one-room vocational buildings at the other white schools in the county; 2 four-room rural schoolhouses and 2 one-room vocational buildings for Negroes. Two white schools were renovated, and two others painted.

The NYA cooperated with the county and the FSA in the building of 1 two-room vocational building, and 7 one- and two-room schoolhouses for Negroes. Six more new one-room Negro schoolhouses have been built by the county and FSA. Arrangements for the building of 4 more combination four-room school and shop buildings for Negroes are now well

---

* Data from records in office of County School Superintendent of Greene County, Georgia.

under way, with the county, FSA, and the patrons of the schools cooperating.

The school improvement program has provided relatively adequate buildings at each of the white schools, and when it has been completed will have done the same for 6 Negro schools, 2 of them wholly rural. In each of these latter cases, 4 dilapidated one-room schools were closed. Three other small colored schools have been consolidated.

Beautification of grounds and improvement of sanitary facilities have come along with the school building program. Progress has been made, but much remains to be done, for a dozen small rural schools are still without privies. One colored school still convenes in a church, at Boswell Chapel. Five other schools in the county have unimproved schoolrooms. They are shabby, unpainted, and unceiled. The County School Board has hopes of improving the worst of these next year.

The schools of the town of Greensboro, white and colored, are operated under a separate system, with its own board. C. C. Wills, wizardly in mathematics, has been superintendent for over a quarter of a century. The white high school now for years has been on the Accredited List of the Southern Association of High Schools and Colleges. Only college-trained teachers are used. Graduates readily enter the best colleges and universities.

The county school system transports its senior high school pupils into Greensboro from all over the county, excepting only those who live in or near Union Point. This year's graduating class numbered a half hundred—15 of these were from Greensboro, 35 from the remainder of the county.

Taking the county as a whole, there has been as much progress made under the Unified Farm Program in the use of trained teachers as in the improvement of school buildings . . . "Schoolhouse don't spell much if you ain't got good teachers."

Eight years ago, 13 teachers out of 47 in the white schools of the county system had less than one year of college training. Last year, all 44 teachers had two years of college training or more, 25 of them had four years.

The training of Negro teachers improved greatly, too. Nearly three fourths of the 48 teachers eight years ago could not qualify for even the lowest grade of state license. Many had only finished the local one-teacher schools, could teach only because they had been granted a license by the county. At that time, only three had any college training. Last year, 37 out of 52 teachers had college training, 14 of them four years, and 12 others two or more. The number of teachers with county licenses has been further reduced. The few remaining ones will likely either attend summer schools and raise their certificate, or be replaced by better-trained teachers within the next few years.

GENERAL INDEX

"A Brighter Day Has Dawned," 376-377;
see also Louisiana Dunn Thomas.
Abolitionists, 45, 51, 55-57, 59-60.
Academies, private, 25, 35-38, 103, 104, 107,
113.
"Acre-Right Law," 71, 78, 89; see also "40
Acres and a Mule."
Adams, John Quincy, 31.
Advance-rent agreements, 243-244, 271.
Africa, 28, 29, 43, 48.
Agricultural Adjustment Administration,
214-218, 359-360; benefit payments of,
199, 208; voting in elections, 200, 217-
218; committee members, 321; payments,
382-383.
Agricultural and Mechanical Association of
Greene County, 92.
Aid to blind, 313.
Aid to dependent children, 313.
Alabama, 27, 42, 44, 61, 292.
Alexander, W. W., Dr., ix, 205-207.
American Red Cross, 301-302, 306.
Andersonville Prison, 75.
Anti-slavery agitation, 45-46, 56-60.
Appomattox, 72, 74, 77, 91.
Asbury, Bishop Francis, 24, 44.
Ashwood Farms, (S. C.), 292.
Athens, (Ga.), viii, 33, 34, 35, 40, 49, 130,
150, 157, 210, 306, 323.
Atkinson, W. Y., 121.
Atlanta, ix, x, 50, 65, 104, 108, 121, 132,
133, 134, 143, 150, 153, 157, 171, 172,
174, 186, 189, 206, 240, 321, 341, 351,
359, 376.
Atlanta Constitution, 133, 169, 197.
Atlanta Joint Stock Land Bank, 160.
Atlanta Journal, 127, 134.
Atlanta University, 189.
Augusta, (Ga.), 10, 11, 12, 16, 19, 33, 34,
35, 39, 46, 49, 80, 94, 114, 157, 205, 206,
353, 368.

Augusta Chronicle, 17, 23, 132.
Augusta Fat Cattle Show, 214.
Augusta Presbytery, 109.
Augusta Tribune, 123, 125, 127.
Australian Ballot, 191.
Austrian Peas, 212, 217.
Automobiles, bought by farmers, 146.

"Bale weevils," 165.
Baltimore, 27, 77, 353.
Bankhead-Jones Bill, 196.
Banks, 117, 141, 160-161, 211; collapse of,
161.
Barbecue, 71, 160-161, 335.
Bartram, William, 11.
Bataan, 345.
Bathtubs, first in farm homes, 141.
Bethune, Thomas, "Blind Tom," Greene, 95.
"Billion dollar bandit," 183-184.
Birmingham, 359.
Bishop Grace, 186.
Blount, H. H., 382, footnote.
Blue, Caroline, x.
Bluecoats, 70-71, 76, 80, 97.
Boll weevil, vii, 155-165; arrives, 149; re-
turns and stays, 151, 329; ruins crop, 152-
153; changes wrought by, 155, 158; fire
and poison for, 163-165; dates set by, 165.
Bonus Marchers' Camp, 189.
Bookmobile, 308, 361.
Booster clubs, come and go, 173-175.
Brick buildings, 53-54, 191.
British Government and the Confederacy,
69.
Brown, Flora, 209.
Brown, John, 60.
Brown, Joseph E., Gov., 62, 69.
Brown, Paul, Congressman, 195, 197, 203.
Bureau of Agricultural Economics, ix, 200,
211, 224 footnote, 380.
"Bushwhacking," 64.
Buttrick, George, 137.

389

INDEX OF PICTURES

All of the pictures in this book were taken in Greene County, Georgia, by photographers of the Farm Security Administration. The pictures were made by Jack Delano, except Plates 23 and 36 by Marion Post, and Plates 11, 37, and 38 by Edwin Rosskam. To locate site of pictures, see Map of Greene County in end papers of this volume.

GREENE COUNTY, GEORGIA—PEOPLE
AND PLACES

399

Underwood Brothers, of Siloam, 183, 229, 231.
Union Manufacturing Company, 315, 316.
Union Meeting House, at Greensboro, 44.
Union Point Normal School, 138.

Van Landingham, S. L., ix.
Veazy, 125, 150, 326; Plate 49.
Veazy, William, 25.
Vincent, C. C., 192.

Ward, Green, 148.
Warner, J. B. Y., 103.
Watson Springs, 141, 185.
Watts, Harrison, 27.
Wayside Home, 67-68.
Weaver, Benjamin, 21, 190.
Weil, R. B., 203.
Weinstein, M., 190.
Welch, Bruce, 306.
Welch, Lucille Stone, ix, 306.
West, Wade H., 163, 171, 289.
White Plains, 32, 37, 44, 66, 68, 94, 107, 112, 113, 114, 115, 116, 117, 125, 150, 161, 162, 163, 166, 169, 171, 173, 189,
191, 192, 215, 231, 246, 265, 306, 308, 326, 345, 355, 376; Plates 51, 67, 68, 76.
White Plains Academy, 35, 113, 190.
White Plains Manufacturing Company, 117.
White Plains Woman's Club, 308, 335.
White, Thomas N., 62-63.
Williams, Carey, ix, 180-182.
Williams, Cranston, 182, 308.
Williams, James Cranston, 176-183, 210, 332-333.
Williams, Ruth, 209.
Williamson, Peter, 15.
Willis, L. B., 101.
Willis, Richard J., 43, 44.
Wills, C. C., ix, 386.
Winslett, J. B., 181.
Woodville, 35, 49, 130, 138, 142, 150, 156, 160, 161, 169, 188, 191, 192, 214, 265; Plates 3, 17, 26, 32, 47, 48, 77.
Wray, Thomas, 190, 192.
Wray, Will, 192.
Wrayswood, 141, 190, 192, 231, 244, 296; Plate 20.
Wright, Edgar D., 189.
Wright, Madison C., Jr., x, 219.
Wyatt, L. L., Sheriff, ix, 316, 318.